W. Roy Niblett and
R. Freeman Butts, Editors

Brian Holmes, Associate Editor

UNIVERSITIES
FACING
THE
FUTURE

Published in Great Britain by
Evans Brothers Limited

 Jossey-Bass Inc., Publishers
San Francisco · Washington · London · 1972

UNIVERSITIES FACING THE FUTURE
An International Perspective
W. Roy Niblett and R. Freeman Butts, Editors

Copyright © 1972 Evans Brothers Limited

First published in 1972 in Great Britain by
Evans Brothers Limited
Montague House, Russell Square, London W.C.1
as *The World Year Book of Education 1972/73:
Universities Facing the Future*

Library of Congress Catalogue Card Number LC 70-186577

International Standard Book Number ISBN 0-87589-133-0

JACKET DESIGN BY WILLI BAUM

FIRST EDITION

Code 7221

The Jossey-Bass
Series in Higher Education

Published in association with
University of London Institute of Education
Teachers College, Columbia University
Evans Brothers Limited, London

Editorial Board

Preface

The evidence provided in *Universities Facing the Future* clearly indicates that lively initiatives in higher education are taking place in many countries. One of the intentions in inviting contributions to this book was to give individuals a chance to tell at first hand of pioneering work within their own colleges or universities and to point out its significance.

The emphasis throughout is on innovation. A number of the twenty or so contributors who write of what is going on in their own institution have been keen to emphasize its representativeness; but for the most part the authors describe what it is doing and leave that to speak for itself. The chapters grouped in Section I, however, pick out and draw attention to trends that are of major import in the rapid evolution of higher education now so obviously taking place.

The chapters in subsequent sections are grouped so as to throw light on the general line along which higher education appears to be developing, the chapters about individual institutions acting as illustrations and examples. The last ten years have been marked by vast increases in student numbers, a proliferating range of functions for higher education, an extended diversity of offerings and of qualifications, and increased flexibility of transfer between courses. These changes have taken place almost equally in low income and high income countries – that is, those countries still dependent upon farming or crops for their wealth as well as those to which industrialization has brought increasing affluence (if not always either happiness or 'success'). Such tendencies bring into prominence problems of the interrelation of institutions of higher education, symbolized by the movement toward comprehensivization in some form – the subject of the final section of the book.

Perhaps we should add that no limitation of any sort, except in matters of length, has been imposed by us on what the contributors say. The author of each chapter is himself responsible for the content of what appears under his name.

London　　　　　　　　　　　　　　　　　　　W. Roy Niblett
New York　　　　　　　　　　　　　　　　　　R. Freeman Butts
September 1972

Contents

SECTION III:

SOME SIGNIFICANT MOVEMENTS IN CONTEMPORARY
UNIVERSITIES OF THE WEST

Contributors

GERALD ANTOINE, *Officier de la Légion d'Honneur; Commandeur des Palmes Académiques; Officier de la Couronne de Belgique; Recteur, Université d'Orleans-Tours*

ERIC ASHBY, *master, Clare College, Cambridge; sometime president and vice-chancellor, Queen's University, Belfast*

S. T. BELYAEV, *rector, Novosibirsk State University, Akademgorodok; member, U.S.S.R. Academy of Sciences*

RICHARD J. BLANDY, *senior lecturer in economics, The Flinders University of South Australia*

DAVID CARNEIRO, JR., *professor, University of Paraná Curitiba, Paraná, Brazil*

LADISLAV CERYCH, *councellor, OECD, Paris*

JOHN FERGUSON, *dean and director of studies in arts, The Open University, United Kingdom*

GERALD T. FOWLER, *assistant director, The Polytechnic, Huddersfield, United Kingdom; visiting professor, University of Strathclyde, Scotland*

DOROTEA E. FURTH, *consultant, Higher Education Section, Educational Investment and Development Division, OECD, Paris*

RONALD GOLDMAN, *professor of education, La Trobe University, Victoria, Australia*

TANKRED GOLENPOLSKY, *head, Foreign Languages Department, Far East Science Centre, Vladivostok*

HILDEGARD HAMM-BRUECHER, *Staatssekretär in Bundesministerium für Bildung und Wissenschaft, West Germany*

TIMOTHY S. HEALY, S.J., *vice-chancellor for academic affairs, City University of New York*

JOSEPH HERMAN, *director, Hungarian Academy of Science; director, Division of Higher Education, UNESCO, Paris*

C. T. HU, *professor of comparative education and director of the Center for Education in Asia, Institute of International Studies, Teachers College, Columbia University, New York City*

ANDREW M. KEAN, *principal, All Saints' College of Education, Leeds, United Kingdom*

PREM KIRPAL, *chairman, Executive Board, UNESCO, Paris*

NORMAN LINDOP, *director, The Hatfield Polytechnic, Hatfield, United Kingdom*

A. W. MARTIN, *professor of history, La Trobe University, Victoria, Australia*

WARREN B. MARTIN, *professor of history and provost of the Old School, Sonoma State College*

LELAND L. MEDSKER, *director, Center for Research and Development in Higher Education, University of California, Berkeley*

FRANCISCO MIGOYA, *general secretary, Universidad Iberoamericana, Mexico*

ALBERTO MONCADA, *professor of university administration, University of Madrid*

W. ROY NIBLETT, *professor of higher education, University of London Institute of Education; sometime director, University of Leeds Institute of Education, United Kingdom*

HAROLD J. PERKIN, *professor of social history, University of Lancaster*

GILDA L. DE ROMERO BREST, *professor of education and director, Center of Research on Sciences of Education, Instituto Torcuato di Tella, Buenos Aires*

DONALD G. W. SCHUTTE, *tutor and head, Department of Curriculum Development, Institute of Education, University of Dar es Salaam, Tanzania*

MICHIYA SHIMBORI, *professor of sociology of education, School of Education, Hiroshima University*

INGRID N. SOMMERKORN, *Education Research Center, Massachusetts Institute of Technology*

SETH SPAULDING, *director, School and Higher Education, UNESCO, Paris*

JAMES F. TIERNEY, *vice-president, Institute of International Education for the International Councils on Higher Education, New York*

TOH CHIN CHYE, *vice-chancellor, University of Singapore*

EDWARD W. WEIDNER, *chancellor, University of Wisconsin—Green Bay*

DOUGLAS T. WRIGHT, *chairman, Committee on University Affairs (Toronto); chairman, Commission on Post-Secondary Education in Ontario*

UNIVERSITIES
FACING
THE FUTURE

An International Perspective

Section I

Directions of Advance:
An Overview

1

Issues and Choices

W. Roy Niblett

The title to this book can be read in two ways: with the implication that universities have decided upon their stance towards the Future and now are facing it – with foresight and firmness; or with the implication that the Future with its threats and its promise is there to be faced – and woe be to universities which do not reckon with the fact. Something of both meanings is intended – either universities or the Future may have the initiative, as it were. What seems improbable with society in such rapid movement is that universities will themselves remain unchanged: to what extent will they change by their own will or be changed by force of circumstances?

Universities today are, especially in advanced countries, more and more obviously part of an emerging whole system of tertiary education. The vast growth of student numbers, the increase in the demand for more technology – i.e. more control over things – and the new public requirement that tertiary education shall make itself useful, are factors tending to alter universities themselves and, rather more gradually, their self-image. Hardly anywhere is it generally believed that the recipe for meeting the next twenty years is to continue to do, only better, what has been done in the last twenty. But to face the future relevantly and with conviction is particularly difficult when what is relevant or right is obscure and often under dispute. It may be helpful to outline some of the main issues regarding which choices have to be made – whether by bringing them up into consciousness and coming to a decision; or by making the decision unconsciously simply by continuing to follow the line already being taken.

Emphasis on Research versus Emphasis on Teaching

The first of the conflicts arises between the concept of the university as a producer of research and of knowledge; and the concept of the university as charged primarily with civilizing and humanizing its members. The conflict is concealed, not resolved, by emphasizing that research fertilizes teaching. There is a consensus of opinion in favour of this view. But how *much* research is necessary for the purpose? Would not much of the research still done in universities be done more efficiently in institutions where the workers could concentrate on the main task instead of being 'interrupted' by having to teach undergraduates – or indeed anybody? After all, many of the professors free to choose 'vote with their feet' by opting out of most teaching, except perhaps when they can draw directly upon their research activities in their lectures or classes.

But it can well be argued that though some of the plea that 'research fertilizes teaching' may be a rationalization, some is not – especially where actual involvement with a problem has not merely made the mind aware of other problems but has etched into it hard a number of the techniques by which those problems may be tackled.

All the same, concentration upon scholarship, laboratory research or even research in social science fields can be 'escapist' in the sense that those pursuing it have of necessity to detach themselves from the world, and may tend to regard the interpreters of their findings, or those who incorporate them in practical policies, as lower in the hierarchy – mere teachers, popularizers or administrators. The investigator thus feels able to separate himself antiseptically out from concern with what becomes of his results – leaving it to industrialists, governments, even speculators, to make what use of them they wish. His own stance is non-committed, a-moral, almost an-aesthetic – and as such dehumanizing. For a detachment, necessary though it is, can so easily breed a remoteness from human concerns. Universities may trade out of the here and now, or even the near future, at a cost it may be beyond human capability to pay.

Should then universities come closer to the market place? Not market place, perhaps, so much as places where fuller revelations of human nature and of the human dilemma happen than are likely to occur in a market. What may be needed is more anxiety to get right inside the human condition, more sensitivity, a greater capacity to be imaginatively and morally aware. This too will involve discrimination and critical judgment; rationality and discipline of mind; a refusal to give way to sentimentality and illusion. But detachment will alternate with identification and both be legitimized as activities proper in universities.

Specialization versus General Education

The second conflict, closely related to the first, is between producing specialists and producing more widely educated people. Traditionally, the university was the only institution of higher education – attendance often bringing social prestige and leading to membership of a profession itself in a position of authority: the church, for example, medicine, law, the civil service. It was, of course, assumed that people would emerge from their university generally educated, and this was more likely before man had entered as technical an age as ours. In medieval times, the Trivium was intended to give a basic general education before even the Quadrivium – itself fairly general in content – was begun. Oxford and Cambridge first degrees were for most graduates essentially non-specialist in character until the later nineteenth century. Without postgraduate schools, which largely developed in the nineteenth century, the Liberal Arts Colleges in America and the great universities in Europe were much more really institutions of general education.

But today the demand is that universities should produce the specialists indispensable to a technologically complex society. Lack of the requisite chemical, surgical or economic knowledge – exact, accurate and immediately available – may spell disaster. And the more complicated our world becomes, the narrower the specialisms may need to be. The pressure to produce an adequate supply of specialists is so intense in every industrialized country that if universities will not do the job, other institutions of tertiary education must and will rapidly be found that will.

Yet the indispensable specialists can be produced at great cost not merely to their own wholeness as human beings, but to the quality of society itself. There is a temptation, frequent enough in industry, to use human beings as tools of a purpose they play little part in forming, and may indeed by the very nature of the education they have received have been made less fitted to form. For they may have been robbed of some of their potential capacities of mind by the need to concentrate on clever manipulation.

What are the ways of resolving this conflict? First by a more widespread realization of its existence. Second by giving more attention to general education. In the USA and in a number of countries influenced by the American tradition, the first two years of a university course have included the study of a variety of subjects chosen by the student himself, though not always in the wisest combinations in spite of the availability of counsellors. On the continent of Europe, where most of the students entering universities have had an academic type of secondary education embodying a fairly rigorous study of eight or nine subjects to the age of 18, the danger of over-specialization once the university has been entered has been real. In England, where a high degree of specialization in a group of three sciences or three arts subjects even now begins for many boys and girls at 16 while they are still at school, the danger of narrowness has been even greater.

Hence the significance of the attempts in many countries to widen the scope of first degree courses, especially in the first year or two. The new University of Keele[1] (founded 1949) in Britain went further than most in introducing a Foundation Year which compelled all undergraduates on entry to the University to study for a year a combination of some science and some arts subjects. All nine of the non-technological universities in Britain founded since 1960 have degree schemes intended in one way or another to prevent too confined an approach to a single subject field, and the tendency in many longer established universities in many countries has been to broaden rather than confine their requirements for a first degree. One recipe is 'to multiply the options';[2] giving the student a still wider and more attractive range of subjects from which to choose the required number; and more syllabuses have been worked out for degrees inter-disciplinary in concept, involving an interrelated study of two or three subjects right up to the first degree examination. But it is easier to invent such combinations than to secure that the Departments concerned with teaching them will modify more than slightly their normal specialist approach to the subjects for which they are responsible.

It is indeed the power and independence of the Departments which acts as a conservative influence in Asia and South America as in Europe, Australia and the USA. Even in some new universities which have tackled with determination the problem of excessive specialization, organizing their degree courses on the basis of Schools rather than Departments and appointing Deans of Schools with considerable powers to preside over them, there are signs that even such safeguards may not be sufficient. The demands of a country's professional associations – of engineers, doctors, lawyers, psychologists – may be a factor here; so may those of industry; so also may be the traditionalism of the academic mind. Most of those who teach a subject in higher education were themselves educated as specialists in that subject up to PhD level.

Perhaps one of the most promising developments is the natural growth of interdisciplinary fields at the postgraduate level. No university or institution for higher technical education can support a Centre for Urban Studies, Pollution Studies, International Studies, Communication Studies or Population Studies without producing far-reaching incentives for inter-disciplinary work. Many graduates from such Centres may go into teach-ing future generations of undergraduates with new insights into the possibility of relevant, interdisciplinary studies at first degree level. Such a recipe will, however, still only be very partially a solution to the problem of reconciling specialized with general education. It is a pragmatic solution, for some areas only, and one which may devote little thought to the principles upon which interdisciplinary studies should or could be based.

At present there is certainly a widespread tendency for university teachers at all levels to blame the previous stage of the student's (or the child's) education for the narrowness he shows. 'That ought to have been attended to earlier – now there is no time, even if I were capable of tackling the job.' This of course is sheer educational irresponsibility, however understandable, and a powerful argument for less cut-offness between higher education and secondary, postgraduate and undergraduate, and between the various stages of the first degree course itself.

Independence versus Integration

The third conflict is that between the university as a self-contained entity and as leading member of an integrated system of institutions of tertiary education. Until comparatively recently, universities were to all appearances independent, self-contained institutions, academically free and having no duty to link themselves with other institutions of higher education, which until the eighteenth century indeed hardly existed anywhere. With the rise of an industrialized society, with science and its applications of basic importance to it, colleges for 'the mechanic arts', technical colleges, and colleges in which to educate teachers to teach children the literacy and numeracy now indispensable, were needed in greater and greater numbers, and as the standards mounted the institutions to which the technologists, technicians and teachers went after leaving their secondary schools became more and more obviously places of tertiary education. In countries as diverse as Egypt, Japan, Brazil and England universities themselves developed faculties of technology; in others – Germany and Holland for example – separate technological universities were created. But it is only of very recent years that it has become clear that technicians and elementary school teachers need a period of higher (as distinct from further) education: one which introduces them to the principles as well as the intelligent practice of a craft. The boundary line between the technological and the technical expert has become harder and harder to draw; that between top management and middle management less precise; that between the essential demands made upon the teacher in an elementary school, staffed chiefly by non-graduates, and those made upon the teacher in a secondary school, staffed chiefly by graduates, less easy to differentiate.

It does not follow, of course, that if institutions of further education are upgraded, they should develop closer links or relationships with universities. But there are many reasons to explain the world-wide tendency for them to do so. First, there is in most countries a strong movement towards greater social equality. In a period when men 'knew their station' there was less upward and downward mobility than there is ever likely to be again. But that period was followed, in many countries, by one of cut-throat competitiveness and naked ambition, which now also seems dated. Injustice is among the most palpably perceived of evils in a modern world. We are far more aware, too, than we were, even up to a few years ago, that the abilities of man are not safely to be categorized in childhood or youth as gold, silver or copper. It is not merely that mistakes can be made in categorization but that what is known as ability depends so much on assumptions about what ability itself consists of, on capacity to recognize its presence, on the self-estimate of its possessor. So that without denying at all differences in innate intellectual potential between individuals we are more and more sure that flexibility of organization in an educational system is important. Ease of transition for students between different types of educational institution at the tertiary stage is likely to become more possible – whether within the same institution, which will then become a 'comprehensive' university, or between institutions retaining their separateness.

Moreover, it is becoming more obvious that the duplication of very expensive research facilities, even library resources, in inviolably separate though neighbouring institutions can be a waste of money. Finally, in future there may well be more natural migration by the staff of one type of higher education to another than there is at present.

In the chapters they have contributed, Drs Hamm-Bruecher and Ingrid Sommerkorn show something of the strength of the current moving in West Germany towards the comprehensive university. One of the motivations of the movement is the conviction that here is a pattern of higher education which will save waste of talent and of spirit. In the Danish concept of comprehensive Centres of Higher Education – not dealt with in the book – the idea is that every Centre should specialize in a few related subjects, some of them less academic, others more so. Transference in each direction between less and more academic types of study would be easily possible, exemptions being given from courses already passed. Every such Centre would encourage research enterprises in some of the subjects it taught. Several Centres might be put near together in a number of areas of the country, contacts between them being encouraged in the hope that joint and interdisciplinary research enterprises would flourish.[3]

But a more common development in higher education in a number of countries is the extension of already existing technical and further education systems to cater for much larger numbers of students, of whom an increasing proportion are full-time. A development of this kind may temporarily leave unsolved the problem of transfer from University to Polytechnic or vice versa as in Britain; from University to College of Applied Arts or vice versa as in Ontario; from University to IUT (*Instituts Universitaires de Technologie*) as in France. Such a gap leaves many questions without an answer – the longer-term future is quite inadequately faced by such a pattern, however satisfactorily the more immediate demand for larger numbers of technicians may be met.

A too little noticed experiment is the implementation since 1946 of the recommendations of the McNair Report in England and Wales by which universities take final responsibility themselves for ensuring that the standards, academic and professional, of practically all entrants, non-graduate and graduate, to the school teaching profession are adequate. The means by which this has been done is the voluntary creation, in every major university but one, of a University Institute of Education, to which all the teacher training colleges in the region belong. Syllabuses and forms and details of examinations are decided upon jointly by members of staff of the university and the colleges with the help of a fairly elaborate mechanism of committees. In recent years a proportion of students from the colleges have been enabled to read for Bachelor of Education degrees of their parent university.

The criteria of future success of the Institute of Education idea include whether means can be found (a) of widening the concerns of the colleges so that their students do not emerge with a qualification to teach which is unserviceable for any other purpose; (b) of opening up higher degrees, and not in Education only, to suitable BEd graduates; and (c) of securing that contacts and relationships between university students and staff on the one hand, and college students and staff on the other, become increasingly close. This is in some ways a test case of the willingness of universities to link themselves more intimately with institutions which many university teachers still regard as socially and mentally inferior places as well as including in the subjects they teach some of dubious academic respectability – physical education, for example, dance, drama, home economics. Others would testify to the broadening effect of its responsibility for an Institute of Education upon a university's own programme and upon its awareness of its function to give leadership of more than a research-oriented sort.

It remains possible as present policy is shaping that the colleges of education in Britain will again revert for a time to the further education sector – but with permission to give degrees of their own, which will then have to win recognition from universities as external bodies if university degree work is contemplated. We may therefore still find ourselves for an additional period with the dichotomy (which has something of a class, as well as an academic, distinction about it) between colleges of education and universities proper that the McNair and Robbins Reports, of 1944 and 1963 respectively, sought to overcome.

Any organization of higher education in a system which makes the university – as the leading member of the institutions of higher education of its region – into a kind of headquarters for educating society assumes that it will have developed an imaginative understanding of what such a function entails; and that is far at present from being the case. Quick evolution towards such a realization of responsibility is not likely to be possible, but it is difficult to see what in the long run is a satisfactory, or even viable, alternative to it.

In future years many more students in higher education in most countries will probably be studying part-time; and a larger proportion will be older men and women returning to update their qualifications or renew their intellectual vitality. These factors by themselves could greatly change the image a university has of its own nature and add to its capacity for developing links easily with other parts of the higher education system. The idea of the Open University in Britain and that of open admission, as to the City University of New York, are experiments to watch, not only because of their boldness but of their broadening of concept of what a university can properly be. What may be gained, however, must not result in what Sir Eric Ashby has called 'the thin stream of excellence'[4] running thinner still. But that is a danger against which, at any rate, some universities are consciously trying to safeguard themselves.

Academic Freedom versus National Interest

Another conflict of purpose with which the university may be faced is that between looking upon itself as an autonomous institution, pursuing its own way in freedom, unhampered by the state; and as having duties laid upon it from the outside so that it furthers national policy and national prosperity. Which of the state's own needs, real or supposed, is it legitimate for it to require universities to satisfy? If it wants to reduce the numbers of surgeons to be trained and add to the number of civil engineers, this may be acceptable – provided that the places of higher education are given time enough to make the change. But if it demands a wholesale switch from arts to technology (or less probably from technology to arts) are universities to have small say in the matter? Has not the university a responsibility for providing not only experts in particular fields, but overall critics – including critics of the state itself, its assumptions and even its policies? There are parts of the world as different as China and California where the state has demanded, not without success, that universities should toe lines, which left to themselves they might well have been unwilling to do. But in almost every country sanctions have been used to bring to heel institutions of higher education thought by the state to be serving it in particular respects inadequately, ineptly or selfishly.[5]

Even to expect universities to produce citizens 'with an active character'[6] who shall be good members of their society may be unduly to underestimate the value to the state itself of some who will not be active in character but shy artists, introverts, meditators, philosophers, yet invaluable to the development of their nation itself. Who shall decide? And who will decide whether an overriding need of the future may not be for more people with an international outlook, which may cause them to challenge merely national interests or what seem to them (mistakenly or not) to be so? The universities on occasion may easily seem to many men in the street, and many in more powerful positions too, to be producers of a mixture of protestors and rebels. And their public image may suffer accordingly. Have they to conform or defend themselves? This raises the much larger question of how far universities have a responsibility for interpreting the needs of their country, some of which it may be barely conscious of at all itself, to those in political office, to the public in general, including the public outside the country as well as inside it.

Such profound issues as these are more not less likely to become urgent in future with the lessening size of the world, the growth in extra-national contacts, the realization of how valuable the contribution of universities can be, not only to the solution of problems of health and tech-nology (pollution rarely has national boundaries), but for clarifying aims in national – and personal – life. Their value is far from utilitarian only.

A resolution of conflicts of this kind can perhaps only be found first in an evolution of consciousness on the part of universities themselves regarding their *de facto* position and secondly, in a widening recognition of their responsibility. No institutions of higher education anywhere have really been such free agents as they may have thought they were. They need a better knowledge of their own history and the functions they have fulfilled in the past. In future they are likely to become more and more dependent upon the public purse for funds – either by payment of grants direct to them, or indirectly through payments for research, subsidization of student fees, loans at lower than the normal rates of interest, etc.

Their way forward cannot therefore be one of seeking to isolate them-selves either from the public or the state. Their importance as centres of research, of new knowledge and new applications of knowledge is not in question. But their public relations work is, in many countries, in need of improvement: what Dr Weidner calls their 'community outreach' could be furthered far more imaginatively than has often as yet been attempted. Yet to develop chiefly on this side could result in an enfeeblement of their capacity to be detached while remaining informedly humane – intellectual consciences of their country and maybe of a whole aggregation of countries.

They are less and less likely in future to cater chiefly for a wealthy elite, whose views are accepted in a community by reason of their assumed social distinction. Yet it was a willing acceptance of this kind of superior-ity which has given universities in the past much influence – largely through their graduates, who occupied so many of the major positions of power. In future, it is the intellectual contribution made by their products which will count. But the concept of 'intellectual' is still often inadequate. Unless it contains within it more than an entirely objective kind of rationality, the universities may still find themselves servants to the state in a way neither can afford. What is in the last resort an aristocratic ideal, that of academic autonomy or freedom, must find a place within the mind of as many as possible of the individual people universities educate, so that they have, as individuals, an ability to be detached, values to which they are committed, and ability to give reasons for holding them important. What is necessary is no longer the elitism of a social class, but the possession by the graduate of an elite integrity of mind, the ability to make judgments that are good, and intellectually good too, because reckoning with moral and aesthetic as well as practical issues.

Quantity versus Quality

The fifth conflict in need of resolution for the future is that between a policy of building a smaller number of large universities or a much larger number of smaller ones. The advantages of large size include economy of construction; administrative efficiency; the presence near at hand of numbers of varied Departments whose close contact may fertilize both research and service enterprises. The advantages of smaller size include the greater ease with which personal relationships between individuals – both senior and junior – can be established and the greater and more obvious coherence attainable by an institution. The 'cluster college' idea;[7] the fostering of relations between institutions of great variety not on the same campus, can help to resolve the conflict.

But future policy-makers will still have to decide where the balance of advantage lies. Is there not a fairly early limit in size even to the cluster college? How important are personal relationships to the kind of higher education we seek to give – or that students want to receive? It may be that some of the most important elements in the higher education needed in future cannot be communicated unless people bring more of their own humanity into the situation than either faculty or students are at present willing to do.

Concern for Objectives versus Concern for Orientation

Without any doubt university lecturers and professors need to raise more resolutely into consciousness the objectives of their teaching – whether in lectures or seminars. This is a preliminary to any effective improvement both in their teaching and their examining. But concern with objectives cannot in itself be a substitute for a concern with 'process', that is, concern for the whole impact a university makes upon its students, and not only for the measurable attainments which may come from efficiently teaching a particular subject or combination of subjects. The more clearly objectives are defined the more likely they are to be attained. But the very clarity itself may result in a narrowing of purpose. It is not enough to make teaching and examining more efficient if the chief purpose is to teach a scholarly discipline with bare regard to the needs of society or of students. The university which is really to face the future, as we have seen, cannot remain the preserve of professors unaware of their broader tasks.

The very success of a clear-sighted, analytic method is due in part to its dividing up the world into manageable aspects or portions, keeping the variables under observation and control. What cannot be controlled tends to get left out of the analysis; the more definable and measurable tend to be preferred to the less definable and the immeasurable. In our entirely right conviction that we must define relatively near at hand objectives more accurately, it is easy to overlook the need even to ask the larger questions.

A number of the chapters in this book touch on this, but rather by implication than overt statement. Yet the passionate concern of Tanzania that its universities should educate good socialists; the interesting reference in the chapter by Belyaev and Golenpolsky that one of the functions of a higher educational institution is to forge 'a materialistic outlook'; the remark by Toh Chin Chye that students tend to be 'educated for an empty life' are all indications that a belief in technology is by no means the only belief really animating civilization today. Great expectations attach to our investment of so much hope and mental energy in controlling further the conditions of living; but dreams also are important. If vision is too completely subjugated to planning, the best we can hope for may be more of the same; extension rather than inwardness; quantity rather than quality.

In the long run the individual may be the ultimately important thing. At any rate it is unlikely that the future can be adequately faced by universities unless this possibility is kept more clearly in mind than it is at present fashionable to do.

NOTES

1. Called at first the University College of North Staffordshire.
2. Cf. p. 386 (Warren Martin).
3. See *Skitse for udbygningen af de højere uddannelser i tiden indtil 1980*, Copenhagen: 1967.
4. In *Any Person, Any Study* (New York: McGraw-Hill, 1971).
5. Cf. p. 32 *infra*.
6. Cf. p. 33 *infra*.
7. Cf. p. 37.

2

On the Threshold of Mass Higher Education

Ladislav Cerych and Dorotea E. Furth

Introduction

Rapid world-wide expansion of post-secondary education is now a well-known phenomenon. Its various aspects have been abundantly commented upon and described most frequently under the headings 'pressure of numbers' or 'explosion of enrolments'. It is also widely recognized that this pressure or explosion constitutes one, if not the major, factor behind the strongly felt (though not often rapidly implemented) need for qualitative and structural transformation of the existing post-secondary education systems. The type of changes which are needed can to some extent, therefore, be derived from an analysis of the patterns of recent quantitative expansion and of their qualitative consequences.

Such an analysis has recently been presented by the Organization for Economic Co-operation and Development[1] and its major conclusions will serve as the main source of the first part of the present article. On the basis of these investigations undertaken by the OECD, the argument will be put forward that quantitative expansion has brought most of the higher education systems to a critical point, which we shall call the 'threshold of mass higher education'. Finally, some general characteristics of mass higher education and alternative structures for a mass system will be identified.

Probability of Further Growth

Expansion of enrolments in post-secondary education during the past two decades is reflected in Table 1. This table shows clearly that almost all countries were subject to a very rapid expansion, whatever the level and ratio of their economic development, the size and structure of their higher education system and the type of educational policy adopted and pursued. It is not easy to identify all the forces underlying this universal phenomenon, much less their relative weight, impact and interrelationships, but it appears that the most powerful role has been played by the development of secondary education which, especially in Europe, has constituted the principal direct cause of expansion at the post-secondary level. A kind of 'Iron Law of Educational Growth' can thus be formulated: universalization of primary education, leading to generalization of

14

TABLE 1

GROWTH OF ENROLMENTS IN POST-SECONDARY EDUCATION

Country	Enrolments (1955=100)			Enrolment ratios (1955=100)		
	1960/1	1965/6	1968/9	1960/1	1965/6	1968/9
Austria	201	255	259	150	213	277
Belgium	136	219	260★	148	204	254★
Denmark	148	238	300★	143	178	202
Finland	141	241	350★	129	185	255★
France	132	243	327★	145	208	232
Germany	167	210	240★	132	189	205★
Greece	136	278	362	147	342	405★
Ireland	139	174	270★	159	174	217★
Iceland	104	147	181	—	—	—
Italy	128	191	247★	134	212	244
Luxembourg	141	214	260	—	—	—
Netherlands	149	216	260★	142	165	173
Norway	168★	380★	458★	161★	281★	303★
Portugal	134	196	246	147	212	335★
Spain	125	216	265★	146	231	273★
Sweden	147	285	455	137	200	268★
Switzerland	142	214	240	122	147	158★
Turkey	180	266	370★	177	246	338★
United Kingdom	141	212	271	138	170	214★
Yugoslavia	202	256	331	210	317	397★
Canada	176	327	464★	168	233	346★
Japan	117	178	245	114	169	199★
United States	135	208	260	123	149	166

SOURCE: Development of Higher Education, 1950–67, Statistical Survey, OECD, Paris, 1970, and Development of Higher Education, 1950–67, Analytical Report, OECD, Paris, 1971, National Statistics for 1968–9.
★Estimates.

secondary, and the latter to a corresponding growth of higher education.

The important question to be asked is whether this process will continue during the seventies and eighties – in other words, whether it is reasonable to expect the growth curves of post-secondary education to climb in future years as they have done since the fifties. At least two facts point in this direction:

(a) The educational policies of most of the industrialized countries are based predominantly on the principle of satisfying social demand for higher education and opening its gates not only to those qualified by traditional criteria (that is, all applicants who have successfully completed general secondary education), but also to students who up to now have been excluded, either formally or in practice, because of their social origin, educational background or age.

TABLE 2
APPROXIMATE ENROLMENT RATES FOR ALL HIGHER EDUCATION

Countries	Age groups	Higher Education				
		1950/1	1955/6	1960/1	1965/6	1968/9
Austria (1)	19–24 years	—	3·0	4·5	6·4	8·3
Belgium	18–23 years	4·0*	5·4	8·0	11·0	137*
Denmark	19–25 years	5·0	5·4	7·7	9·6	10·9
Finland	19–24 years	4·2	5·5	7·1	10·2	14·0*
France	18–23 years	4·8*	6·0	8·7	12·5	13·9
Germany	20–25 years	3·8	4·4	5·8	8·3	9·0**
Greece	18–24 years	—	1·9	2·8	6·5	7·65*
Ireland	18–22 years	3·9*	4·6*	7·3	8·0*	10·0*
Iceland	—	—	—	—	—	—
Italy (2)	19–25 years	4·2	4·1	5·5	8·7	10·0
Luxembourg (3)	20–25 years	—	—	3·8	6·1	—
Netherlands	18–24 years	4·4	5·2	7·4	8·6	9·0
Norway	19–24 years	3·4*	3·1*	5·0*	8·7	9·4*
Portugal	18–24 years	1·4	1·7*	2·5	3·6	5·7**
Spain	18–24 years	—	2·6*	3·8	6·0	7·1*
Sweden	20–24 years	4·8	6·3	8·6	12·6	16·9**
Switzerland	20–25 years	4·5	4·5	5·5	6·6	7·1**
Turkey	18–23 years	1·0*	1·3*	2·3	3·2	4·4**
United Kingdom	18–22 years	5·2*	6·3	8·7	10·7	13·5*
Yugoslavia	19–25 years	2·7	2·9	6·1	9·2	11·5**
Canada (4)	18–23 years	6·5*	8·1	13·6	18·9	28·0**
Japan	18–22 years	4·9	7·1	8·1	12·0	14·1
United States	18–23 years	16·8	21·1	25·9	31·4	35·0

[1] Austrian students only.
[2] 1951, 1956, 1961 and 1966.
[3] 1960 and 1966.
[4] 1951, 1956, 1961 and 1965.
* Estimate of enrolments.
** Estimate of age group.
See Table 1.

(b) This social demand for higher education will most probably continue to grow; no major constraints or ceilings can be identified which would lead to its decline in the foreseeable future.

The first point can be illustrated by a number of official statements which have been made in different countries,[2] while the second point – that social demand for post-secondary education will very probably continue to grow in the future – is supported by several important circumstances:

(i) Higher education, even in the most developed countries, still serves a minority of the age group. As seen in Table 2, in 1968 no European country exceeded an enrolment ratio of 17 per cent, and eleven enrolled 10 per cent or less of the relevant age group. Canada, and particularly the USA, are far ahead in this respect; the gap is even more striking when considering that in 1965 no European country had reached the 1950 enrolment ratio of the USA. Thus it seems highly unlikely that a decline in growth rates, or even a stagnation of enrolments, would take place in the coming years as a result of the approach of some kind of assumed ceiling.

(ii) As already mentioned, the most powerful driving force behind the expansion of higher education in Europe has been the development of secondary education. But, here again, the potential is far from being exhausted. At present, in no European country does more than 50 per cent of the respective age group finish secondary school, and in most the percentage is less than 30 or even 20, as against 60 per cent in the USSR and around 80 per cent in Japan, Canada and the USA. Consequently, there is no reason why the 'Iron Law of Educational Growth' should not continue to exercise its influence wherever secondary school enrolments still fail to include the large majority of the relevant age group. On the contrary, it may be expected that the effects of this law will be reinforced by continuing reform of the conditions of admission to universities. Until recently, in most countries, those entering universities were almost exclusively those who had been successful in completing a course of general (academic) secondary education; the new measures – which so far have had only slight quantitative impact – foresee admission from all branches of secondary education, and even from among those without complete secondary schooling.

(iii) Another important growth potential derives from existing inequalities of educational opportunity. The fact that present enrolment ratios of women in higher education constitute in most countries only one third to one half of male ratios; or that students from working class families represent no more than 25 per cent of the total number of students, and often less than 10 per cent, whereas these classes constitute up to 50 per cent or more of the population; or the low participation rates of students from certain regions – all these and similar sources of inequality will necessarily add to the pressure of social demand for higher education. In fact, the policies which have already been pursued – albeit, often with insufficient rigour – have begun to have a significant impact. Thus, for example, new higher education establishments have been created in areas or regions where up to now the absence of such facilities, or geographical distance, represented either psychologically or materially a serious obstacle to attendance at post-secondary institutions.

(iv) It must also be borne in mind that of the various factors correlated with the rate of participation in higher education of different social groups, by far the most significant is the educational level of parents. An increase in the number of fathers and mothers with university degrees (or merely secondary school diplomas) inevitably implies more children demanding entry into higher education a generation later. The seventies (or, at the latest, the early eighties) will be precisely one generation span from the beginning of the great expansion wave which took place in most countries during the course of the fifties.

(v) Finally, it is increasingly recognized that higher education should not be the privilege of a specific age group (e.g. 18 to 25 years) or of full secondary school graduates only, but that it should be available to all those capable of benefiting from it. This leads to the concepts of, and requirements for, remedial education, adult education, retraining, or recurrent education, all of which imply the entry into post-secondary institutions of a new type of clientele and of additional students who were scarcely represented in the past.

Limits of Expansion?

All these factors of determining the probable future growth of post-secondary education are sometimes considered as insufficient to counterbalance two basic constraints which, theoretically, might impose strict limits on the expansion curve: the impossibility of devoting a continuously increasing proportion of public funds or of GNP to higher education, and the decline in the rate of return to higher education resulting from an over-supply of graduates. Neither of these constraints can be substantiated as being a force with more than short-term effects. Most of the European countries devote between 0·8 per cent and 1·5 per cent of their GNP to post-secondary education. The USA has now passed the 2 per cent level and expects to reach 3 per cent in 1976. Again, therefore, if there is any theoretical and practical ceiling, it is far from being reached. This is equally true of the danger of over-production of graduates; here it should suffice to recall that Japan, with a GNP per capita of about half that of the most advanced European countries, provides employment to almost three times as many graduates; and, on the other hand, the USA, with a per capita income about double that of Europe, absorbs every year four to five times as many degree holders as an average Western European country.

Clearly, bottlenecks – general or sectorial – might and probably will arise and could seriously disrupt the functioning of the system; but nothing in the long-term trend points towards an inherent absorption limit of the economy which would be sufficiently powerful to reverse the growth propensity and pressure of social demand for higher education.

The End of Elitist Higher Education

The recent expansion of enrolments, combined with the influence of various other socio-economic factors, has created a situation the nature of which can probably best be characterized by a set of new problems to be faced by higher education systems in most developed countries.

(*a*) Society expects higher education to fulfil a much *larger and varied number of functions* than those assigned to it in the past; its value and goal structure is becoming different from the value and goal structure of traditional higher education systems;

(*b*) The demand for higher education has led not only to massive expansion of enrolments but also to a *change in the clientele* of higher education, i.e. to a considerably increased variety and greater heterogeneity of aptitudes, abilities, motivations and expectations of students with regard to their future education, professional career and life in general;

(*c*) The role of higher education as a *key factor of production* in terms of economic theory becomes progressively more important than the role of capital, in the same way as the latter replaced land in the nineteenth century;

(*d*) Higher education, by the sheer mass of resources it requires in budgetary and personnel terms, is assuming a *political weight* incommensurate with its traditional role.

Few systems can cope with these new problems without first undergoing a number of radical reforms, not only in their different parts and aspects but in their overall structures. And such reforms become even more urgent when one considers the high probability of further growth in the course of the coming years.

This also leads to the main thesis of the present article, already formulated in a recent OECD document:[3]

> Most countries are at an intermediary and critical stage between elitist and mass higher education, the former having to be abandoned under the pressure of numbers and of a series of socio-economic factors, the latter requiring structures, content and organizational arrangements which have not yet been developed and only partly identified.

The situation is of course more critical in some countries than in others, but, as shown in a chapter in the 1971/72 *World Year Book of Education*,[4] practically all Western systems, whatever their relative level of development, suffer from a certain number of common deficiencies: inequality of opportunity, inadaptation to manpower needs, financial difficulties, lack of flexibility, and lack of response to the quest of new generations for self-fulfilment. Whether the crisis is of a similar nature in most European systems with 5 per cent to 15 per cent enrolment ratios on the one side, and the USA or other countries with ratios between 20 per cent and 40 per cent on the other, is not quite certain. To some extent it can be argued that for several decades – and possibly even since the end of the nineteenth century – the USA (and a few other countries) have had a system which facilitated the advent of mass higher education: a diversification of curriculum, the development of a service function for universities, the mobility of students between various sectors of the system. And it may be that these characteristics explain why the USA attained present European enrolment ratios some 20 to 30 years ago with, at that time, a GNP per capita significantly lower than the one prevailing in Europe today. This might also explain why, in general, the present pressures for reform and innovation in North America do not question so much the institutional framework of higher education, while in Europe a quest for completely new types of institutions is increasingly becoming the *leitmotif* of higher education planners. Several groups and individuals have, of course, recommended a virtually total revision of some of the basic principles of American higher education. In this respect, the Carnegie Commission on Higher Education represents probably the most comprehensive and massive effort, the effects of which cannot yet be assessed, but which might easily become a significant model for an overall reappraisal and planning of higher education.[5] Recently also the Federal Office of Education and the Ford Foundation sponsored the preparation of a report[6] which questions some of the basic assumptions of the American higher education system and recommends many completely new approaches to its development.

But very few, if any, of these recommendations have produced proposals to abolish or to change drastically the overall institutional structure of the system or any of its major components. Scarcely anybody wishes to abolish, say, the Junior Colleges or private universities; no one suggests a completely new comprehensive organization of higher education, as reflected, for instance, in the German *Gesamthochschule*, the Danish University Centre or the French *Loi d'Orientation* proposals. The question can therefore be posed whether the present difficulties encountered by US higher education are a corollary of a new stage – a passage from mass to universal higher education[7] – or whether they result simply from an imperfect and/or partial assimilation of mass higher education requirements only, and from the persistence of some components of an elitist structure.

Comparative educationists, historians, sociologists and economists of education will, it is hoped, throw more light on this possibly very significant question of the USA/Europe 'enrolment gap' and institutional versus content reforms of higher education. In the meantime we can only restate our main point, namely that most of the European countries, after having increased their enrolment ratios from about 5 per cent or less to

10–15 per cent, are facing a situation to which their systems are not adjusted; in other words, they are facing the 'threshold of mass higher education' (while in the USA the 'threshold of universal higher education' may already have been reached).

Among the factors causing this inadaptation and thus the crisis characterizing most European systems, it is not sufficient to mention the classic argument of the rigidity of present elitist structures. Underlying this situation are the predominant attitudes, expectations and aspirations of many groups concerned (including professors and students) which seem to be in conflict with some of the basic conditions and prerequisites for the establishment of a system of mass higher education.

Main Characteristics of Mass Higher Education

Setting up structures of mass higher education will involve profound changes in many areas. Four of them will be briefly examined in the following section:

(a) relations between secondary and post-secondary education;
(b) the content of higher education;
(c) the relation between higher education and employment;
(d) the relations between higher education and society in general.

Subsequently, a more detailed analysis will be presented of the different overall institutional structures of mass higher education which seem to be emerging.

(a) Relations between secondary and post-secondary education

Mass higher education cannot become a reality without mass secondary education. The quantitative or statistical evidence for this thesis is irrefutable, as Table 3 shows.

The development of mass secondary education in Europe implies, however, much more than raising student numbers to present US, Canadian or Soviet standards – it implies a fundamental change in the traditional qualitative relationship between the two levels. The on-going reforms of secondary education mentioned earlier,* all of which tend towards a 'dehierarchization' of various types and streams of secondary schools, if not towards the concept of comprehensive secondary education, must become both an institutional and a sociological (in the sense of their social prestige value) reality of the concept of equality of educational opportunity at the post-secondary level is to have any practical meaning. This, of course, has, among other things, important consequences for curriculum planning and development, and leads, in general, to the concept of post-compulsory education in which upper secondary and post-secondary education are considered as an integrated and articulated whole.

---

* See p. 17.

TABLE 3

NUMBERS OF SECONDARY SCHOOL-
LEAVING CERTIFICATES AS A
PERCENTAGE OF THE POPULATION OF
THE CORRESPONDING AGE-GROUP
(COLUMN I) AND ENROLMENT RATIOS
IN HIGHER EDUCATION (COLUMN II)

(1965 or 1966)

	I	II
Austria	11·7	7·5
Belgium	29·6	14·9
Spain	6·6	8·7
France	17·4	17·4
Italy	18·0	11·3
Netherlands	18·8	13·6
United Kingdom	18·7	11·9
Sweden	18·5	13·1
Switzerland	4·3	7·7
Yugoslavia	21·0	13·1
Canada	71·6	23·7
United States	75·7	40·8
Japan	50·5	12·0
USSR	58·4	31·0
—of which full-time	—	12·7

SOURCE: Development of Higher Education, 1950–67, Analytical Report, OECD, Paris, 1971.

(b) *The content of higher education*

Traditional systems emphasize only a small number of well-established and academically recognized disciplines and are in this sense only a continuation or a rather timid extension of the famous Trivium and Quadrivium of the medieval university. Mass higher education, on the contrary, must offer a wide and perpetually changing range of fields of study. Without going quite as far as the American and Soviet systems in the fifties or early sixties (the USA offering 1,600 types of degrees from mathematics to caretaking), higher education in the future simply cannot afford a rigid classification of disciplines to which both professors and students are obliged strictly to adhere. The ideal of individualized education is a corollary to this requirement, as is, in more general terms, the concept of equality of fields of study, whether they correspond to highly theoretical and historically-rooted disciplines or to practically and problem oriented (and usually interdisciplinary) areas of knowledge.

Even more important in this domain, however, seems to be the problem of the structure of studies. Traditional pedagogy as reflected in the majority of existing systems postulates only unilateral relationships and flows: from general to specialized, from theoretical to practical, and from education to job. In the emerging mass systems it is necessary not to reverse these relationships but to provide alternatives; in other words, to take into account the wide range of abilities, experiences and motivations of the new enlarged student clientele, some of whom will be more successful in their learning if they follow the traditional path, others if they are allowed to go in the opposite direction – from special to general, from practical to theoretical and from work to education.

(c) Higher education and employment

The relationships between education and employment in mass higher education will be much more diffuse than formerly. In the elitist system, as a rule, each level and type of education corresponded closely to a specific type of job or profession, while in mass higher education a particular degree will give access to a substantially greater variety of occupations. This situation corresponds to at least two other circumstances. On the one hand, as a result of technological progress, the structure of the labour market changes much more rapidly than in the past, and its flexibility is one of the main conditions of economic growth. If the supply of qualified manpower is not sufficiently elastic to meet this situation, the system will inevitably become blocked and will simultaneously face graduate unemployment and a shortage of skilled personnel. On the other hand, it is clear that growing demand for higher education leads to an upward shift of qualification requirements, even when such a shift is sometimes technically unjustified. Sooner or later, however, the extra-employment objectives of higher education, whose weight is certainly increasing, will compensate for this 'employment devaluation of graduates'.

As stated earlier, a mass system therefore renders meaningless the theory of 'overproduction of graduates'. This seemingly radical thesis – considering the present situation and complaints or fears of students and policymakers in many countries – has already been illustrated by the examples of the US and Japan.

(d) Higher education and society

In this respect, the new situation of higher education derives principally from the additional and broader functions which it is expected to fulfil and, in general, from the central role which knowledge occupies in the total life of society. Hence its closer links to, and more direct participation in, the economic, social and cultural development of the national and surrounding community. In the words of Clark Kerr: 'Knowledge has certainly never in history been so central to the conduct of an entire society. What the railroads did for the second half of the last century and automobile for the first half of this century may be done for the nd half of this century by the knowledge industry: that is, to serve as the focal point for national growth. And the university is at the centre of the knowledge process.'[8]

A corollary to this central position of the higher education sector is a whole range of new tasks: adult and continuing education in its various forms, extension services of all kinds, active involvement in the local, regional and national planning effort, etc. Many of these functions were assumed by universities in the past, but to a great extent they were always marginal or a simple addition to the traditional roles of providing teaching to students within a rather narrow age group and of undertaking so-called pure research. In a mass system, on the contrary, it is indispensable that all these new tasks become an integral part of the goal structure of higher education, and assume an importance equal to that of its long-established functions. Most probably this can, and will, best be achieved by a greater interpenetration between teaching and research on the one hand, and on the other by extension services, participation in local, regional and national development and planning, as well as adult (or continuing) education. Tasks related to the latter functions should, to a certain extent at least, become subjects of the former.

Towards Mass Structures

Clearly, all the above characteristics of mass higher education (as well as those not mentioned here, such as a different profile of the teaching profession, new pedagogical relations, etc.) have to be accommodated within an appropriate institutional framework. Whether such a framework must already be in existence before these characteristics can be developed, or whether the institutional structure will inevitably follow from changes in the content methods and objectives of higher education, is to our mind a pointless question. They are obviously interrelated and one without the other will sooner or later lead to a blockage of the system. Only the specific national context can determine the strategic advisability of starting with new institutions because they are necessary to modify content and attitudes, or of adopting the reverse procedure.

The main problem arising in all countries where new structures of post-secondary education have to be planned and developed seems to be one of the compatibility of two types of requirements. On the one hand, higher education must maintain and even strengthen its standards, it must ensure excellence both in teaching and research; on the other hand, it must provide adequate educational opportunities to a mass of students whose interests, abilities and aspirations are extremely heterogeneous and often do not correspond to the traditional functions of universities. The crucial point is that these new mass educational opportunities are not allowed to develop into an isolated sector of 'second-class higher education', considered by both students and society in general as a cheap substitute for traditional full-time university education. In other words, mass higher education must avoid the situation which exists in most European systems today, namely a sharp split into 'noble' and 'less noble' higher education. A differentiation between the more and the less prestigious institutions or types of higher education will always exist; this might be an unavoidable and, in a sense, even a desirable consequence of the quest for the highest possible standards and excellence. Thus a 'parity of esteem' between institutions or courses employing different lengths of study, different conditions of admission, or leading to different levels of degrees, can probably never be achieved. The important thing is that this inescapable difference does not lead to a rigid hierarchy which blocks the flow of students, preventing many of them, whatever their merits, from reaching the top of the educational ladder, and thereby strengthening inequality of educational opportunity. In practice, this means allowing the transfer of students from one institution or course to another, and a minimum of effective co-ordination and of integrated planning of the various components of the post-secondary system; and, parallel to this, a diversification of the system, which implies basically a greater variety of educational opportunities in terms of different lengths and patterns of study, of types of degrees offered and ways in which to obtain them.

We face here another problem of compatibility (which is perhaps only a different formulation of the first problem between high standards and mass opportunities): compatibility between the imperatives of diversification and integration of the system.*

In practical terms, the search for this compatibility most often implies the transformation of a value structure in which pure research, development of knowledge for its own sake, and theoretical or abstract disciplines are placed at the top of the scale, while technically, vocationally and practically oriented studies are on the lowest echelons. Undoubtedly, it is this value scale which constitutes the most formidable obstacle to effective structural change. In fact, if structural changes take place and are not accompanied, or do not produce, corresponding changes in the value system, their consequences will be limited or distorted. Thus, new educational opportunities might be emerging, new institutions might be developing and expanding outside the universities, but the very powerful influence of the traditional standards of the universities will make it difficult for the new components of the system to acquire sufficient prestige without to some extent imitating the former and thereby rejecting their own specific functions.

---

* The authors, in their chapter in the 1971/72 *Year Book of Education*, and in several OECD documents, speak of 'diversification and unity of the system'. It appears, however, that the term 'unity' might also suggest unified control of the system, which is certainly not a necessary or even a desirable goal. Thus the term 'integration', or possibly 'articulation' is probably more suitable.

On the threshold of mass higher education, three main institutional models seem to be emerging: (*a*) the comprehensive university model, (*b*) the binary model, and (*c*) the combined model.

(a) The comprehensive university model

In this system all types of post-secondary education are put under the umbrella of a single regional unit which thus becomes the tool both of diversification and integration of the system. This new kind of university includes both short- and long-cycle courses, vocationally and academically oriented, part- and full-time education.

All teachers and students belong to the same institutions and, theoretically at least, status differences disappear because the common formal denomination implies easy transfer from one type and level of course to another, joint affiliation, sharing of equipment, etc. The German *Gesamthochschule* or the Danish University Centre seem to be the prototypes of this model, in which the degree of integration (or of articulation) may vary from a mere 'co-operative comprehensive university' to a fully integrated one. In the former, the regional unit is a simple confederation of formerly independent institutions which retain a large degree of autonomy; in the latter, a basically new entity is born comprising a central administration and a unified decision-making process.

At least two fundamental conditions will have to be fulfilled if this model is to succeed. In the first place, profound changes must take place in the attitudes of the university community, which will not only have to accept as equal partners the formerly 'less noble' institutions, but, more difficult, they will have to adjust their own rules and standards to those of the former non-university establishments. Secondly, the functions previously fulfilled by the non-university sector (short-cycle higher education, technical and professional studies) must continue to be assumed by the new unit. If this is not the case and all the activities of the comprehensive university become progressively oriented towards traditional university goals, diversity will remain a meaningless slogan.

(b) The binary model

Essentially, this model postulates the continuation of a separate development of the traditional university and of a reformed non-university sector. It may be justified in cases where universities either refuse to change their goal structure and/or remain highly selective, and do not or cannot respond to mass demand for higher education. But, in this situation, the non-university sector must become much more than it is in the elitist system; it must, in a sense, be 'ennobled', which means acquiring at least some of those characteristics from which the universities derive their prestige: possibilities for students to be awarded degrees at all levels, higher status and research possibilities for teachers, etc. Clearly, the present UK pattern is the best example of this model.

Such an 'ennobling' of the non-university sector (and its increased quantitative weight) might eventually facilitate an 'integration among equals', i.e. a closer link with universities, which for the moment seems impossible because the prestige difference between the two sectors is too great.

The danger of course is that this separate development approach may give rise to protracted conflict, with consequent overlapping, wastage of scarce resources and failure to meet some of the main overall objectives of post-secondary education.

(c) The combined model

The majority of countries will probably follow this model,* which consists of two closely related sectors. The bulk of non-university institutions will cover the first two or three years of post-secondary education and their graduates will have the choice of entering the labour market or going on to further studies at university. This means, in fact, that the non-university institutions must be multi-purpose – they must offer both the first cycle of full university education, and vocationally oriented short-cycle higher education. In some instances, all students who intend to pursue studies after secondary school have to pass through them (for example, the CEGEPs in Quebec); in other cases they represent an alternative and a student can either start there or in the university sector (for example, Junior Colleges in the USA). The important point about this model is that it must eliminate the 'blind alleys' which characterize many European systems, both past and present, where entry into a non-university institution represents an irreversible choice which strictly limits the student's educational and professional career.

The major difficulty here is that the transfer function may be stressed too much by authorities and by students, which makes the non-university institution lose its other equally important function of providing more practically oriented and shorter higher education. In the long run, the only solution seems to lie in a change in the attitudes of society itself, in the relative values people place on the various types of education. In the more immediate future, improvements in the employment conditions of short-cycle and vocationally oriented degrees might be the most important measure. It would also undoubtedly help if the flow of students between the two sectors could develop in both ways, not only from non-university to university institutions but also from universities into the

---

* Because of the large number of countries where this model is expected to develop, different solutions will probably be applied. However, it is too early at this stage to establish any comprehensive classification.

more specialized non-university sector (this objective is already being emphasized in several countries, such as France, Norway and Belgium).

Whatever model or combination of models is adopted, the main institutional characteristic of mass higher education seems clear: its structure must offer considerably enlarged facilities for post-secondary study in terms of more widespread geographic location, of access conditions in relation to educational backgrounds, of patterns, forms, lengths and fields of study, and in terms of possibilities for transfer of students from one level and type of study to another. More or less monolithic universities, even if their size or number could be multiplied, cannot represent the principal feature of mass higher education; a much broader institutional framework is necessary which can accommodate not only the increased numbers of students but also the different functions which post-secondary education has to fulfil in the years to come.

REFERENCES

1. Development of Higher Education, 1950–67, Statistical Survey, OECD, Paris 1970, and Development of Higher Education, 1950–67, Analytical Report, OECD, Paris 1971.
2. Norway: Committee on Higher Education (Ottossen), Volumes 1 and 4. Ministry of Education, Oslo, 1966 and 1969.
   Sweden: Directives to the 1968 Commission on Post-secondary Education (U68) and proposals of the Commission on Entrance qualifications (KU).
   U.K.: Report of the Committee on Higher Education (Robbins), London, HMSO, 1963.
   Germany: Minister for Education and Science, Report of the Federal Government on Educational Policy, Bonn 1970.
3. Towards New Structures of Post-Secondary Education, Preliminary Statement of Issues, OECD, Paris, June 1971.
4. L. Cerych and D. Furth: 'The Search for a Global System: Unity and Diversity of Post-Secondary Education', World Year Book of Education 1971/2.
5. See the contribution to this volume by Sir Eric Ashby.
6. US Department of Health, Education and Welfare: Report on Higher Education, Washington D.C., March 1971. (Prepared by an independent Task Force under the chairmanship of Professor Frank Newman.)
7. Martin Trow: 'Reflections on the Transition from Mass to Universal Higher Education', Daedalus, Winter 1970.
8. Clark Kerr: 'The Uses of the University' (Cambridge, Mass., 1964), p. 88.

3

The Great Reappraisal
A Progress Report on the Work of the Carnegie Commission on Higher Education in the USA

Eric Ashby

Introduction

From 1870 to 1970 the number of students enrolled in full time higher education in the USA has doubled every 14–15 years. In 1900, 4 per cent of the age group went to college; in 1970, 40 per cent were at college. The output of graduates has become one of America's biggest industries, consuming some 2 per cent of the gross national product. Side by side with this massive educational activity there is an enormous output of research, much of it indeed trivial, but some of it superb.

It is the most impressive achievement in education which the world has ever seen. And yet it is in trouble. The system will have to continue to expand to meet consumer demand, but if expansion means no more than the extrapolation of present trends, the system is heading for crisis. It has been estimated that by the year 2000 there may be 14–16 million enrolled students in American universities and colleges. But it has also been estimated that already about 1 in 6 students are unwilling 'captives' of formal higher education, attending against their will:[1] in 30 years' time that might mean some $2\frac{1}{2}$ million 'captive' students. Already 6 out of 10 students who enrol in American universities and colleges fail to get the ultimate degree to which they aspire, an overall dropout rate of about 60 per cent:[2] in 30 years' time that might mean some 9 million students leaving without their desired diplomas. The hierarchy of institutions – community colleges, four-year colleges, universities – is not stable and secure: many institutions low in the hierarchy neglect the functions they are supposed to perform and strain themselves to take over the function of institutions above them in the hierarchy. Community colleges, for instance, tend to emphasise para-academic courses which exempt students from the first two years of the degree curriculum; four-year colleges agitate to set up doctoral programmes at the expense of their work with undergraduates. And the unit costs of producing a graduate, far from exhibiting economies of scale, are constantly going up: they are said to have increased by about 5 per cent per annum in recent years.

29

It is against this background that the Carnegie Foundation for the Advancement of Teaching established in 1967 a Commission under Clark Kerr (formerly President of the University of California). Its mission is to make a systematic appraisal of higher education and to suggest guidelines for its future development. The Commission's final report is still some way off, but it has already (October, 1971) published nine interim reports and twenty-one monographs; and many more are to follow.

Reappraisals of higher education are nothing new: Britain is, rightly, proud of the monumental report which carries Lord Robbins' name; Germany has the equally impressive series of publications from the *Wissenschaftsrat*. But the reappraisal by the Carnegie Commission goes far beyond these; the monographs being produced under the Commission's sponsorship cover an astonishing range of topics and its interim reports are setting out not just logistics, but a comprehensive philosophy for American higher education.

Diagnosis

The Commission began by defining the more urgent problems to be solved, and it suggested ways of solving them. Chief among these is a persisting inequality of opportunity, still painfully evident two centuries after the architects of the Declaration of Independence had asserted that all men are created equal, that they are endowed by their creator with certain inalienable rights. The inequalities are caused by differences in socio-economic status, differences in colour, and differences in place of residence. The effects of socio-economic status are illustrated by the figures in Table 1.

TABLE 1
PERCENTAGE OF MALE HIGH SCHOOL GRADUATES
WHO WENT TO COLLEGE THE FOLLOWING YEAR

Academic	socio-economic status			
Aptitude	Low	Middle	High	Total
Low	10	15	40	14
Middle	30	46	67	46
High	69	81	91	85
Total	24	53	81	49

(From a sample of 50,000 boys, in 1960. Data taken from a report of the Commission on Human Resources and Advanced Education.)[3]

The effects of ethnic group are illustrated by the fact that in 1968, when 27·5 per cent of the 18–24 age group of white persons was enrolled in college, only 14·5 per cent of the same age group of black persons was enrolled.[4] (It has to be remembered that even this lower percentage exceeds the percentage of the age group of British youth enrolled in universities!) As for the effects of place of residence, 'young persons in the Pacific Southwest attend college at twice the rate of those in the Deep South'.[5]

The Commission's first concern has been to urge that the inequalities suffered by the present generation should not become the legacy of succeeding generations. In two special reports[6] the Commission proposes a vigorous and imaginative campaign to tackle this problem. The first difficulty is that both students and institutions need financial help. For students the Commission recommend a great expansion of educational opportunity grants, derived from federal funds. In 1966–7 nearly a quarter of a million undergraduates from low income families received grants from this source; but this was only 3·7 per cent of the total enrolment. By 1976 the Commission wants 32 per cent of the total enrolment to be beneficiaries under the federal scheme for educational opportunity grants. Any qualified student who needs financial support should receive enough money to attend a local low-cost college. The money would not all come from a federal grant: there should be a basic grant of $1,000 p.a. supplemented by 'work study payments' of $1,000 p.a. – these are payments for jobs of various kinds, on the campus or in non-profitmaking institutions off campus, occupying not more than the equivalent of two days a week, and generated by federal grants to the bodies which offer this part time employment.

Many students from low income families, particularly those of high intelligence, wish to get their higher education elsewhere than at a local low-cost college. For these students the Commission proposes that the federal government should charter a national student loan bank which will lend up to $2,500 p.a. to students for approved undergraduate study (there is a similar proposal for graduate study). Repayment, with interest, would be recovered by the Internal Revenue Service, and there would be sensible humane arrangements for deferring annual repayments.

Grants and loans are not sufficient, of course, to dispel the shadows of inequality. Schools attended by the underprivileged have to be improved; 'equal opportunity centres' ought to be set up to help those who aspire to higher education; even recruiting centres might be desirable to persuade young people to enter college. And remedial courses should be laid on to bridge the gaps, where they exist, between poor schooling and college.

It would be a serious strategic error to swell the flow into higher education without some corresponding federal financial support for colleges and universities. The first need is to build more city community colleges so that everyone in a large city is within commuting distance of a place where the first steps in higher education can be taken. This, writes the Commission, will require the building of some 280 new community colleges by

1980. Another need is a subsidy to many existing institutions: the Commission recommends that all accredited institutions which enrol a student who holds an educational opportunity grant should receive a subsidy of $500 per undergraduate in 1970–1, rising to $1,000 in 1979–80.

By the year 2000 the Commission hopes there will be what it calls universal *access* to higher education, though it distinguishes this from universal *attendance*. But will the American public distinguish between universal access and universal attendance? One of the intractable problems which arise from the policy to provide universal access is that young Americans may feel obliged to go to college, whether they want to or not and whether or not they want jobs for which a degree is a necessary qualification. The risk, already apparent, is that higher education will become *socially* compulsory; universities and colleges will become flooded by students who have neither the inclination nor the need to study, and this will divert resources away from the minority of students who seriously desire and need higher education. The distinguished American sociologist Martin Trow put it well when he said that unless high quality education is protected in some way, the autonomous functions of universities (which is the prime contribution they make to society) will be swamped by their popular functions. It is as though the Bodleian or Weidner libraries had to expend the bulk of their energies on supplying readers with light fiction and magazines.

The Carnegie Commission is alive to this danger; indeed its first report is called *Quality and Equality*, and its recommendations comprise a package deal which includes massive federal support for research: grants for university-based research based on 1967–9 figures, which are increased annually at a rate equal to the five-year moving average annual rate of growth in the gross national product. But this measure alone will not be enough to protect the thin stream of intellectual excellence upon which, in the long run, the nation depends for innovation and change. Reconciliation of the autonomous and popular functions of higher education remains a formidable problem for which the Commission still has to find a solution.

The Goals Reconsidered

The introduction to this chapter paints a gloomy picture of the future of American higher education if the system merely gets bigger and spends more money without reconsidering its goals. In Britain, where the picture is similarly gloomy, though in a more remote future, there has been practically no reconsideration of goals. Two exceptions to this should be noted. The first is the proposal by A. B. Pippard for a two-year generalist degree, which has evoked the kind of doctrinaire opposition which has stifled so many moves for reform in British higher education.[7] In the USA the Commission is boldly reconsidering goals. Its first contributions are published in three works: a monograph on the structures of academic degrees,[8] a critical examination of the functions and aspirations of four-year colleges,[9] and a special report, based largely on these two books, which makes imaginative and radical proposals about patterns of higher education.[10] The nub of the problem is the value – some of it genuine, some of it false – which society sets by university degrees. Obviously the medical practitioner, the engineer, the teacher, must not be let loose on society unless they hold certificates of competence. But the newspaper columnist, the television producer, the book publisher, may not want their formal education in a solid block of 16 continuous years, from the age of 6 to the age of 22. If they go straight from high school into a job, they may forfeit the chance of higher education except as evening students. If they attend a university for two years and leave, without a degree, to be 'where the action is' they are labelled dropouts. If they want to alternate stretches of study with stretches of employment, they find in the rigid British system no opportunity for this, and in the American system inadequate opportunity. If they want a long and deep experience of higher education they are offered only one pattern: a PhD course which is a vocational training in research, not a discipline in scholarly reflection. These constraints did not matter when the university was a specialized institution, attended by a small fraction of the age group, content to fit their lives into a traditional pattern. Today the constraints are unacceptable and it is too late now for universities to close their doors to all except genuine scholars, for they have allowed their degrees (it was partly their own fault) to become status symbols, useful for promoting inter-class mobility and attracting higher salaries from society. Therefore, coupled with plans for universal access to higher education, there must be arrangements for honourable exit from higher education. To come to college willingly, as and when you want some intellectual nourishment, and to leave college willingly when you have got what you came for: this should be the aim of colleges and universities in the 1980s. Universities, like museums and libraries, should be entered through a revolving door.

Such thoughts as these require major changes in social attitudes toward higher education. The Commission's special report, *Less time, more options*, specifies some of these changes and points a way toward their achievement. Young people, the report declares, should be given:

> more options (a) in lieu of formal college, (b) to defer college attendance, (c) to stop out from college in order to get service and work experience, and (d) to change directions while in college. . . . Opportunities for higher education . . . should be available to persons throughout their lifetimes. . . . The sense of isolation (at college) would be reduced if more students were also workers and if more workers could also be students. . . . The emphasis on certification through formal higher education should be reduced.[11]

The Commission does not content itself with these pious hopes; it suggests administrative mechanisms for fulfilling them. The prime need is a revision of degree structures, with five exits from higher education, each carrying with it a certification. A summary is given in Table 2.

TABLE 2

Years from High School	Qualification	Years of study after BA
2	associate in arts	–
4	bachelor of arts	–
5	master of arts	1
6	master of philosophy	2
8	doctor of philosophy } doctor of arts	4

The innovations in this scheme are:

(*a*) That accelerated courses should be provided so that students could, if they chose, complete an associateship in 1–1½ years and a BA in 3 years.
(*b*) That the associateship should be taken by all students, whether it is a terminable degree or not and that it should become the 'standard degree' for an increasing number of students, with the expectation that some of them will return later in their careers to study for higher qualifications.
(*c*) That the masters' degrees should be standard credentials for secondary schoolteachers.
(*d*) That the time necessary to complete a PhD, which is at present disgracefully long (Table 3) should be reduced.
(*e*) That there should be a new kind of degree, the doctor of arts, for those who want a higher qualification as a scholar and university teacher without commitment to a career of intensive research.

It is doubtful whether some of these proposals are realistic in the present social climate of the USA. The associate in arts is likely to be regarded as a consolation-award, rather than the 'standard degree' for those who are incapable of getting a BA. (The situation in Britain is similar: no teacher's diploma or higher national certificate or City and Guilds award compensate for the handicap of being unable to wear a gown and coloured hood on ceremonial occasions.) And, at the other end of the scale, it is at present unrealistic to suppose that a doctor of arts degree (already introduced in some American institutions, e.g. the University of Washington), will attain parity of esteem with the PhD. Before that could become practicable it would be necessary to transform the whole scale of values used to

TABLE 3[12]
TIME WHICH ELAPSES BETWEEN BA AND
COMPLETION OF PHD, 1964–6

Field	Median	Mode (*years*)
physical sciences and engineering	6·3	5
biological sciences	7·3	5
social sciences	8·0	5
arts and humanities	9·5	6
professional fields	10·8	7
education	13·8	15

estimate merit in American academic life, and to attach to scholarly wisdom as much prestige as is now attached only to the publication of what are called advances (though they are often no more than prolifer-ations) in knowledge. That the transformation is possible is evident from the status accorded to tutors in Oxford and Cambridge, many of whom publish very little and whose aim is to produce 'not a book but a man'. But American academia shows no sign yet of a sympathetic attitude to this scale of values. However, the Commission's proposals have to be taken very seriously, for – quite apart from their educational merits – the Commission estimates that both time and money could be saved if its recommendations were to be adopted. The length of time spent in undergraduate college education (the Commission states) can be reduced roughly by one-fourth without sacrificing educational quality; and the reforms proposed in the report could, by 1980, save $3–$5 billion a year in recurrent expenses and, over the decade 1971–80, $5 billion in capital expenses.

Finance

The choice before American educationists is to reduce the unit costs of higher education to levels which satisfy the public, or to persuade the public that higher education is so important that it deserves support not-withstanding its high unit costs. It is hard for an Englishman, accustomed to modest budgets of British universities, to realize that many American universities are suffering grave anxiety about their finances. The Carnegie Commission has focused attention upon this in a study with the ominous title *The new depression in higher education*,[13] which examines the financial state – or, for some institutions, the financial plight – of 41 universities or colleges. What appears to be an impressive growth of income is being overtaken by increased costs due to the obligation to accommodate more students, and, of course, to inflation. The study estimates that the income of many institutions would have to increase at the rate of 6·5 per cent per student per year, if they are to balance their accounts; and the projections, based on such hard evidence as is available, are for annual increases of no more than 5 per cent. Among universities, in the sample surveyed, already 'in trouble' are Stanford and the University of California at Berkeley; and 'heading for trouble' are the universities of Harvard, Chicago, Michigan, and Minnesota. All these institutions are making cuts in expenditure and some have had to go to the length of discontinuing courses. The greatest embarrassment has occurred in universities heavily committed to federal research projects, the funds for which have been used in some cases to finance tenure appointments. The only thing which can be said in favour of this crisis is that it is compelling reluctant academics to decide what activities in their universities are really important!

The people of the USA are committed to a policy of mass higher education. They do not dispute the need for universal access to college, nor the need for high quality in teaching and research. Why, therefore, have so many of their universities been plunged into acute financial embarrassment? The reasons are complex: the costs of a foreign war and anxieties about economy at home; a certain disenchantment with scientific research – federal support for research and development which had been increasing at the rate of about 20 per cent per year, shrank in 1970 to an increase of only 2 per cent, not enough to keep pace with inflation; and – the most significant reason given by harassed university presidents – 'the need to restore public confidence in education'. There is undoubtedly a crisis of confidence. Taxpayers, legislators, private donors, want universities to demonstrate (i) that they can govern themselves in reasonable tranquillity; (ii) that they are being run efficiently, on the criterion of cost-effectiveness (a dangerous and – some believe – irrelevant criterion to apply to academic operations); and (iii) that they can restore a consensus about 'a unifying set of purposes – purposes that the supporting public can understand and defer to'. This third cause for concern is the most perplexing one; it runs through the whole gigantic enterprise; a commitment to a system whose very practitioners cannot agree as to its purpose. There is no difficulty in defining the purpose and defending the programmes for vocational and professional education. But in practically all universities half the four-year undergraduate course, the freshman and sophomore years, is occupied by general education, commonly composed of about one-third humanities, one third social sciences, and one-third natural science. To say that there is no consensus among academics about the purpose and value of this general education would be an understatement. The curriculum (as one critic wrote) does not represent the outcome of any defensible and rational intellectual process. It is not unreasonable that the American public should require a more purposeful policy than this for 50 per cent of undergraduate education before allocating to universities and colleges an even higher proportion of the gross national product.

A Constellation of Studies

Considerations such as these led the Carnegie Commission to arrange for a whole constellation of studies around the core of higher education. A list of these is given in an appendix. In the compass of this chapter there is room to expand on only two of these studies: one on the epidemic of dissent and disruption which has put severe strain upon American higher education; the other is the changing relation between institutions of higher education and their social environment.

(a) *Dissent and Disruption.*[14] This study contains a careful, and on the whole reassuring, analysis of the attitudes of students toward the episodes of dissent and disruption in many American institutions from 1964 to 1970. Data in social science surveys are easy enough to get, provided people can be persuaded to fill in questionnaires; but they are hard to interpret, for the very activity of conducting a poll affects the attitudes of those who are polled, and it is misleading to suppose that data collected in this way have a validity comparable with that of the objective data of natural science. However, the Carnegie study rests on a massive enquiry under the direction of Martin Trow, in co-operation with Seymour Martin Lipset, both of whom have a reassuring scepticism toward quantitative data and whose conclusions are, therefore, trustworthy. Trow surveyed opinion in 300 institutions (almost one-eighth of the total number in the USA); he obtained opinions from over 60,000 college and university teachers and over 100,000 students. His conclusions are that the overwhelming majority of college teachers and students oppose violence and disruptive demonstrations on campuses; there is wide agreement on the need for reform in American society; the majority of students and teachers are generally satisfied with the institutions in which they work (though there is wide agreement on the need for some specific reforms). The Commission, reflecting on this and other documents of evidence, has prepared some proposals for campus stability. Dissatisfaction and disaffection, the Commission believe, will persist 'for a substantial period of time'. Policy should, therefore, be directed not to suppressing these attitudes but to guiding them into activities, which (to use the modern jargon) are not counterproductive. The Commission's proposals are – amid so much polarity toward far left and far right – courageously liberal. 'Dissent' they tersely say 'must be protected. Disruption must be ended.' To this end they propose a model 'bill of rights and responsibilities for members of the campus'. Bills of rights and responsibilities are proliferating all over American colleges. The Commission's draft embodies some simple and sensible principles. It embraces the whole university community – students, teachers, administrators, trustees – not just students; a contrast to the provision in some British universities, which require students, but not teachers, to behave 'modestly and becomingly'. The draft also specifies the rights of the *institution*; for example that it should have the right to forbid its name or its finances to be used for commercial or political ends.

The press coverage to the Commission's interim report on dissent and disruption, released on 14 March 1971, was widespread and favourable. This is an important sign, for in America the backlash against students had assumed alarming proportions. (Statistics published by the Commission indicate that 65 per cent of people over 50 years of age condemn even legitimate demonstrations permitted by the local authorities!) It is to be hoped that the Commission's quantitative survey will dispel the popular belief that the student population is seething with discontent. Even after the invasion of Cambodia in the spring of 1970, which sparked off the most extensive campus protests in American history, and led to deaths at Kent and Jackson State, only 4 per cent of American campuses experienced violent protest and even in these, only a small minority of students took part.

(*b*) *Institutions of Higher Education and their social environment.* Several of the Commission's studies converge on this theme. The most interesting (and controversial) are *The capitol and the campus*[15] which examines the responsibility of the states for higher education; and *The city and the campus*[16] which discusses the responsibility of higher education for the cities of America.

It would not be an exaggeration to describe *The capitol and the campus* as 150 pages of dynamite; for it exposes astonishing differences among states in their provision for higher education. Nineteen states have consolidated governing boards to supervize higher education in the state, and twenty-seven states have co-ordination boards. These bodies aim to avoid wasteful duplication and harmful competition between institutions within states, but they clearly have made little progress toward uniformity of standards between states. There are revealing 'league tables' showing the per cent of per capita income spent on public higher education (with Wyoming at the top and New Jersey at the bottom); number of undergraduates enrolled per 100 in the undergraduate age group (with Utah and Massachusetts near the top and Maine and Virginia near the bottom); and the amount of migration of students in and out of states for their higher education (with an 'immigration' of 37,000 students into Massachusetts and 26,000 into Indiana, and an 'exodus' of 21,000 students from Connecticut and 98,000 from New Jersey). New Jersey has been described else-where as a 'disaster area' for higher education, and California as an 'El Dorado'. Statistically, at any rate, these labels are appropriate.

The great differences between states in their provision for higher educa-tion are not accounted for solely by poverty. New Jersey, a rich state, has nearly 60 per cent of its high school graduates enrolled as students, but only 29 per cent of them are enrolled in New Jersey. By contrast Mississip-pi has 64 per cent of its high school graduates enrolled as students, all but 1,300 of them in their own state. States which spend less than 0·6 per cent of per capita income through taxes for higher education include Pennsyl-vania, Ohio, and Delaware. States which have to 'export' over 15,000 students a year to find college places include New York and New Jersey. Notwithstanding the inequalities of opportunity set by state boundaries, the Commission come down squarely in favour of state sovereignty (as opposed to federal sovereignty) over higher education. They oppose a single national system. Federal support (which the Commission call for on a massive scale) should nevertheless be for specialized and supplemental purposes. There is a strong plea that states should support private institu-tions, which – although they now enrol fewer than 30 per cent of students (compared with 50 per cent a dozen years ago) – remain an important source of diversity in American higher education. And, added to these highly charged statistics, there is in the Commission's report a firm and statesmanlike defence of academic autonomy in state institutions, in-cluding – as danger signs – quite an astonishing list of the powers which a state governor can, and sometimes does, exercise over higher education under his jurisdiction.

In a totally different way, the Commission's views on the city and the campus touch the exposed nerves of American society. For cities, once a splendid triumph of civilization, have become civilization's disgrace. In America, as in parts of Europe, the founders of universities and colleges commonly chose placid towns rather than busy cities: for Michigan, Ann Arbor, not Detroit; for Illinois, Urbana-Champaign, not Chicago. The land-grant college movement in the 1860s reinforced this choice. It was a time when well over three-quarters of the American people lived in rural areas. Now two-thirds of the American people live in cities and the proportion will rise to four-fifths by the 1980s. The Commission are wise, therefore, to press for more and more city colleges (even if they are only two-year community colleges) so that the maximum number of Ameri-cans can live within commuter distance of some place of higher education. In response to this concentration of population in cities, city colleges and universities have multiplied greatly in recent years. The campus of the city university is not remote or withdrawn; it is threaded with public streets and in some cities – Philadelphia's Temple University, for instance, or the University of Chicago – adjacent to decaying slum property. The daunting social problems of the city – crime, racial prejudice, poverty – are on its doorstep.

These circumstances prompt the Commission to examine an important concept. Should urban-grant universities be established, analogous to the land-grant universities established a century ago? An urban-grant university would bias its teaching and research toward problems of the city, as its predecessors did toward rural problems. The analogy must not be pressed too far, for land-grant universities were concerned with primary industry: increasing yields, controlling plant and animal disease, distributing and marketing agricultural products. It is noteworthy that the Massachusetts Institute of Technology, which in fact received a land grant in 1862, has made contributions to secondary industry comparable with the contributions which Wisconsin (say) has made to primary industry. But an urban-grant university of the 1970s would be concerned rather with the social problems of cities: transport, crime, racial segregation, poverty. That consideration of such problems as these should be included in the curricula of law schools, faculties of economics, departments of sociology, there is no doubt. The controversial question is whether universities should become involved in policy-making for cities, either through advisory services or even more directly. On the one hand there are those who maintain that the only field in which universities can claim expertise or authority is education: 'We cannot believe' wrote Sidney Hook, 'that the mission of the university is to lead mankind to a new Jerusalem'. Sidney Hook may not believe this, but many other people do: they see in higher education the most powerful instrument for injecting rational thought into political action, and for dispelling prejudice and passion.

The Commission, in its present mood, does endorse the urban university's commitment to urban problems. So do many American universities and colleges. There are in the United States no fewer than 200 research centres concerned with urban problems. In some places the effort is directed to bringing precision into municipal decisions through what are called 'urban observatories', which collect the raw material out of which policies can be made. In another place (Buffalo) the university is offering some of its services to the city through 'Storefront Centres' which aim to bring the university's expertise to the 'slum inhabitant' and, through direct involvement, to permit the university to learn more about the problems of poverty. These activities do great credit to the conscience of American intellectuals. Those who have been engaged in these activities know how perplexing and frustrating they may become. One big urban university, for instance, in the ghetto of a big city, was pressed by students to put on courses which were relevant to its neighbourhood. The university complied; it put on a course in criminology, for the most acute neighbourhood problem was crime. The result? The students protested because police were coming on to the campus to attend the course.

Coda

This very brief summary does scant justice to the scope and detail of the Commission's activities. In addition to books on the two themes I selected as examples of its work, the Commission has published monographs on higher education in Catholic colleges and Negro colleges;[17, 18] a valuable resume of patterns of higher education in nine countries outside the USA;[19] an analysis of the finance of medical education;[20] and a number of books which set out the opinions of observers of the educational scene from inside and outside the country.[21, 22, 23] Among the Commission's interim reports which are not discussed in this chapter is an important one on policies for medical and dental education, which received widespread publicity and comment when it was published.[24] A list of reports and books published up to June 1971 is given at the end of this chapter.

This is a coda, not a conclusion, for it is too soon to draw conclusions. The Commission plans at least ten more two-day meetings during the fifteen months ending in December 1972 and a dozen or more monographs sponsored by the Commission are likely to appear during this period. It has yet to be ascertained whether this gigantic mound of evidence can be refined into clear and simple principles for the reform of higher education. There are, in my view, grounds for optimism that the principles will emerge; for as the facts and opinions build up, they seem to flow toward some common conclusions, such as these:

(i) another generation, perhaps, before there is genuine equality of opportunity for young Americans to benefit from higher education, but a compelling current of opinion and legislation toward that end;

(ii) the establishment of a code of conduct, with effective sanctions, for both teachers and students, bringing a basic stability (though never freedom from tension) to the campus;

(iii) increased support and influence from the federal government, but with safeguards against the hazards of over-centralization;

(iv) realization, as more and more of the age-group go to college, that a degree is no longer a passport to upward social mobility – a realization which may lead to a disenchantment with higher education on the part of those who have no genuine motivation for learning;

(v) a new pattern of attendance at universities, where students enter college as they enter libraries or museums: to satisfy an intellectual need, and to leave, not necessarily with a scroll and a gown and hood, when their need is satisfied – resulting in a much wider age-spread among students.

But this is to anticipate the great synthesis which, at the time of writing, still lies ahead of the Commission. Even if no synthesis were to be attempted, the material assembled and published (or soon to be published) constitutes the most thorough analysis of a nation's higher education which has ever been made. And even if the synthesis, when it is delivered, fails to lead to reforms in American higher education, it would remain the most massive and courageous effort to plan the future for American youth that any group of men have ever attempted. Many of the Commission's reports and monographs have a relevance far beyond the United States. The purpose of this chapter is to urge those in other nations who have responsibility for the planning of higher education to benefit from the Commission's work.

REFERENCES

Most of the references are to books published by the Commission. The titles are given in full in the appendix.
1. *Less time, more options*, p. 7 (Commission).
2. ibid, p. 9.
3. John K. Folger, Helen S. Astin, and Alan E. Bayer. *Human resources and higher education* (New York, 1970), p. 310.
4. *A chance to learn*, p. 2 (Commission).
5. ibid, p. 2.
6. *A chance to learn* (Commission), and *Quality and Equality* (Commission).
7. See: E. Ashby. 'Science and antiscience', *Proc. Royal Society, London, Series B*, 178 (1971), pp. 29–42.
8. *Academic degree structures: innovative approaches* (Commission).
9. *Colleges of the forgotten Americans* (Commission).
10. *Less time, more options* (Commission).
11. ibid, p. 1–2.
12. ibid, p. 45.
13. *The new depression in higher education* (Commission).
14. *Dissent and disruption* (Commission).
15. *The capitol and the campus* (Commission).
16. *The city and the campus* (Commission).
17. *From backwater to mainstream* (Commission).
18. *Between two worlds* (Commission).
19. *Higher education in nine countries* (Commission).
20. *Financing medical education* (Commission).
21. *State officials and higher education* (Commission).
22. *Recent alumni and higher education* (Commission).
23. *Any person, any study* (Commission).
24. *Higher education and the nation's health* (Commission).

APPENDIX

Carnegie Commission on Higher Education: publications up to June 1971: All publications are by the McGraw-Hill Book Co., New York.

Reports of the Commission
A chance to learn: An action agenda for equal opportunity in higher education (1970).
From isolation to mainstream: Problems of the colleges founded for negroes (1971).
Higher education and the nation's health: Policies for medical and dental education (1970).
Less time, more options: Education beyond the high school (1971).
Quality and Equality: New levels of federal responsibility for higher education (1968).
Quality and Equality: Revised recommendations, new levels of federal responsibility for higher education (1970).
The capitol and the campus: State responsibility for post-secondary education (1971).
The open-door colleges: Policies for community colleges (1970).
Dissent and disruption: Proposals for consideration by the campus (1971).

Monographs
Eric Ashby, *Any Person, Any Study: An essay on Higher Education in the United States* (1971).
Frank Bowles and Frank A. Decosta, *Between Two Worlds: A Profile of Negro Higher Education* (1971).
Barbara B. Burn, Philip G. Altbach, Clark Kerr and James A. Perkins, *Higher Education in Nine Countries: A Comparative Study of Colleges and Universities Abroad* (1971).
Earl F. Cheit, *The New Depression in Higher Education: A Study of Financial Conditions at 41 Colleges and Universities* (1971).
E. Alden Dunham, *Colleges of the Forgotten Americans: A Profile of State Colleges and Regional Universities* (1969).
Heinz Eulau and Harold Quinley, *State Officials and Higher Education: A Survey of the Opinions and Expectations of Policy Makers in Nine States* (1970).
Rashi Fein and Gerald I. Weber, *Financing Medical Education: An Analysis of Alternative Policies and Mechanisms* (1971).
Andrew M. Greeley, *From Backwater to Mainstream: A Profile of Catholic Higher Education* (1969).
Oscar and Mary F. Handlin, *The American College and American Culture: Socialization as a Function of Higher Education* (1970).
Robert W. Hartman, *Credit for College: Public Policy and Student Loans* (1971).
Dale M. Heckman and Warren Bryan Martin, *Inventory of Current Research on Higher Education, 1968* (1970).
Harold L. Hodgkinson, *Institutions in Transition* (1971).
Morris T. Keeton, *Models and Mavericks: A Profile of Liberal Arts Colleges* (1971).
Dwight R. Ladd, *Change in Educational Policy: Self-Studies in Selected Colleges and Universities* (1970).

Eugene C. Lee and Frank M. Bowen, *The Multicampus University: A Study of Academic Governance* (1971).

Lewis B. Mayhew, *Graduate and Professional Education, 1980. A Survey of Institutional Plans* (1970).

Leland L. Medsker and Dale Tillery, *Breaking the Access Barriers: A Profile of Two-Year Colleges* (1971).

Irwin T. Sanders amd Jennifer C. Ward, *Bridges to Understanding: International Programs of American Colleges and Universities* (1970).

Joe L. Spaeth and Andrew M. Greeley, *Recent Alumni and Higher Education: A Survey of College Graduates* (1970).

Stephen H. Spurr, *Academic Degree Structures: Innovative Approaches Principles of Reform in Degree Structures in the United States* (1970).

Ron Wolk, *Alternative Methods of Federal Funding for Higher Education* (1970).

4

Speculations from an International Perspective

Seth Spaulding and Joseph Herman★

The model for a university as an institution was created in another time and even in the most progressive of universities there are many trappings which found their origin in the middle ages. Most would agree that one of the functions of the university is to preserve the wisdom of the past. The problem arises when this is interpreted as a preservation of the past itself, rather than of its wisdom that might relate to the present and the future.

The Symptoms of Discontent

The symptoms of discontent are many. Governments see the universities as a sizeable investment in the human resources of the future and in knowledge that will serve national goals and aspirations. Many in legislative and executive posts in government are questioning this tremendous investment and wondering if the needs of the state (the people) are indeed being well served.

Students see the university as a place where they spend valuable years of their early adult life, and they want these years to be productive and relevant to their life styles as they see them. The newspaper headlines testify that they often do not see this relevance and they do not hesitate to make this discontent known.

Parents see the university as the open door to social mobility of their children. In every country, more and more parents who never saw the inside of a university themselves have the aspiration of sending their children to one. Even in the United States where virtually any high school graduate can find a place in some university, parents are never quite satisfied with the quality of educational opportunity which they feel is available to their children. This frustration is intensified in those countries where only small percentages of children will have university places.

Employers look to universities to provide young people who can do the jobs they want done. Most industries are not satisfied with the quality

---

★ The views expressed in this paper are entirely those of the authors and do not necessarily represent those of Unesco.

of university graduates and many feel that they have to retrain the graduates themselves. In at least several of the so-called under-developed countries there is an apparent unemployed-university-graduate problem, in part because the university spaces available are so geared towards the preparation of young people in traditional academic areas of which there is limited demand, and in part because there has been inadequate definition of what new kinds of people are needed for the future.

Finally, the university is seen by the university professor as a sanctuary where he can pursue his academic interests in a somewhat protected environment. A degree of protection, of course, is necessary for creative and innovative scholarship but there are those that would claim that professors have not been as zealous in formulating and complying with their responsibilities as they have been in articulating their right to autonomy. Community interests are forcing the academic to temper his notion of what makes for a proper university environment.

All of these and other issues raised by the various clienteles of the university have enmeshed the university as an institution in a web of political tensions in many countries. There are those who now say that political concerns are being used to judge academic performance. There are those who decry the polarization that is being produced by this political atmosphere, students against professors, the university against the government, groups of faculty against other groups of faculty and so on. Indeed, the notion of a university where scholars search and teach in an atmosphere of collaboration and respect for divergent ideas may be in danger.

Universities in their Societies

The factors which have provoked what is sometimes called the 'crisis' in the universities are well known. There is the 'demographic explosion' in the university, caused by profound social, economic and cultural changes and by resultant changes in government policy. There is the 'knowledge explosion', especially since the Second World War. This has meant (1) an exceptionally sudden quantitative increase in knowledge of man and the world around him; (2) a transformation of many basic concepts in each discipline; (3) the interpenetration of traditional disciplines, and (4) the almost constant birth of new disciplines. The labour market has changed: public and business enterprises, research facilities, intellectual professions of all kinds, are waiting for recruits. These must not only be well trained but educated so that they can adapt to the continuous enrichment of knowledge, to rapid social change, to the transformation of often fundamental concepts and methods, including those in their own professions. All of this is fully obvious in the industrialized countries, but these same factors come also into play in the developing countries. Here they bring forth even more complex problems because the university systems of these countries are often more or less imported forms from another society.

As a result of all these interrelated forces, universities in both the developed and under-developed world have become theatres of tensions and conflicting needs. These contradictions often take the form of open confrontations, especially where certain strata of the university community, and most often the students, are sensitized to the conflicts by problems social, economic and political beyond the university itself. With the healthy concern which characterizes young intellectuals, they feel partially responsible for these tensions. Authorities who are farsighted or happily inspired have succeeded in keeping the university conflicts within the framework of discussion – often passionate – with an outcome of a more or less organized series of reforms.

What are these conflicts? We shall simply mention a few of the more obvious. There is a conflict of needs which is surely not without resolution, but nevertheless serious and complex. It has to do with determining (a) the very nature of the content of university studies and (b) the structures which should develop once this has been determined. It is obvious that the need to democratize higher education combined with the increasingly 'open' nature of the disciplines, and the re-definition or disappearance of the boundaries between different scientific spheres, demand a rethinking of the traditional academic model. They also demand a considerable advanced interdisciplinarity on the part of the student as well as on the part of the institutions. They demand freedom of choice and mobility for the student within the university, abolition of the traditional major examinations with the unavoidably rigid programmes they spawn, and individualized relationships between teachers and students. The teachers should be guides and intellectual companions to the students, rather than agents transmitting a pre-established knowledge.

But there are also other factors. Most intellectual professions are not content merely with flexibility. In a beginner they demand systematic and intensive study of a specialized and complex conceptual system and techniques related to the use of them. This is surely so in scientific fields, and especially in applied sciences such as medicine and engineering. Furthermore, for those who finance a university, studies are very expensive. They are therefore justified in being concerned that intellectual workers be prepared in a reasonable length of time, without too much wastage and at the least cost. The full solution to the problem of democratizing the university, making its teaching more flexible and at the same time satisfying all the professional and financial requirements for professional specialization does not seem to have been found.

There is another fairly obvious and often painful conflict between the fact of the numerical increase of students and available places in the labour market. It is a noble ideal and an irreversible trend that a larger segment of each generation should reach the highest level of education available. If to the universities as such one adds the various para-university courses, in-service training courses, correspondence courses, etc., some large countries such as the USA and the USSR already have an infrastructure which in theory should permit all those who want, and are capable of doing so, to participate in some kind of higher education.

Even so, in many countries the very rapidity of social change, the in-adequacy in planning and preparing for the future or the praiseworthy desire not to direct by administrative methods the professional choices of the students, easily creates situations of partial unemployment. This can create a kind of floating and rootless 'intelligentsia', and, at the same time, a lack of trained manpower in certain sectors. One often sees in one and the same country students demonstrating for the abolition of examinations, for flexible curricula, for open higher education, and, on the other hand, for an education which leads to pre-determined positions and protects them from unemployment. The situation naturally becomes especially serious when the threat of unemployment and social maladjustment co-exist with rigid and archaic university structures.

Within the context of these conflicts, there is much academic concern as to how to maintain quality education. Not, of course, quality in the sense of preparing some aristocratic and archaic elite, but a quality which has become even more necessary because of the evolution of knowledge and growing flexibility of the structure of the university. Related to prob-lems of quality is the continuing false dichotomy between teaching and research. There is a kind of 'mandarinism' espoused by certain researchers who are unable or unwilling to transmit their knowledge, and there are, on the other hand, teachers who have lost contact with the progress of their own discipline and who fall back on pedagogical virtues the existence of which is difficult to prove. It should be evident that the living bond between teaching and research is part of the very essence of university life, but even this bond must be the subject of reflection as we ponder on the future of the university.

Curriculum

In the more innovative universities, one clearly can note the trend for the boundaries between disciplines to become blurred as each discipline seeks to relate more directly to problems of the present and the future. This is happening not only in the basic and applied physical and natural sciences. Boundaries between the social sciences and the professions are becoming less distinct too. Anthropologists, sociologists, psychologists and econo-mists are finding homes in schools or faculties of public and business ad-ministration, law, international affairs, public health, education, and even schools of engineering and/or library science. In essence, there is a trend toward the application of social sciences to professional problems of our day and age. This fits with demands of students for personal and meaningful experiences other than the memorization of information which may be out of date before they leave the university.

Parallel to this is student resistance to curricular approaches which come in a pre-planned package of three or four years. Universities which allow students to plan a diverse programme which may indeed be the basis for multiple careers are finding considerable success.

At least one new university (the University of Wisconsin at Green Bay)* is structured entirely around environmental studies. Although this is a unique institution in a country which can afford bold experiments, it is likely that new universities even in the developing countries will begin such innovative approaches around problems which are pressing for them, and especially around problems of development.

Disappearance or, at least, a softening of the borders between disciplines and the stress on relevance to life problems thus is causing re-thinking of the way the university is structured for curriculum purposes. In many countries, faculties traditionally have been self-contained and the students in one faculty would never take a course in another faculty. This is giving way to the integrated university concept already practised in some countries whereby most disciplines which have relevance to students preparing for a number of careers are considered as horizontal programmes which serve students in many faculties.

The nature of faculties themselves is changing and there is some likelihood that the university in some countries will be structured in smaller units in the future so as to make change and innovation more easy to accomplish. At the other end of the spectrum, in some universities, especially in Europe where senior professors traditionally have managed miniature institutes and chairs in almost total isolation, there is a trend towards grouping of these minute specialities into larger units. This is effectively broadening intellectual co-operation in teaching and research, and, at the same time, is diminishing the absolute control of senior academicians.

Changes in the structure of the curriculum, of course, will have little impact on society without parallel changes in the society in which the university lives. For instance, many deplore the small numbers of university graduates in agricultural subjects, especially in countries which are still heavily dependent on agriculture. It is unlikely that large numbers of agronomists and agricultural specialists will be prepared by universities until such time as these specialists can command positions of salary and

* See Chapter 19.

prestige comparable to those trained in other areas. Reform of the agricultural industry must go hand in hand with university reform if there are to be dramatic improvements in this sector.

Similarly, it is often said in developing countries that graduate engineers will not do the kind of practical engineering work when they finish their studies that engineers in highly developed countries are doing. 'They will not work with their hands', one often hears. Again, in highly developed countries a graduate engineer may perform a greater variety of practical tasks than a graduate engineer in a developing country but he also earns substantial income for doing these tasks. This is often not the case in the lesser developed countries.

Teaching Method

It is an almost universal practice to train teachers in teaching method if they are to teach at the elementary or secondary level. At the higher education level it is often assumed that if a man has a degree in his speciality he surely must be able to teach it. This assumption is being increasingly questioned.

The physical size of many universities has produced a number of problems. The concept of young scholars (students) working closely with the advanced scholars (professors) in research and study is no longer a reality on most campuses. Even in universities where seminars and tutorials have been a tradition, teaching has tended to become a series of lectures to large groups of students who take notes and attempt to memorize enough information to pass an examination. If the students have personal contact at all at the undergraduate level, it is often with teaching assistants whose main interest is in getting a graduate research degree themselves and who are teaching simply to pay their way. Undergraduate seminars and tutorials seem to be a thing of the past in some universities.

Attempts to remedy the situation range from experimental programmes to teach professors more innovative approaches to teaching and learning, to technological approaches to the packaging of curriculum in the form of self-instructional materials, television courses, computer-assisted instruction, and teaching-learning laboratories. Organizational innovations include attempts to encourage 'peer teaching' whereby students work together on problems of common interest and learn from one another. There is also an increased interest in bringing non-professional teachers into the classroom, people who have distinguished themselves outside the university and who have a great deal to share with the students. Students, in some experimental programmes, are encouraged to undertake research and service projects in the community for which they get credit.

There is the beginning of a recognition that good teaching should be a ground for advancement as an academician, and some universities do not base promotions on research and publications alone. Proposals have been put forward that universities should give two kinds of advanced degrees: one for people who intend primarily to teach and another for those who intend primarily to do research. The danger here, of course, is that teaching might crowd out research interests and thus alter the basic uniqueness of the university as an institution which both creates as well as transmits knowledge.

Certainly, during the seventies there will be much foment in the way we organize teaching and learning resources on the university campus.

Students

A *de facto* selection policy is at work in most countries whereby young people from the most privileged families tend to have a better chance to enter the university. This applies whether there is a very rigorous selection for a very few places at the university or whether there is an almost open system whereby there is a place for anyone who wants to attend.

Since most countries now profess egalitarian ideas, this situation is of concern. There are and will be increasing attempts to provide greater opportunity for young people from less advantaged families and these will often take the form of special pre-university programmes to prepare underprivileged youngsters for university careers.

In countries where there traditionally has been a rigorous selection process, often when the child is 11 or 12 years old, this early selection is rapidly vanishing. There is general agreement that such selection processes are wasteful of human potential, since the performance of children at this age on examinations is dependent on so many factors other than inherent ability.

The students who do make it to the university, in any case, are not the students of yesterday. The pace of involvement in the real world has quickened and students are no longer content with the university life of yesterday. There is some evidence that among the dropouts from the universities in many countries are the more self-sufficient, creative and innovative people.

Students are looking for new relationships, new meaningful involvements, and new directions for their lives. The university must change to satisfy this search for relevance.

Student Evaluation

There are two general approaches to student evaluation. Some universities prefer to give periodic examinations which purport to judge a student's performance over a lengthy period. Others prefer the cumulative evaluation approach whereby small bits of information are accumulated and the sum total of this is the assessment of the student. With more diversity in the curriculum, more options open to the student, with more kinds of learning experiences included in the curriculum than simply listening to lectures, it is likely that the trend in most universities will be toward the cumulative evaluation approach.

The concept of grades is being questioned even in the universities where there is cumulative evaluation. Many universities are now offering the students the option of choosing a number of courses for which they will not receive a grade, but rather a pass/fail notation. It appears that this approach encourages students to widen their interests and does not, as some have feared, encourage students to work less.

There is some speculation that, with computer-assisted instruction and other methods of packaging learning experiences, cumulative evaluation of a much more detailed character is possible than even with the grading by course as now practised in some universities. Computer capabilities are such that they can keep track of individual tasks accomplished by students and the feasibility of handling phenomenal amounts of information on student performance is now a reality. It remains to be seen if these approaches are administratively and conceptually practical.

Research and Public Service

It has been said that research and public service go hand in hand, for significant research, after all, is a service to the public. Accepting this, there is nonetheless a great trend for university professors to be more directly involved in public service activity and in community goal-setting and decision making than was the professor of days gone by who did little but research that which he conceived of as important in his own discipline.

With public investment at high levels in tertiary education, it is reasonable to expect the concentration of expertise at the university to be available to government and industry, and to community service organizations. Such experience is also a quality input for the university inasmuch as the professor keeps in this way in constant touch with problems of the real world. There are those universities who discourage this kind of involvement with the notion that it interferes with university autonomy. This, certainly, is a short-term view since autonomy must accept responsibility and cannot be interpreted to mean isolation. Most large universities now accept government and industry contracts for all kinds of scientific development and research work. This research tends, however, to be largely along disciplinary and professional lines and the best interdisciplinary research in most countries is still done outside the university by industry and government. Trends in the future toward interdisciplinary curricula may affect the vitality of research and service activities in the university community.

Certainly, large scale research and service activities are possible only with a full-time faculty. In a number of countries there is still a tendency to run a university with a very limited full-time faculty, the majority of the faculty being employed part-time to give courses which consist of series of lectures and nothing else. Certainly, it is good to involve community leadership in university teaching, but this must be balanced with full-time residence scholars if it is to be effective.

Finally, there appears to be increased interest in research on university teaching. It is indeed strange that an institution which exists in large part for teaching has not been more interested in research on this process in the past. It is, however, increasingly respectable for an academician in a discipline or a profession to spend a considerable amount of his time on research on how to structure the teaching and learning process more effectively and on how to prepare new kinds of teaching and learning materials for use in higher education.

It has been said that universities exist in order to replace faith with reason. Students no longer, however, have faith in reason alone. They wish their professors to be sharpened with experience in applying reason to real problems confronting society and civilization. This, of course, implies as well a questioning of basic issues in society. Some would express concern at too much involvement of the professor in service activities, since these activities are serving the *status quo*. Indeed, the university must not be so dependent on the *status quo* that it can not participate effectively in proposing alternate goals of the future.

University Governance

Increasingly being questioned are the ways that universities go about managing themselves and making their decisions. Traditionally, decisions in a university are made by the senior academic faculty and the administration. Such governance is based on personal power in a hierarchical structure much as in any bureaucracy. The trend is toward much greater participation in university decision-making, both by the various constituent groups on campus and by groups off campus. Since decision-making in the past was based largely on the predispositions of limited numbers of senior people, it was never clear to others how decisions were made and what went into making them. The trend now is toward transparency in the decision-making process with those who are interested on and off campus able to see exactly what goes on in making the decisions. The closed system tends to perpetuate rather than create. The new open approach brings into question many traditional modes of action and will make way for innovative new programmes and structures on campus. When the councils of university government were limited to very few, there was a distinct gap between the decision-makers and the junior faculty and students and community. As broader forms of participation are emerging, this gap is less noticeable.

Such participation in governance is being attempted in a variety of ways. The simplest is to simply include representatives of the different constituent groups on policy boards of the university. But the very structure of these policy bodies is being questioned at other universities. Representative government in any form limits participation to the elected representatives. Students are increasingly demanding a more flexible representation open to all who may be interested in an issue of the moment. Some students and professors are also suggesting that the endless committees and commissions are slow and irrelevant to the kinds of immediate and rapid decision-making which must take place in an innovative campus. They are urging structures which will allow for *ad hoc* decisions related to the present.

University Planning and Development

Many universities are finding that, no matter what their decision-making structure, they are often making decisions based on ignorance. They do not have adequate information on matters being discussed, either on their own campuses or comparative information about other campuses. Accordingly, many universities have established planning and development units, with extensive management information systems, in order to gather appropriate data to help decision-making bodies in making intelligent decisions. These data often include statistical information on the reality of the situation under discussion, projections as to future effects of alternate decisions, analyses of cost implications of alternate decisions, information on the experience of other institutions on the same matter, and relationship of the decision under discussion to other policy and programme matters.

The danger is that such offices become mechanistic structures which attempt to make decisions at the same time as they are providing information for decision-making. If this occurs, the university can find itself being managed by budget officers and systems analysts instead of by the participants in the academic process. The academic community needs information on which to base decisions but they must make the decisions themselves.

Often a part of the planning and development structure, but usually separate from it, one increasingly finds centres for institutional research and innovation. These centres take a variety of approaches toward the stimulation of innovative activity in curriculum and methodology. Some do this by providing exceptional learning resources and facilities for those academic departments who wish to innovate, others do it by attempting to stimulate and financially support new kinds of academic programmes, interdisciplinary activities and the like. When headed by a senior official of the university and supported substantially, such a structure can be very useful in stimulating change.

Finally, there is a trend toward inter-university planning and development offices which help all universities in a country to understand the collective effect of individual decisions. In several countries, these offices are the mechanisms through which government support for universities is channelled. Such mechanisms help bring order out of chaos in countries where many universities have often proceeded with their own development plans with little or no detailed knowledge of the present programme or future plans of other universities.

Autonomy and Accountability

On the one hand, universities generally claim autonomy and on the other, the public is increasingly demanding greater accountability. The two concepts are not necessarily in conflict.

Universities will increasingly have to justify to the public the large amounts of monies invested in them. Faculty, students and administrators in universities will have to be individually accountable for performance. Some universities now encourage continuous evaluations by students of the performance of their professors. Others even encourage careful scrutiny of the performance of administrative staff to the level of the chancellor or president. Productivity of individual departments in terms of teaching, research, and service are constantly under scrutiny. Criteria for judging performance are sorely lacking in many institutions and the development of criteria and methods for assessing these criteria will be a major task of the future in many institutions.

New Structures for Life-long Higher Education

With a greater emphasis on accountability, many institutions will be looking toward new structures in order to increase their performance. There are exciting new ventures under way that may change our notions on how a university should offer its wares. The Open University in Britain is one of them.*

In socialist countries of Europe, there are a number of popular or workers' universities which allow workers to undertake university studies part-time. In Cuba, the 'University of the Fields' includes work in the countryside as an integral part of the university programme, and university credits are given for such work. In Poland, a television university has existed for over a decade, primarily for workers, who are given three weeks of paid vacation for laboratory and seminar work each year if they are enrolled.

---

* See Chapter 29.

In a new experiment in the United States, a group of 19 universities, ranging from small experimental colleges to large state universities, are banding together to form a 'University Without Walls'. This university will allow young people to participate in a variety of learning experiences in the community and in any of the participating universities and to receive a university degree after demonstrating ability to perform in the context of the problems of the world around them rather than in the context of a traditional university classroom.

The effect of most of these new structures is further to democratize the university, and often to relate the university more directly to development needs of the country. The emphasis is away from the mechanistic manpower production model to the emphasis on broad development of man who must participate in the renewal of society.

Universities and National Development

The fact that there is great diversity of structures has not, as yet, resolved a basic question of the developing countries, namely, what kind of a university do they need in order that it contribute most effectively to national development? It is almost commonplace to say that the exportation of duplicates of European or North American universities is inappropriate. There is, however, today a certain tendency to export not only traditional European or North American university models, but their innovations and experiments, often controversial and far from mature. But, if universities in developed countries should not be slavishly copied, what is the structure, what are the varieties, the models of universities which the developing countries and, in particular, the youngest countries of Africa and Oceania need? Study of this problem has scarcely begun. It seems to be clear that the needs of the countries to which the new universities must be adapted cannot be identified simply as immediate needs in trained manpower, even if these needs must be considered in the short run. The long-term needs of these countries are more far-reaching: these countries need a place for discussion and deep analysis of the characteristics and foreseeable trends of their development; they need more people capable of foresight and independent judgment; they need a basis on which research in vital scientific domains can develop, because the real independence of these countries lies in the achievement of human-development goals.

This long-term service to the countries, which could appear superfluous to those who observe only immediate manpower needs, cannot be ensured outside the university or the universities of the countries. The setting of development goals and strategies in highly industrialized countries is assisted by a series of institutions and milieux where long-term thinking and research can be undertaken (i.e. academies, research institutes, associations of intellectual professions, etc.). In a great number of new countries, the university is the only place where the intellectual energies of the nation can be concentrated. One example of the limitations of short-term manpower approaches will suffice. In many developing countries it is assumed that they cannot afford advanced graduate training facilities, and that after undergraduate preparation students may go abroad for further specialization. This decision, in essence, shapes the entire undergraduate sequence toward preparing students who will be accepted in foreign universities. Is this tolerable when the university should be doing other things, more related to development needs of the country, than those which are primarily geared to standards of foreign universities?

Equally crucial in developing countries is the effect of the university on the rest of the school system. Even in countries where only one child in a thousand has a chance of entering the university, the elementary and secondary levels tend to be distorted toward a linear curriculum suitable for preparation for the university. This means that the great majority of children who never get to the university are probably receiving less than the appropriate education to enter life at the level at which they leave school. A new kind of university, more clearly related to development needs, would have profound effects on what happens at lower levels of education.

But the concept one has of development is crucial too. Most governments assume a kind of linear development model whereby the university provides certain manpower inputs. Such a model assumes that poor countries will develop in much the same way as rich countries have developed. There are some who would question this assumption, especially when the experience of the first development decade is considered. The gap between rich and poor is widening and it may be that universities should be looking for new, non-linear models of development, and should be pursuing other long-term goals than those related to simple manpower development for known jobs in the existing economy.

University Financing

In most countries, universities are supported almost entirely by the government. Even in countries where there are large numbers of private universities, these private universities are finding it increasingly difficult to function without government support. In some countries, university autonomy is so well established that the universities receive a certain percentage of the government's budget to do with what they may. In many countries, however, governments are attempting to establish formulae for the support of higher education that are consistent with the functions the universities are expected to perform.

In essence, governments in some countries will probably increasingly provide categorical support for different aspects of the university's activities. They will provide support for students, often through grants to the students who can then study at any university they like, support research activities in areas of concern to the national interest, and provide grants for the construction of facilities. In cases where governments continue to give so-called formula grants to universities to do with what they may, there will be an increased emphasis on institutional accountability and a demand that the institution provide evidence of the effectiveness of its programme. This will have both good and bad effects. On the positive side, it will force universities to examine carefully their programme and structure in terms of performance criteria. On the negative side, it will undoubtedly cause increasing conflicts between governments and universities, since the university may see its goals as different from those as seen by the government. This will be especially the case in countries where the university may wish to take leadership in setting development goals and its notion of development may be in conflict with that of the government.

Unesco's Role in Higher Education

The future of institutions which deal in the transmission and creation of universal knowledge must be considered in the international context. Perhaps for this reason, the authors of this chapter have been asked to briefly describe the role of the United Nations Educational, Scientific and Cultural Organization (Unesco) in facilitating appropriate international collaboration in the study and resolution of university problems.

Although problems of education in general have traditionally been at the forefront of Unesco's concerns, it is only during the past few years that *higher* education in particular has received increasing emphasis and attention within the programme of the Organization. The reason is fairly obvious. Unesco is, in a sense, a forum where the Member States bring their anxieties, their problems and, to a lesser extent, their hopes, for discussion, comparison and analysis in a regional and international perspective. If Unesco now is facing university problems more resolutely than, say, eight or ten years ago, this is because university problems have been, for the past few years, much in evidence in most of the Member States.

This does not mean that Unesco can have a university policy or its own conception of a university. It is not Unesco's function to favour or impose policies or models and, in any case, the extreme contextual diversity and needs in the various countries would make one model impossible and without any sense. Nevertheless, its central position permits the Organization to have some internal consistency in its programme which expresses itself in the exchange of experiences, in the sorting out and making known of new trends, in providing Member States, upon request, with advice and assistance of various kinds. Through these activities Unesco can and must contribute to the renovation of higher education, and especially of universities. Renovation is the key word, not because of a taste for novelty for its own sake but because the universities must adapt to the changing cultural and scientific needs of the societies which created them.

The Organization sponsors periodic meetings of Ministers of Education where long-term goals and targets are established. Studies, conferences and seminars are undertaken on many of the university problems discussed in this paper. A joint programme with the International Association of Universities and the Ford Foundation has assisted in the creation of a Regional Institute for Higher Education in Development in Singapore. Plans are currently under way for the establishment of a Unesco Regional Centre for Higher Education in Europe, and a feasibility study is proceeding, in co-operation with the United Nations in New York, for the establishment of a United Nations International University, which would collaborate with all existing national universities in exploring problems requiring international academic collaboration.

The Organization has recently assisted the United Arab Republic and the Syrian Arab Republic in a thorough study of their higher education system, and is working with a number of African, Latin American and Asian countries on university problems. A number of science and engineering faculties have received Unesco-United Nations Development Programme assistance in the form of experts and equipment. A major emphasis in many of these activities is the provision of information to national universities on the basis of which they can make more informed decisions. One aspect of this work has been to assist national universities in understanding the nature of the curriculum of other universities in order to move toward a better understanding of equivalencies in various institutions and programmes. A series of guide books is now available to assist universities in understanding the content of programmes in other universities in various countries.

In essence, the Organization places high priority on helping governments and institutions in setting up the structures necessary to set their own policies and construct their own programmes on a continuous basis of positive renewal. The Organization attempts to impose no policy on any government or institution but stands ready to assist its 125 Member States in exploring alternative approaches to the making of the university of the future.

Section II

University Progress in Rapidly Developing Countries

Introduction

W. Roy Niblett

The distinction between developing and developed countries, or between low-income countries and high-income ones, is bound to be arbitrary in a number of ways and for several reasons. Even in wealthy countries there are underdeveloped areas; the decaying centres of great cities are low-income neighbourhoods surrounded by suburbia. Moreover the concept of development itself contains many presuppositions about what constitutes human progress: it certainly relies too much upon superficial economic dogmas to be accepted uncritically.

What is remarkable is that underprivileged though many African, South American and Asian countries are, as compared with affluent North American and European nations, the *general* direction of development of their higher education systems is pretty closely akin to that of their wealthier sisters. Sometimes no doubt economic aid from the treasuries – and occasionally guidance and advice (not always taken) from the scientists and academics – of richer countries have been an important factor here. Sometimes, as in the case of China, they have entirely cut themselves off from this. But they have almost all enormously expanded their provision of higher education, have shown an increasing flexibility in determining entrance qualifications, and are developing a broader concept of the proper content of a higher education curriculum. Students in most of them have tended to gain in power to influence the state of things. It becomes clearer that though, by and large, institutions of higher education in underdeveloped countries may be at an earlier stage of evolution than those in affluent ones the line of evolution along which they are going raises many of the same problems about how they should face the future – and about the very nature of the future to be faced – as elsewhere.

The countries and the universities dealt with in this part of the book are instances only which might be paralleled by many others. We wish we could have included a chapter about Chile, for example, where remarkable developments have taken place in recent years in fostering University Centres in various parts of the country which have developed an organic relationship with the expanded University of Chile in Santiago; or chapters on particular universities – typifying others – in, say, Nigeria, whose university population has gone up so fast, Kenya, Gabon, Iran, Indonesia, Malaysia.

The general movement (though like a snake going forward, parts of the body may point in different directions at the same time) is one that will inevitably bring to light many of the same conflicts regarding the place and function of universities as appear in more advanced countries. The conflict between what Martin Trow has called the elite and the popular functions of higher education is an obvious example. How reconcile the need in many nations for producing informed leadership with that of producing large numbers of people awake and aware enough to follow an intelligent initiative? Higher education needs in these days to fulfil both tasks. But it is by no means easy for one not to become subjugated to the other – especially in universities that have been strongly elitist in tradition.

The inclusion in this section of the book of a chapter on a Japanese university is not to be taken to imply that the Editors do not regard Japan as an affluent country; but it *is* rapidly developing and its universities are moving with extraordinary speed, not without turmoil, from a pre-twentieth century to a post-twentieth century world.

The Regional Institute in South-East Asia with which the last chapter deals is a prototype of a kind of development likely to become much more common in the future: the region concerned includes a number of countries and the Institute's remit involves a number of disciplines and fields of study. Here is a parallel in an international field and in a developing region to the useful postgraduate interdisciplinary Centres of Study increasingly common in individual universities – and in groups of universities – in several more affluent countries.

5

The Chinese People's University: Bastion of Marxism–Leninism

C. T. Hu

It may be suggested that the true significance of China's revolution under Communism lies in the single word 'people'. In Chinese the term 'people' is formed by the two characters of *jen*, meaning man, or human, and *min*, meaning people or subjects of a state. While *jen-min* as a term is probably as old as the Chinese language, its usage in the current context and its clearly understood connotations are unmistakably peculiar to the Communist phase of modern China. The crucial character *min* is often rendered as people by itself. But in both Imperial and Republican China the character *min* had been used in conjunction with modifiers other than *jen*, thereby giving the resulting combinations meanings quite different from the term *jen-min*, which is currently in use. Among other things, the term *jen-min* or people implies the Communist concept of class struggle: the common man and woman who form the masses and who in pre-Communist days had been victims of oppression and exploitation by the privileged classes. The Communist revolution brought about the overthrow of the oppressors, both foreign and domestic, and the 'liberation of the people'. Consequently, the Chinese nation-state was proclaimed to be Chung-hua *jen-min* kung-ho kuo, or The Chinese *People's* Republic. The highest legislative body became known as *jen-min* tai-piao ta-hui, or the National *People's* Congress. And the armed forces of the state are called *jen-min* chieh-fang chun, or the *People's* Liberation Army.

Though the word 'people' is neutral and normally implies collectivity of human individuals, Communist ideological stress upon class struggle has qualified its usage by making it non-all-inclusive. People, in contemporary Chinese context, refers to the four classes of workers, peasants, petty bourgeoisie, and national bourgeoisie, the two former working classes constituting quantitatively the majority and qualitatively the source of revolutionary strength. 'The feudal class and the bureaucratic capitalist class, together with their political representative, the Kuomintang reactionaries, are definitely not people of New China; on the contrary, they are the Chinese people's enemy.'[1]

Until the founding of the People's Republic in 1949, the Communist movement, being insurrectionary in character, had adapted its educational efforts to the needs of revolution. The few institutions of higher learning or, more correctly, the few schools bearing the designation of either a university or college, such as the Resist-Japan University in Yenan, were as a rule highly informal and unstructured schools for the training of party activists. With their accession to power, the Communists inherited from the Nationalists some 270 universities and colleges which they proceeded to reorganize and reform as early as 1950. At the same time, the need for ideologically correct and professionally dedicated party workers grew more urgent as the task of national reconstruction became more demanding.

The Beginnings of the People's University

The Chinese People's University came into existence as early as the end of 1949, when the Administration Council of the central government passed a resolution for its establishment. Preparatory work was assigned to some of the members of the faculties of three institutions in north China and in early 1950 post-graduate students were admitted into such research departments as Foundations of Marxism–Leninism, Problems of Chinese Revolution, Public Finance, Economics, Law, and Diplomacy. On October 3, 1950, the University was formally opened with an inaugural ceremony, with a full-time teaching staff of fifty-five, and a total of thirty-eight Instruction and Research departments.

Major objectives of the new university were declared to be the training and supply of teaching personnel in the field of theoretical foundations of Marxism–Leninism, of high-ranking cadres in the fields of public finance, economics, and the social sciences, and of managerial talents for industrial enterprises. For the supply of students, the university relied primarily upon the ranks of older and experienced party cadres, while the more progressive elements among the young and the non-Communist intellectuals were also admitted for their development and reform, in order for them to develop into 'fighting heroes dedicated to the party, revolutionary cadres, progressive personages, and labour models'.[2]

Although the Communists have consistently demanded the 'proletarianization of intellectuals' and emphasized the importance of eliminating class differentials in education, education in the first seven or so years retained many features of the earlier periods. A 1957 report claimed that in Peking higher institutions, eighty per cent of the students came from landlord, bourgeois, or petty bourgeois families. At approximately the same time, a survey of members of higher institutions teaching staff, involving nearly 2,500 individuals in forty-six colleges and universities, showed the majority to have come from landlord and bourgeois families, and that as high as 98 per cent of them received their education in old China, 'soaked with the class spirit of the bourgeoisie'.[3] It is in this particular respect that the Chinese People's University has stood out as a unique and a sort of model institution. A strictly 'party' institution in keeping with the spirit of the revolutionary days, the People's University drew both its faculty and students largely from middle ranking party functionaries who, through many years of faithful service, had proven their loyalty and devotion to what the party stood for.

Unlike most comprehensive universities and other higher institutions of education whose faculties had been educated in old China, the People's University from its inception was staffed primarily with individuals who had served in one of the several pre-liberation institutions. For more technical subjects, such as public finance and statistics, the instructional personnel came from party or state organizations with more practical experience than academic training. At times, special arrangements were made for party dignitaries to serve on the faculty on a part-time basis. In 1958, in the early days of the Great Leap Forward, K'ang Sheng and Ch'en Po-ta, both members of the Communist Party's Central Committee, together with Chou Yang, then Vice Minister of Culture of the party, were among the dozen or so distinguished adjunct professors.[4]

Student composition showed a similar pattern. Of the 2,279 students who formed the first graduating class in 1954, 67 per cent were members of either the Communist Party or the Communist Youth League, while close to 60 per cent were cadres of peasant-worker background.[5] This is entirely in agreement with the policy of the University, for until the summer of 1956, student recruitment had been restricted to cadres in active service. All cadres under the age of thirty, whether in party, state, or productive units of all types, and members of the armed forces and veterans, were eligible for admission to the People's University as long as they applied with the necessary recommendations from their respective organizations.[6] It was made clear that admission of active cadres served the dual purpose of improving the ideological and technical competence of the individuals selected and at the same time raising the morale of the rank and file of party activists through the provision of higher education opportunities. Since the overwhelming majority of the so-called 'old' cadres had had highly inadequate formal education as a result of their early participation in the revolution, and since enrolment in or graduation from a higher institution of education still carried considerable prestige, the People's University, as a special institution of higher learning, sought to satisfy the educational and psychological needs of party cadres of proven quality.

The People's University was designated as one of the relatively small number of comprehensive universities in which several major subject areas were covered in the instructional programme. As such, to have for its student body only over-aged and academically ill-prepared cadres would in the long run reduce the University to the status of a political training institute. It was, therefore, obviously for reasons of academic upgrading and with it its public image that the University decided in the summer of 1957 to accept high school graduates through the nation-wide system of unified entrance examinations. To insure its so-called special 'party character' and to implement the policy of 'opening the doors for peasant-workers', the People's University took over the Peking Experimental Peasant-Worker Accelerated Middle School in 1952 as an appendage of the University, into which graduates of the Middle School were automatically admitted.

Expansion and Development

Beginning in 1952, the People's University embarked upon an ambitious expansion programme. In that year, the Marxism–Leninism Research Centre was established, for the express purpose of training qualified teachers for various types of higher institutions in this field of paramount importance. In early 1953, a Correspondence Department was added for the benefit of party cadres in active service, with as many as twelve subject areas, including philosophy, industrial economics, law, and the like. In the fall of 1954, a Marxism–Leninism Night University came into existence, with its own buildings and facilities away from the main campus, but administratively forming a part of the University. Following the general trend apparent in the mid-1950s, all regular departments within the University lengthened their residence requirements from four to five years, and by 1956, the University felt sufficiently confident to introduce a doctoral programme, accepting twenty-five post-graduate candidates for advanced degrees in such specialities as Foundations of Marxism–Leninism and dialectical materialism. In 1958, in the wake of the Great Leap Forward Movement and the Socialist Education campaign, the Correspondence Department was elevated to the status of college, under which more than ten Correspondence Centres were established in major cities in North China.

Over a period of fifteen years, the People's University developed from a relatively little known institution for political indoctrination with a faculty of fifty or so experienced cadres and a student body of several hundred to become the leading university in Communist ideology in the entire nation. Even during and after the Cultural Revolution, which plunged China into a state of utter chaos, the University had an enrolment of more than ten thousand students and a faculty and staff of over 1,600.

In spite of the very rapid rate of expansion, the People's University has through the years adhered faithfully to the overriding principle of stressing political consciousness and class background. While the national percentage of higher institution students of proletarian background rose from 19·1 in 1951–2 to 29·2 in 1955–6 and to 48 in 1958–9, the People's University had more than 70 per cent of peasant-worker origin from the very beginning. It was this fact that earned for the University the title of 'cradle of China's worker-peasant intellectuals'.[7] This has been made possible by a special set of admission requirements which differ considerably from those that obtained in other institutions. Only individuals in the following four categories were eligible for admission:[8]

1. Those who have participated in the revolutionary movement for a period of eight years, under the age of 35, and with formal education equivalent to junior middle school (approximately 9 years of formal schooling).

2. Those who have participated in the revolutionary movement or having served in party or state organizations for three or more years, under the age of 32, and with formal education equivalent to junior middle school.

3. Those who are between the ages 17 and 32 and who have been progressive workers with formal education equivalent to junior middle school.

4. Those who have graduated from senior middle schools, under 27, and who are politically progressive.

Because of the generally low level of educational attainment on the part of the majority of party activists, the junior middle school requirement was clearly a concession to most of the aspirants. Even that, however, proved difficult to meet and consequently the further concession in the form of 'equivalence'. In the absence of unequivocal guidelines, what is 'equivalent to junior middle school education' could be subject to all kinds of interpretation; hence the People's University's student body in the earlier days has been characterized by a highly obvious inadequacy in educational preparation. For example, 80 per cent of the freshman class of 1950 had no more than junior middle school education, with many of them at a level slightly above the completion of primary grades.[9]

Even after the stiffening of academic requirements in 1955, when admission called for equivalence to senior middle school graduates in Chinese language, political knowledge, history and geography, and proficiency in mathematics comparable to junior middle school graduates, enrolment continued to be largely restricted to revolutionary cadres on active duty, to industrial workers, and to demobilized members of the armed forces.[10] By and large, the unevenness in academic preparation reflected itself in two ways: 1. the regular full-time programmes conducted by the nineteen academic departments tended to attract academically better prepared students, whereas all short-term training classes and correspondence schools catered almost exclusively for active cadres with insufficient formal education; 2. the more intellectually and professionally oriented departments generally had higher academic standards than those primarily concerned with Marxist–Leninist ideology.

To an appreciable extent, the same pattern held true in the teaching staff. As the University expanded, teachers from the 'old liberated areas' proved inadequate both in number and in quality. The introduction of subjects other than those purely political gave rise to the need for experts with formal training, and the need was met by two major means which may be described as borrowing and training. The former involved the practice of seconding from 'fraternal institutions' teaching personnel in a variety of technical and professional subjects. The Chinese Academy of Sciences, the Peking University, and other higher institutions in the city of Peking have been sources of supply. The latter called for the up-grading of the University's own personnel through intensive training pro-grammes.

For this, the role of Soviet experts until their recall in the early 1960s can hardly be exaggerated. Of the considerable number of Soviet experts serving in China before the Sino-Soviet split, a significant portion was assigned to educational institutions of all types, and the People's Uni-versity received its share. These experts concentrated their efforts on the training of teachers and research students, on the preparation of textbooks and similar teaching materials, and on designing scientific research pro-jects and instruments. Up to early 1953, most members of the People's University faculties had been 'teaching while learning', generally under the guidance of Soviet experts. From 1954 on, the Soviet experts began to shift their areas of concentration to the preparation of special reports and the formulation of pedagogical policies. The utilization of Russian teach-ing materials gained wider currency, as 'the University mobilized all instructors who know Russian to translate and edit Russian materials for use in classes. Between September 1950 and August 1955, they completed more than two thousand syllabi, lecture notes and references which were printed in 7,650,000 copies for distribution among more than a hundred institutions of higher learning.'[11] Furthermore, the more promising and younger instructors were encouraged to enrol in the doctoral pro-gramme for the degree of Kandidat, which required sophistication in dialectical materialism, proficiency in one or more foreign languages, and thorough command of subjects in a chosen speciality. In addition to assistance of an academic nature, special leaves and reduction of teaching responsibility were granted those who wished to take advantage of the doctoral programmes. It was reported in 1956 that most instructors were determined to obtain the Kandidat degree within five to twelve years.[12]

The People's University's deliberate effort in safeguarding and developing the so-called revolutionary tradition of the pre-1949 period, which called for special emphasis upon politics in terms of content and proletarian class quality in terms of student composition, determined in a fundamental way the direction in which the University must go and with it the quality of its students and instructional staff.

Instructional and Other Programmes

The uniqueness of the People's University as an innovative institution can also be seen in its instructional programmes. Although known as a comprehensive university, it has only the three faculties of arts, finance and economics, and politics and law. Beginning with eight departments in the regular programme – economic planning, finance and credit, trade, co-operatives, factory administration, law, diplomacy, and Russian – and eleven short-term training programmes – economic planning, finance and credit, domestic trade, foreign trade, co-operatives, factory administration, statistics, law, diplomacy, education, history and geography – the University gradually expanded its offerings not only to cover more subject fields but more importantly to suit the specific needs of individuals coming from a variety of professional background.

In the course of expansion, there emerged the unmistakable pattern of duality, in that 1. the regular full-time departments tended to be more academically rigorous in comparison with those short-term training programmes, and 2. the non-regular courses were, with rare exceptions, basically technical or professional in character, largely for party workers whose ideological correctness was more or less taken for granted. In 1952, for example, the University offered only advanced courses in political theory 'for the training of teachers of political theory for institutions of higher learning and a number of cadre schools throughout the country'.[13] These courses were restricted to philosophy, political economy, history of the Chinese Communist Party, Marxism–Leninism, and similar subjects. When the Correspondence Division was established in 1953, ten areas of specialization were offered, all of which in the general field of finance and economics, including such specialities as domestic trade, trade statistics, consumer co-operatives, and banking.

By 1961, the University had altogether six major types of programmes: 1. regular university course of four or five years duration; 2. short-term specialized classes; 3. evening school; 4. correspondence school with more than one area of specialization; 5. correspondence school with multiple subjects in one field of specialization; and 6. correspondence school with one single subject.[14] The number of departments in the regular programme increased from eight in 1950 to ten departments and fourteen specialities in 1954. In 1957, the University began to offer five-year courses in the following departments and areas of specialization:[15]

Faculty of Arts: 1. history, 2. philosophy, 3. historical archives (4 year), 4. journalism.
Faculty of Finance and Economics: 5. Economics (political economy), 6. planning and statistics (planning and national economy, statistics), 7. industrial economics, 8. agricultural economics, 9. trade economics, 10. finance.
Faculty of Politics and Law: 11. law.

According to a more recent survey, the People's University had nineteen departments in the middle of 1967 in its regular programme, fifteen in the special programme, and fifteen courses in the research programme. The new departments added to the regular programme were Chinese language and literature and Russian for the Faculty of Arts; finance and statistics for the Faculty of Finance and Economics; and international politics, diplomacy, fundamentals of Marxism–Leninism, and history of the Chinese Communist Party in the Faculty of Politics and Law.[16] The short-term special studies programme as well as the research programme duplicate, on the whole, the regular offerings, the former designed for the in-service cadres while the latter for more advanced students.

There are usually several instructional and research units and/or specific fields of specialization within a department. These units form the basic teaching organs which are responsible for the organization of pedagogical activities, promotion of scientific research, improvement of the instructors' ideological level in Marxism–Leninism, and the training of research personnel. In short, they determine and carry out programmes of instruction and research.[17] One department from each of the three faculties and their fields of specialization are given below to indicate the range of coverage:

Faculty of Arts: Department of Philosophy
    Logic
    Ethics
    Philosophy
    Dialectical materialism and historical materialism
    Foundations of natural science.
Faculty of Finance and Economics: Department of Political Economy
    Political economy
    Economic geography
    Foundations of Marxism–Leninism
    Philosophy
    History of Chinese revolution
    Political theory and economic science.

Faculty of Politics and Law: Department of Diplomacy
  History of International relations
  International law.

Under this system, a student majoring in one department may choose one or more sub-fields of specialization. The purpose is to turn out 'quickly more and better qualified men through intensive training in a particular subject for their special profession'.[18]

The most outstanding characteristic of the People's University lies in its unremitting emphasis upon what in China has been broadly referred to as 'politics', with 'redness' as the ultimate goal. This is reflected in the composition of its faculty, its administration, its student body, and in the types of its programmes and curricula. A substantial portion of both its programmes and students has been devoted to strictly political indoctrination. The course and number of hours required in the Marxism–Leninism Night University, which forms an integral part of the People's University, are given below as an illustration:[19]

Fundamentals of Marxism–Leninism	150 hours
History of Chinese Revolution	120
Theory of People's Democracy	32
Political Economy	150
General Chinese History	114
Selected Works of Mao Tse-tung	174
Dialectical Materialism and Historical Materialism	100

Even for the trusted cadres who enrol in such technical subject areas as public finance or trade, approximately forty to fifty per cent of their class time had to be devoted to political subjects similar to those listed above. In addition, all persons connected with the University have been required to take part in special lecture and public discussion sessions from time to time. For the promotion of Socialist Education, the University organized a series of public lectures in 1957, with the leading party functionaries serving as lecturers. Putting aside one day each week for this purpose, the series covered the following topics:[20]

The great significance of struggle against capitalist rightists
The question of standpoint
Socialist revolution
Socialist construction
Concerning the consolidation of People's Democratic Dictatorship
Oppose liberalism and anarchism
Concerning the consolidation and strengthening of Party leadership
Concerning the consolidation of democratic centralism
Oppose individualism and professionalism

Oppose absolute egalitarianism
Concerning the consolidation of Socialist International unity and the
  unity of peoples of the world
Oppose chauvinism and regional nationalism.

The efficacy of so enormous a dosage of ideological injection remains
questionable, if for no other reason than the oft-repeated need for further
efforts and the equally often lamented undependability of many individuals. Long before the Cultural Revolution, Party leaders within the University repeatedly sought to uproot the so-called rightist tendencies which
ranged from the 'nostalgic feeling' about purely academic and intellectual
courses to outright anti-Party views and advocacy for the overthrow of
Communism.[21]

To fight against the growth of politically unhealthy modes of thinking
and to ensure compliance with the principle of 'combining education with
productive labour', the People's University initiated a wide range of programmes to enable all students to reinforce their learning through practice. While some took part in specially designed projects undertaken in
conjunction with specific areas of specialization, the majority, especially
since the Cultural Revolution in 1966, had been 'sent down either up to
the hill or down to the fields', a widespread practice known as *hsia-fang*
and sometimes aptly rendered as 'rustication'.[22] In order to engage
actively in production, the University built a paper mill at the height of
the Great Leap Forward, and it was reported that the mill, fully utilizing
student manpower, was capable of producing nearly four tons of paper
daily in 1960, and that between January and September of that year, the
mill increased its productivity by more than 40 per cent, at the same time
reducing the cost of production by twelve per cent.[23] For students in
departments concerned with finance and economics, the University
opened a department store in the western suburbs of Peking in 1958. The
response of the 'people' in the neighbourhood was said to have been
exceedingly favourable because of the students' proletarian spirit in conducting their business.[24] Students of law and journalism have likewise
been engaged in productive labour of one form or another, giving the
over-all impression that 'the hsia-fang movement has resulted in the total
renewal of thought on the part of all students'.[25]

The Cultural Revolution and its Consequences

Despite its commanding position in Chinese higher education as the
bastion of Marxism–Leninism–Maoism orthodoxy, the People's University was as much shaken to its foundation as all other institutions of higher
education. There seem to be two major factors that were responsible for
its inability to escape what must have been the most violent storm that

ever hit China since 1949. One has to do with the reform efforts under the auspices of Liu Shao-ch'i and begun in the early 1960s which, among other things, resulted in a sharper distinction between politics and academic pursuit, and therefore between 'redness' on the one hand and 'expertness' on the other. As the University expanded, 'students who do not even know the English alphabet, who are ignorant of the most elementary mathematics, and who cannot tell that ice is a form of water'[26] found it increasingly difficult either to gain admission or to remain in attendance. Greater attention to the academic and professional aspects of university life meant lesser concern with politics, on which the academically ill-prepared students thrived. To those whose only credential or qualification happened to be their ideological correctness, the swing of the pendulum in the direction of intellectuality posed a serious threat. When the storm broke, they formed the vanguard in bringing about literally the destruction of China's educational system.[27] The second factor was purely party politics. Since the top leadership of the People's University was largely identified with the Liu Shao-ch'i faction, and more specifically with the Peking Municipal Committee, the purge which came at the heel of the Cultural Revolution swept across its campus, resulting in the forceful removal of a good number of responsible party committee men and their followers.

However, the People's University followed rather than led the educational part of the Cultural Revolution. The revolutionists echoed the demands made by students in other universities. In July, 1966, seven students of the People's University made demands for the complete revamping of higher education and urged that 'the writings of Chairman Mao be used as standard texts and class struggle be made the key subject for study'. They wanted the period of schooling on all levels shortened, so that they could participate in the three revolutionary movements to reform themselves. Moreover, higher education must be made available to workers, poor and middle peasants, and demobilized servicemen of the armed forces.[28]

Like other schools, the People's University at present is under the collective leadership of a revolutionary committee, and all personnel are being re-educated by the Mao Tse-tung Thought Propaganda Team sent by the People's Liberation Army. As of 1971, a semblance of normalcy has returned to the campus, but the pendulum has clearly swung to the extreme left, with even greater stress upon political indoctrination to ensure 'redness', upon practical and manual labour to prevent social aloofness, upon 'self-reliance' to create a truly Chinese socialist culture, and upon 'proletarianization of the intellectuals' to forestall any possible resurgence of revisionism in the future. In all these formidable tasks, the People's University, by virtue of its revolutionary tradition, is expected not only to succeed but also to provide national leadership in its 'privileged position as the bastion of Marxism–Leninism'.

REFERENCES

1. Ch'ien Chun-jui, 'Our present educational principles', *New China Monthly*, June, 1950, p. 407.
2. Wang Chun, 'A Survey of The Chinese People's University', *Studies of Chinese Communism*, Vol. 1, No. 10, Taipei, Taiwan, October, 1967, p. 59.
3. *Hsueh Hsi Semi-Monthly*, November 18, 1957.
4. *Peking Daily*, August 22, 1958.
5. *Kuang Ming Daily*, June 28, 1954.
6. *Peking Daily*, April 28, 1957.
7. Ts'ao Yu, 'The People's University of China: The Cradle of Builders of Socialism', *Wen-I Pao* (Literary Gazette), No. 13, July, 1955.
8. *People's Daily*, March 15, 1950.
9. *People's Daily*, June 7, 1950.
10. *People's Daily*, June 3, 1955.
11. Immanuel C. Y. Hsu, 'The Reorganization of Higher Education in Communist China', *The China Quarterly*, No. 19, July–September, 1964, pp. 139–41.
12. *Kuang-Ming Daily*, March 1, 1956.
13. *Kuang-Ming Daily*, February 23, 1963.
14. *Kuang-Ming Daily*, December 2, 1961.
15. According to a brochure issued by the Ministry of Education dated March, 1957, cited in *China Topics*, August, 1968, pp. 20–2.
16. Wage Chun, op. cit., pp. 60–6.
17. 'Hu Hsi-k'uei tells about the Aims and Methods of the People's University', New China News Agency, July 4, 1953. Hu was Vice-President of the University at the time.
18. Immanuel C. Y. Hsu, op. cit.
19. Wang, op. cit.
20. *People's Daily*, August 23, 1957.
21. *Hsueh Hsi Semi-Monthly*, Nov. 18, 1957; *Chung-Kuo Ch'ing-nien pao* (China Youth News), January 30, 1955.
22. *Wen-hui Daily*, Shanghai, March 26, 1955.
23. *Kuang-Ming Daily*, November 23, 1960.
24. *Kuang-Ming Daily*, September 2, 1958.
25. *People's Daily*, January 7, 1959.
26. *Wen-hui Daily*, Shanghai, January 13, 1953.
27. For a general discussion of the impact of the Cultural Revolution on Chinese higher education, see C. T. Hu, 'The Chinese University – Target of the Cultural Revolution', *Saturday Review*, New York, August 9, 1968.
28. *People's Daily*, July 12, 1966.

6

The University of Dar es Salaam: A Socialist Enterprise

Donald G. W. Schutte

The University of Dar es Salaam has a brief past and faces the future with limited precedents. It is the future which holds the promise of the fulfil-ment of aims and purposes put forward by the Chancellor, Julius K. Nyerere, at formal inaugural ceremonies on the 29th of August, 1970. He said:

> This is the background to Tanzania's decision to establish its own University. Our nation has decided to divert development resources from other potential uses because we expect to benefit by doing so. We believe that through having our own higher educational institution in this country, we shall obtain the kind of high-level manpower we need to build a socialist society, and we shall get the emphasis we need on investigating the particular problems which face us. In other words, we expect that our University will be of such a nature that all who pass through it will be prepared both in knowledge and in attitude for giving maximum service to the community.
>
> In its teaching objectives and in its research for new knowledge – the aim of the University of Dar es Salaam must be service to the needs of a developing socialist Tanzania. This purpose must determine the subjects taught, the conduct of courses, the methods of teaching and the manner in which the University is organized, as well as its relations with the community at large.[1]

The Creation of the University

The University was created by an Act[2] of the National Assembly of the United Republic of Tanzania with effect from 1st July, 1970. On that date the University of East Africa, with its constituent colleges in Dar es Salaam (Tanzania), Nairobi (Kenya), Kampala (Uganda – Makerere) ceased to exist. In its stead were three fully-fledged independent East African universities.

Co-operation between the three universities, however, did not cease. Under the auspices of the East African Community an Inter-University Committee was formed, as a vehicle for exchanging ideas on University Education and reports on courses being developed in each university.[3]

Further,

> ... as a result of good intentions of the three partner states ... it was also agreed
> to send our (Tanzanian) students to the Universities of Nairobi and Makerere ...
> for those courses for which our own faculties do not meet the national manpower
> requirements. Similarly, the University of Dar es Salaam will continue to admit
> a certain number of students from Kenya and Uganda. ....[4]

Historical Development

The former University College which provided the foundation on which
the new University will be built grew up over a period of nine years.
Instigated by the controlling party, the Tanganyika African National
Union (TANU), and TANU Government, the University College opened
its doors on 25th October, 1961, in buildings in the city centre borrowed
from TANU, with 14 students of law. Later, in 1964, the main campus
was located 13 kilometres from Dar es Salaam on Observation Hill. It
has since come to be known familiarly as University Hill, or just – the
Hill.

At the time of the inauguration, the student body had grown from 14
to 1,316 citizen undergraduate degree students and 36 citizen graduate
degree students. 350 non-citizen undergraduates and 30 non-citizen graduate degree students were also being catered for as well as 323 non-degree
students.

Undergraduates were distributed in faculties as shown in Table 1
on the next page.

The distribution shown above may be compared with the projected
growth in the faculties to 1975–6 (Table 2, p. 78).

Primary and Secondary Feeder System

Since National independence in 1961, and the opening of the University
College the same year, the primary and secondary schools' feeder base has
continued to expand. The magnitude of the expansion between 1961 and
the time of the inauguration ceremonies (August, 1970) is shown below in
Table 3 (p. 79). The goal of national planners is universal primary
education by 1989. Secondary educational opportunities will be expanded
to meet man-power needs in relation to the growth of the national
economy.

Looking at Table 3 one comes face to face with a fact which, when
coupled with other facts, reveals a problem facing the nation generally,
the University specifically. At the same time as the feeder base expands at
the bottom educational levels, it is constrained on the upper levels by
manpower needs which are determined by the expansion (or contraction)
of the national economy. The number of places in post-primary schools,
colleges and the University depends on the number of government,

TABLE 1

| Faculty | Year Opened | Location | Degree | Length of Course | Tanzanian | | | Non-Citizen | | | Grand Total |
					Male	Fem.	Total	E.A.	Other	Total	
Law	1961	Hill	LLB	3 years	88	8	96	62	0	62	158
Arts and Social Science	1964	Hill	BA	3 years	337	72	409	170	7	177	586
			BA (Ed.)	3 years	249	81	330	35	4	39	369
Science	1965	Hill	BSc	3 years	17	7	24	36	5	41	65
			BSc (Ed.)	3 years	238	45	283	18	2	20	303
Medicine	1968	Muhimbili Hospital	MBChB	5 years	104	9	113	8	3	11	124
Agriculture	1969	Morogoro	BSc (Agri.)	3 years	57	4	61	0	0	0	61
TOTALS					1,090	226	1,316	329	21	350	1,666

parastatal,* or private enterprise posts available. The colonial heritage left a huge gap between the number of qualified middle and high level posts to be filled and the number of local persons to fill them. As the University does one of the jobs it was created to do, the gap narrows but the limited posts available are filled with Tanzanians who are young and have many

TABLE 2

Faculty	1970–1	1975–6
Law	96	98
Arts and Social Sciences	739	810
Science	307	386
Medicine	113	349
Agriculture	61	231
Engineering (To open 1972–3)	0	371
TOTALS	1,316	2,245

productive years ahead of them. The result is a low turnover rate in a limited number of posts. Unless there is a rapid expansion of the economy, the number of University places relative to the size of the feeder base will decrease. For example, when the secondary schools' teaching posts have been localized and the rate of secondary school expansion slows to adjust to the demands of economic growth, there will be fewer government bursaries offered to candidates in education. Bursaries will be diverted as incentives for potential candidates to follow courses in other faculties, e.g. engineering. But when all the faculties have reached full capacity in terms of reflecting manpower needs, what then? It is at this point when the full effects of pegging higher education to manpower needs will be felt. Up to this point rapid expansion of places to fill the manpower gap will have largely obscured the effects. It is also at this point when the full import of the policy of education for self-reliance will become apparent. The question is whether, having arrived at this point, the people will understand the economic constraints on educational opportunities in this developing country or whether they will force an over-production of unemployable middle and high level manpower by exerting political pressure.

Primary schools, for all intents and purposes, are fully staffed by Tanzanians trained in the ten Colleges of National Education. The preservice training of secondary school teachers is a responsibility of the

* This refers to non-governmental institutions in which government has controlling interests. The University itself is a parastatal organization. It is not under the control of any single Ministry, but is fully supported by government. Salary scales and working conditions for University non-academic and academic staff have been brought into line with civil service scales and conditions.

TABLE 3
Tanzania Mainland* Primary and Secondary Schools: Feeder Base 1961 and 1970

	Male	+ Female	= 1961 Total	1970 Total	= Male	+ Female
Primary Standards ** 1–8 (1961) 1–7 (1970)	316,366	170,104	486,470	802,413	486,651	315,762
Secondary Forms 1–4	8,142	3,278	11,420	28,322	20,719	7,603
***5–6	362	50	412	2,895	2,429	466
1–6 Total	8,504	3,328	11,832	31,217	23,148	8,069
Grand Total	324,870	173,432	498,302	833,630	509,799	323,831

*Statistics for Zanzibar not available. For the past two years, 1969–70 and 1970–1 Zanzibar has not sent any degree candidates to university.

**The number of standards in primary schools has been reduced to 7; selection at the end of standard 4 has been eliminated.

*** Successful completion of Form 6 is a prerequisite for university entrance.

N.B. Estimated Population, Tanzania Mainland – 1970: 12,890,000: adjusted growth rates 2·7.

Department of Education within the Faculty of Arts and Social Sciences. The manpower needs of secondary schools is and has been treated as a matter of urgent priority. This is reflected by the number of education students in two Faculties supported by government bursaries. 45 per cent of all citizen students in the Faculty of Arts and Social Sciences are education students (BA (Ed)). The percentage in the Faculty of Science is even higher; 95 per cent of all citizen students in this Faculty are Education students (BSc (Ed)). The goal is to fully staff Tanzanian secondary schools with citizens by 1977. All students on government bursaries are bonded for five years to serve the Tanzanian Government. The effort to localize staff is reflected in Table 4 below.[5]

TABLE 4
LOCALIZATION OF THE SECONDARY SCHOOL TEACHING FORCE

Year	Total Teachers Required	Total Citizens Available	Balance of Non-Citizens
1969–70	1,346	656	690
1970–1	1,360	890	470
1971–2	1,406	1,106	300
1972–3	1,452	1,282	170
1973–4	1,498	1,378	120
1974	1,545	1,465	80
	. . . .	. . . . (1977)	0

Growth of New Faculties

A Faculty of Engineering is to be opened in July 1972. Still in the planning stage are two additional Faculties. A Faculty of Commerce and Management is envisaged as an outgrowth of the Department of Management and Administration, at present a part of the Faculty of Arts and Social Sciences. No opening date has been agreed upon. A Faculty of Veterinary Science which had been seriously considered, has for the moment been laid aside. Manpower needs for veterinary scientists will be met by sending students to Nairobi University.

Students

As in any university, students, the basic unit of need, are what the university is all about. The restlessness that has characterized student bodies throughout the world has not had a major effect on this campus. The problem is 'elitism' – real and imagined. Real, when, in the face of social and economic need, the society creates in its university educated leaders more concerned with serving self than society. Imagined, when those who occupy leadership posts by virtue of their educational qualifications, or students following a course which results in the achievement of qualifications necessary to hold a leader's post, are accused of being self-serving because they accept the normal perquisites and economic rewards attached *by regulations* to the post. The problem is to create leaders who are socially conscious and whose social conscience demands service as a moral purpose.

The problems surrounding student 'elitism' first came to the forefront in 1966 when large numbers of students at the University College protested against the terms of compulsory national service. At that time, the President of the United Republic expelled over 300 students, sending them back to their fathers to work the land and learn 'something of humility and service'.[6] Most were readmitted a year later and have since passed through the University. The lesson has not been forgotten by those who are now on campus. The President's actions have made for a rather docile student body with quite a different make-up. The emphasis has shifted to 'guiding and encouraging the enthusiasm of a more militant minority' (on the radical left) while 'containing and transforming the preconceptions and activities of the bulk of students'.[7]

J. S. Saul, a political scientist at the University, provided a small window into the student world in his article 'Radicalism on the Hill'.[8] He pointed to the existence of various groups within the student body. One group, the general mass, was characterized as being apolitical, cynical about *ujamaa* (Tanzanian Socialism) and the leading role of the Party under Tanzanian conditions, bureaucratic and technocratic in outlook. They are, he said, 'more interested in their perquisites and economic well being than in the imperatives of Tanzanian Socialism'.

He characterized another group, the 'radicals', as having 'always been under fire on the hill'. They are accused of being 'opportunists', 'fanatics', and ' "infantile" in their oversimplified version of Fanon's views on violence'. But, for Saul, 'the fact remains that this group has comprised the most admirable and dedicated members of the student body and the clearest ideologically, the most concerned about Southern Africa liberation . . . and the most sympathetic (if sometimes sympathetically critical) towards Tanzania's own efforts to construct a socialist society . . . they must be considered the saving remnant whose energies can and should be harnessed to the national effort and whose enthusiasms must be fed into the developing debate about national purposes and programmes.'

Saul also pointed to a third or middle group. These are those 'who are sincere patriots and attracted to socialism, but who are offended by or put off by the shrillness on the part of their fellows (the radicals)'. They might be, Saul suggests, drawn into a 'more overt and self-conscious commitment' if other tactics were used.

In the reorganization process which accompanied the creation of the new University, the radicals, as radicals, seem not to have gained the favour for which Saul pleaded. A single student organization, the Dar es Salaam University Students Organization (DUSO) was formed. Its membership comprises the entire student body, citizen and non-citizen. Officers are freely elected by secret ballot to handle student affairs, and they, with other members serve on the official administrative bodies of the University. At the same time, the University branch of the TANU Youth League, which is exclusively Tanzanian, was put in charge of political activities on campus related to national politics. DUSO has a 'Ministry' of African Affairs to handle matters which fall under that heading. DUSO elected a Kenyan student as its president, some say because he would be less subject to political pressure than a Tanzanian president would be. The international militant group, University Students African Revolutionary Front (USARF) along with its publication *Che-Che* were banned by the university administration, even though TYL members were a part of the organization. TYL members at the University have since come out with a new publication, *Maji-Maji*.

The student disciplinary authority is vested in the Chief Administrative Officer. By-laws concerning discipline are made by the Senate and enacted by the Council of the University. Students have a right to appeal cases to the appeals committee of the Council.

Dormitories are segregated by sex. Visiting regulations are in effect and enforced. 'Students may not entertain visitors in their rooms after 10.00 p.m. and before 9.00 a.m. The term "visitors" refers to students of the opposite sex and to non-members of the university of either sex.'[9] Of a total of 2,058 degree and non-degree students, 1,595 were in residence on the main campus, 223 at Morogoro, and 123 at Muhimbili. No special provision is made for married students although they are allowed to live off-campus.

Staff

At the time of the inauguration ceremonies, August, 1970, the student-teaching staff ratio was approximately 1 : 8. There were 266 teaching staff, 32 per cent of whom were Tanzanian citizens. The remaining 181 members represented 36 nationalities, though 62 were British and 31 came from North America. Obviously, the matter of localizing the University teaching staff is of great concern. The Minister of National Education presenting the Bill to establish the new University made the following points:

> The University of Dar es Salaam will continue and increase its efforts of recruiting academic staff who have distinguished themselves in their subjects from any part of the world provided that they are prepared to serve this nation under the conditions laid down in this Bill. Since we have openly made known to all other nations what our policy is, I have great confidence that educational experts from

many parts of the world will continue to show their interest in coming to help us. There are some who have already indicated to us that they would be happier to come to teach in our University after it has become a national university. At the same time we shall increase our efforts in preparing suitably qualified Tanzanians to take up teaching posts in the University of Dar es Salaam. This year alone twenty Tanzanians who have done very well in their first degrees at the University have been sent abroad for post-graduate courses, so that on their return they will be teachers at the University.[10]

National Service

National Service lasting an aggregate of two years is compulsory for all students, male and female, granted government bursaries to prepare them to fill high level professional posts. There are a variety of ways to fulfil this obligation:

1. The student does a five month stint of in-camp military training. Preferably this is done before coming to the University between Form 6 and Year 1. He/she is paid at a rate of twenty shillings per month. Wearing of the uniform is mandatory at all times.

2. The student takes up his/her degree course. One week-end per term he/she returns to camp for a refresher course. During this week-end wearing of the uniform is mandatory.

3. When he/she successfully completes his/her degree course, he/she is posted to his/her professional civilian job. For the next eighteen months, wearing of the uniform is mandatory at all times in and off the job and 60 per cent of his/her normal salary is paid to the National Service. The remaining 40 per cent is taxed according to the tax structure which affects all citizens.

4. After eighteen months, he/she spends one final month in camp. This completes the requirement.

The University Institution

The objects of the University, as set out in the Act, are:

(a) to preserve, transmit and enhance knowledge for the benefit of the people of Tanzania in accordance with the principles of socialism accepted by the people of Tanzania;

(b) to create a sense of public responsibility in the education and to promote respect for learning and pursuit of truth;

(c) to prepare students to work with the people of Tanzania for the benefit of the nation;

(d) to assume responsibility for University education within the United Republic and to make provision for places and centres of learning, education, training and research;

(e) to co-operate with the Government of the United Republic and the people

of Tanzania in the planned and orderly development of education in the
United Republic;

(*f*) to stimulate and promote intellectual and cultural development of the
United Republic for the benefit of the people of Tanzania;

(*g*) to conduct examinations for, and to grant degrees, diplomas, certificates and
other awards of the University.[11]

Socialism and Control

The essence underlying the organizational structure is quite clearly *control*
by and in the name of the people of Tanzania for whom it was created to
serve. This was made clear by the Minister of National Education presenting the Bill for the Act to the National Assembly:

> It is certain that the University of Dar es Salaam will not be like an ivory
> tower or like an isolated island in a vast ocean. The University of Dar es Salaam
> is a vital organ of the people because it was founded by TANU, and it will serve
> the people who are financing it. The University of Dar es Salaam can never be
> used as a centre for opposing the policy of TANU and Afro-Shirazi Parties.[12]

He cited several facts concerning the organizational structure which

> ensure that the University of Dar es Salaam will be fully under the leadership of
> this nation which is lead by TANU and Afro-Shirazi Parties as indeed all other
> national affairs are under their guidance.[13]

These facts as provided for in the act are that:

1. the President of the United Republic shall be Chancellor;
2. the Chancellor will appoint key officers which include (*a*) the Vice-
Chancellor, (*b*) the Chief Academic Officer in consultation with the Vice-
Chancellor, (*c*) the Chief Administrative Officer in consultation with the
Vice-Chancellor, and he will approve the appointments by Council of
Deans of Faculties and Directors of Institutes.[14]

Thus he states, this

> . . . is evidence that the administration and management and academic control of
> the University will be in hands of the people who have been appointed by the
> Chancellor who is at the same time the President of the United Republic.[15]

Further, the Act provides that the main administering body of the University, the Council, comprising of twenty-nine members '. . . will be
chosen by our national organs and, therefore, will be under the jurisdiction of our parties'.[16]

An analysis of the composition of the University Council supports the
Honourable Minister's statement immediately above. It also reveals two

surprises. One is the size of student representation which the Minister calls 'revolutionary'. The other is the inclusion of representatives from other Universities in East and Central Africa. The latter however supports the national objective of promoting African unity and indicates the intention to foster good relations with former sister colleges and the University of Zambia.

The Chairman of the Council, Mr A. J. Nsekela, is at the same time the Chairman of the National Bank of Commerce. The Vice-Chairman, Mr C. D. Msuya is the Principal Secretary to the Treasury. Mr P. Msekwa, who is ex-offico member of Council by virtue of his post as Vice-Chancellor, moved into that post from the post of Executive Secretary of TANU. Of the seven members of Council appointed by the Vice-Chancellor, three are Vice-Chancellors at the Universities of Zambia, Nairobi, and Makerere, two are from Ministries of Education and Health and National Insurance in Zanzibar (in spite of the fact that Zanzibar has not sent a candidate to the University in the past two years), one is the Headmistress of a secondary school and another is an Adult Education Officer. Of the three persons appointed by the Minister of National Education, one is the Principal Secretary of that Ministry, one an Assistant Director of National Education with responsibility for Technical Education, and one is the Headmistress of a secondary school. The Ministry of Economic Affairs and Development Planning is represented by its Principal Secretary. There is one member from the National Union of Tanganyika Workers (NUTA) and there are two members from the Co-operative Union of Tanganyika, Ltd. Three members are MPs, and three are Deans of Faculties (Medicine, Agriculture and Science). DUSO has five members one of whom is the President of the Organization. Old students are represented by one member elected by the Convocation.

Neither the Chief Academic Officer nor the Chief Administrative Officer are members of the Council. Both, however, have the statutory right to attend and participate in meetings, although neither have voting rights. At least one, and usually both, are on all Council Committees and both are ex-officio members of the Executive Committee of the Council. The Chief Academic Officer, Dr I. N. Kimambo, Professor of History, was Vice-Principal of the University College. The Chief Administrative Officer, Mr A. C. Mwingira, was appointed to this post from the post of Principal Secretary in the Ministry of National Education. Except for the three Vice-Chancellors from the international academic community and the President of DUSO all members of the Council are Tanzanian as are those staff members appointed to key University offices.

By statute the Council must meet not less than four times during a financial year and at other times fixed by the Chairman on fourteen days' notice. Ten members may request the Chairman to summon a meeting within thirty days of such request in writing. The Chairman, or in his absence, the Vice-Chairman, who is elected by the Council from amongst its members, presides at all meetings. A quorum consists of one-third of the members in office for the time being. Decisions are made by majority vote in meetings or by the expressed views of the majority in writing concerning matters about which relevant papers have been circulated to members. In the latter case any member may request any such decision be deferred and made the subject matter at a regular meeting.

There is an Executive Committee of the Council which acts in case of emergency and to consider urgent affairs. It has eight members which is sufficient to constitute a quorum in a regular meeting. Both the Chief Administrative and Chief Academic Officers are ex-officio members of this committee. As presently constituted the eight members include: the Chairman, who is Chairman of the Council, the Vice-Chairman of the Council, the Vice-Chancellor, the Principal Secretary of the Ministry of National Education, two of the members elected to Council by Senate and the President of DUSO.

Other committees of the Council appoint non-Council members. Three are statutory, five are created by the Council. The statutory committees are: the Appeals Committee (Student Discipline), the Appointments Committee (Academic), and the Appointment Committee (Administrative). The five created committees include: the Finance and Development Committee, the Estimates and Development Sub-Committee, the Estates Committee, the Student Affairs Committee, and the Staff Development Committee. The Vice-Chancellor is chairman of the three statutory committees. The student Affairs Committee is chaired by the Principal Secretary of the Ministry of National Education, the Estimates and Development Sub-Committee is chaired by the Vice-Chairman of the Council. The remaining committees are chaired by the Chairman of the Council.

Control is important to giving Tanzanian and, therefore, socialist direction to the future activities of the University. A primary reason for its emphasis in the organizational structure stems from the historical frustration of self-reliance experienced by the former University College.

In his speech to the National Assembly,[17] the Minister of National Education spoke of the nature of this frustration:

> When it was realized that the efforts to form an East African Federation would not be fruitful in the immediate future, it became apparent that in certain essential matters of national development each country should arrange to take full responsibility. Each of our countries made its own internal development plans in accordance with its own political philosophy. We in Tanzania chose the policy of Socialism and Self-Reliance as guided by our Arusha Declaration.
>
> Mr Speaker, Sir, the founder of our nation, President Mwalimu Julius K.

Nyerere, has taught us that the aim of education is to transmit from one generation to the next accumulated wisdom and knowledge of the nation. If we accept this truth, we must realize that it is impossible to expect the University of East Africa to be a vehicle for transmitting to future generations more than one political ideology. For it is evident that we Tanzanians have decided to transmit to our future generations the TANU and Afro-Shirazi Party Policy of Socialism and Self-Reliance. Our Colleagues too, have freely chosen their own political philosophies which they wish to transmit to their future generations. So, immediately it was realized that each nation was choosing its own political philosophy, we undoubtedly knew that the day would come when each of these nations would decide to effectively control its entire educational system from primary to university.

That day has now come, and this Honourable House ought to rejoice whilst recognizing its significance in the development of education for our nation and in transmitting to future generations the culture and wisdom accepted by Tanzanians. Moreover, this step is in accordance with the basic principles of our nation of non-interference with internal affairs of other nations and of not allowing other nations to interfere with our internal affairs.

Every nation has the full right of deciding for itself the traditions and customs which they want to be transmitted to their future generations through the medium of education. But in those matters in which we agree, even if touching internal affairs of each nation we are prepared to co-operate for the benefit of all nations.

Thanking Dr W. Chagula, who served the University College first as Deputy Principal and later as Principal for five years, the Minister gave further emphasis to the frustrations experienced within the framework of the University of East Africa. He also sounded a note of hope for the future.

Dr Chagula, in co-operation with his colleagues, struggled very hard to inject the legitimate Tanzanian national spirit into the life of the Dar es Salaam University College. To dare to inject this spirit into the College, while the College was part of the University of East Africa was a difficult task. All of us understand that it is difficult to serve many masters. There is nobody to blame for this state of affairs for we all know that it was due to historical circumstances Dr Chagula and his colleagues achieved a considerable measure of success especially in training the manpower that was required by our Development Plan and also in giving the University College a Tanzanian outlook. I request Dr Chagula to receive my own personal thanks and those of the Government and of this Honourable House for the service which he and his colleagues have rendered this nation.[18]

Barzun[19] identified seven resources which university administrations must distribute to the best advantage. His list included men, space, time, books, equipment, money and reputation. The question is: to whose best advantage? The answer in socialist Tanzania is: to the advantage of the university, not as an institution separate from the people who created and finance it, but one used as a tool to bring about the human and economic development of a self-reliant nation.

The reputation of the new University of Dar es Salaam depends on distributing the other six resources in such a way as to create high level manpower from a 'selected few'. At the end of their University course, the selected few should be in possession of knowledge, skills and research abilities. They should be imbued with an attitude of 'service to the many'[20] – free of intellectual arrogance or the self-seeking attitudes of a fortunate elite which forgets that its fortunes were provided by the peasants and workers of the nation.

The creation of the new University eliminated the prime frustrating factor – lack of control. Henceforth the administration would be free to 'inject the legitimate Tanzanian national spirit' into the life on the campus.

The fact of control changed the University's reputation overnight. In a *rites de passage*, the new Vice-Chancellor, moving from his office as Executive Secretary of TANU to his new offices at the University, was accompanied by a joyous, singing, chanting, banner- and palm-waving crowd of TANU members as he took over the people's University. The following day, a TANU flag was raised on a new pole in front of the administration building to wave triumphantly in the breeze next to the national flag of Tanzania.

Other factors, however, did not change. For a short while the University can trade on the reputation which TANU has for serving the needs of the people. After that, it will be judged by its own actions and the attitudes of its students and staff. The new administration must deal with those factors which complicate the life of university administrators in most developing countries. Development of a modern economy demands that an emphasis be placed on technology and specialization of function in a contractual society. Both are dependent on education. Tanzania has adopted a policy of Education for Self-Reliance. It is predicated on the assumption that universal primary education (a goal for 1989) will provide a literate, numerate, politically educated citizenry qualified by way of their educational experiences to live well, to work in and to develop the rural sector with the help of local leaders who emerge from amongst themselves and their government and party leaders. Post-primary education will be for a few who are selected for the purpose of serving the many.

Quantitatively, the selection is constrained by prediction of high and middle level manpower needs set out in the five year development plans. Government bursaries are awarded to those selected to do post primary courses in secondary schools, national colleges of education, technical and business colleges, and the university.

Qualitatively, selection must be fairly and carefully done. 'O' and 'A' level examinations are set by and monitored by the East African Examinations Council which remains associated with the Cambridge Syndicate for the purpose of maintaining international standards. They measure knowledge, skills, achievement and say something of aptitudes. Attitude assessment is done by teacher observation, character assessment scales and principals' reports. At present the need is still felt to measure Tanzanian standards on an international scale. This arrangement however has all the aura of the type of external control which will eventually lead to the creation of three separate universities. It remains to be seen how long Tanzania will continue the arrangement. One wonders if Tanzania has its own standards set out in measurable terms, and if these standards are relevant to Tanzania why the nation needs to appeal to some vague international standards. Again, one wonders if the early 'Land Grant' agriculturally oriented colleges in the USA worried about international standards in their formative years.

Putting educational qualification in the hands of a few selected individuals tends to distribute those individuals throughout the society in the most remunerative jobs – remunerative in terms of money, power, and privileges. Thus, unless the product of the university is one which provides a citizen product who serves the nation – and is seen to serve the nation – by his efforts to bring about human and economic development, the reputation of the new University will suffer. It will be accused of having created an educated elite in a classless society. Thus, the moral problem which confronts individual students is also a prime problem, in terms of reputation, for the new administration.

Control and Academic Freedom

The question may and should be asked, 'Does the emphasis on socialism and control mean the end of academic freedom at the new University?' The answer, of course, depends on one's concept of academic freedom.

There are few who would suggest that academic freedom be equated with academic anarchy. The 'academy' is rooted in the body of experience of the society in which it grows. The range of tolerance for unregulated liaisons amongst individuals and organized groups within any society is small. For society inculcates its own norms, its own values and beliefs. It develops organizational structures which are used as instruments in promoting those norms, values and beliefs amongst its own citizens. A British or American university, a Russian or Chinese university are just that – British, American, Russian, Chinese. The University of Dar es Salaam aspires to be a Tanzanian institution. Thus it is not surprising that its stated values and beliefs are socialistic, as are those of the society in general. Nor, is it surprising that its administration should act as an instrumentality to build a socialist society.

Speaking to this point in his inaugural address the President said:[21]

And because this is a Tanzanian University, it must do these things (provide facilities and opportunities for the highest intellectual enquiry, encourage and challenge students to develop powers of constructive thinking, and encourage its academic staff to do original research and promote intelligent discussion of issues of human concern) in such a manner that the thinking is done in the framework of, and for the purpose of serving the needs of Tanzania's development towards socialism. The University of Dar es Salaam must be a University; and it must be OUR University – relevant to the present and future society of Tanzania.

In this connection I must add that we have a past error to correct, and a present danger to avoid. For we have always recognized that Harvard University must try to understand American society, and be understood by it, in order to serve America. And we have always known that London University and Moscow University must each try to understand, and be understood by, their respective societies in order to serve their nation's people. Yet it is only recently that we have realized a similar necessity in Africa. Our universities have aimed at understanding Western society, and being understood by Western society, apparently assuming that by this means they were preparing their students to be – and themselves being – of service to African society.

This fault has been recognized and the attitude it involved has been in the course of correction in East Africa – and particularly in Dar es Salaam – for some time. But there is now a danger of an understandable – but nevertheless a foolish – reaction to it. The Universities of Africa which aim at being 'progressive' will react by trying to understand, and be understood by Russian, East European or Chinese society. Once again they will be fooling themselves into believing that they are thus preparing themselves to serve African society. Yet surely it is clear that to do this is simply to replay the old farce with different characters. The truth is that it is Tanzanian society, and African society, which this University must understand. It is Tanzania, and the Tanzanian people who must be able to comprehend this University. Only when these facts are firmly grasped will the University of Dar es Salaam be able to give full and proper service to this society. The University of Dar es Salaam has not been founded to turn out intellectual apes whether of the Right or of the Left. We are training for a Socialist, self-respecting and self-reliant Tanzania.

The values which underly the socialist ethic in Tanzania are:

(a) love – expressed in terms of equality of sovereign citizens and respect for human dignity;
(b) sharing of resources produced by one's own efforts in co-operation with others;
(c) work by all; exploitation by none; and
(d) democracy – free discussion and participation in the nation's decision-making processes.

These values, held by the nation's citizenry, are seen as the preconditions for building a socialist society. They affect the direction of the activities and the relations amongst individuals and groups at work in the nation's institutions, including the university. They form the basis on which society operates

> . . . and no advocacy of opposition to these principles can be allowed.
>
> To say this is not a negation of the freedom which the principles claim to uphold. There can be – indeed must be in a changing situation – public discussion about whether particular measures which are proposed support or nullify the principles. But, for example, there can be no public advocacy of inequality between citizens, and no actions which degrade one law-abiding citizen in relation to another.[22]

There are those who would challenge these principles in the name of some abstract notion of 'god', 'nation', or 'flag' – who do not see man in society in all cases as the purpose of society. And there are those who challenge them on the basis that they are too idealistic for large groups where members do not know each other.

> This criticism is nonsensical. Social Principles are by definition, ideals at which to strive and by which to exercise self-criticism. The question is not whether they are capable of achievement, which is absurd, but whether a society of free men can do without them.[23]

On the sixteenth anniversary of the birth of TANU, the President cited TANU beliefs which follow from the socialist values listed above: All men are equal; work is essential for mankind; no exploitation of man by man; all major means of production must be in the hands of the people; and there should be a classless society. He called on TANU members to understand and discuss these principles.[24]

These, then, are the value and belief asymptotes in Tanzania. They are the moral constraints which affect human relationships and economic development activities in general and academic freedom in particular. They illumine purpose and practices with concern for one's fellow man rejecting self-interest and individualism, which to many are as repugnant and dangerous as slavery.

The purpose of academic freedom and those who administer it should be neither to tend men nor to tame them, but to release the power of men in loving, sharing, working, democratic relationships – to participate in building a better society.

Within the constraints of socialist values and beliefs, members of the university community have the same freedoms as all other members of the Tanzanian community for which it seeks to produce educated leaders. They are free to determine their own future, govern themselves without interference from non-Tanzanians, to live in dignity and equality with all other citizens, speak freely without fear of arbitrary arrest because they happen to annoy someone in authority, participate in making decisions which affect their lives, and to know. They seek freedom from hunger, poverty and disease; in short, through their intelligent and educated efforts, they seek economic and social development of Tanzania.

In his inaugural address,[25] the Chancellor defined a university as an institution of higher learning: a place where people's minds are trained for clear thinking, for independent thinking, for analysis, and for problem solving at the highest level. He noted the three important functions of the university as being:

(a) to transmit advanced knowledge which serves as a basis of action and springboard for research;
(b) to provide a centre for intellectually capable people free of day to day administrative and professional duties with a library and laboratory facilities necessary to advance the frontiers of knowledge;
(c) to provide, through its teaching for the high level manpower needs of the society.[26]

He sees the purpose of all learning as being to increase man's power over himself and his environment; its function to be the development of man. Development automatically means there is need for relevance between man and learning. Noting that knowledge is international, the Chancellor provides the key to relevance as being the selection of the kinds of problems which are examined at the university.

> The laws of chemistry . . .; an economic analysis is valid or invalid wherever it is made. But the kinds of problems which are examined at the university, the means through which advanced and theoretical knowledge is taught does and should vary according to the background and the anticipated requirements of the students.[27]

Such requirements are related to the needs of the student's society if he is provided with the opportunity by education to serve that society.

The Chancellor does not interpret relevance to mean cutting 'ourselves off intellectually from the rest of the world on any grounds, whether these be geographical or ideological'.

> For even if we succeeded in doing that, we should certainly not be able to deflect the effects on us of others' ideas, knowledge, and actions – indeed, we should be less capable of doing so because of ignorance!
>
> Thus we would be inviting our own destruction if we gave too narrow a definition to the word 'relevant' when using it in relation to our University studies. Knowledge is international and inter-related. We need to know and to

understand as much as we possibly can; we need to learn from the past and present of all parts of the globe. All knowledge is relevant to us, even if we consider ourselves only as Tanzanian citizens and ignore our existence as human beings.

It is only by starting from that basis that we can avoid blundering into national disaster through deliberate blindness.[28]

Nor does he interpret relevance to be a question of drawing up syllabuses which talk about Tanzania all the time . . .

It is a question of intelligent and knowledgeable tutors relating their discipline to the student's, and the society's past, present, and anticipated future experience.

For ultimately this question of the relevance of a particular subject, course, or lecture, can only be determined by those who are familiar with the subject as well as knowledgeable about our social goals. Certainly the academics must be able to explain to laymen the importance of a particular study and its relationship to the society. But we must avoid the trap of allowing unqualified people to decide on its inclusion in the University teaching just by looking at the name of a course, or at a syllabus outline, and then stating firmly, 'this is relevant, that is not'.

This does not mean that all the planning of teaching and research at the University can be left to the sole discretion of the academic staff. The community has too much at stake to allow any one group such complete control. Ideas about what is needed, and can be done, should come both from University staff and from the community at large. The decisions must then be made on the basis of whether a particular course is likely to contribute to our development; whether it is one which is appropriate to a University institution rather than some other (and possibly less expensive educational body; and whether this use of our resources is justified in the light of possible alternate uses in other sectors of the economy. Such decisions must necessarily be made by the representatives of the whole society. But they must be reached in the light of advice given by those qualified to tell what can be gained from a particular study. And once a course has been decided upon, the academic staff must be allowed to decide how to conduct it. If they cannot do that properly, and for our service, then they should not be employed by the University.

And ultimately, the community has to judge the University by results . . .[29]

And it will judge by whether or not the results achieve the aims stated by the Chancellor.

We aim to revolutionize the conditions in which our people live, so that everyone is assured of the basic necessities of life and is able to live in decency and dignity. But we are not only trying to develop; we are determined to do this on the socialist basis of human equality. We want to establish a free society where all citizens are assured of justice. And while doing all this, we need to safeguard our national independence against all external or subversive attacks.[30]

It is in relation to the final aim of safeguarding national independence against external or subversive attacks that university administrators face a fundamental problem of judgment. For it is at this point at which the concept of control intersects the concept of academic freedom to teach and do research. In a developing nation which desires to build a society which is socialist, yet uniquely Tanzanian – the question becomes: What is external attack? Or who is subversive? Only Tanzanians themselves can subvert; outsiders attack. Must those who control the University – the Council, the Senate, the Faculty Boards, the administrators – be suspicious of all expatriates? They make up a large percentage of the teaching staff. Must they be suspicious of Tanzanians who – in the arena of free debate disagree with particular measures suggested by the Government Party as supporting socialist principles? Will they be accused of being tainted by their contacts with associates or their previous training abroad? If so, how can they teach and do research? Must those in government ministries which have been 'purified' by localization of staff suspect the new University which has been administratively 'purified', but which has a large number of expatriates or Tanzanians trained abroad teaching and doing research? If so, how can they in good conscience issue permits which certify the legitimacy of the researcher? Research is essential if the courses taught are to be relevant to Tanzania.

Africa in general, Tanzania in particular, has behind it the colonial experience; her people have been betrayed many times by results, if not by intentions. Thus, they have cause for suspicion. However, living in the shadow of past suspicions, will not promote real learning or research. Caution is necessary to the preservation of life. Suspicion, on the other hand, destroys life. Without faith in the good intentions of one's co-workers, until and unless they are proven untrustworthy, the University as defined by the Chancellor cannot exist. Changing suspicion to cautious faith is thus a major human problem which faces the University. Its accomplishment will be the measure of its maturity. There is every reason to believe that the University of Dar es Salaam will meet the full measure if the Chancellor's words are heeded:

> ... We have then to trust those we employ and those we select to attend it (the University). We can watch and warn. We can demand that they should explain what they are doing and why – and we can tell them to change if that is necessary! We can instruct the staff to examine themselves and their work every year – to conduct 'post-mortems' with the students at the end of every course and to use the experience as they gain it. But we should be stupid to try to bind the University staff hand and foot, and move them like puppets.
>
> The University must be allowed to experiment, to try new courses and new methods. The staff must be encouraged to challenge the students and the society with arguments, and to put forward new suggestions about how to deal with the

problems of building a socialist Tanzania based on human equality and dignity. Further, they must be allowed, and indeed expected, to challenge orthodox thinking on scientific and other aspects of knowledge. . . . The staff we employ must lead in free debate based on a concept of service, on facts, and on ideas. Only by allowing this kind of freedom to our University staff will we have a University worth its name in Tanzania. For the University of Dar es Salaam will be able to serve our socialist purposes only if we accept that those whom we are paying to teach students to think, must themselves be allowed to think and speak their thoughts freely.[31]

REFERENCES

1. J. K. Nyerere, *Speech as Chancellor at the Inauguration of the University of Dar es Salaam, 29th August, 1970*. (Brochure: Public Relations Office, University of Dar es Salaam, Dar es Salaam, Tanzania, 1970), p. 5.
2. *The University of Dar es Salaam Act*, 1970. Bill Supplement to the Gazette of the United Republic of Tanzania, No. 23, Vol. 11, dated 5th June, 1970 (Government Printer, Dar es Salaam).
3. C. Y. Mgonja, *Speech by the Honourable C. Y. Mgonja, M.P., Minister for National Education, Presenting to the National Assembly the Bill for an Act to Establish the University of Dar es Salaam 16th June, 1970* (Government Printer, Dar es Salaam, Tanzania, 1970), pp. 11–12.
4. ibid.
5. United Republic of Tanzania. *Tanzania Second Five-Year Plan for Economic and Social Development, 1st July, 1969–30th June, 1974*, Vol. I: General Analysis (Government Printer, Dar es Salaam, 1969), p. 151.
6. J. Cameron and W. A. Dodd, *Society, Schools, and Progress in Tanzania* (Pergamon Press Ltd, Oxford, 1970), p. 220.
7. J. S. Saul, 'Radicalism and the Hill', *East Africa Journal*. December, 1970, Vol. 7, No. 12, p. 27.
8. ibid, pp. 27–8.
9. *By-Laws and Regulations* of the University of Dar es Salaam. Appendix L (Mimeograph, Dean of Student's office).
10. C. Y. Mgonja, op. cit., p. 14.
11. *The University of Dar es Salaam* Act, 1970. op. cit., p. 5.
12. C. Y. Mgonja, op. cit., p. 13.
13. ibid, p. 12.
14. ibid.
15. ibid.
16. ibid.
17. ibid, p. 11.
18. ibid, p. 14.
19. J. Barzun, *The American University: How it runs and where it is going* (Harper & Row, New York). Reviewed by P. Woodring, *Saturday Review*, 21st December, 1968.
20. J. K. Nyerere, 'Education for Self Reliance', *Freedom and Socialism* (OUP, Dar es Salaam, 1968), p. 281.

21. J. K. Nyerere, Inaugural Speech, op. cit., pp. 5–6.
22. J. K. Nyerere, *Freedom and Unity* (Oxford University Press, 1967), p. 14.
23. ibid, p. 13.
24. 'TANU's Task "to Fulfil Socialism" ', *The Standard* (*Tanzania*), 8th July, 1970, p. 1.
25. J. K. Nyerere, *Inaugural Speech*, op. cit., p. 1.
26. ibid, p. 4.
27. ibid, p. 7.
28. ibid, p. 8.
29. ibid.
30. ibid, p. 6.
31. ibid, pp. 8–9.

7

Higher Education in Latin America in an Era of Change

James F. Tierney

Universities in Latin America cannot be adequately understood apart from the societal context. But there is one feature of Latin American society which unites the region, however profound the differences between the nations – the phenomenon of change. The nature, degree and pace of change have varied from country to country, but no part of the region has completely escaped its impact. In a real sense, change in Latin America means modernization – the transformation of a feudal, agrarian and closed society to an urban, industrial and open society. The process is long-term and, inevitably, disruptive – of systems, institutions and values. The outcome of the struggle between the competing philosophies of change – reform or violence – is by no means clear. Even less clear is the shape that the future society will take. In Latin America today, change is the only constant.

Higher education in Latin America has mirrored the breakdown of traditional society, and there is every reason to believe that stress and instability will continue to dominate the university scene throughout the seventies. Many of the causes of this situation result from internal weakness and contradictions within the institutions themselves. Others are quite beyond the power of universities to control. We shall isolate four major trends in the region and analyze their present and projected impact on institutions of higher education.

Population Growth

Latin America as a region has the world's highest rate of population increase – almost 3 per cent per year, and it is unlikely that this trend can be significantly reversed during the 1970s.[1] Barring unusual conditions, the population will increase from 284 million in 1970 to 379 million in 1980. Moreover, should the present rate of growth continue, the population of Latin America will double in less than 25 years, with economic, political and social consequences of a magnitude which can only dimly be perceived today. The major components of this growth rate – continuing high rates of fertility* coupled with rapidly declining mortality rates due to dramatic advances in medicine, public health and sanitation – have resulted in a very young age structure, with a high proportion of children and young people and a low proportion of aged people. Looking at the region as a whole, the population breakdown by age is roughly: 0–14 years – 42 per cent; 15–64 years – 55 per cent; over 65 – 3 per cent. This age structure has significant implications for education at all levels. According to data compiled by the United Nations, the percentage of the total population enrolled in schools in Latin America rose from 13·3 to 17·1 between 1956 and 1965. Percentage increases by educational level during the 1960s were: primary – 57·6; secondary – 110·6; higher – 92·3. Although it is risky to extrapolate the enrolment trends of the coming decade from present statistics, it nevertheless seems clear that student pressures on educational facilities will become even more severe in the next ten years.

It is doubtful that education can continue to command a major share of public funds in the coming decade. Public policy will be under pressure to assign a larger share of public expenditures to other social services, and with the cost of higher education increasing in the face of limited resources, it seems reasonable to anticipate a reduction of funds available to the education sector. Nevertheless, enrolment estimates for higher education in 1980 total 3 million, compared with less than 1 million in 1970.

Urbanization

The shift of the Latin American population from rural areas to cities, and especially to the capital cities, seems to be irreversible, at least in the short run. During the sixties, the rural population grew at an annual rate of only 1·5 per cent while the rate of increase in urban centres approached 4·5 per cent. In 1960, 47 per cent of the population lived in cities; this percentage increased to 54 in 1970. The number of urban centres of one million or more inhabitants will have increased from nine in 1970 to 28 in 1980. At least four of the centres will have ten million or more inhabitants.

The appeal of the city is obvious and pervasive, and since universities in Latin America are largely urban institutions, the impact of urban growth on their structure, functioning and future policies will certainly be massive and perhaps revolutionary. Greater economic opportunity – more jobs and higher wages – is only one facet of the urban pull. The city offers amenities and access to public assistance which far exceed anything available in rural Latin America. Perhaps most important of all, the city provides the facilities and the motivation for mass political visibility.

---

* Except for Argentina, Chile, Uruguay and Cuba, where growth rates range from 2·5 to 2 per cent per annum.

Even the casual visitor to the major urban centres of Latin America is struck by the sharp contrast between areas of wealth and areas of poverty. The barrios, barriadas, favelas, cinturones de miseria – the 'belts of misery' – describe with bleak accuracy the overcrowded slums in which rural migrants settle and live. For increasing numbers of poor people, the promise of the city seems fraudulent. There are more jobs, but there are many more applicants. In many of the overcrowded slums, true unemployment is equalled only by 'hidden' unemployment in poorly-paid 'service' activities which add little to income but contribute greatly to personal inadequacy and frustration. Yet the difference between rural and urban marginality lies in the perception that the urban poor are acquiring, albeit slowly, an escape-hatch through the school system. This perception, largely an urban phenomenon, will lead sooner rather than later to a demand for wider access to the university, posing challenges to educational and political leadership which are not likely to be met by the system of higher education as presently constituted.

Political Unrest

Violent political change is hardly a new phenomenon in Latin America. The 1960s seemed to continue a trend long familiar to students of the area. Elected governments were overthrown in four major countries – Brazil, Argentina, Peru and Bolivia – and replaced by military regimes. In Uruguay, long a showcase of representative democracy, the government has been unable effectively to cope with a radical terrorist group whose activities threaten the viability of the system. A recent election in Colombia came close to returning to power a former dictator bent on destroying the political compromise which ended the period of extreme violence in the 1950s.

There were clear signs, however, that the political unrest of the 60s was not simply more of the same. For example, the military regime in Peru has adopted a strongly nationalist policy with left-wing reformist overtones. And in Chile, a popularly elected Marxist government, led by Dr Salvador Allende of the Socialist Party, has embarked on a programme aimed at fundamental redistribution of wealth and political power. The traditional palace revolt, which changed nothing but the leadership element at the top of the pyramid, is giving way to a revolutionary movement which questions and in some cases rejects the premises and institutional arrangements of society as presently constituted.

The struggle to shift the base of political power in Latin America has important consequences for higher education. Whatever else may be said about universities in the region, it is a central fact that they are highly politicized institutions. Far from serving as havens of contemplation and reflection for disinterested scholars, they are a crucial element in the struggle for power. This is not to say that teaching and research do not get done in the Latin American university. It is meant to suggest that the university, whether it likes it or not, is an instrument of change and, as such, its role is at least as much political as it is educational. In periods of national upheaval, the political role dominates and, indeed, in some cases, the university ceases to function as an educational institution. In the view of the writer, this should come as no surprise. The university can devote its full attention and its resources to educational pursuits only after the society has reached a level of development in which political power is reasonably stable *and* is accepted as legitimate by the intellectual leadership of the country. There is very little evidence that the fundamental institutional and attitudinal changes which this level of development requires has as yet come about in the region.

The Drive for Development

The 1960s were proclaimed the Development Decade by the United Nations which, among other objectives, established a 5 per cent annual growth in income as a major goal for the developing countries. It is neither possible nor necessary, given the scope of this paper, to assess the Latin American experience in the light of UN and Alliance for Progress objectives. Suffice it to say that certain indicators depict substantial progress: the growth in income goal was achieved; gross investment was high, and largely financed by internal savings; government savings increased markedly, reflecting improvements in tax structures and collection mechanisms; and the overall balance of payment position of the region was far stronger at the close of the decade than at the beginning. Much of the economic gain was absorbed by the rapid rate of population increase, as other economic indicators made clear. For example, per capita income remained at a low level throughout the decade. Moreover, the income gap between Latin America and the developed nations increased significantly over the decade. Social indicators of development present an equally spotty record. While mortality rates declined and life expectancy increased, large blocs of the regional population were unaffected by these statistical improvements and were still denied adequate medical and dental care. The data show a percentage decline in illiteracy (although there was an increase in the number of adult illiterates) and a rise in the percentage of children in school, and yet there is increasing frustration over the inequities and qualitative deficiencies of the educational system.

Whatever the successes and failures of the development effort in the 60s, it was evident that all the Latin American countries, irrespective of political colouration, were firmly committed to economic growth and modernization in the coming decade. In this effort, institutions of higher learning have been assigned a special role. Dr Felipe Herrera, a Chilean economist and until recently President of the Inter-American Development Bank, in a recent address echoed and reinforced the charge to the universities made earlier by politicians, planners and business leaders in Latin America:[2]

> Needed in the 1970s will be leadership by our universities in redefining national and regional goals. I look to the universities to help create a better understanding of the aspirations of emerging Latin America. . . . I know the universities will be reservoirs of skills for political, social and economic development. In large measure, the transfer of technology that is essential to modernization in agriculture and industry will be possible only because of the research and training on [university] campuses.

The State of Higher Education in Latin America

It is against the backdrop of rapid population and urban growth, political unrest and region-wide commitment to modernization and development that an assessment of the problems and prospects facing higher education can most usefully be made. This assessment is attempted on a global basis in full awareness of the need to generalize without opportunity to take note of any but the most significant exceptions to the generalizations made. A brief description of the evolution of the Latin American university will be followed by a section on the structure and functioning of the contemporary university. A concluding section will discuss trends and emerging concepts, with some comment on the problem of adjusting higher education to development needs.[3]

The Evolution of the Latin American University

Both in terms of structure and orientation, the university in Latin America is a heritage of the colonial era. Spain and Portugal transferred almost intact to the New World the academic structure of centres such as Bologna, Paris and Salamanca, at the core of which was a faculty or school of theology together with faculties of canon and civil law and medicine. At their founding in the mid-sixteenth century, the three oldest universities in the western hemisphere – at Santo Domingo, Lima and Mexico City – conformed to this pattern. In the course of the next two centuries, however, the gradual expansion and diversification of economic activity, together with the drive for political independence, led to a decline in theological teaching (gradually replaced by philosophy and letters – the humanities) and the introduction of engineering instruction. By the nineteenth century, the orientation of the Latin American university had become completely secular, and its structure had crystallized around the professional faculty as the basic organizational unit. Legal and financial responsibility for higher education during this period rested with public authorities, either national in the case of the older and larger institutions, or state-provincial-local in many of the newer universities. By 1900, thirty-six universities were operating in the region. During the twentieth century, universities grew in number, size and complexity, but with exceptions to be noted later, the basic pattern remained much the same as it had existed at the turn of the century. It is well to look closely at the main elements of that pattern.

Emphasis on Professional Training

The root objective of the Latin American university is the production of graduates qualified to practise in one or the other of the professional fields in which instruction is offered. Traditionally, these included law, medicine, humanities and engineering. Their number has since proliferated in response to new situations and demands, but the pattern remains the same. In many institutions, professional training was the exclusive objective; in others, it dominated lesser goals, including high-level scholarship and original research. The rationale for the utilitarian purpose assigned to higher education was based upon two assumptions. First, by the time a student entered the university, he had been sufficiently exposed to 'general education' at the secondary-preparatory levels to have acquired the breadth of knowledge and the intellectual ability to master the skills and techniques of his chosen career. Second, in its self-image as an elitist institution, the university set out to train the future members of governing and professional classes. To the extent that many university graduates never did practise their professional calling (and moreover that many apparently had no intention of so doing), the university degree became an end in itself – a status symbol and an entrance card into the halls of power and influence.

Neither of these assumptions could stand unquestioned even in the light of late nineteenth-century reality, and it is obvious that both are untenable today. Certainly the great national universities are no longer elite establishments catering to the needs of upper-class children, and it has become increasingly apparent that the product of the secondary school system is something less than the well-trained generalist capable of intelligent career selection upon entry to the university. Recognition of this has been reasonably widespread among educational leaders in Latin America, and more than a few universities have introduced reforms – general studies programmes and guidance and counselling services are two examples – designed to come to grips with the new reality. But the imbalance in favour of professional training remains predominant in the region. Institutions change slowly, especially when vested interests have the power to block or divert the forces of change. And such is the case in the typical Latin American university today.

The Professional Faculty as the Basic Organizational Unit

Because of the preponderant and, in some cases, exclusive commitment of the Latin American university to professional education, and because the faculties were the body to provide this type of training, it follows that faculty is a basic unit organizationally in the university structure. Faculties were directed by deans who were, in a very real sense, autonomous in the exercise of their authority. Faculties have their own libraries and other physical resources and, in fact, in the time frame in which we are speaking, faculties of universities were scattered in different parts of the city and there was very little physical communication among them. As a result of this situation, the university was not, in fact, a unified whole, a community of scholars, but rather an umbrella organization under which an ever increasing group of autonomous or semi-autonomous faculties existed to provide training for the particular group of students who chose to follow that particular career. The faculties varied greatly both in number of professors and number of students. For example, in a study of higher education in Mexico, it was found that the smallest faculty had three professors while the largest had 617. The range of students was also considerable. One faculty had only nine students while the largest had over 6,000.

In general, it is fair to say that the strength of the faculty reflected, at least in part, the size – in terms of both the professors and students – and also, perhaps even more important, the ability of the dean or director to compete successfully in the budget process. In many cases, the director was able to raise funds for his particular operation outside the normal budgets. The most successful faculty deans or directors were adept at the political process and were effective in political in-fighting. It was in the nature of the case, therefore, that co-operation among faculties was not a built-in requisite of the system. In fact, the independence of faculties in instruction was reflected in university rules and regulations. For example, students who were enrolled in one professional faculty were unable to earn credit for courses or programmes taken outside their faculty. There were several results of this situation. One of the more obvious is the existence of significant duplication of course offerings. This was especially true in basic sciences courses which were offered in much the same way in faculties of engineering and medicine. Moreover, the system had the effect of squandering scarce human resources and resulted in offerings in some faculties which were clearly second-rate and mediocre. Moreover, the rigidities of the system worked against the possibility of problem orientation approaches to training and did not permit the possibility of experimental course offerings which cut across the faculty lines. The faculty structure was deficient in another respect. Because the system was geared to the production of graduates who could pass an examination for a professional certificate, the emphasis of instruction was largely limited to rote-learning – the transmission of knowledge accumulated by the professor who was himself a member of the profession. In fact, the typical makeup of the faculties reinforced this method of instruction. The predominant number of professors were part-time: they appeared at the university twice or three times a week to offer a course of lectures and then left immediately to return to their professional practice. Full-time professors were the exception. There was little opportunity for the members of a faculty to conduct research and, in fact, the typical structure of the faculty separates teaching and research. In some cases, research institutes do not exist. In cases where they do, there is little interaction between the personnel who are responsible for research and the teaching faculty whose responsibility it is to train the students.

One reason for the situation is found in the very low rate of pay of university professors. Except for a very few full-time professors, many of whom had independent means aside from their salary, the pay scale was insufficient to support the faculty member. It was essential for him to have another means of earning a livelihood. In such a situation, it was unrealistic to expect that he would spend more than the minimum amount of time in preparing and meeting his classes and that, in fact, he would regard his university post as anything but a status symbol and largely extracurricular to his main pursuit.

Political Interference

Throughout the nineteenth century, the Latin American university was fair game for national political groups who had no hesitancy in using it to serve their own ends. During the periods of independence and after, universities were largely in recess, and, when they were in session, in constant turmoil. The universities were the seed-beds of future political leadership and became the training ground of individuals and groups whose principal objective was not to acquire an education or a degree, but to move into the national political arena. It was understandable in this situation that the political authorities of the moment viewed activities within the university as a threat to their own existence and did not hesitate to take action to dissipate that threat. The universities during this period reflected the instability of the larger society around them and it was soon to be evident that fundamental changes would have to be made if they were to continue to exist as educational institutions.

At the beginning of the twentieth century, then, the typical Latin American university looked somewhat as follows. It was a publicly supported and financed institution with a strong, almost exclusive commitment to training for the professions. Its basic organizational unit and the locus of its power was the individual faculty. As a creature of the state, it became enmeshed in the political struggles of the day. There were forces at work, however, which were to undermine the university as it then existed and the earliest and, perhaps, most significant erupted in the rebellion in Córdoba, Argentina, in 1918 which led to a series of reforms which had an impact on the structure and orientation of the present university in Latin America.

The Córdoba rebellion was instigated and led by student groups who sought a voice in the affairs of the university. Student complaints, however, were not limited to their lack of a role in university governance. The Córdoba Manifesto complained of the dependence on the university of politicians and political decisions; part-time and inadequately trained teaching faculty; lack of research; weak and uninterested administration; the sterile scholasticism of much that was offered in the university curriculum; the value-laden and formalistic methods of teaching; and the great gap which students believed to exist between what went on in the university and the social problems of society. In essence, the Córdoba reform movement demanded that students assume some responsibility in the running of the universities and that, in addition, they help to reorient the universities along the lines of community service.

Not too many years ago, it could be said with reasonable accuracy that Latin American university students differed from students in other countries by participating in the governance of the university and, in many cases, by engaging in political activity of considerable importance. The situation has changed and the Latin American university student is no longer unique in this respect. Since the student riots at Berkeley in 1964, a chain reaction spread throughout the university world. Student disturbances have broken out in both the industrialized West and the developing nations of Asia and Africa. As a result, universities have more and more acceded to one of the principal student demands, which is a role in university decision-making.

In this one respect, however, the Latin American university student had taken the lead many years ago. Student co-government has been, since 1918, a distinctive characteristic of the Latin American university. The system took many forms; in some cases, students participated directly by vote in the election of rectors, deans and other governing principals. In other cases, co-government tended to mean participation of students in university affairs but with no vote. Students sometimes shared voting power with faculty and with alumni and this pattern, so-called tripartite co-government, was by far the most common.

Since its widespread adoption after the Córdoba reforms, student participation in university government has become an established fact in Latin

American higher education. Of course the extent and importance of student participation has varied considerably among countries and within the same country, depending upon the institution. The role of the student has often reflected the struggle for political power. For example, at the present time, student participation in university affairs is severely limited in those countries which have military regimes. Exceptions to this are Peru, where an activist student role is encouraged, and Brazil, whose universities permit limited student participation in university decision-making under circumscribed conditions. In general, students have been and are more active in public than in private institutions, and in large universities rather than in small institutions.

Co-government was not the only accomplishment of the Córdoba reform movement. For example, university autonomy has become a legal and in some cases a constitutional requirement, although formal autonomy is often meaningless to institutions largely dependent upon government for economic support. Aside from the financial aspect, however, most public universities in Latin America are territorially autonomous in terms of government intervention. In some cases, this principle has been carried to ridiculous extremes. For example, during the disturbances in Venezuela in the late 1960s, the Universidad Central de Venezuela was in fact a privileged sanctuary for groups of street fighters, not all of whom were students, who proceeded from the university base to commit acts of violence in the capital, after which they returned to the university and regrouped in preparation for the next assault. The political authorities finally realized that the situation was intolerable. When the police were authorized to enter the university campus, they found large stores of weapons and ammunition in dormitory buildings. In spite of these aberrations and abuses, it is fair to say that autonomy and student participation in university decision-making have been, by and large, a constructive force in university life in Latin America.

In the decades following Córdoba, the number of new universities increased significantly in response to forces which were destined to change radically the orientation of higher education in Latin America. The knowledge explosion, particularly in the scientific and technological fields after World War Two, was spectacular. As was noted earlier, another revolution was taking place throughout the educational system in Latin America, the revolution of student enrolment. By and large, the early response of higher education to these developments was *ad hoc*. The basic university structure remained largely unchanged but there was improvement within the structure. For example, new faculties were created out of fields of specializations within the traditional ones. Out of engineering faculties, which tended to focus exclusively on civil engineering training, came new faculties of electrical, mechanical and chemical engineering. In the social sciences, faculties of anthropology, sociology, and economics were added to the university. Most recently, faculties of political science began to appear on the scene. In addition to the creation of additional faculties, new research institutes were established, generally within the faculty structure but largely independent of it in terms of a union of teaching and investigative activities. In a few cases, high-level post-graduate programmes were established within the university, especially in the natural and physical sciences.

The rapid increase in student enrolment, in some cases a faster increase than the growth of the general population, posed a number of serious problems for higher education. There were not enough facilities – build-ings, libraries, books, equipment – to service the increase in student popu-lation. Even more serious was the dearth of trained university teachers. This was due to at least two causes: (1) the university system was simply not geared to the production of the necessary number of faculty required by the rapid increase in enrolment, and (2) the attractions, in terms of salary and job security offered by industry, commerce and government, drained off talented individuals who, at another time, might have opted for a university career. The net effect of this was to lower the quality of instruction within the university system.

Higher education in Latin America attempted a number of solutions to deal with this problem. In the mid-1960s, for example, the National University of Mexico required that all entering students take an additional year of intermediate education before their application for admittance to the University would be considered. This regulation was unusual and re-flected the peculiar characteristics of the Mexican situation in which the National University controls a large segment of preparatory-level educa-tion in Mexico City. In other universities individual faculties required students to take additional preparatory work before admittance. Many faculties and schools required an additional entrance examination with the dual objective of improving the quality of students and reducing the effect of overcrowding. In general, however, these solutions did not come to grips with the real problem and tended to place the burden on secondary and intermediate levels of education – a responsibility which these levels were ill-equipped to meet.

While traditional institutions were experimenting with modifications in the existing structure, new universities were free to take bolder steps in the direction of major educational reform. In part this was a reflection of growing private sector commitment, both religious and secular, to social innovation. Government itself also played a role in the educational reform effort. In specialized fields, particularly in agronomy and the agricultural sciences, institutes were established outside the university system. In some cases, these institutions were under the direct control of Ministries of

Agriculture; in others, control was shared by several government ministries. These developments gave evidence of vigorous growth in higher education in Latin America but, at the same time, emphasized the *ad hoc* response to problems whose solutions seemed to demand much more systematic planning at all levels.

The Contemporary Latin American University

In spite of the diversity of higher education institutions in contemporary Latin America, it is possible to sketch a profile of the typical university based upon a set of criteria which most institutions have in common. In general, institutions of higher education fall into one or another of three broad categories. First is the traditional public university, presided over by an assembly consisting of professors, students and alumni and whose basic function is to elect a rector. This university is administered by an administrative council which is responsible for the general direction of the university and it is normally composed of administrative officials and faculty within the university itself, with some representation from government and from the student body. The chief executive officer is the rector, who is usually elected for a fixed term and is normally a person who has had considerable experience within the university itself either as a dean or director of a faculty, or a leading professor. In a few cases, however, the rector is chosen from outside the university system. Finally, the professional faculty, described above, remains the principal academic unit within the university. The second major type is the private university which is organized along much the same lines as the public institutions but with a governing and administrative structure that points up the power and influence of the founding groups, whether they be ecclesiastical or secular in composition. The third type, either public or private, is typified by the new institution which has been set up along quite different academic lines. The professional faculty has been replaced by the department or institute, based upon academic disciplines or groups of disciplines, permitting institutions in this category to avoid some of the problems associated with the traditional university. Courses in basic disciplines are organized to service the total institution, and upper-level interdisciplinary teaching and research programmes are the rule rather than the exception. Teaching and research responsibilities are combined – the typical faculty member is expected to do both.

Institutions falling within the first and the second categories are attempting, in one way or another, to modernize their structures in accordance with the third category model. The introduction, in the University of Costa Rica and in other institutions, of a general studies programme for the first year or two, required of all students, is an attempt to break away from the dilemmas posed by the rigid professional faculty structure. Students enter the university without commitment to a professional career and are required to follow a common course of study. The choice of a professional career is thus delayed until students have had some exposure to university-level education, with the presumption that decisions involving career selection will be improved.

There is no typical Latin American university in terms of size. One finds extreme variations. The University of Buenos Aires and the University of Mexico have upwards of 100,000 students. At the opposite end of the spectrum, over 100 institutions have an average of about 500 students each. However, the existence of a single dominant university (dominant in both size and prestige) provides a useful means to distinguish between two major groupings of Latin American countries. Argentina, Uruguay, Venezuela, Mexico and the five Central American republics conform roughly to the dominant institution pattern. Brazil, Colombia, Bolivia, Ecuador and, to a lesser extent, Peru, are countries without a principal university. Brazil is unique. All Brazilian universities were founded in the twentieth century in the traditional pattern: the grouping of independent faculties under a university umbrella. The reason why Brazil has no dominant university is found in the broad geographic and regional distribution of the population. The same is true for Colombia, a country of distinct and separate regions, each with its own university. Bolivia and Ecuador have no single dominant university for largely historical and traditional reasons. Peru for many years did have a principal university, one of the oldest in the hemisphere – the University of San Marcos. However, developments in the last thirty or forty years have changed the picture considerably. New universities have grown in size and stature to challenge the leadership position of San Marcos.

Much has been said relating to university students in Latin America. In completing the profile, however, it is necessary to point out that, tradition-ally, public universities have been open to all students who have graduated from secondary schools. As we have seen, the pressure of student popula-tion has resulted in the imposition of special entrance examinations. More-over, the public universities generally provided free tuition. In recent years, there have been developments requiring enrolment fees, for ex-ample, and other incidental charges. However, it is estimated that approxi-mately 80 per cent of the university students in Latin America pay no tuition fees whatsoever, a situation unique in countries in the West. The other 20 per cent are either in private institutions or in institutions which are exceptions to the tuition-free rule. It is important to bear in mind, how-ever, that free tuition does not necessarily mean equal access to higher education. In practice, the free tuition system tends to favour middle- and upper-class groups and, indeed, it has been charged that the free tuition system constitutes an outright subsidy for children in upper-income categories.

The typical university faculty is still dominated by the part-time professor. However, increasing numbers of full-time faculty have been employed in the newly established faculties and departments, particularly in the physical and social sciences.

The traditional geography of the Latin American university, i.e. a series of faculty buildings scattered in different parts of the city, is undergoing radical change. In the recent past, a number of university cities have been created. These are, in effect, central campuses. Examples of these are the National University of Mexico, the Central University of Venezuela, the National University of Colombia, the Central University of Ecuador, the University of Concepción in Chile, and the University of Costa Rica. Many of the newer universities, both public and private, have opted from the very beginning to set up university cities. The motives for these are several, perhaps the most important of which concerns the academic and social life of the student and the need to provide an opportunity for students to live apart from the pressures of society. There are, as one might imagine, political motivations for this as well. Violence which breaks out in a university with a central campus can more easily be isolated and controlled than if the university were physically scattered in the old geographical pattern.

To summarize the profile, the typical Latin American university is a public university with an organizational structure headed by a university assembly and administrative council, governed by a rector, with the basic academic unit still lodged in the professional faculties. Organizationally, however, because of pressures from the outside, the situation is changing and, in almost all cases, universities are attempting to modernize their structure, particularly with respect to a shift from professional faculties to academic departments based upon specialized disciplines or groups of disciplines. Efforts to modernize are one of the principal characteristics of the contemporary university. There are great variations in size both in terms of physical plant, students and budget. The part-time faculty situation is slowly giving way to full-time professional staff, particularly in new faculties and in the newly created institutes and departments. The physical plant of the university is undergoing change with the creation of the university city or central campus concept. This has been adopted not only by the newer institutions but by some of the old and established ones as well. Free tuition for students remains an important feature of the Latin American university.

Emerging Trends and Concepts

In looking toward the future development of higher education in Latin

America, it is possible to discern certain major trends. Many of these, of course, are rooted in past experience and have been stimulated by the trends in society noted at the beginning of this chapter. In general, one sees a marked willingness to experiment and to innovate, and to adapt foreign models to local needs. This is perhaps the most significant characteristic – a change in attitude on the part of university leaders.

There are four major trends in higher education in Latin America which deserve special comment:

1. *Regional and international co-operation*   Several efforts are under way among universities in the region to pool resources for the solution of common problems and for the achievement of common goals. One of the oldest of these, the Central American Higher University Council (CSUCA), has been in operation for over twelve years and it has to its credit a number of significant accomplishments.[4] As an organization of the six national universities in Central America – Costa Rica, El Salvador, Guatemala, Honduras, Nicaragua, and Panama – CSUCA was established to pool individual resources in higher education for the benefit of the whole, and, more important, to serve as a catalyst for reform and innovation. The principal mechanism for university reform was the General Studies programme now in operation in each of the universities. As noted above, General Studies was viewed both as a corrective of low quality secondary education and as a means to undercut the traditional power of the professional faculties through the establishment of discipline-oriented departments independent of faculty control. CSUCA has also promoted the development of regional courses at both the undergraduate and graduate levels (e.g. sanitary engineering at Guatemala, chemistry at Costa Rica) and regional research institutes (e.g. social and economic research at Costa Rica). Economy and efficiency were motivating factors for these innovations, which were designed to serve regional needs. Although plagued by administrative and financial problems, the Central American regional training and research programmes are soundly based and have served as models for similar efforts in other sections of Latin America. At the present time, over thirty-five regional institutions are in operation, with substantive fields ranging from demography and public administration to journalism, nutrition, and urban planning. Most of these institutes are sponsored by international agencies (Unesco, World Bank, etc.), are multilaterally financed, and draw their students and faculty from several or all countries in the region. Although most of them are separate from the national higher education system, their close relationship with universities in the host country gives them a leverage which may well prove a significant factor for future innovation.

2. *Curriculum modernization*   There is increasing emphasis in the Latin

American universities on development-related training and research. For example, data compiled by the Inter-American Development Bank in 1967 indicated the existence of 313 research institutes in the scientific and technological fields, and 41 in the social sciences.[5] The majority of these are new, having been established during the past fifteen years. Notable advances have been made in the physical sciences, as illustrated by the meeting of the Presidents of the American Republics at Punte del Este in 1967, which gave special attention to the need to strengthen education in science and technology; and the Organization of American States, which is a developing multinational strategy to implement the Punte del Este declaration. Evidence of growth in the social sciences is seen in the establishment, in 1968, of a Latin American Council of Social Sciences (CLACSO) representing all of the existing institutes. CLACSO seeks to strengthen national institutes and to promote collaboration among them through joint research projects and exchange of staff. Academic programmes focusing on major problems – population growth, urbanization, resource conservation and environmental pollution – have been established or strengthened in a few universities, notably El Colegio de Mexico, the University del Valle in Colombia, the University del Oriente in Venezuela, and the Federal University of Rio Grande do Sul in Brazil.

3. *Inter-level educational co-operation* There is increased awareness of the need to strengthen links between higher and intermediate educational levels in Latin America. Although universities for many years have been concerned about low standards in the secondary schools, only recently have action programmes been developed to deal with the problem. The most significant of these efforts relates to the training of secondary school teachers. Experimental projects aimed at improving teacher education are under way in several countries, notably Costa Rica, El Salvador, Chile, Mexico and Brazil. It is encouraging to note that many of these were developed through the co-operation of universities and government ministries of education. Many of the experiments are based upon new developments in educational technology, particularly television. Colombia and El Salvador have major projects underway in ETV, and universities generally are beginning to explore the educational possibilities offered by other mechanisms and procedures, ranging from radio and film strips to computers, satellites, and programmed learning. Happily, many of the educators involved in such explorations have approached their task with due caution, reflecting an awareness of the need to clarify educational goals and objectives as a prerequisite to the introduction of the new machines and materials which technological advances have made available.

4. *Research on higher education* A growing awareness of the university as a crucially important institution in the developing societies of Latin America

has stimulated a body of studies which seek to shed light on university objectives, structures and functions. This constitutes a new departure and has important implications for the future of higher education reform. In a recent article surveying this field, Professor Robert Arnove of Stanford University noted that 'Literature on the Latin American university is largely of a polemical and speculative nature, generally devoid of empirical grounding and theoretical significance. Research, in the sense of a systematic quest to enhance our powers to understand, predict and control relationships among variables, is of recent origin.'[6] The evidence presented in his survey suggests that the university world in Latin America is not likely to remain the *terra incognita*, once described by S. M. Lipset. Many of the recent studies, necessarily descriptive and exploratory, raise doubts about the validity of commonly held views of Latin American higher education; others, especially those dealing with educational planning and manpower analysis, have spearheaded major reforms in university administration and curriculum development. One illustration will suffice. Evidence collected in the course of a recent study on the availability and use of instructional aids in the universities of Mexico raises questions about the accuracy of much of the conventional wisdom. To quote from the study:[7]

Several common stereotypes about instruction in Latin American universities did not seem to be borne out in the data. In some cases there was solid evidence, and in other cases one can merely speculate. The short tenure of most administrators tends to confirm the stereotype about the lack of continuity in policy and direction because of short or uncertain tenure, but even though the Directors reported short tenure in their administrative posts many had had long tenure in the institution as professors, so the problem may not be as grave as the stereotype makes it.

The generally held belief in Latin America that Law is the most traditional and conservative and in some senses the poorest of all faculties is confirmed again and again in this study. Law is lowest in the possession and use of all kinds of instructional aids, in the use of flexible teaching arrangements and in the use of central facilities. Law professors tend to spend no time on research and to spend most of their hours outside the university.

There is a general stereotype that Latin American universities are made up of autonomous and completely independent faculty or school cells and that professors and administrators go their own individualistic and unco-operating way. This study tended to cast doubt on this stereotype. First, the university seemed to exercise considerable influence on school and faculty possession and use of instructional aids, particularly the larger kinds of media and facilities. There was much more budgetary dependence than one would have thought. There was much less isolation between administrators and their staff within schools and faculties. Administrators' opinions and professors' opinions were much closer than one would expect. There were many more collaborative teaching arrangements among professors than one generally expects in Latin American universities. These arrangements also ran across faculty and school lines, contrary to expectations. Nor were universities and schools isolated from the outside world as much as is believed. Many professors reported field trips and visits to installations and industries outside the university. There was more contact between professors and administrators than we imagined existed.

A Concluding Comment

Change does not necessarily result in improvement, and there can certainly be no assurance that the changes taking place in Latin America today will produce a just and equitable and vigorous society tomorrow. Yet there is reason to sound a note of cautious optimism on the future of higher education. In so far as it is a proper role of a university to serve society in a direct and immediate manner – to act as an instrument of change – the Latin American university is far better equipped to perform this role in the 70s than it has been in the past. And there is little doubt that Latin American society expects its universities to spearhead and undergird change. In spite of the many problems and shortcomings of the system of higher education, it can no longer be said that the universities of Latin America are elitist institutions isolated from the mainstream of national life. And that is no mean accomplishment.

REFERENCES

1. Statistical data are taken from: Economic Commission for Latin America, *Social Change and Development Policy in Latin America* (N.Y.: United Nations, 1970) *passim*.
2. 'Inter-American Co-operation in the '70s: The Role of Youth', address by Felipe Herrera, University of Miami, Florida, 4 June 1970.
3. Much of the material on the Latin American university has been drawn from the *Annual Reports of the Social Progress Trust Fund* (Washington, D.C.: Inter-American Development Bank, 1961–9).
   See also Ronald Hilton, *The Scientific Institutions of Latin America* (Stanford: California Institute of International Relations, 1970).
4. See W. H. Mitchell, *CSUCA: A Regional Strategy for Higher Education in Central America* (Lawrence: University of Kansas, 1967).
5. *Social-Economic Progress in Latin America. Social Progress Trust Fund. Seventh Annual Report* (Washington, D.C.: Inter-American Development Bank, 1967), pp. 366–7.
6. R. F. Arnove, 'A Survey of Literature and Research on Latin American Universities', *Latin American Research Review*, III, 1 (Fall 1967), p. 45.
7. Noel F. McGinn, with R. G. Davis and R. G. King, *The Technology of Instruction in Mexican Universities* (N.Y.: Education and World Affairs, 1968), p. 3.

8

The University in Brazil : Expansion and the Problem of Modernization

David Carneiro, Jr

The Brazilian higher education system is in a state of turmoil. From outside of the system, the increasing numbers of candidates who apply for places, the modernization of the economy at large, the urge for more research, and the need of society for more graduates, are pressing the system to expand. From inside, the opposing forces of conservatism, the inertia resulting from vested interests, enlarge the resistances to change. In this chapter I shall attempt an analysis both of the forces of inertia and of the sources of modernization.

Brazilian Universities in Retrospect

The university in its modern form did not exist in Brazil until twenty years ago. It is true that a special form of the French system of *grandes écoles* was started in the nineteenth century, and new schools or faculties continued to be created in the same pattern. But it was at the University of Brasilia, in the new capital, that the integrated and organic form of university was started in the early sixties. Even within the system, however, the old structure still prevails and its characteristics are strong in influencing the whole system. This is probably the origin of the strongest force of reaction.

Medical schools were the first to be established, soon to be followed by Faculties of Law and in the latter half of the nineteenth century, Schools of Engineering were started. They were all isolated institutions and only in this century have they been aggregated to constitute universities. They still, however, retain their previous identity and autonomy within a university of which they become a part. Other schools (or Faculties) which were founded later, such as those of Dentistry, Pharmacy, Veterinary Medicine, Philosophy, Sciences and Letters and of Economics still retain the same isolation. The influences of the earlier schools, i.e. of Law, Medicine and Engineering have been strong in shaping the university structure as well as in having a definite social and political bearing on the life of the country. The 'bacharel'* attitude is typical of the conditions that have continued to prevail.

Higher education in Brazil still comprises two classes of institution: the university proper, i.e. the agglomerates of independent Faculties which have been incorporated as universities and the 'isolated' institutions of higher education. The latter are not necessarily second- or third-class institutions. Indeed the opposite is true: they provide instruction to degree level and some have excelled by their academic standards, for instance the Ouro Preto School of Mines, the Itajubá School of Electrical Engineering and the Ribeirão Preto Medical School.

Among the isolated schools professional or teachers' training colleges predominate, usually small units operating as private, semi-private or public institutions under the strict – but only too formal – rules laid down by the Federal Council of Education. When several of them have been established in the same geographical area, especially in the same city, they may aggregate and be incorporated as a new university. But they still retain an individual character and independence in the new incorporated body.

Recent legislation (Decrees Nos. 53/66 and 252/67) has been passed which requires universities to adapt their internal structure to a more unified type. One of the main ideas of this Reform, which is slowly being implemented, is to organize the universities around Central Departments which provide instruction to all courses on the same subject instead of there being separate, independent, and in many cases rival, chairs, one in each school. In the old administrative setting, Schools of Engineering, of Sciences, of Economics would have their independent Departments of Mathematics, of Physics or of Economics, where teaching in those fields was done. Today the aim is to have one Mathematics Department, another Physics Department and an Economics Department (or Institute) where appropriate courses can be taken by students of Engineering, Mathematics or whatever the case may be. Several permanent or *ad hoc* financial instruments are available to back up the legislation and accelerate these and other changes.

The existence of the 'great schools' within the universities has tended to continue to influence in several ways the administration, type and quality of instruction both in the new universities and, especially, the old. First because of the influence of their prestige upon governing bodies; second, because they provide better facilities than newer schools may do; third, because Law, Medicine, and Engineering are traditionally the professions preferred by the intellectual and the political elites which dominate the

---

* 'Bacharel' which is equivalent to the Bachelor degree, in Brazil and in this context, is the Bachelor of Law. The word has acquired several connotations which go far beyond the simple idea of a 'Bachelor of Law' as such: some of these deserve sociological examination.

sources of funds and otherwise attract the best brains; and fourth, because in most cases the staff of 'other' schools have been recruited from among traditional professionals (those same barristers, doctors and engineers) from the 'great schools' though representing new interests, find it hard to match the importance and the power of their rival colleagues.

Part-time versus Full-time Study

In the past it was assumed that, owing to the insufficient supply of special-ized professionals, part-time work at the universities should not only be encouraged but endorsed by law. When the economy was underdeveloped and individual, isolated faculties were small and this perhaps yielded good results. But the system as formalized in the legislation permitted one teaching job to be held 'simultaneously' with some – correlated – technical occupation. With industrial development and the need for graduate work and scholarly research this remained a great anachronism; and since the 'morus' had created vested interests in the appropriation of the extra income and prestige the system permitted, its abolition became difficult.

As part-time study in the universities was general, little time was left for research and most, perhaps all, of the staff's time was devoted to teaching and the magistral lectures which constitute the most important component of Brazilian academic folk-lore. It is easy to deduce from such circumstances that salaries should be low. Therefore, as salaries were only paying for work actually done, they were extremely low – hardly comparable with earnings in private occupations. In these, full-time work has always been the rule. Elsewhere I have described this state of affairs as professorial work being on the one hand too cheap, in terms of money per lecturer, and on the other too expensive, in terms of amount and quality of product obtained, and the additional numbers or teaching staff required.

Low student-staff ratios were general and as part-time prevailed in special cases where they were above average, they certainly indicated – as in Law courses – poor teaching conditions as well. The average national student-staff ratio has been around 4·5 students per teacher (the figure today must be higher, given the new conditions) but in Law courses it can be as high as 30 and in others such as Nursing, as low as one. Attention has only recently been given to these indicators of efficiency and several corrective measures are now being taken.

If lecturers devoted little of their time to students and their contacts remained restricted to the couple of hours they met in the classrooms, the natural and obvious consequences was for students to work part-time as well. Very little attention has been given to the possible bad results of this to academic work at large and to poor professional training, so much so that there are several national and local programmes which offer facilities for part-time work for students in industrial and commercial activities. This, it is assumed, will give students the practical knowledge they need and which university courses do not provide.

The conditions of part-time study I have mentioned were also reproduced in the secondary schools, with two important additional consequences. First the poor training of school leavers led to a concentration on passing the entrance examinations to universities: and as their numbers increased the screening at the moment of admission to university – known as the *vestibular* – became an acute social problem, which is still reproduced every year all over the country. Students working in part-time jobs tend to pay too little attention to theoretical knowledge; their attitude becomes too empirical and they have too much in mind the learning of practical rules which are of immediate use.

Second, that the way out of the non-correspondence between the numbers of candidates for admission to universities and the numbers of places available has encouraged the introduction of *cursinhos* (the English translation is small-courses) placed between the last year of the secondary schools and the first year of university. These courses serve to coach students intensively in answering entrance examination questions.

The typical Brazilian attitude of extolling self-taught scholars is in itself a denial of university scholarship. Yet it continues. We also lament the brain-drain from the underdeveloped countries, especially Brazil, to the developed ones, especially the United States. Both phenomena seem to me to be clear and obvious consequences of the inadequacy of training in the universities for the needs of the labour market.

In a simple social structure as prevailed in Brazil until the thirties and up to the forties, with generalized excess supply of labour and strong family influences, there was little need for technical qualifications. These could be supplied from foreign countries. University courses only remotely corresponded to the demand for labour generated by the economy. With the greater proportion of the labour force employed in agriculture, which was responsible for the larger share of output and of income, hardly any training was provided in universities for agriculture. Concentration upon training appropriate to academic occupations (as lecturers or professors) attracted interest mainly for the social prestige that came with it. This explains, at least in part, the preference for courses in Law, Literature and Philosophy while there was, and still is, a great shortage of science teachers and of the technical skills needed in industry.

The Creation of New Universities

Until the late forties the establishment of higher education and of universities was a result of a slow, somewhat random, and usually individual initiative. Two great exceptions to this are the Federal University of Rio de Janeiro (then called the University of Brazil) which was, from its earliest days a federal entity and the Schools or Faculties established in São Paulo under State Law, with state funds, and which were assembled to become the University of São Paulo.

With increasing economic demands, schools and universities had great difficulty in expanding facilities, and the fifties mark the period of federalization, e.g. grants of Federal funds, with increasing Federal control, for some of their more ambitious programmes. Another alternative would have been to concentrate resources in two or three great national universities, one obvious choice being, at the time, the then University of Brazil whose expansion programme remains delayed until today. The decision is typical: if corrective measures are not going to be painless, then additional new units are created and the older ones are left to fend for themselves.

In the sixties the universities were under strong political pressure and under a storm of criticism both from students' organizations (backed by the Government before 1964) and from top members of Government. By 1962 one magic solution to the universities' pressing administrative, financial and cultural problems suggested by students was their transformation into 'Foundations' supported by public funds. The model was the University of Brasilia. Typical of the changes in the student politics is the fact that after 1964 (the year when the Goulart Government was taken over by the military under the leadership of Marshal Castelo Branco with the support of some liberal technocrats) the same students, while they had complete freedom to meet and to exert pressure on the Government, publicly denounced such a proposed transformation of universities into 'Foundations'. It was argued that this would really put them under the influence of private industry and the forces of US imperialism.

In spite of such restlessness and of so many contradictions I do believe that the important decision then taken – in 1961 – was the creation of the University of Brasilia. Organized as a public Foundation, placed in a new campus, it tried to adapt the American and European models to Brazilian conditions. Full-time work was demanded from both staff and students, special care was devoted to research, tutorials were introduced, a credit system, a simplified entrance examination and graduate work.

Several political circumstances have disturbed the natural evolution of the University of Brasilia. Both Governmental authorities and activist groups of left leaning within the University had a share in the events which more than once, and not only after 1964, disturbed academic life. The significance, however, of the establishment of this type of new university was that it led to new official legislation demanding that all universities in the country should adopt its structure as a model. As often happens, the legislation is taking over long to be implemented.

The sixties were distinctive in being years of more fundamental analysis of university administration and finance and of their adequacy – or inadequacy – to rapidly changing economic conditions. This permitted both the universities to know themselves better and the authorities to define more appropriate educational goals. New funds for education were created: the US Agency for International Development, the Ford Foundation, the Inter-American Development Bank, all devoted more resources to education. Top priority was given to education in the Federal Government's Development Plans. Conditions were ripe for results. Nevertheless, changes within individual universities were still slow to come – partly because the Government required programmes and projects to be presented before resources could be allocated. Then in 1968 strong student manifestations, with street disturbances and clashes with the police, occurred all over the country. These disturbances started in Brazil some months before 'less évenements de Mai' in Paris and reached the same intensity.

Events progressed into a 'crescendo' and after control by force of street confusion and anarchy, a top level Federal 'University Reform' working group was formed to draft a report to the President and propose practical suggestions. This report marks a turning point in the situation because it oriented the Government to make changes in university finance as well as in administration. But one has to be realistic: because legislation is passed things will not automatically occur the day after. The important points were tackled: emphasis was placed on full-time work (and resources were provided for it) on graduate work and research, on the opening of university government to a much wider range of suitable people – including suitable members of staff who were not full professors.

The same period is important because of the universities' decision to organize themselves as a collective body and to sponsor some joint research into higher education administration as well as agreeing on more united action. Typical of this new position is the formation of a non-Governmental council on which practically all university 'Reitores' (Vice-Chancellors or Presidents) are represented. I shall refer to their work below.

Generally indeed the pressure upon the universities obtained a response. This can be felt by the quantitative expansion of the whole system both in terms of new courses offered, and by the increase in places. The numbers of students registered has increased substantially in the last ten years and continues to do so, accompanied by qualitative changes. But resistance to change has not been eliminated, and has contributed to slowing down modernization efforts. The need and desire to modernize are, however, pressing the system to adapt itself to new and rapidly changing economic and social conditions; and this is facilitating reform.

It should not be thought that because student movements have been stopped by force, and because resources have been devoted to expanding and modernizing the universities, student concern has died. Though it is more difficult and certainly more risky for students to assemble, they are alive and watchful of events. If the speed of reform does not increase and if more efficiency is not imposed rapidly on the system, student movement may soon start again. One of the main pressure valves in operation today, impeding explosions, is the Minister of Education himself. With great ability and political sense he has been able to hold the lid and reduce the pressure in the tin where students have been kept.

Some Quantitative Data

In the period 1960–8 the number of universities increased by more than 100 per cent from 23 to 48. Between 1965 and 1968 ten universities were founded. The greatest efforts have been concentrated in the new frontiers: the North, i.e. the Amazon Valley, and in the Centre, i.e. the vast uplands of the West which have Brasilia as their nucleus. Even in the South and in the East, where higher education has been widespread for several decades, the number of universities more than doubled from 14 to 31. The areas where population is greatest, and where economic development is more rapid, also keep the greatest share in the higher education system.

The Federal Government's share in supporting the system has increased more rapidly than the shares of the states or of the private sector, the increase in the number of universities under Federal Government direct control being 77 per cent between 1960 and 1965, whereas the private sector share increased by only 50 per cent.

Taking all higher education institutions together, i.e. inclusive of universities and other higher education institutions, the total number of registered undergraduate students increased by 58 per cent between 1960 and 1965 and again by 79 per cent in the next three years. In the initial year there were slightly more than 93,000 students and the figure almost trebled to over 278,000. These numbers alone indicate a considerable effort from all sectors of society.

As far as subjects are concerned, the Social Sciences have led the way with more than 300 per cent increase; Natural Sciences increased by 279 per cent, followed by Engineering with 176 per cent increase. These were the outstanding advances.

Important reductions in relative participation, but with increases in absolute numbers occurred in Arts (from 4·7 per cent to 2·8 per cent) and in Law (from 22·6 per cent to 18 per cent) and, surprisingly in Medicine (from 19·1 per cent to 14·3 per cent). I want to stress the surprise because these courses seem to be in high demand.

Graduate courses were the characteristic feature of higher education in the sixties in Brazil, and the rates of growth of students becoming greater, an indication that the expansion has high momentum. Starting from 1,700 students in 1960, one reaches 2,355 in 1965 and 4,169 in 1968. This shows a 38 per cent growth in the first five years and a 77 per cent increase in the next three years.

There is little doubt that the very large universities, São Paulo and Rio de Janeiro, will soon reach their maximum sizes – can 20,000 students be considered a limit? They will have to concentrate upon graduate work and scholarship and upon special programmes to enable the other universities to support their effort of improving their staff. The seventies will see such changes.

One peculiar aspect of the Brazilian universities' evolution in the sixties has been the influence of what I would call 'exogenous' programmes to distinguish from the day-to-day planning of each institution. Because of the strong resistances to change, for about twenty years several obviously necessary improvements have had to be carried on in special organizations, which acted as academic bodies but were not universities. One outstanding example is that of the Getúlio Vargas Foundation which started undergraduate courses in Public and Business Administration, and graduate courses and research in Economics. It is not clear whether the universities will absorb these as their Departments or whether they themselves will become universities in due course.

Six special programmes have to be mentioned because of their effect on different sectors of research and scholarship: FUNTEC (Fundo de Desenvolvimento Tecnico-Cientifico) administered by the National Development Bank (BNDE), the Ford Foundation programmes for teaching and research in Economics and other disciplines, the 'Conselho de Reitores' (CRUB) effort to modernize administrative methods, the US Agency for International Development (AID) programmes and those of the Inter-American Development Bank (IDB), and the National Research Council (CNP).

Concluding Remarks

Two clearly opposing forces are in operation in the university system in Brazil. One results from the rapid opening-up of universities to the large numbers of candidates that knock at their doors eager to compete for places – in 1971 there were some 450,000 registered undergraduate students in the system, and by the end of the decade Brazil may have overtaken the one million mark. The other comes from the urgent need to modernize both in cultural and in administrative terms: graduate courses are starting rapidly and research is catching up.

The first round has been won: increasing numbers have flooded the universities which will have to adapt themselves to the resulting pressures and problems. The second round is just beginning to be fought. Then resistance to change may be more difficult to overcome. What it is not yet possible to see is whether the simultaneity of operation of those two strong forces will be compatible one with the other, i.e. if the greater numbers will not delay or even impede modernization and then, even expansion.

It is imperative that during the seventies there should be an adequate selection of first-class executives to run the universities and to guarantee order with expansion, without permitting quality to deteriorate. It is important also to obtain more co-ordination among the several entities that operate in the system, particularly of those within the Ministry of Education itself.

9

Ten Years of Change at the University of Buenos Aires, 1956-66: Innovations and the Recovery of Autonomy

Gilda L. de Romero Brest

We chose the University of Buenos Aires and the period 1956–66 for three reasons: first, Buenos Aires University holds a position of great importance among the country's universities; second, that era is the closest to our day of those periods noted for the pioneering spirit; third, and most important, because the energy expended in the direction of innovation during this time was possibly the widest in range, the most profound and most consistent in the history of the Argentine universities. The initiatives were aimed as much at defining the constitution and function of the university *vis-à-vis* society in general, as at modernizing its internal operation.

To be able to judge the achievement in its true perspective, and to understand the motives of its agents and supporters, it is necessary to place it in its appropriate context in Argentine history. This particular period of change in the University coincided with a moment of optimism and a desire to overcome the profound crisis in politics and in social and economic conditions which had gripped the country for more than four decades, a crisis for which no solution seemed forthcoming, or to be at least very distant and uncertain.

The ten years of renewal 1956–66 fell between two 'revolutions'. In 1955 Peron's government fell, and in 1966 the military once again overthrew the legitimate government and installed a *de facto* regime. It is also necessary to point out that this period, when the University acted autonomously, was preceded and followed by long periods of intervention in University affairs by the government.

During these ten years the efforts to reconstruct the University paralleled those to reconstruct the country; as had happened before, the worsening of the national situation was paralleled by a worsening of the situation in the University. 'If the times we have just lived through can teach us anything' said Tulio Halperin Donghi in 1962, 'it is that the constant effort to achieve cultural and scientific renewal is frequently brought to a halt by the results of a crisis in the country, which affects the University along with all other national institutions. Ever since the start of the era of renewal which began with reform of the University in 1918, the University wanted to develop not only in order to adapt more completely to the new social climate, but also to extend its scientific and cultural achievements. However, this desire for growth was arrested time and again, often with brutal suddenness, by the deviously unforseeable consequences of the national crisis.'[1]

But reconstruction, as Donghi points out, did not mean exactly the same thing for the government as it did for the University. For the government, it implied mainly the restoration of the 'rule by the Right and a sincere return to the democratic institutions established by the constitution'. For the University restoration was only part of the re-building process, which was principally aimed at recovering its autonomy (also an aim of the revolution and one which was thoroughly accomplished), and repairing the damage incurred.

The University programme, however, went beyond mere restoration and proceeded resolutely towards the construction of a new University. The government nostalgically overlooked the vices and defects of the past, but encountered insoluble difficulties in its attempt to recreate it. Because it did not wish to go back to the bad old ways, and wanted to create a programme aimed at the future, the University was faced with the difficulties inherent in this divergence of viewpoints. Although the paths along which the government and the University chose to advance at first ran parallel, they did not stay together, but in fact often diverged widely, and sometimes ran in totally opposite directions. It must be made clear, however, that in spite of this increasing difference the government did not reverse its decision on the self-governing status of the University.

The above difficulties were not the only ones which faced the University. There were also the obstacles and hardships which any attempt at reform encounters. But the instigators of university change had a very clear conception of the risks of the enterprise they had undertaken, and the uncertainty of a fate which had, inevitably, to be closely linked to the national future. In spite of all this the University community began, and brought directly to its conclusion the programme of reform detailed below. But government and University, however, were both trapped by the forces of the unresolved national crisis, and a new revolution once more brought these efforts to nothing.

There follows a description of what was achieved in the University of Buenos Aires during this decade. Those aspects which are most relevant from the point of view of University reform are as follows:

(i) Government
(ii) The teaching staff
(iii) Courses, study plans and academic organization
(iv) Teaching
(v) Research

  (vi) Social function and extension of the University
 (vii) University Press
(viii) University secondary schools
  (ix) Campus
   (x) Auxiliary University services
  (xi) Autonomy.

The University of Buenos Aires, founded in 1821, consists of ten faculties, located in various parts of the city (Agriculture and Veterinary Science; Architecture and Town Planning; Economics; Pure Science; Law and Social Science; Pharmacy and Biochemistry; Philosophy and Letters; Engineering; Medicine and Dentistry). In 1966 it had 5,876 staff (excluding contracted and honorary lecturers) and according to the University Census of 1964, 65,328 students.

Government–Student Participation

In 1958, the Convocation approved the University Code which set up a tripartite government of university, faculties and departments. The three ranks, professors, students and graduates thus took part with voice and vote in all the decisions of the University, including the election of professors, deans and the Chancellor.

In each faculty, the council was made up of the Dean, eight representatives of the professors, four from the students and four from the graduates. 'All regular students on a University course, and having passed the University first year, may vote for the student representatives', and, 'students who have completed at least half of the course for which they have enrolled, or students in their final two years may stand for election as student delegates.' (University Code, article 119c.) The students accepted the Convocation's decision, and the Code it adopted, in spite of the fact that the solution did not satisfy the demands of large sectors of students and graduates who were hoping for equal representation in the senate.

In this fashion a most significant experience in self-government by a University, with full student participation, began in 1958. Student participation in University government had already been established in 1918, and it was one of the triumphs of the student movement of that year, which became known as the Reform of the University. This movement had wide repercussions in Latin America, not only in the university field but also in politics. This was largely due to the fact that university reform was based on a wider-reaching ideology, radically anti-oligarchic in nature, which had grown up with the emergence of the middle classes of both town and country on to the social–political scene.

The inclusion of the students in the governing body of the University in 1958 meant that the positive value of what they could offer in the way of new suggestions as to the fulfilment of the University's obligations had been clearly recognized, as well as the right to participate in decisions concerning their education. Equally, it was due to the power of the student body, and to a certain extent, to the ideology of the Reform. The active and wide-ranging intervention of students in university matters – as well as in political and social ones in critical moments for the nation – has a long history in Argentina. The student movements and organizations destined to change the future of the University, came into being at the beginning of the century (the Medical Students Centre was formed in 1900, the Engineering Centre in 1903, and the Law Centre in 1905). As early as 1903 a body of 1,000 law students went on strike (over examination regulations) and caused a crisis in the University which lasted a year, exposing faults in the teaching system and its outdated structure. The conflict went beyond the University and reached parliament, turning public opinion in favour of the students.

The growing strength of the student body showed itself once again in the period with which we are dealing. The first man designated by the Minister of Education to reorganize the University was chosen from a trio put forward by the University Federation. In the era which was ending the students had formed a valid and strong opposition. It should also be made clear that student participation in University government since its formalization in 1918 corresponded with those periods of a state of law and democratic awareness. The *de facto* governments which followed restorations of the oligarchy were accompanied by a weakening of democratic liberty; they put an end to University autonomy, brought back a policy of intervention and naturally considered as totally intolerable the participation of youth – increasingly radical – in university government.

This experience, although difficult, was of the greatest value. Student participation represented without doubt a force of great importance in the modernization and reform of the University, and this fact was particularly obvious in the first years.

It also presented many difficulties arising from two main sources. One of these was the growing ideological division, one sector growing steadily more radical, on the other hand, a strengthening of groups of Catholic democrats. Both these parties gave birth to a criticism which turned to direct opposition of many of the new reforms, and this turned the task of the senate into an arduous and difficult one. Other difficulties sprang from the way in which the administration was implemented. Problems apparently arose because the fields of decision and action were not clearly defined. The decision-making bodies went beyond the boundaries of their area of responsibility into the field of administration, thus limiting and obstructing action, or at least making it much more ponderous. This constant deliberation was often unnecessary, and wasted a great deal of time and energy. Nonetheless the experience was no doubt very useful in perfecting forms of government with student participation, a factor not only beneficial but vital to the life of the University.

The Teaching Staff

Several innovations were made in this period with regard to the teaching body, considered a key element in the reforms. The most important measure was the introduction of full-time lecturers and research workers. In 1956 only ten lecturers were actually full-time and in 1966 the number in this category had reached 678. Thus an attempt was made to overcome the situation where the lecturer was only responsible for his own course of lectures, and to make him part of the overall aims and the daily life of the University. This was to ensure that continued and full attention was given to the students and their development, to make sure the staff did participate in the government and activities of the faculties and departments, and finally to stimulate scientific research.

At the same time the structure of the teaching pattern was altered and the system of four-month terms introduced. One of the aims of this modification was to enable the professors to dedicate one four-month session to teaching and the next to research. However, in many cases the increase in the number of students exceeded the corresponding growth in teaching staff and so it was not always possible to fulfil this objective. Nevertheless, this reorganization of the terms, together with the introduction of full-time lecturers, not only had very good results on teaching itself but also gave a significant boost to research.

The University Code, adopted in 1958, set up a system of electing professors by competitive examination and limiting the length of time they could hold the chair. Under the new system this was for a period of seven years, at the end of which time the post became open for reallocation. This was – as the Code states – 'to create an atmosphere which will stimulate intense intellectual activity, and the greatest possible concern for efficient teaching'.

At the same time the Code set up 'freedom of teaching'. This was another effort to broaden and enliven lecturing, through the contributions of other lecturers with different perspectives on their topics of the regular professors. Freedom of teaching opened up the possibility of starting new or parallel courses, on the request of those interested, or of members of faculties, subject to the approval of the Governing Council.

The length of time a professor held his chair, and freedom of teaching, had been fundamental questions in the Reform of 1918, as ways of combating a stagnant system and the feudalism of the chairs.

The other important aspect of the reform with regard to the teaching staff was the establishment of a 'course for the formation and stimulation of students with a vocation for university lecturing'. This course was to provide Assistant Lecturers. These were organized into three categories: Second Assistants (advanced students); First Assistants (graduates) and Chief Assistants. The course 'demands attendance at lectures and seminars on themes allied to the chosen subject, and participation in these lectures and seminars, as well as attendance at and participation in lectures on methods of teaching and research'. 'The University organizes the special lectures required by the Faculties to achieve this desired end . . .' Promotion from one level to another was by fulfilling certain requirements and an examination. Those who completed the teaching course satisfactorily in all respects were designated Assistant Lecturers in the specific subject by the senior Council of the University.

The effects of these measures were widespread. They added to the general activity of the University, and speeded up its tempo. The four-month term intensified the work of the students. The same was true for the lecturers. Their teaching function acquired compactness and continuity by the number of hours spent weekly on lectures and associated activities, which the system demanded. There was a noticeable change in the traditional pattern of sporadic attendance at the faculty – often only two or three times a week, and that exclusively for the time needed to give lectures. Thus the teaching function grew ever more professional because of the increased demands which were made on it, and the wider activities it had to undertake.

Finally, the general duties of the lecturers also increased under the new system, which demanded their participation in administrative and other University affairs. This meant they had to spend more time in the University and become more involved in it as an institution.

Academic Structure – New Courses – Replanning of Courses

During this period attempts were also made to change certain traditional aspects of the structure of the University. Before this, it had consisted of a collection of isolated faculties, and it had offered a profusion of faculties, few being scientific ones.

Fundamental changes to the structure were not in fact made. An attempt to integrate the pure sciences into a system of central research and teaching departments met with much resistance and did not have the desired results. All that was achieved was some collaboration between the chairs of Odontology, Agriculture and Veterinary Science, Pure Sciences, Medicine and Pharmacy and Biochemistry.

However, the idea of linking faculties was not abandoned, and they tried to achieve it by another, less ambitious method. For this reason several departments and centres were created, responsible direct to the Chancellor: i.e. the History of Science Department, and centres for Higher Art Studies, Technological Investigation, Town and Country Planning,

Psychology, and Psycho-pathology of Youth. Although no more changes than these were achieved in the structure of the University as a whole, one major advance was made in the internal unification of the faculties, when the departments were created as unifying teaching bodies for the respective courses. Traditionally, the chairs were completely autonomous in laying down their courses; professors often ran these as they pleased. Organization into departments was adopted by several faculties. The government of the departments was the responsibility from the start of a departmental junta, one of whose main functions was to integrate the teaching of the different subjects and give coherence to the lectures on each course. This organization was completed by the adoption of the system of choosing lecturers for the departments and not for a specific subject which gave a greater flexibility so that each lecturer, within his own field, could initiate different courses to fit in with the needs of the course and its professors.

An important advance was made in scientific courses. The most outstanding example was undoubtedly in the faculty of Natural Science which made notable progress. It not only became one of the most advanced groups in the University, but also achieved a scientific standard of international level. The creation of modern courses on the one hand and the organizing of some new short study courses and the replanning of old ones on the other, is another aspect of the reforms worthy of mention.

Some other important new features were the School of Public Health, of Political Economy and Administration, and of Nursing. Courses of Anthropology, Sociology, Psychology and Computer Science were introduced. Other courses were reorganized. The course in Pedagogics, for example, was refurbished as a course on the Science of Education, and new curricula were drawn up in Pharmacy and Biochemistry, Agriculture and Veterinary Science into a basic course. Thus a flexible curriculum was set up in many subjects with optional courses added to a basic lecture course. Courses were also set up on subjects linked to the economic development of the country (Agriculture, Veterinary Science, Statistics, Economics, Industrial Chemistry, Industrial Engineering and Chemical and Mechanical Engineering). Naturally, there were many difficulties to be overcome which slowed down or halted the improvements which it was hoped to make.

Teaching

A large proportion of the innovations centred on the quality of the teaching and on the growth in efficiency of the University. The high level of failure, the high dropout rate, and the excessive length of studies, all problems arising from the low efficiency of the University, were attacked on various fronts. From the methods used we will quote a few: the adoption of the four-month term, the improvements in teaching – such as the reduction in the number of formal lectures and the increase in practical and laboratory work etc., changes in the system of promotion, the increase in the number of full-time professors, the increase in the number of teaching staff by the creation of assistant lecturers, the extension of timetables to enable students who were working part-time to attend more lectures if they so wished, a system of grants for students, etc.

The interest focused on teaching aroused attention and study and this led to growing awareness of the learning process itself, and to some improvements in teaching methods. The four-month term system (together in many faculties with obligatory attendance at practical classes, or small seminars), meant on the one hand that students had to concentrate on a limited number of subjects, and on the other led to an increase in the sustained and systematic work of teachers and students throughout the course. This was accompanied by periodic evaluation. All this brought fundamental changes to the organization, dedication and work patterns of both lecturers and pupils. Especially from the viewpoint of the lecturer, the change was far-reaching. Traditionally, his role had been confined, in many faculties, to dictating a course *ex cathedra*, without assuming the least responsibility for whether the students learnt anything or not, and then holding an examination at the end of the year. This system was upheld by the lack of obligation to attend classes, as this meant that many students only appeared to sit the examination.

Thus, examinations were the main objective of both lecturer and student. The four-month term, obligatory attendance at lectures and periodic evaluation (which sometimes replaced a final examination altogether) meant that the focus was moved from the examination to a continuous teaching effort by lecturers, and equally continuous and sustained application by students. The formal lecture and the final examination began to be seen in their true perspective within the learning/ teaching structure, which grew to be recognized as the true centre of effort. The obligation to hold practicals, or to hold weekly discussions with students, meant the work had to be divided between a team of teachers – lecturers and assistants. Thus, the responsibility of the lecturer, previously centred on the formal lectures, was expanded and given new life. Not only was a direct contact created and maintained between himself and the student, but it also became necessary to review teaching methods and aids. Lecturers had to become more professional as teachers, and they had recourse to modern teaching methods. Thus, the teaching standard was raised considerably. However, we must not minimize the difficulties and opposition the new system had to overcome, which did partially limit its success.

Research

The policy of innovation which had taken roots in the University naturally drew its strength from people strongly biased towards the advance of science through research.

One of the main deficiencies which the University was trying to overcome was the fact that it had been dedicated almost exclusively to the teaching of professionals, and was notorious for its neglect of research and for the almost non-existent number of scientists and research workers it produced.

An attempt was made to end this situation and to change the concept of the University's role. In the long debates in the Consejo Superior on this topic, two main points became apparent. The first was that research in all its forms is the main source of inspiration for good lecturing and closely connected with it; and the second, that to contribute to the advance of science and to the formation of scientists and research workers is a central function of the University. We should also make clear the importance which was assigned to research into problems of national development, including the growing needs of the process of modernization.

Various measures were employed to achieve these aims. Some have been mentioned above, such as the appointment of full-time professors and the four-month term which allowed research to be concentrated into the intervening four-month period. This new system was complemented by the introduction of grants for graduates, to stimulate scientific investigations. In 1958, the University agreed to create 100 annual grants for graduates to study in their home country or abroad. Following this, it was decided to institute a system which would ensure 'the incorporation of graduates on grants into the Faculties and Institutes of the University'.

Next came the formation of Institutes as research centres in all the faculties. This was in accordance with the statutes of the University Code, where the relevant section states 'that for the adoption or creation of Research Institutes, recognition of the following conditions is indispensable: (*a*) They must carry out work which will add original knowledge to the existing fund of knowledge. (*b*) They must educate research workers through their teaching, which should be specifically directed to this end.' There was also a special fund created for the Promotion of Science, to finance works of scientific investigation.

Social Function and Extension of the University

Section III of the Code approved in 1958 defined the relationship and the duties of the University towards society. It pledged itself to provide equal opportunities to students and graduates by means of grants and other aids and services. It undertook to spread knowledge through courses and seminars, and also to make known, through publications 'the intellectual achievements of its members . . . and the most significant works of both Argentine and world-wide culture'. It also accepted a responsibility to play a part in the education of the people. Lastly it undertook to stimulate and encourage 'any activities which will help, in any degree, the social advancement of the country . . .'. Courses of action were planned around these objectives; the more important achievements are described below. For students, 200 grants were instituted in 1958 and 500 in 1959, and in 1964 and 1965 the number reached 998 and 994 respectively. The volume considered essential by the University authorities was never attained because of the lack of resources allocated to the University.

The spreading of knowledge and culture as one of the functions of the University was attempted in various ways. The *University of Buenos Aires Review* became more forward-looking and broader in its publications, and Bulletins were published giving information on the University and the faculties. Then there was the creation of the University Press, and we will devote the next section especially to this, as it was one of the most ambitious and successful projects of the decade. The other way in which knowledge was broadcast was by setting up courses beyond the normal University range. Two in particular of these types of course warrant special mention – the Seasonal Courses, and courses run by the Department of Graduates.

The Seasonal Courses were started in response to the objectives of the Inter-university Regional Council (set up in agreement with the Universities of Chile and of the Eastern Republic of Uruguay in 1958). These courses ran for several weeks – in summer and winter – in each of the Universities, and were on themes particularly relevant for the region at that time; they were run by professors from all three Universities, and in addition lectures were given by specially invited professors. They were supported by very large numbers of students, graduates and the general public and also attended by about 100 grant-assisted students specially selected for the courses from national and international universities.

The Department of Graduates, created in 1958, to co-ordinate and encourage graduate activities, organized in 1960 integrated university courses to 'offer to graduates a panorama of the problems and achievements of this century'.

In 1956, the Department for the Extension of the University was set up. This Department tried to go beyond the traditional concept of extension and to bring university culture to groups of the population who had not previously had access to it. It centred its action on 'efforts to educate the people, in line with the social development of the community'. Its end was to achieve the integration of the University into its social context through tackling the vital social function of the University.

The Department also attempted to put the students in contact with the less favoured sectors of the population, give them an understanding of the problems which faced them. It began to evolve techniques of investigation suited to real problems, and techniques of action helpful to their solution. Thus, a pilot scheme in education as a means to social development, aimed particularly at the industrial zone of Greater Buenos Aires was introduced; the Department managed to achieve community service and direct action through the Centre for Development of the Community, the Joint Health Service, etc.

The commitment of the University to studies concerning the economic, scientific and technological development of the country became clearer as did the need for it to help with investigations into the actual problems of the nation. The creation of the Centre of Applied Research was a way of ensuring the 'continuity of such studies, and the participation of specialists in the various branches of knowledge'. One of its duties was to 'carry out a selection of problems of particular interest to the country, for closer study', and to place the results of these studies 'at the disposal of the government and the public'. All this was aimed at bringing about agreements between the faculties and national bodies and institutions, to facilitate research into problems of agricultural technology, geology, and natural resources, marine biology, cattle breeding, atomic energy, medical physics and radio isotopes, public health and hospital organization, radio astronomy, atmospheric contamination, town planning, education, human resources, etc. Other links were established with various organizations in order to set up postgraduate schools in subjects such as civil engineering, hydraulic engineering and marine engineering. Thus a change was brought about in the concept of university research, and the area of investigation in technology was widened. Another result was the direct participation of the university in efforts to secure national development.

The University of Buenos Aires Publishing Company

This was undoubtedly one of the most important creations of the decade, and one which exemplified the nature of all the other changes. Its functions were those of any publishing company, but additionally it was committed to the spread of learning among the general public. These aims were amply fulfilled, so that within four years it became the most important publishing company in Latin America. An idea of the size of its work can be given by these figures: between 1958 and 1966, 800 titles were published and put into circulation, and more than 10 million copies printed.

Secondary Schools connected with the University

There are two of these, the National College of Buenos Aires which runs courses leading to the *bachillerato* (school leaving certificate), and is the oldest and most venerable school in the city, and the Carlos Pelligrini Commercial School. Before the decade we are considering, both were preparatory schools for the university. Several important changes were made to them. First, they were turned into experimental schools, and second, because of the experimental nature of the teaching, many reforms in method were made. Co-education was introduced and changes were made in the curriculum, in techniques of teaching, in systems of discipline, as well as the change to full-time teachers, the organization of educational and vocational services, etc. However, especially in the National College, because of its long history and prestige, the reforms met with enormous resistance and many difficulties were encountered in implementing them.

The Campus

Until the start of this period, the university buildings were scattered throughout the city, many of them were very old, and almost all were far too small to accommodate the growing numbers of students or the many new university activities.

One of the first reforms tackled was the construction of a university campus. The project was quickly set in motion and the first buildings started. The increasing restrictions on the money available to the university slowed down the initial spurt, however, and the development became slow and arduous.

University Auxiliary Services

During the decade there were set up two distinct groups of Departments and Auxiliary Services, one centred on the students and their needs, and the other on teaching techniques. In the first group was the Department of Vocational Guidance, non-existent until this time in the university; there was also the Department for Student Welfare, concerned with grants, lodgings, travel and holidays; also the University Health Service and the Department of Physical Education. In the second group there was the University Planning Council, the University Statistics Centre and the Department of Higher Education.

University Autonomy

The ethic of most universities in Latin America is based essentially on the principle of autonomy. This principle, which is inviolable for them, is jealously guarded, and intervention by any outsider is seen as a profanation. This Latin American ethic has led to a singular compromise. It has chosen to make autonomy a more sacred principle than the freedom of the professorial chair. This probably derives from a sense of belonging to a community, whilst the defence of the freedom of a professor would find its strength in a more individualistic climate. It is also possible that the sense of social responsibility and of commitment to the nation and its problems is strengthened by a watchful defence of the university charter.

This concern about freedom could, on another level, be linked to the fact that in our countries it is hard not to be constantly aware of the existence and potential of the universities, whereas in more sophisticated societies, they are lost in the vast web of other more varied institutions. We suppose that, in part for this very reason, members of the university feel themselves more obliged to take up a definite position on all problems of national import, and that this is expected of them, at least by some sectors of the community. On the other hand it is extremely irritating to other sectors because they wish to set themselves up as guardians of the future nation. Criticism and the reformatory zeal were therefore either intolerable or threatening to them. This gave rise to many clashes, and finally in the name of law and order, the universities were silenced by government intervention.

The myth of university neutrality was used many times as a justification for these actions, but this neutrality was based on unrealistic thinking and ingenuous reasoning. In the name of these principles, a new *de facto* government intervened in the affairs of the Argentine universities, sacked 1,315 lecturers (professors, demonstrators, and assistant lecturers) and put an end to the reform movement.

This reform of the University of Buenos Aires was the work of a group of rectors, deans, vice-deans, professors, young graduates and students, belonging for the most part to the two non-professional faculties of the University – Pure Sciences, and Arts (Philosophy and Letters). We should in justice quote some of their names, even at the risk of unjustly omitting others; these were Risiere Frondizi, the Chancellor, and Jose Luis Romero, Rolando Garcia, Jose Babini, William L. Chapman, Manuel Sadosky and Gino Germani.

REFERENCE

1. Tulio Haperin Donghi, *Historia de la Universidad de Buenos Aires* (Editorial Universitaria de Buenos Aires, 1962), p. 219.

10

Universidad Iberoamericana, Mexico: The Ongoing Reform

Francisco Migoya

When the President of the Universidad Iberoamericana declared to the Press in 1970 that he was in favour of exchanging traditional examinations for other methods of control, there was a reaction of surprise, and even of scandal among the reporters and faculty. And it was evident that a large part of the faculty would not collaborate in a radical reform of educational methods and systems which the country's condition, at least 50 years behind the times, demanded. What could not be expected from some of them, however, was what others urgently demanded. The Academic Committee, an organization representing the various faculties at the University, suggested that the different schools should take part in a self-analysis at depth, to include the question of the location of schools within the University; the relationship of the University with other organizations, the aims, both immediate and remote, to be pursued by them; academic and social goals of the university and the means by which they could be reached; in other words, its future plans and trajectory.

Both the schools and the Student Councils received these ideas with great enthusiasm, and promised to collaborate in undertaking such a self-analysis. This has marked the beginning of important reform in structure, methods and systems.

Reforms of Structure

The structural reforms being planned are of two kinds: departmental organization, and the introduction of student representation on two executive committees.

(a) *Departmental Organization* Latin American universities have traditionally functioned through organized departments within each professional field. This puts members of each Department into complete isolation from the rest at the university, makes institutional co-ordination difficult and results in a lack of unity in the life of the university as a whole.

The Rector is now leading a team which is working to introduce an academic reform based on departments – by which the departments are regarded as basic units, responsible for academical studies within specific

137

fields, but are linked to each other in Schools. Though the Departments assume the responsibility of providing the Schools with the required courses, they enjoy complete autonomy in carrying out their work.

The following are the advantages of organization through Departments: (1) instead of having a pre-established set curriculum, the student can arrange, within limitations, through the flexibility of credits, his own curriculum. Although strictly speaking departmental and credit organization can function separately, in practice they condition each other. (2) There is greater communication within Schools between professors of kindred subjects. (3) There is a more favourable opportunity to revise plans and study programmes. (4) Duplication of courses is avoided, leading to considerable savings. (5) There is a great deal more co-ordination in research work. (6) In offering only one course to different schools, the students have to make an effort to adapt it to their needs. (7) There is a more favourable possibility to plan the training of prospective faculty. (8) Waste of space and equipment in laboratories and workshops is avoided.

In order to organize departmentalization, it is essential to start from a careful revision of study plans and programmes. This responsibility is placed on the Heads of Departments. The Schools request the necessary courses from the Departments, and these have to offer what is satisfactory to each Dean of a particular School. The project is divided in various stages, but it is hoped that it will start to function during the 1972–3 session.

(b) *The Representation of Students* The students are allowed to have five representatives sitting at meetings of the University Council, which comprises thirty persons. They do not have an equal participation in reaching decisions, but they can both speak and vote. On the Council of each individual School, they form a percentage of practically one-third. They also participate in a similar way in managing the University magazine. This moderate participation permits us to know the students' opinion, leads to a more responsible and mature attitude on their part, once they become familiar with the problems the institution has to face, and establishes an easier relationship between the authorities, the faculty and the students.

Theoretical-practical Courses in Laboratories at the Engineering School

The subjects included in the studies of this School require careful and graphic exposition. Because of that, a good number of the classes are taught with the aid of slides, which show the design of machinery and the different processes. Next semester, all the subjects related to Hydraulics and Soil Mechanics will be taught in special laboratories. The idea is that all courses in Mechanics of Materials, Soil Mechanics, Structures and Hydraulics, should be taught in laboratories which permit the use of aids and equipment which can complement theoretical exposition. The student will no longer find the costly facilities of previously used laboratories, but he will make models with disposable materials, which will help his comprehension of the phenomena being studied. He will also participate in drawing up the programme and budget of the project that each model implies, and in seeing the best ways of putting it into practice. It is expected that these laboratories will become an important means in the education of students.

Solving Problems through Electronic Computers at the School of Chemical Engineering

Considering the great scientific advance and the recent discoveries and new technology within this field, as well as the complexity and difficulty of problems connected with it, electronic computers have become an indispensable tool in teaching at this School. In order to obtain practice in their field, chemical engineering students spend several hours a week at the Electronic Computer Centre at the University. This permits the programming of problems whose mathematical solution would be time consuming, but which with the aid of computers can be worked out in a few minutes. As is well known, the use of computers has increased the numbers of books in the field of cybernetics and design of reactors. The Universidad Iberoamericana has already contributed to this literature.

Throughout the two years that the students have been practising at the Centre of Electronic Computation it has been observed that the students' enthusiasm towards it has increased; so much so, that it has been necessary to provide all the branches of engineering with more hours at the Centre. The Computer Centre aims to expand its services to the non-technical schools, such as Business Administration, Industrial Relations and Accounting. This would mean the introduction of an adequate language, for instance COBOL.

The School of Design is already using a programme for the designing of new types of equipment. The teacher prepares a programme giving the mathematical model of the design for a machine, the student provides data for this programme, and the computer provides them with a fair number of alternatives to be analyzed. This permits the advantage of reckoning with a number of alternatives before the design is finally chosen. If done manually, this would imply a considerable limitation in the number of possibilities to be studied.

We think that in the future some courses of programmed instruction, controlled by computers based on remote terminals could be established. In this case, the student would have a terminal connected to the computer.

The student would introduce a certain code in the machine, and, as an answer, the computer would ask him a number of multiple choice questions. The student then would have to choose the right one, feeding it to the computer through the same terminal. The computer would have to be programmed so that, depending on the correctness of the answer presented, the student would continue with the next step of the course, or make him go back to review what he had previously studied. In this way, the student's progress would be directly connected to his own capacity, and not to the need to conform to that of the group. In traditional schools the class has to conform to the average level, while programmed teaching is adapted to the students' personal needs.

Administration of the different schools is being partially done through computers. This means that officials and administrators have to adjust to the schedules offered by Centro de Calculo, which limits the freedom of action previously enjoyed by them; on the other hand, results are more accurate and uniform. This system permits the detection of any departures from regular procedures on the part of administrators – departures not always completely justified. Nevertheless, there is some fear among administrative personnel, that computers may gradually become substitutes for human beings.

Seminar on Chemical Research

The course called Experimental Chemistry requires 20 hours a week. The students taking it at UIA do not perform the traditional chemistry tests, but are trained to do research work, which begins within the course. Instead of having a theoretical lesson, the students take part in a seminar, called a research seminar, in which they discuss scientific methods and practise chemistry research. The seminar is formed by teachers, research scientists at the University, and guests from other institutions, who, along with the students, actively participate presenting their own results, and those of other persons, actively working in the same field. The number of full-time teachers assisting UIA students is considerable, and, especially during the last few semesters, they have established a close relationship with the students as well as supervising their work more effectively. According to some opinions, the great number of papers written by undergraduates which have been published by international journals is one of the outcomes of this system.

Methods of Investigation Applied to Communication

Until a few years ago means of exchanging information in Mexico were very deficient. In 1960 UIA opened the School of the Science and Techniques of Information, the first in the country. This School aims to prepare real professionals in the field of communication. Because the field is so new the school has yet to undergo many changes in order to become adjusted to the demands of advertising and other firms which depend upon efficient communication. Anyone who is to be professionally educated in communication needs a solid humanistic training, as well as a socio-economical one; and at the same time, he has to master the way to project this knowledge. This duality gives a special character to the school, and has lead to its becoming one of the most popular at UIA. Such popularity permits a more careful selection of students. In 1965, the school accepted 84 new students. In 1970, the number went up to 106, but the number of applicants rejected was much larger. A novelty within the field of communication is the study of the different methodologies applicable to social communication. As a preparation there is a course on theory of information, which is practically a resume of the investigation done in the United States and in Europe in this field. An original investigation on the different methods that could be applied to communication is done later.

The senior group is now doing some investigation on 'The possibility of classifying society on the basis of the values it serves and not only on money'. They expect to have a possibility of evaluating the reaction of public opinion to an event, and to inquire why it is that people react in one way rather than another when faced with a fact or some piece of news. It is not yet possible to judge the results of an investigation which is just beginning, but the project has been received very enthusiastically by the students, and has given them an incentive to work. Nevertheless, the school will have to define its future and definite orientation. Is it to be of socio-philosophical tendency, concentrating in the most meaningful formative aspects, or to give communication a more ample practical place?

Two courses on communication are being filmed in videotape. The first is on Hispano-American Culture, consisting of fifteen lessons, lasting 25 minutes each; and the second, on Universal Culture, which covers thirty lessons. The idea is to use these lessons in courses taught at the University, but also considering the possibility of renting them to other institutions which may request them. In fact, it seems that some North American Universities are interested in buying them to be used in Spanish. There are videotapes of other material which the Schools of Industrial Design, and of the Sciences and Techniques of Information always use as an introduction to group discussion. This system is favourably accepted by the students, but both the elaboration of the programmes and the maintenance of equipment for closed circuit television is quite expensive, so the projects are not generally carried out owing to lack of the necessary finance.

The use of Teletype is a very useful practice for students at the School of

Science and Techniques of Information. Eight students receive information each day from 7 to 8.15 a.m. and prepare two news programmes lasting 15 minutes each. Later, these programmes are discussed and graded by the teacher and the entire class. Within this telex programme a student spends a complete day following all international information, and later joins his class to make a plan to inform students who have not read the day's newspapers. At a later stage, they compare their own work and their programme with what the newspapers outside have published that day. This permits a re-phrasing of headlines, and they learn to help the readers obtain all the necessary information on what is really happening. This helps to develop their critical attitude towards some informative organizations who lack a definite ideology.

The Programme in Psychotherapy

The Psychopedagogical Orientation Centre offers therapy services to those who request them and at the same time prepares the Psychology School graduates as therapists. In order to carry this out, they offer a postgraduate course, the first of which began in 1968, and will last four years. During the first two years of the course students prepare for their Master's Degree in Psychology, and at the same time work in the Centre. During the four-year programme, they should also go through therapy themselves. The project aims to have the future therapist get to know himself better, and at the same time equip him to put into effect what he has learned through personal experience. This should become easier, since he will have lived what his future patients will experience later. This programme is inspired by modern pedagogical systems, combined with the existential type of therapeutic theory advanced by Rollo May, Carl Rogers and Abraham Maslow.

The grading system is quite new, because, in order to evaluate the student's performance, three opinions are considered: that of the teacher, that of the student himself, and his own classmates. They all get a grading form, and in order to fill it out they have to consider two aspects: the formal, which consists in evaluating: (1) the ordering of the elements, (2) clarity, (3) appearance, and (4) self consistency, and (5) critical judgment. Naturally the evaluation of the contents is much more significant than that of the formal aspect.

It usually happens that the most accurate and effective evaluation is the one provided by the student himself, probably because knowing that his own classmates will also judge his performance, he is forced to be more realistic and objective. The teacher's intervention helps to form a criterion. He requests explanations regarding the student's and the class's evaluation.

It is still too soon to give an exact opinion on the results of this system, since the first group taking the four-year course has not yet graduated, but it has been observed that, since the students are not used to this type of procedure, they find it difficult.

Vocational Orientation Sessions

Sessions of Vocational Orientation are another service that the Psychological Orientation Centre will offer all students applying for entrance at UIA during the registration period in 1971. Its aim is to provide information about the professional studies the applicant has chosen, and also about the functioning of UIA.

Lectures are given before entrance examinations, and last for two hours. They are divided by areas, so that the student can attend two lectures within the area of his preference. These lectures are given by three persons: a lecturer – usually a teacher at the particular school. He takes up (*a*) aims of the professional studies, (*b*) the structure of the academical programmes, study plans, and their meaning, (*c*) subjects to be taken during the first school year and degree of difficulty, (*d*) aptitudes and interests which are required, (*e*) work rhythm, (*f*) registration demand, and (*g*) social projection of the professional practice. The lecturer then chooses a senior student in the same field, whose contribution consists in helping the teacher and actively participating at the stage of 'questions and doubts'. The idea is that beginners get in touch with the senior students who have gone through the same experience and problems they will have to meet. It also helps them to feel more at ease and to ask questions more openly.

A representative of the Student Council is elected whose function is to inform the new students about the administrative functioning of UIA, as well as about the Students' Association. This person is previously informed that his contribution should be free of any political aim, and should be kept at a strictly informative level.

Group dynamics are organized with registered students. This service is offered to all those entering UIA, the purpose being to facilitate their adaptation to university life, and to establish a better relationship with their classmates, as well as to their obtaining more knowledge regarding their motivation in choosing it. This is done through discussion of all these aspects. These groups are co-ordinated by a psychologist and a senior student. They last two hours. The experience obtained from these sessions is quite limited since they were started only two years ago, but they do have an advantage over the previous system, which consisted in giving orientation talks in schools. The fact that representatives of the University went into the schools gave the idea of a commercial and proselytizing aim. The new system is carried into effect by announcing the sessions as a service to students; and only those who are interested attend them. Nevertheless, it has been observed that the number of people wishing to attend is usually larger than there is capacity for.

Field Work in the School of Social Anthropology

Field work is a novelty in the teaching system of social anthropology. It is an academic requisite that the students of Social Anthropology undertake a month of research, generally in Indian communities, or at other peasant or factory working areas. The location for such field practices is previously chosen, bearing in mind the necessary requirements for obtaining the desired results, that is: the teaching of investigation techniques which are not standardized, mostly regarding so-called 'participating observation'. The practice is conducted by a teacher accompanying each group of students. There are three different groups, each led by a teacher working in three different communities at the same time.

Besides the knowledge obtained through direct investigation of anthropological and social data, field work serves a more important purpose: to enable the student to experience at first hand, and get to know socioeconomic and cultural situations which are different from those in his own environment. This, specially in countries like Mexico, where the differences in socio-economic status are so great, impresses the students deeply. They are forced to face a different reality; which generally results in their being awakened and stimulated to evaluate their own environment more critically.

The nature of the field practices involves certain risks whose control depends on close contact between the student and the teacher leading the group and participating in its work. It is also important that the project should be carried out with the idea of establishing close contact, but without idealizing its purpose. The student is there to learn, not to fake an integration. Interrelationship is a means, not an aim. Field practices undoubtedly improve academic relationships; whether they lead to the formation of a socially-minded conscience, it is impossible to say. But it is hoped that they do. Those who have participated in field practices up to now, confronted with the living conditions of a great majority of the Mexican people, are in favour of a more fair distribution of the available resources.

Independent Study

Conventional educational institutions function under the assumption that learning is directly connected with the students' attendance at a pre-established number of classes, throughout a pre-established number of weeks. Education is given in four-hour a week packages, either by semester or other periods. Independently from the size of the package, credits in learning are closely related to the regularity of attendances at classes.

The honour programme, and the independent study programme, are both reactions against these systems. Independent study is work which is requested from the student, sometimes to be done alone, sometimes as a member of a small group, but always without the presence of the teacher, and instead of attending the regular class periods. It is a study programme based on topics selected by the student, with the approval of the appropriate Department, and supervised by the instructor. Independent study is frequently associated with the honour programme. This course is designed to permit capable students to carry out their studies in an independent manner, but under the direction of a member of the faculty. The student has to report on his work, and to take a final examination. The programme is limited to exceptional students, implies independent or tutorial work, makes the student more responsible for his own work, emphasizes reading and self instruction, gives the student freedom from class attendance. It gives an opportunity to accelerate studies. It can comprehend all the curriculum or only part of it. There are many varieties. It is given individually, under supervision; individually, without supervision; in small groups without an instructor; in small groups with an instructor. It is expected that the student will work on his own for most of the time. This programme provides freedom for the professor, and as a result makes the student more resourceful.

This type of programme does not eliminate the teacher from the business of teaching, but rather makes him ask: to what kind of learning experience should we expose the student? What kind of combination of classwork and independent work makes learning more effective?

Having the above-mentioned points in mind, the Academic Committee approved the following norms to carry out the honour and independent study programmes: the honour programme permits able students to undertake their studies independently under supervision and guidance of a professor within his School, and/or Department. The student has to report on the work assigned to him, and can do so by means of written work, on examination in particular subjects, or by general examinations. The honour programme at UIA can be granted to students of the fifth semester or above, on request from the student. Candidates should have an average above what is normally established at each school. It can be applied to all the subjects taken by the student, or only to some. In cases where the academic load includes subjects not corresponding to the main area, these are eliminated from the programme, unless the student has sufficient knowledge to go more deeply into them. If subjects offered by another Department are authorized, the previous approval of both Directors would be necessary. Authorization to follow the programme is granted for only one semester, but it can be renewed if the student obtains an equivalent or a superior average to what he had at the beginning of the programme. Granting authorization for the programme implies a bilateral commitment between the Department or School and the student.

Conclusions

This presentation of new ideas may give the impression that what is lacking is an overall rational plan to develop the particular programmes. The different initiatives do reflect an awareness that there is a problem, and show a preoccupation in solving it. Some of the experimental systems may be valuable, but others may have to be changed for more positive ones.

We have to bear in mind, however, that higher education in this country has only just started to depart from the passive attitude that used to characterize it. One can say that almost all the institutions that seriously face the problem are new, both the Secretaria de Educación Pública and Universidad Nacional Autónoma de México, and also other universities that have created departments specializing in providing higher education with new and more effective teaching methods which are in agreement with the current situation. No doubt one of the more promising future projects is communication and sharing, and exchanging programmes between universities, since the cost, and required personnel, to develop them exceeds the possibilities of a single institution. This communication and joint effort would result in common objectives and a greater possibility of basic problems being detected. Such a joint effort might help to increase necessary resources for providing the right solution.

11

Higher Education in India: Priorities and Problems

Prem Kirpal

The need for a radical reform of Indian higher education in the context of emerging national tasks and objectives was expressed as follows in the Resolution of the Government of India setting up the Education Commission in July 1964:

> The attainment of independence ushered in a new era of national development founded upon: the adoption of a secular democracy, not only as a form of government but also as a way of life; the determination to eliminate the poverty of the people and to ensure a reasonable standard of living for all through modernization of agriculture and rapid development of industry; the adoption of modern science and technology and their harmonizing with traditional spiritual values; the acceptance of a socialistic pattern of society which will secure equitable distribution of wealth and equality of opportunity for all in education, employment and cultural advancement. Greater emphasis came to be placed on educational development because of the realization that education, especially in Science and Technology, is the most powerful instrument of social transformation and economic progress and that the attempt to create a new social order based on freedom, equality and justice can only succeed if the traditional educational system is revolutionized, both in content and extent.

In the light of these high expectations from the working of educational institutions and centres of learning, the Indian Education Commission (1964–6) identified some special responsibilities of universities in the present state of India's social and educational development. The universities are exhorted to encourage individuality, variety and dissent, within a climate of tolerance, and to learn to serve as the conscience of the nation; they are invited to assist the schools in their attempts at qualitative improvements and to develop programmes of adult education, especially through the network of part-time and correspondence courses; they are asked to shake off the heavy load of their early tradition which gives a prominent place to examinations and strive to improve standards all round by a symbiotic development of teaching and research; and they are expected to create at least a few centres of excellence which would be comparable to those of their type in any other part of the world.

To realize these special objectives and other broad functions shared in common with all universities, the Education Commission visualized a well-conceived and comprehensive plan for the development of higher education, spread over the next twenty years and directed, among other things, to the following three programmes of high priority: a radical improvement in the quality and standards of higher education and research, expansion of higher education to meet the manpower needs of national development and, to some extent, the rising social ambitions and expectations of the people; and improvement of university organization and administration.

In the twenty-three years since Independence the number of universities in India has increased from 19 to 83; in addition there are 14 institutions having the status of university under special Acts of Parliament. Regional and political pressures as well as the expansion of enrolment tend to increase the number constantly. Institutions multiply faster than adequately qualified teachers and the necessary financial resources. The inevitable shortage of amenities and dilution of standards militate against qualitative improvements. In such a situation new strategies of development are required to establish and nurture some centres of excellence within a rapidly expanding system.

Centres of Advanced Study

The Education Commission thought that the most important reform in higher education was the development of a few 'major universities' where first-class postgraduate work and research would be possible and whose standards would be comparable to the best institutions of their type in any part of the world. The concept of 'major universities' was seriously considered and debated upon, but finally abandoned in favour of the more broad-based and egalitarian approach of establishing Centres of Advanced Study in selected departments where the conditions of staffing and postgraduate research were favourable. It was feared that the 'major-university' approach would relegate the larger number of universities to a second and inferior rank, depleting them of talented staff who would inevitably migrate to the major universities. The larger diffusion of departments as centres of excellence at as many university centres as feasible was preferred. To establish and strengthen Centres of Advanced Study, the Ministry of Education and the University Grants Commission secured assistance from Unesco and the United Kingdom. This external assistance brought to the advanced centres a number of Soviet professors under Unesco's programme and specialists from British universities in addition to training facilities and research equipment. The stimulus and contacts afforded by these programmes of external assistance and liberal grants from the University Grants Commission were utilized for developing Centres of

Advanced Study. By 1968, thirty university departments – 17 in science subjects and 13 in humanities and social sciences – were selected on the basis of their work, existing facilities and potentialities for further development to function as Centres of Advanced Study in specific fields. These Centres were intended to encourage the pursuit of excellence and to provide suitable conditions and facilities for advanced studies and research which could be utilized by talented students from other universities through a liberal system of grants and scholarships. With six Advanced Centres in Botany, Chemistry, Physics, Zoology, Economics and Sociology, the University of Delhi functioned virtually as a major university, followed by Madras, Bombay, Calcutta and Chandigarh with more than one Centre.

The development of Centres of Advanced Study had some wholesome effects. Apart from raising standards of teaching and research, they have reduced the need for sending students for study abroad and tend to check the so-called 'brain-drain', or flight of talent to foreign countries. Their number is, however, still very small compared to the size of higher education and its rapid tempo of expansion. Some even of these few may fade away for lack of resources and staff. It is too early to say whether they have exercised beneficial influence on other departments and universities; too often they seem to work in comparative isolation, without sufficient relationship with other departments in their own and related fields. A start on the right path has, however, been made and the experiment promises the building up of strong and lasting centres of excellence, disseminating their example and influence widely and developing relations on a continuing basis with similar centres in other countries.

Collegiate Education

An attempt was also made to upgrade higher education at the collegiate level. More than 3,000 colleges affiliated to universities cater for over 85 per cent of the student population in higher education. With a few notable exceptions most of these institutions are little better than schools, providing dull and mechanical teaching of what is often out of date information and rarely offering any stimulation of mind and independent thinking. The main defect of the collegiate system was that it held the affiliated colleges in a uniform mould of mediocrity, ridden by examinations and fearful of experimentation and change. The Education Commission recommended that where there is an outstanding college (or a small cluster of very good colleges) within a large university, it should be granted an 'autonomous' status. This would reduce the parent university's role to that of general supervision and conferment of degrees, conceding to the autonomous college the power to frame its own rules of admissions, to prescribe its courses of study and to conduct examinations. The

Commission thought that it should be possible to bring at least fifty of the best colleges under this category before 1974. So far there has been little progress in this direction and the affiliated colleges continue to languish in the traditional grooves denying to the mass of students enrolled the benefits of better and more relevant education.

Some improvements were effected in teaching and education by the use of better libraries and laboratories, encouragement of independent study, and reform of the examination system. The Education Commission underlined the need for experimentation, especially in the way of handling larger numbers of students without a proportionate increase in educational expenditure or the number of faculty members, and by entrusting a certain amount of teaching to research students and selected postgraduate students after their first year. This too has remained largely a pious hope, without generating much experimentation.

Greater success was achieved in the organization of student services, including orientation for new students, health services, residential facilities, guidance and counselling, especially vocational placement, student activities and financial aid. Deans of Student Welfare were appointed to administer these services. The working of Student Unions was improved and assisted and attention was given to problems of student unrest and indiscipline. The University Grants Commission has given financial assistance for such activities. Many universities have improved facilities for games and sports and Government have launched a programme of social service which requires from students disciplined service in rural areas and town slums. Emphasis on character-building, patriotism and moral and spiritual values is loudly proclaimed even though concrete action to promote these objectives lags behind.

The Medium of Instruction

The question of medium of instruction at universities has aroused heated controversy. The switch-over from English to the regional languages was recommended by the Radhakrishnan Commission in 1948–9, but little progress was made in this direction. Lack of textbooks and reading materials in the regional languages, the rapid growth of knowledge, especially in science and technology, and the deficiencies of language teaching retarded the progress. The use of Hindi as the all-India language met with serious opposition from non-Hindi speaking States. The Government resolution of July 1968 outlining a national policy on education stated:

> The energetic development of Indian languages and literature is a *sine qua non* for educational and cultural development. Unless this is done, the creative energies of the people will not be released, standards of education will not improve, knowledge will not spread to the people, and the gulf between the intelligentsia and the masses will remain, if not widen further. The regional

languages are already in use as media of education at the primary and secondary stages. Urgent steps should now be taken to adopt them as media of education at the university stage. . . . Special emphasis needs to be laid on the study of English and other international languages. World knowledge is growing at a tremendous pace, especially in science and technology. India must not only keep up with this growth but should also make her own significant contribution to it. For this purpose, the study of English deserves to be specially strengthened.

This settled the problem of languages at the university stage. No time limit was prescribed for the switch-over and the choice in this matter was left mainly to the universities. A special position was accorded to the study of Hindi and Sanskrit. The adoption of regional languages as media of instruction in universities poses formidable problems. Universities are encouraged to produce textbooks of good quality in regional languages and considerable financial grants are available for this task. Progress, however, is necessarily slow and everywhere a bilingual situation, in which both the regional language and English are used, is developing at the first degree stage. Postgraduate work continues to be done in the English medium. National institutions for development of languages have been established, notably one in Hyderabad for English language teaching and another in Mysore for regional languages, in addition to several university departments and a few Centres for Hindi and Sanskrit. Complementary to the measures for developing Indian languages is a large programme for production of books on all subjects, including translations of standard works from English and other European languages. Facilities are provided for learning important international languages in addition to English; many universities provide teaching in Russian, French and German. Area studies at selected centres have been organized to provide facilities for the study of languages and civilizations of important cultural areas of the world.

New Institutions for Research and Development

Attempts to improve the range and quality of higher education are reflected in the creation of new institutions. For example, the establishment of the National Council of Educational Research and Training in 1961 was a recognition of the importance of education as a significant area of study which had been grossly neglected in the past. The Council undertakes, aids and promotes research in all branches of education, organizes advanced pre-service and in-service training and disseminates improved techniques and practices. It also organizes extension service for institutions engaged in educational research and training of teachers. The research and teachers training programmes of the Council are developed through the National Institute of Education at New Delhi and four regional colleges of education at Ajmer, Bhubaneshwar, Bhopal and Mysore. The Institute's programme is at present being implemented by its constituent units

– Development of Teaching Aids, Field Services, Basic Education, Adult Education, Educational Psychology and Foundation of Education, Science Education, Social Sciences and Humanities, Educational Administration, Pre-Primary and Primary Education, Teacher Education and Textbooks, and units for Educational Survey and Publications. In addition to the publication of the *Year Book on Education*, the Council brings out three periodicals: *School Science*, the *Journal* of the National Institute of Education, and a half-yearly research journal *Indian Educational Review*.

The National Council of Educational Research and Training with its constituent units and programmes of research, study, training and publications have broken new ground and their example has to some extent influenced developments in the States, who have set up similar institutions at the State level. It has up-graded educational research and teacher education. But the hope of the Education Commission that strong inter-disciplinary studies of education would develop at universities has not been fulfilled. In general, universities remain indifferent to educational research and training.

To rectify the balance in favour of Social Science and Humanities which were neglected owing to a major deployment of resources to Natural Science and Technology, the Government of India established at Simla in October, 1965, the Indian Institute of Advanced Study. It conducts advanced study and research on social sciences, historical sciences, philosophy and literature. The aim is to 'study Man in the Context of Nature and Human Society in given times and spaces'. The Institute receives various categories of academic personnel, visiting professors, lecturers and guest Fellows – and offers facilities for research, group discussions and writing. Its publication section has already published nine volumes of translations containing the papers and proceedings of many seminars and conferences. To strengthen the social sciences, the Government has also established an Indian Council of Social Sciences which gives grants to institutions and individuals. Along with some Centres of Advanced Study at universities, these new institutions have developed greater interest in social sciences and humanities. In general, however, humanistic studies have not developed to the same extent as natural sciences and technological education. There are very few centres of excellence for the study of Indian culture and civiliz-ation and the interest in Social Sciences and Humanities lags behind more practical and utilitarian fields.

Developments in Rural Higher Education

The problems of rural India and its main occupation of agriculture have given rise to some interesting innovations in higher education. The University Education Commission had in 1949 recommended the establish-ment of rural colleges and rural universities to promote the advancement of rural India. A National Committee appointed for this purpose in 1954 evolved a pattern of education suited to the needs and resources of rural areas. Consequently fourteen Rural Institutes of High Education were organized to offer facilities to rural youth to acquire that training and skill which would make them effective leaders of the community. In 1966, a National Council for Rural Higher Education was constituted under the Chairmanship of the Union Education Minister to advise the Government of India and the State Governments on all matters concerning the development of rural higher education in the country and to conduct examinations for the various courses approved by it. Eight different diploma, post-diploma and certificate courses of one to three years' duration were developed in subjects like rural economics, rural sociology, civil and rural engineering, agricultural science, etc. The curricula and the courses in the Rural Institutes, were designed as an integrated whole comprising study, research and extension. The curricula were geared to the needs of rural people.

The programme of rural higher education, which was in the nature of pilot projects, soon ran into serious difficulties. The students demanded equivalence with university courses and degrees which the traditional universities denied them, and on completion of their courses not all of them found work and employment for which they were trained. Consequently, some of the rural institutes reverted to the traditional pattern and became part of universities.

The eight new Agricultural Universities established after Independence were more successful and followed the new pattern of integrating teaching with research and extension on the lines of the land grant colleges of the USA. Postgraduate work became a distinctive feature of the agricultural universities which were co-ordinated by the Indian Agricultural Research Institute. The new agricultural universities are less conservative and tradition-bound than other universities and have already shown a capacity to change and innovate. Some of these universities have broadened their courses and range of subjects. They have taken up several research and training programmes directly related to agricultural production. Their contribution to the extension of the so-called 'Green Revolution' to the Indian situation has been considerable, and they have influenced the growth of agricultural institutions at the university level in other countries of Asia. In this sector India received valuable assistance from the Government and some specialized institutions of the USA.

The Jawaharlal Nehru University

Perhaps the most innovative event in Indian higher education in recent years was the establishment in 1968 of the Jawaharlal Nehru University in New Delhi. Intended to be a tribute to the work of a great national leader who was also a citizen of the world and a student of human affairs, the University named after him was conceived as an experiment in the pursuit of the ideals and tasks which distinguished Nehru's life. A grateful nation resolved through its Parliament that the Jawaharlal Nehru University should be new and unique in its concept, relevant and dynamic in its functioning and devoted to the pursuit of excellence in the creation of knowledge and culture, and the ordering of a society looking to the future rather than the past. The Nehru University is still in the early formative stage of planning and the building of foundations. In the process of this planning, some of the most distinguished scholars, scientists, educationists and management specialists have been involved, and some of its emerging features point to developments elsewhere in India in the years to come.

The Jawaharlal Nehru University is developing its programmes on the basis of the following broad principles.

1. With its nation-wide jurisdiction, the University should have a national character, broader than the regional concerns and horizons of other universities. While developing the institutions and centres on its campus at Delhi on a priority basis it should, right from the start, develop some programmes and institutions in other parts of the country also.

2. It should function mostly at the postgraduate and research level. Undergraduate work should be small in scale but of the highest level of excellence and undertaken only on exceptional and compelling considerations.

3. It should develop studies centred round major problems of national significance, especially those which were dear to Jawaharlal Nehru's heart, and emphasise an inter-disciplinary approach to their pursuit in preference to the traditional approach of discipline-oriented departments and programmes. These important problems could include: Secularism (including a comparative study of religion); National Integration (with emphasis on the study of all types of social tensions); the Problems of the Backward Classes; the problems of development of Traditional Societies (with special emphasis on planning for development), etc.

4. It should concentrate on the development of those disciplines and programmes which are not adequately developed at present and avoid repeating the set-up common to other universities.

5. It should strive to maintain the highest standards possible, especially as it will be free from the pressure of numbers and aim at producing the highest quality of trained manpower, particularly for the system of higher education itself.

To implement these principles in terms of concrete programmes, seven Working Groups in the area of Social Sciences have planned for the organization of the following Centres: (1) for Historical Studies; (2) for the Study of Social Systems; (3) for the Study of Political Development; (4)

for the Study of Regional Development; (5) for Educational Studies; (6) for Social Medicine and Community Health; and (7) for the Study of Interactions of Science and Society.

In addition, two other Centres for Disarmament Studies and for Studies in Diplomacy have been planned. In the area of Natural Sciences a great deal of thought has been given to the development of a school of Life Sciences and a school of Environmental Sciences. In the School of Life Sciences it is proposed to put special stress on Cell Biology, Developmental Biology and Neurobiology. The School of Environmental Sciences will require the joint participation of applied mathematicians, physicists, geophysicists, geochemists, life scientists, meteorologists, hydrologists and oceanographers. A School of Computer and Systems Sciences has also been visualized.

It was expected that some existing institutions in Delhi and elsewhere would be admitted to the complex of the Nehru University and developed in accordance with its new principles and approaches. The first institution to join the University in 1969 was the Institute of Russian Studies, set up a few years earlier. The concept of a university-level institution devoted to a major foreign language and combining with language studies special facilities for the translation of scientific and technical books and serving as an 'information centre' in this field, was a new development. Soon afterwards the Indian School of International Studies joined the University. It is hoped that all-India institutions in medicine, agriculture and engineering, located in Delhi would find ways of participation in the programmes of the new University.

Much work lies ahead and substantial resources of men and money will be needed to get the Jawaharlal Nehru University firmly established. One of its important roles will be to serve as a catalyst for educational development of parts of the country lagging glaringly behind in education, particularly in subjects of crucial importance for industrial and agricultural development. The new University is a daring concept of combining different disciplines and areas of study for undertaking concrete projects and programmes required for the service of man. In its pronounced concern with problems in the pursuit of peace, development and human rights, the Jawaharlal Nehru University could grow on the lines of an International University, the feasibility of which is under study by the appropriate organs of the United Nations.

To build a great design it is necessary to have clear priorities and a strong will for dedicated action. A wide gulf still exists between dream and reality. If the Indian scholars and specialists in younger and middle groups working in India and abroad could be attracted to the service of the new University and it could continue to receive influences from all quarters, it might grow into a great institution, capable of making a significant impact on the concept, content and structures of higher education in India, and perhaps in other developing countries also. One of its immediate tasks should be to develop co-operation among Indian universities which remain isolated from each other and not sufficiently receptive to ideas and influences from outside.

The Threat of Numbers

The ambitious plans to develop the Jawaharlal Nehru University as a great centre of excellence, unique in concept and function, and other schemes and projects to improve the quality of higher education, are threatened by the pressure of mounting enrolments. During 1960–9, the biggest enrolment increase in India was in the sector of higher education (128 per cent), and added nearly one million students. In 1969–70, the enrolment in the University of Calcutta alone was 210,000 with 190 affiliated colleges. The tempo of increase continues unabated. With 62 per cent of its population under 25 years of age, and the pattern continuing to alter in favour of the younger age groups, the explosion of numbers at all levels of education, and especially at the tertiary level, in the coming decades appears truly frightening. The educational expenditure as a percentage of national income increased from 2·4 in 1960–1 to 2·9 in 1968–9; but a major part of it goes to meet the costs of higher education, starving the crucial sectors of elementary and mass education. In recent years India has spent proportionately more on university education than perhaps any other country in the world. With the growing need of mass education for economic and social developments this high allocation of resources to higher education can no longer be sustained. At the same time, the limitation of enrolments through selective admissions is not practicable; the demand for higher education is insatiable and students from backward areas and classes, especially from the rural areas, must catch up with the more fortunate urban youth.

To meet this situation of expanding enrolments and shrinking resources, the Ministry of Education decided upon the introduction of correspondence and part-time courses. The innovation met with stubborn resistance from university vice-chancellors and academicians who feared the lowering of standards and, after some difficulty, a department of correspondence education was started at Delhi University on an experimental basis. The Department attracted large numbers and soon it swelled into a massive undertaking. The experiment revealed that the performance of a slightly older age group in correspondence and part-time education compared favourably with regular whole-time students, and it reduced considerably the pressure upon the university and affiliated colleges. The Delhi Institute of Correspondence Education led the way to a large expansion of similar facilities at other universities. The Education Commission recommended that opportunities for part-time education should be extended widely and should include courses in science and technology. The Commission estimated that by 1986 about a third of the total enrolment in higher education could be provided through a system of correspondence courses and evening colleges. The Resolution on National Policy on Education (24 July 1968) declared that education through part-time and correspondence courses should be given the same status as full-time education, 'Such facilities will smoothen transition from school to work, promote the cause of education and provide opportunities for the large number of people who have the desire to educate themselves further but cannot do so on a full-time basis.' The new system has justified itself and is expected to expand rapidly.

More recently a plan to start a University of the Air, based largely upon the educational programmes of the All-India Radio and the new medium of television has been evolved in consultation with specialists from Britain and USA. The use of broadcasting and television for strengthening education at all levels is now fully accepted and efforts to extend facilities are being made. To develop the new educational technologies and programmes the involvement and participation of educationists should be greater than has been the case so far.

Higher Technical Education

In conclusion, a reference must be made to a phenomenal expansion of technical education at university level, and the establishment of new institutions and programmes of study and training in this important field. By Independence in 1947, a total of 17 engineering colleges with 5,348 students had been established. By 1964–5, a total of 133 such colleges were teaching 78,114 students, of which 1,719 were at the postgraduate and research levels. In 1967–8, enrolments in engineering and technology had reached 104,266, an increase of almost 400 per cent over the 1956–7 enrolment of 21,237.

In 1945 the Federal Government appointed the Sarkar Committee to consider whether India should have several regional technical institutions or one central all-India technological institution with affiliated colleges. The Sarkar Committee recommended that at least four regional institutions should be established – one each in the North, East, South and West. In 1950 the first regional technological institution, the Indian Institute of Technology at Kharagpur, was founded; and in 1956 Parliament declared it a degree-granting institution 'of national importance'. Soon afterwards came the Indian Institutes of Technology at Bombay in 1958, at Kanpur and at Madras in 1959, and at Delhi in 1961. All five Institutes were incorporated as institutions 'of national importance' under the Institutes of Technology Act of 1961.

Each Institute is expected to provide residence and courses of study for 1,600 undergraduate and 400 postgraduate and research students. The education offered is not only theoretical but practical, because Indian industry does not provide practical training programmes such as are given by industries in the United States and Britain. As the Institutes, working in close collaboration with industry, develop engineering and technical courses based on the most modern technologies, they are helping to lay the basis for an industrial economy. Each of the five Institutes receives some international aid: the one at Bombay from the Soviet Union, the one at Kanpur from the United States, the one at Kharagpur from several international agencies, the one at Madras from West Germany, and the one at Delhi from Britain.

The Institutes are set apart from the typical Indian university by the following common features.

1. A unitary form of organization, which allows for fast changes of curriculum and methods.
2. Freedom to experiment and change.
3. Aid from foreign countries and international agencies.
4. A board of governors and a director.
5. Conferences of all five directors several times a year on each other's campuses.
6. The IIT Council, set up by the Institutes of Technology Act of 1961, which approves admission standards, budgets, 5-year development plans, scales of pay, various conditions of service, and common policies concerning degrees, duration of courses, fees, scholarships, and other matters of common interest.

Enrolment at all the Institutes in 1965–6 was almost 10 per cent of the total engineering and technology enrolment (85,555) for the same year.

Although not patterned after the Indian Institutes of Technology, the Indian Institute of Science (in Bangalore) was designated after Independence by the Federal Government for major development grants for advanced study and research in technology. In 1963 this institute taught over 600 postgraduate students, more than a third of the total postgraduate and research enrolment in the country. A two-year postgraduate course leading to the master's degree, recommended for various technical fields by a special Committee on Postgraduate Engineering Education and Research, has been introduced in 10 universities.

India's experience clearly proves the axiom that the development of technical education should be correlated to industrial and economic growth. In 1968 it was estimated that some 11,000 engineers and some 46,000 technical diploma holders were unemployed. This experience also showed that in a developing country, the planning of technical manpower is not a foolproof process and that technical manpower planning needs continuous review and correction at the appropriate time. The present emphasis in technical education has shifted from quantitative expansion (which resulted in the surplus of trained manpower) to qualitative enhancement.

The rapid development of higher education in India, briefly and selectively described above, has undoubtedly resulted in many innovations and some qualitative improvement. The paucity of financial resources and the poverty of management continue to be the main obstacles to the kind and level of transformation required by the challenges of the emerging future. In spite of these difficulties Indian universities have reared talent which has often blossomed in the more congenial academic climate of foreign universities, trained high level personnel which has not been used effectively at home, and offered facilities to classes of population who were denied equal opportunities in the past. Educated unemployment looms as a great social danger, but for this the educationist is only marginally responsible. Despite the lowest per capita expenditure on education in India, educational achievements have surpassed the performance of the economy and the effectiveness of planning and management.

12

Hiroshima University in Evolution: The Question of Autonomy

Michiya Shimbori

The Peculiarities of Japanese Universities

Superficially, Japanese universities have a structure quite similar to their counterparts in western countries: they have the same faculties, divisions and departments, the same type of staff hierarchy with professors, associate professors and lecturers or instructors, and a legally established institutional autonomy similar to that of western universities. Competent Japanese professors are as superior in ability and achievement as their western colleagues. Foreign observers therefore who are in touch with the formal structure of Japanese universities and their distinguished scholars, who are full members of the international academic community, may conclude that Japanese universities have little peculiar about them, and that if they have their problems, these must be of the sort common in western universities.

In fact, Japanese universities were founded in order to import and assimilate the sciences and technologies of the then advanced western nations, and to train the modern bureaucrats, after Japan opened her shores to the world a hundred years ago. They were organized on the model of the western universities. Japan has now 850 universities, 470 of which are junior colleges, with 90,000 full-time teachers, 15,000 of whom are in junior colleges, and 1,620,000 students, of whom 26,000 and 40,000 are in junior colleges and in graduate schools respectively. Naïve persons may think that this wonderful expansion of higher education is responsible for the contemporary economic development of Japan and shows the high level of her education and culture. A quarter of the male and a fifth of the female population of college age in Japan are in fact enrolled in universities and colleges. But those who are a little sceptical may think that there cannot be so many universities in the western sense. Indeed those who have studied Japanese universities, or who have frequented a Japanese university even for a year, are ready to admit that Japanese universities are different from western ones to a considerable extent. Then what are the differences? At least these must be mentioned:

1. *Institutional uniformity* Japanese word for university is *daigaku*, and that for junior college is *tanki-daigaku* (short-term *daigaku*). So the latter are included in a broad category of universities. According to the School Act, Japanese universities must 'aim to teach broad knowledge extensively, to teach and research professional scholarship intensively, and to develop intellectual, moral and applied abilities, as academic centres'. All institutions which are accredited by the Committee on University Accreditation are entitled to call themselves universities. Universities must put equal emphasis upon general education, professional education and research; no university may lay special stress upon any one of these three functions. The period of residence is determined formally, *viz.* two years for junior college students, four years for undergraduates, two years for candidates for masterships, and three years for candidates for doctorates; every student is required to obtain the same number of credits everywhere in the nation. Teachers of national universities are paid upon a scale common to all. The budget of every university is predetermined by the national standard per student and teacher.

2. *Paternalism* Many professors, especially of the humanities and social sciences, do not appear in their office except when they have to take a class. The average teaching load per week is eight or ten hours; in the remaining hours they can do anything and be anywhere they like. One credit is composed of one-hour of class-teaching for 15 weeks in one term (half year), but few teachers fulfil this duty completely. Tenure is afforded to quite young teachers, and they are promoted automatically in a seniority system irrespective of ability and effort. Accordingly among teachers the climate of severe academic competition is lacking in the individual campus as well as in the national academic community. This is also the case with students. When a professor teaches too many students, as in private universities and in the lower division responsible for general education, he knows too little about them to assess them as persons. But students are generally given quite generous marks. Their attendance at classes is scarcely checked; nor are they allotted home-study. Idle students who have hardly attended classes can expect to get credit if they pass the term examination, nay if they merely present the answer paper. Even when they do not get any credit, they can keep their status as students for eight years if they pay their annual tuition fee, which is surprisingly small, i.e. little more than $30 US in the national university, which entitles them to attend any class. Whenever a university punishes or dismisses a problem student, except in a case of defaulter who is dismissed automatically, a revolt against the punishment occurs, so that every university is extremely reluctant to take this step. In these matters there is a kind of paternalism among teachers as well as students. There is in fact little severity and competition in a Japanese university generally, except

for those who are sincerely committed to research and learning. The general climate is one which fosters professors who are concerned with money-making activities or with campus politics, and students who devote themselves to recreation, sports, dating or political activism.

3. *Isolationism or exclusivism* This too can be observed everywhere. Japanese universities are characterized by little internationalism. The majority of teachers are Japanese nationals, with the exception of a few foreign language teachers. Even Japanese who are graduates of foreign universities are seldom employed as teachers; Japanese professors are widely known for their poor linguistic ability; most of them live in an academic community composed only of Japanese scholars: they publish usually only in Japanese. Surprisingly few foreign students study in Japan. Thus Japanese universities are in a state of isolation. Even domestically each institution is isolated from others. Major universities employ their own graduates only. Once employed by a given university, a member of staff will work there for his whole career: there is little transfer either of staff or students between universities. So that in the name of academic autonomy, a university is inclined to be isolated from and independent of outer society. Although private universities have a board of trustees who are its financial sponsors and are representative alumni, it is out of the question for national universities to be administered by layman trustees. Officially at least, the government and industries are looked upon as the great potential threats to university autonomy and freedom. Few universities are interested in extension work and refresher courses. Even within the campus, the component parts exclude one another; the autonomy or self-administration of university means substantially that of each faculty; when there is a conflict of interest or opinion among faculties, even the president can do almost nothing in making the final decision. Likewise departments and chairs are independent of each other within a particular faculty; in a chair there is an atmosphere combining paternalism and feudalism, with a full professor who has the greatest power at the top and undergraduate students at the bottom in a seniority hierarchy.

The extent to which everything said above is true differs from university to university. But Japanese university organization is clearly anachronistic in considerable measure. If, for instance, the university is to be a research institution, paternalism and exclusivism are contradictions, since research ought to be universalistic in Parsons's sense, cosmopolitan in Merton's sense, and achievement-oriented. A university should be renamed a professional school if its functions of education and social service are separated from research.

Since professors and students who are capable of research of high quality must be limited in number, it is an illusion to expect it from the rank and file of all universities. Moreover it may be quite unreasonable and unrealistic to categorize in a uniform way all the institutions with their vast varieties of professors and students. The expanded universities of today are so heterogeneous in quality and social function that it is hard to treat them as homogeneous. The contemporary university can no longer exist without responding to social demands without, and social support in its training or research functions; it can no longer defend its traditional autonomy as an ivory tower.

In a contemporary society which has become international, the university alone cannot remain parochial. It is unreasonable for the university alone to be paternalistic in this age of domestic as well as international competition. Now that the interdisciplinary approach, new science methods and project research are making great progress, traditional sectionalism and departmentalism must lead to defeat in world academic competition. The contradictions peculiar to Japanese universities have become clearer and clearer. It was the demands of student radicals for university reform which escalated finally to a stage of destroying the universities, that forced academics and society to become aware of these contradictions. Stimulated by them, many universities reluctantly began to reform themselves.

Hiroshima University as a Case Study

After the defeat of the Second World War, attempts were made to reform the Japanese system of higher education thoroughly, and there appeared new universities, called *shin-sei daigaku* (universities of new system). Hiroshima is typical of them and has directly suffered from many difficulties which accompany, and must be tackled by, any thorough reform. Before the war, Japan had 48 higher institutions with a title of *daigaku*, 19 of which were national, i.e. founded and financed by the central government. Along with them there were many other higher institutions: *koto-gakko*, high schools, with the function of preparatory education, chiefly liberal, for university; *semmon-gakko*, advanced professional schools, such as technical, commercial, agricultural colleges, which trained professionals of middle rank; *shihan-gakko*, normal schools, to train elementary teachers; *koto shihan-gakko*, higher normal schools, to train secondary teachers. In the pre-war educational system, a small proportion of those who finished six years of compulsory elementary education went on for five years to secondary schools, middle schools and vocational schools. The majority of high school graduates and a few from other higher schools went on to universities for three years. While before the war there were higher institutions of different social functions, scholastic standards, characters, etc., after the war all of them were named *daigaku* on a principle of equal and widely-open opportunities for higher education and became uniform and homogeneous legally and formally.

It was the national institutions which were reformed to the extreme extent. All national higher institutions within every prefecture were integrated into one national *daigaku*. Each of them became a faculty of a newly-born university: a technical college became a faculty of engineering, a normal school a faculty of education, etc. The aim of the new university was to train cultivated citizens with the broad, general and critical views in various faculties, rather than to train professionals with only the narrow, special and uncritical perspectives in a one-faculty school.

This reform of integrating varieties of higher institutions meant that a new university was composed of faculties of different levels and characters and that it was extremely difficult to attain its unity as a whole. Not only was there inter-faculty conflict of interests and prestige, but often component faculties were located far from each other. Hiroshima was typically faced with these difficulties. The core of the new Hiroshima University was the Hiroshima University of Arts and Science of the old system, which had been one of the two highest training centres of educational leaders as well as researchers at the national level. Under it was Hiroshima Higher Normal School, which functioned as a preparatory school for the former and at the same time as the highest training college of secondary teachers. These two became Faculties of Arts, of Science, and of Education. Having such a tradition, the New Hiroshima University is national and academic in these faculties. They are of the same quality as the other old universities. Another faculty which is an offspring of an old university is the School of Medicine. It had been the Hiroshima Medical University. Together with these old universities, Hiroshima High School, as a preparatory school for old national Imperial Universities like Tokyo and Kyoto, had stressed liberal and general education, the Hiroshima College of Advanced Technology, which had served regionally by its professional and terminal education, and the Hiroshima Normal School, which had trained elementary teachers in the prefecture, were incorporated into the new University as faculties of general education, of engineering, and as a branch of faculty of education respectively, while faculties of fishery and husbandry, of government and economics were newly added. Accordingly the new Hiroshima University has faculties which developed from old universities, from old professional colleges, from a liberal arts college, in terms of level, which were academic, professional or liberal in terms of curricula, and which were national, regional or local in terms of service or recruitment. It was composed of very varied faculties, so that it was difficult to integrate it into a true unity.

Second, as mentioned before, since Hiroshima University has a long tradition as a national centre of educational research and training, it has been more deeply interested in Education as a subject than other universities, and has been distinguished in research in this field. Not only in the

Faculty of Education, but also in Faculties of Humanities, Science, and Liberal Arts there are many teachers who graduated in the old Hiroshima University of Arts and Science, and are interested in Education. Of five presidents after the war two were distinguished educationists and one was a former Minister of Education. Such an education-centred character cannot be observed in other institutions, and it has been deeply concerned with university reform. Among many other universities there are only a few who study university education; Hiroshima is one of a very few having research workers in this field.

Thirdly, Hiroshima University became a centre of the most radical student movements. The relation between university reform and student unrest is an interesting subject for research. All the institutions from which the present Hiroshima University developed had before the war only several hundred students and an academic atmosphere. Hiroshima University of Arts and Science, as distinct from other multi-faculty Imperial Universities like Tokyo, had no faculties such as business or engineering which had a vast body of rich students and alumni. Clearly the new University was forced to overcome great material hardships in the city of Hiroshima, destroyed absolutely by the A-Bomb. Both teachers and students felt that the reconstruction of their campus should depend on *esprit de corps*. When students were taught in ex-barracks without even a windowpane, calmness prevailed in this University. When, however, it became more fully equipped on a more consolidated campus, it became a centre of radicalism. In 1969, the campus was blockaded by radicals for several months, and the six-storey main administration building occupied by them had to be recovered finally by armed police. This battle was as fierce as at the Yasuda Hall of the University of Tokyo at the beginning of the year. While Hiroshima University had tried to reform and improve itself before radical destructive movements occurred, a revolt against the University could not be prevented.

A reformed system or improved facilities may be accompanied by student radicalism. True, a student revolt makes the university often aware of the necessity of further reform, but it often prevents it from putting new plans into practice. Student radicals point out the defects of the university and where the blame lies. Teachers and administrators become conscious of the defects and propose additional plans for reform; but then students refuse to talk with the university, because they now assume that discussion, negotiation, compromise and communication with it means the surrender to, and incorporation into, the established authority. Looking upon the university as a power structure and as an agency for preserving the conventional power of the whole society, they resist every reform the university proposes. In a big university where the final decision is made independently by individual faculties, it is hard for the university as a unit to attain a consensus. It is harder still for various groups of students, such as the New Lefts who refuse all decisions made by the university, the orthodox Communists who insist upon participation in all fields of administration, and general students who are apathetic, to do so. Often bloody struggles take place among various factions of radicals. The 'good old days' of Hiroshima University when there were few radicalisms, could anticipate relatively more reforms, while the widely recognized necessity of further reforms, with more plans proposed for carrying them out, has not been followed by corresponding action in these days when there are more student movements.

This tendency can be observed in all other universities. While Hiroshima and, say, the University of Tokyo, Tokyo University of Education and Tokyo Institute of Technology, have made more reform plans than other national universities, few have been put into practice. It may lead to a feeling among teachers that any effort to reform means a fruitless waste of time and energy. It follows that thorough university reform can be enforced only 'from above' by the government. But before the war the state controlled universities so much and so often that there is strong antipathy, distrust and allergy toward the state, and reform initiated by it is always resisted both by universities and students. Accordingly, existing universities are hardly reformed enough. Many think it most realistic to stimulate the existing universities to reform themselves by establishing new ones to compete with them. In this way the government is trying to promote a new university in the suburbs of Tokyo, an Open University, a United Nations University, etc. Of the existing universities, private institutions can be reformed of their own accord to a greater extent than national ones whose range of reform is restricted by law and budget requirements.

Ongoing Reform of Hiroshima University

Hiroshima University shows typically many difficulties which a university must tackle in a period of great and rapid change.

In size it has greatly expanded. In 1959, when the new university was almost completed, there were 909 teachers and 861 clerical staff, while in 1970 there are 1,482 teachers and 1,411 clerical staff. In contrast to 1959 when the capacity for new undergraduate and for graduate students was 1,400 and 197 respectively, in 1970 the numbers are 2,010 and 457. Now 8,281 undergraduate and 754 graduate students are enrolled. In terms of student-teacher ratio, undergraduate education has remained almost unchanged while the graduate one has greatly deteriorated during this period. Japanese universities have no professors exclusively responsible for graduate education, so that when graduate schools are attached the teaching staff is not expanded to correspond with the heavier teaching load. Every

university, however, tries to acquire a graduate school for increased prestige and to add to its research funds.

Another change in structure is the geographical consolidation of divisions. As seen earlier the institutions from which the new university was
composed had been independent and small. Since one of the leading
principles for post-war universities was to train students in broad and
general culture in an academic community composed of different majors,
the aim was to consolidate the institutions on the same campus. The central administration office was placed on the small site of the former Hiroshima University of Arts and Science and Higher Normal School, to which
the Faculties of General Education, of Government and Economics were
moved in 1961. As the Faculty of General Education is responsible for the
lower division, namely freshmen and sophomores, half of all undergraduate students are enrolled in it. Thus the small site is grossly overpopulated.
A survey in 1967 showed that on this central campus of 114,655 square
metres there were 5,118 students; in other words only 22·4 square metres
were allotted per student, one of the worst ratios in the country; the space
is utilized to the fullest extent with buildings, few trees and open spaces
being left.

It is the faculty of General Education that suffers most from these conditions. It is responsible for the general education of students who have
not received specialized education and it has no graduate school, so that
there does not exist a close tie based upon academic majors between
teachers and students, with a much poorer research fund and heavier
teaching load. For example the statistics for 1969 students/teacher ratio is
26·5 : 1 in the Faculty of General Education in contrast to 8·1 : 1 in other
faculties. Of the general education curricula, students complain saying
that they are nothing but a repetition of upper secondary education, that
they are too specialized, or that they are taught in an impersonal and
passive way. Students, who have passed the severe entrance examination,
find disillusionment in their dreamed university.

In order to solve these difficulties and dissatisfactions, the Faculty of
General Education has made many efforts. The main measures are:
guidance and orientation offered to the new entrants; tutorials, in which
one teacher is responsible for the guidance of a group of ten or twenty
students; counselling; a comprehensive or problem course, in which
several teachers of different disciplines give a lecture one by one on a
common theme, such as 'The State and Human Rights', 'Problems of
Post-war Democracy', 'Social Organization', 'Human Nature', 'The
Modernization of Japan' etc.; a general education seminar, which is different from seminars in upper division in that a teacher trains a small group
of students of different majors by means of discussion and writing; a
special class, which trains speaking and writing of foreign languages and

literary appreciation; a language laboratory, etc. Compared with these, convention ruled in other faculties in the upper division, with little effort for reform, before radical student movements.

The post-war change was remarkable, though further evolution is still necessary. As compared with the professionalism, elitism and nationalism of pre-war higher education, the new universities were based upon the idea of giving the widest opportunity to the general mass of the people so as to train a cultured and critical citizenship. Each of around fifty prefectures has a national multi-faculty university, which opens its door to all the graduates from upper secondary schools. Tuition fees are low, more stress is put on general rather than professional education, and academic autonomy is secured. As a result, university education has been rapidly expanded. Apart, however, from various transitional conflicts and confusions necessary in all changes, many essential dilemmas have appeared, such as:

1. The statistical distribution of ability indicates the incompatibility of quantitative expansion of human resources and a maintenance of their quality. This contradiction becomes clearer especially when a university is oriented to research.

2. Quantitative expansion and integration of different kinds of higher institutions are accompanied by an extreme variety of teachers and students. This may add to broad perspectives but makes for a weakened sense of unity and community.

3. Differentiation and specialization within the sciences tends to result in sectionalism and a fragmented education.

4. There are many new trends in science, e.g. towards 'big' science, the use of machines such as computers, which encourage bureaucracy in administration. Often there is research which cannot be managed by one single university, however much it is expanded, but needs help from without the university. If we take into consideration the important part played by science and technology in the contemporary world, the university of today cannot remain aloof from society.

5. While education requires personal relation and a collegiate principle, the bureaucracy natural in the large university tends to impersonality and formality.

6. As a university becomes open to social expectancy, serving and depending upon the society, it tends to be more manipulated and controlled by it – and especially local rather than cosmopolitan society.

7. Universities, having lost their individuality, tend to be too uniform, subject to evaluating themselves on the single scale, all seeking to imitate the very top in prestige hierarchy.

8. Into a university which is open to mass influences, contemporary fashions of society will enter. The university now ceases to be objective,

neutral and critical, and becomes involved in social, especially political, movements. The ideological oppositions within outer society appear on the campus itself. The university ceases to be a place of ideological tolerance and coexistence.

Since 1967 Hiroshima University as a whole has been aware of the importance of further reform and worked upon its plans. That year saw the rapid escalation of student unrest all over the country. Student radicalism in Hiroshima University was led by a most militant faction, and nearly 30 were arrested in these affairs. The government suspended the provision of scholarships to the arrested. Students protested to the University, which had recognized this stoppage, by hunger-strike and by so-called collective bargaining with the President, who was held captive for a whole day and finally carried to hospital. He never appeared on the campus thereafter. In place of the old president, a young and active professor was elected in April, 1969. At once he began to take the reform problem up, to communicate with many teachers and students. In July he recovered the campus occupied by the uncompromising activists by means of armed police. Since the end of that year the nationwide storm of student radicalism has been calmer, and there were few troubles in 1970. Hiroshima like other universities has regained calmness. Ordinary students, aware of the fruitlessness of radicalism, have not supported it morally and physically. Some teachers who feel easy in this apparent peace seem to lose the motivation to reform, returning to their previous authoritarianism and conventionalism. After all, a student movement in one university is a part of the national one, and like epidemics and fashions it disappears soon without any relation to reform – so many teachers think. This may be true, but the questions the movement raised are still fundamental questions to the university and common students and even teachers remain discontented with the status quo.

But Hiroshima nevertheless has made great efforts to assess the problems and to diagnose the further reforms necessary. In May 1970, the Preparatory Committee on the Hiroshima University Problems submitted a report which advised the President to organize a Committee on University Reform. In July it published a report: *Proposals for the Reform of Hiroshima University*, and invited all members to react to it. This sophisticated Report, in recognizing and analyzing the reality that changes in science and society have led to the making of the university into a 'knowledge factory' or 'education factory', insisted that instead of adapting passively to this state of affairs, we should construct a new philosophy of higher education. It defined the reform as a continuing process in which reformable problems should be tackled one by one constantly in the light of the highest ideal, and in which a newer university should be constructed 'from within' through discussion and criticism among all its members.

Many fundamental reforms were proposed, like autonomy for all members instead of for faculty only, university extension, financial autonomy, the federation of many universities, internationalization, a separation between research institute and office, the abolition of the traditional entrance examination, the reform of curricula, especially in general education, the inauguration of a university court, a new system of vice-presidents, the abolishment of tenure, and periodical assessment of achievement of teachers.

A total of 2,500 people, composed of 54 per cent teachers, 48 per cent clerical staff and 16 per cent students, expressed their opinions upon the Report, in consideration of which the Committee published in September 1970 'A Basic Way to Reform Research and Education'. Nine *ad hoc* committees were established with a hundred members in all, and a Liaison Committee was formed between faculty committees and central committees. Each worked out and published reform plans, among which the feasible were to be put into practice upon approval of the Academic Council. Since Hiroshima University is too small in area to function well, another *ad hoc* committee was organized to obtain and plan a new large campus. The main reforms already instituted include:

1. The bi-monthly *Campus News* published by the Committee on Public Relations to help overcome the lack of communication on the campus since June, 1969.

2. The Institute for University Problems was organized in August, 1970 with a staff of nine, expected to develop into a larger Centre of Higher Education. At present it collects the data, provides information and studies the reforms accomplished abroad.

3. University Extension was initiated in the summer of 1970. Three courses on 'Environmental Pollution and Human Life', 'Computers' and 'Youth Problems' were offered, each of 30 hours, and attended by a total of 300 citizens.

4. The Office of Students was reorganized. In 1969 a professor was appointed the Dean of Students and to improve service to students. In 1970 a Centre for Health was established in charge of health examination, mental hygiene, counselling, etc. for students and teachers by specialists in medicine, psychiatry and psychology.

5. Curricula were reformed, especially in the Faculty of General Education, where so-called wedge-shaped curricula were introduced in 1969. While formerly freshmen and early sophomores were not permitted to take specialized subjects relevant to their major, now they can take some of them. Correspondingly, juniors and seniors can take general education, which before was open only to the lower division. Other faculties have broadened their range of electives and increased the number of small-scale seminars they offer.

6. Facilities were improved and established such as the Computer Centre, University Ground, Gymnasium etc.

7. Many researches on university problems have been done by independent groups of young assistants and graduate students, as well as surveys and plan-making by official committees.

Concluding Observations

There are two kinds of reform in Japanese universities, reform on a nation-wide scale, forced as it were 'from outside', and spontaneous reform in each university 'from within'. Change from the pre-war system to the post-war one is an example of the former, while reform achieved or now being done in Hiroshima represents the latter. For national universities there is relatively little scope for their own reform, restricted by law and money. Thus reform at national level has been seriously considered by the Central Advisory Council for Education, which is presided over by a former Minister of Education and former President of Hiroshima University. Most problems and defects in contemporary higher education are recognized both by the government and the Council and by the universities themselves. But once the government proposes a reform plan to solve problems, however reasonable it may be objectively, the universities refuse to accept it, simply because it is proposed by the state, from above and from outside. They consider it incompatible with academic autonomy to agree to it. Between the state and universities there is a vast psychological distance. This lack of mutual trust, together with the lack of students' unity, is responsible for the incomplete reform.

The same situation can be seen within an individual university. Egoism and insistence on autonomy rules an individual teacher, a department and a faculty. They refuse to accept a reform plan made above, say in the central administration, if it contradicts with their own interest. There are always a few teachers in revolt, who make the consensus difficult. On the other hand, ordinary teachers tend to leave the reform to official committees or administrators, and tend to neglect daily reforms they can effect themselves immediately.

REFERENCES

Those readers who want to know more of the background details of Japanese universities are recommended to consult:

P. G. Altbach, Japanese Students and Japanese Politics, *Comparative Education Review*, vol. 7, no. 2, Oct. 1963.

J. E. Blewett (ed.), *Higher Education in Post War Japan: The Ministry of Education's 1964 White Paper*, 1965 (Tokyo: Monumenta Nipponica Monograph, no. 22, 1965).

B. B. Burn, Higher Education in Japan, in his *Higher Education in Nine Countries*, chap. 9 (Berkeley: Carnegie Foundation for the Advancement of Teaching, 1971).

R. J. Lifton, Japanese Youth – The Search for the New and the Pure, *American Scholar*, vol. 30, no. 3, summer 1961.

H. Passin, *Society and Education in Japan* (New York: Teachers College Press, 1965).

The most comprehensive bibliography in English is offered in:

P. G. Altbach, *A Select Bibliography on Students, Politics, and Higher Education*, revised edition (Cambridge, Mass.: Center for International Affairs, Harvard University, 1970).

P. G. Altbach, *Higher Education in Developing Countries: A Select Bibliography* (Cambridge, Mass.: Centre for International Affairs, Harvard University, 1970).

K.B.S. Bibliography for Education and Students' Problems in Japan, forthcoming, Tokyo: Kokusai Bunka Shinkokai.

H. Passin, *Japanese Education: A Bibliography of Materials in the English Language* (New York: Teachers College Press, 1970).

The present author has written the following articles in English, which may be of some use too:

The Fate of Postwar Educational Reform in Japan, *School Review*, vol. 68, no. 2, summer 1960.

Graduate Schools in Japan, *Education in Japan*, vol. 2, 1967, Hiroshima University Institute for International Education.

The Sociology of a Student Movement – A Japanese Case Study, *Daedalus*, winter 1968.

New Student Radicals, *Annals of the American Academy of Political and Social Science*, May, 1971.

Introduction to *K.B.S. Bibliography*, cited above, forthcoming.

There is much material directly relevant to the reform of Hiroshima University, all in Japanese, the most important of which are the following booklets:

Committee on University Reform, *Proposals for Reform of Hiroshima University*, 1969.

Preparatory Committee on the Hiroshoma University Problems, *Report to the President*, 1969.

Ad hoc Committee on Curricula, Committee on University Reform, *Basic Plan for Curriculum Reform*, 1970.

Ad hoc Committee on Curricula, *General Education*, 1970.

Ad hoc Committee on Curricula, *Professional Education, Basic Education, Foreign Language Education and Physical Education*, 1970.

Ad hoc Committee on Administration, *Provisionary Report*, 1970.

Committee on University Reform, *Memo on the Future of Research and Education*, 1970.

Committee on University Reform, *Basic Principles of Reform of Research and Education*, 1970.

Committee on Administration, *Reform of Administration*, 1970.

Central Library, *White Paper on Library*, 1970.

Faculty of General Education, *Plan for Reform of Faculty of General Education*, 1970.

Outline of Hiroshima University, annual.

Collection of Campus News, annual.

Catalogues of Faculties, annual.

Armed Police of Hiroshima Prefecture, *The Longest Day, how we recovered Hiroshima University* (Tokyo: Nikkan Rodo Tsushin-sha, 1970).

13

A Regional Institute of Higher Education and Development in South-East Asia

Toh Chin Chye

In 1959, Unesco and the IAU formed a Joint Steering Committee with the collaboration of the Ford Foundation to make a study on the 'Role of Institutions of Higher Education in the Development of Countries in South-East Asia'. These studies, which were begun in September 1961 and concluded in April 1965, were embodied in three volumes, being the Director's Report, Country Profiles, High Level Manpower and Language Policy. One of the recommendations made by the Committee was the establishment of an Institute of Higher Education and Development.

This proposal found support at the 4th General Conference of the IAU in 1965 held at Tokyo, and the Conference of Asian Ministers of Education and Ministers responsible for Economic Planning organized by Unesco at Bangkok in 1965. The establishment of the Institute was also endorsed at the 14th General Conference of Unesco in Paris in 1966. A Preparatory Commission was then established in 1968 to look into matters pertaining to the overall organization of the Institute. This Commission, through both formal and informal approaches, concluded that there was sufficient interest by South-East Asian Governments and their University Communities for the establishment of such a regional Institute (RIHED).

A Conference, hosted by the Singapore Government, was held in February 1969 to discuss the establishment of this Institute. Official and University representatives of Cambodia, Indonesia, Laos, Malaysia, Philippines, Singapore, Thailand, and the Republic of Vietnam were present. Representatives of ECAFE, FAO, ILO, Unesco, IAU, Association of Southeast Asian Institutions of Higher Learning, South-East Asian Ministers of Education Organization, the Asian Development Bank and the Ford Foundation were also there as observers.

The chief role foreseen for the Institute was to promote co-operation between universities and governments in the solution of problems affecting the region in general and in the study of factors affecting economic and social development of individual member countries in particular. The Conference established an interim committee of management to seek the views of governments, and to lay the groundwork for establishing the

Institute. To date seven countries have agreed to participate in the Institute, viz. Cambodia, Indonesia, Laos, Malaysia, Thailand, Vietnam and Singapore.

In April 1970, a meeting of government representatives of these countries and representatives of IAU, Unesco and the Ford Foundation was held to discuss the set up, administration and funding of the Institute. The Institute will be located in the campus of the University of Singapore. It will be an autonomous institution which will be administered by a Board of Governors comprising government representatives of participating countries and representatives from their university communities. The meeting also adopted the Articles and Memorandum of Association of the Institute and the budget of the Institute. The Institute will be funded by contributions from participating governments and the Ford Foundation has approved a grant of US $436,000 to support the Institute over a six-year period.

Post-war Development

It is noteworthy that with the exception of Thailand, the six member countries were once under colonial rule and their independence has been a post-war phenomenon. This historical background has led to the existence of different educational systems in the South-East Asian regions. These systems and curricula were modelled upon those of the colonial powers with little or no consideration of their relevance to the indigenous social environment. Euro-centricism was exemplified by tropical medicine being studied in temperate countries and oriental studies pursued in the west. With the coming of independence, nation-building became a preoccupation in South-East Asian countries and education is seen as an important vehicle for this effort. It was against this background that the Unesco/IAU studies on institutions of higher education in South-East Asia were carried out and the committee concluded that it was impossible to apply the same definition of higher education to all countries because of the wide variety of institutions to be found in the region. This difficulty was compounded by the lack of demographic and educational statistics in some countries while the uncertainty of the political situation in the region defeated any attempt at projections for the future.

Regional co-operation in South-East Asia has only recent beginnings because this was never encouraged during the period when the greater part of South-East Asia was under colonial domination. A South-East Asian Ministers of Education Organization (SEAMEO) has been set up with the objective of promoting regional co-operation in education. SEAMEO has established regional training centres for English language, educational innovation and technology, tropical medicine and public health, science and mathematics, tropical biology and agriculture, these

centres being distributed among member countries. The Regional Institute of Higher Education and Development (RIHED) however does not
propose to duplicate the activities of SEAMEO; it will essentially be an
institute which will conduct research into economic and social problems
of member countries especially those which are inter-regional in character.
In South-East Asia, most universities are dependent upon government
funds and the best of each nation's intellectuals can be found within these
universities. It is not unnatural that universities have come to be regarded
as potential forces in economic and social development but there is a gap
between aspiration and achievement. Historically this gap has been due
on the one hand to academics wanting to be left alone in the 'niches' that
they have created for themselves within the universities and, on the other
hand, because of academic distrust of the government lest their autonomy
be disturbed. Quid pro quo there is also a lack of confidence of government bureaucrats in the ability of academics to handle problems of real
life or in real time. So long as such a gap continues to persist, governments
in South-East Asia will never be able to mobilize their national intellectual
and social forces to solve the multifarious problems which developing
countries face. RIHED in attempting to bring together both government
and university representatives, so that they can apply their minds on
national and regional problems together, is making an attempt to break
through an artificial barrier of mistrust between bureaucrats and academics, between commissars and yogis. In this context, it is interesting to note
that in Thailand members of universities are regarded as civil servants and
in Indonesia they work part-time in government ministries, while in
Singapore, they are seconded as ambassadors or sit on boards of management of public statutory bodies. Whether South-East Asian universities
shape themselves after the model of western universities is unimportant;
what is important is whether developing countries in this region can
fruitfully use their indigenous intellectual resources towards social and
economic development.

As part of RIHED's functions, the institute will gather statistical data on
institutions of higher learning and organize seminars and workshops in
areas where universities can actively contribute towards national development. A major problem facing governments of South-East Asia is the
rapid increase in population in their countries where the natural growth
rate has varied from as low as 15 per thousand to as high as 35 per thous-
and. The total population of countries who are members of RIHED was
199·2 million in 1970. These demographic statistics conjure up immediately
major economic and social problems and with the birth rate in some
countries soaring at 40–50 per thousand, there are problems of meeting
demands for educational facilities and opportunities for employment. In
recent years, South-East Asian universities have shared with their western

counterparts campus unrest and student rioting, for reasons and causes which are indigenous and bear no similarity to the causes of unrest in western universities. While it is true that students have manned the barricades and gone rampaging in the streets for political reasons, it will be a failure on the part of governments not to understand that the major underlying deep-rooted causes for such mass frustration is a sense of hopelessness induced by an educational system in which young men and women are educated to a level for whom there are no prospects of employment. This is particularly true with regard to an over-supply of university graduates who are accustomed by their social environment to expect minimum standards of living for their university qualifications. Such an attitude towards higher education has become a concern of governments and the community has begun to question the choice between quantity universities and quality universities.

The need to utilize manpower for economic and social development has now been accepted as a top priority objective in governmental planning. If this is so, then logically no university should ever have been built without a study having been first made on manpower requirements and on the cost effectiveness of establishing a university. The calculations of the accountant and the analytical logic of the economist in developing manpower resource are more often than not overridden by emotive political pressures for the status which a university diploma is supposed to give and by the intuitive but fallacious belief that universities are the chickens that will lay the eggs of economic prosperity. The present despair of young men and women educated for an empty life has driven them to supporting extremist and insurgent movements. The current difficult position in which higher education finds itself in South and South-East Asia proves that countries with a low level of economic development have only a limited capacity to absorb university graduates, and setting up more universities which offer the traditional type of courses only helps to accentuate the problem of arousing expectations and frustrating them. The problem of unemployment is exacerbated by the migration of the rural unemployed to the towns and cities. A balance between the cities and the countryside needs to be achieved but the problem of rural unemployment on the South-East Asian mainland and archipelago is hard to resolve without first understanding rural attitudes and acquisition of quantitative data.

RIHED is just beginning to be organized but a full programme of possible problems has already been drawn up for its attention. Projects encompassing the region were:

1. To assess the impact on the region of the established as well as the rapidly increasing regional organizations and programme.

2. To reveal the implications of the high birth rate and increase in population of urbanization and of population mobility for South-East Asia.

3. To facilitate the sharing of faculties among the universities of the region.

4. To establish criteria in institutions of higher learning in order to facilitate interchange of students and faculties.

5. To study means of transforming the competitive economies found in South-East Asia into complementary ones.

6. To identify institutions in South-East Asia that can provide training which is most appropriate to the needs of South-East Asian countries.

7. To discover the best means of preventing the pollution of air, water and soil.

Problems which are more national in character include:

1. Learning how the technical and economic development projects and programmes have affected the social, physical, cultural and spiritual lives of the people who have been dislocated and whose customs, habits and living have changed.

2. Improving the selection of those who should attend institutions of higher education at public expense.

3. Securing co-operation between government and universities in formulating and implementing development plans.

4. Identifying the most appropriate criteria for the allocation of the limited resources of developing countries for mass education and for selective higher education.

5. Reviewing, on request, the university system of a country by a qualified team to recommend development plans that would meet the needs of the country and region yet avoid wasteful duplication. This could be done by assisting new universities to identify problems in development and build graduate programmes that will be most productive.

6. Finding what universities can do to assist in providing a team approach to total community development.

7. Investigating the correlation of the manpower needs with the production of the required trained personnel.

8. Exploring the relationship between the security of a country and its development by examining the changes in the attitude of people who have benefited from improvements in such fields as agriculture, health and roads.

9. Encouraging the development of interdisciplinary studies to focus on problems of development.

RIHED does not pretend to be able to solve the problems of South-East

Asia or succeed where the politicians have failed and the planners have miscalculated. The Institute can, however, through its connexions both with the universities and the governmental sectors, do research in depth for which the universities are admirably equipped and point out more realistic approaches towards social and economic development which the politician and civil servant find credible and can implement.

Section III

Some Significant Movements in Contemporary Universities of the West

Introduction

W. Roy Niblett

Most of the universities which figure in this section were creations of the recent past and are still in rapid development. Some of them were certainly established without much regard to their relations to other sectors of a national system of higher education: such relationships are still in the course of being worked out or are waiting to be worked out at some future time. The choice for a new university of a rural site, even if it is not far from a city of some size, offers challenges to it (cf. Orleans–la Source, Konstanz, Sapporo, Simon Fraser, Warwick). It cannot be said of most of the new universities created in England in the 1960s that their physical position made it easy for them to be part of a 'higher education neighbourhood unit'. That consideration at the time hardly entered into the reckoning.

But in one way or another all the universities of which accounts are given in this section were encouraged from the start to be experimental in outlook – even Navarre in Spain in the early 50s. It is significant that in a number (and this could be paralleled in many other new universities not covered here) the power of the Department, representing an established discipline, has acted as a conservative influence and sometimes a severe brake upon the development of the institution as a pioneer. The reasons for this include the effectiveness of the achievement that can result from studies made coherent by following recognized subject lines; the demand that university teachers should either 'publish or perish' *does* yield dividends in the form of research and thinking directed to useful and achievable social ends, though it may inhibit some kinds of reflectiveness that are also necessary. If new universities are to establish themselves in the eyes of their older companions they must toe at least some of the 'proper' lines. For one thing if members of their faculties do not so establish themselves they will not be able to move to other universities, and their best students may well be handicapped in getting places in postgraduate schools of study in older (and more orthodox) universities whose reputations are already made.

Included in the section is a chapter about Wisconsin-Green Bay, an institution with ideas of far reaching significance about a possible new shaping of an undergraduate curriculum; and Akademgorodok where in a fertilizing contiguity are some twenty institutes of postgraduate study. It may be that upon the degree of the contiguity the fertilizing power will more and more depend. Each points one of the ways forward; and both accounts have natural links with Section V of the book.

14

A British University Designed for the Future: Lancaster

Harold J. Perkin

The University of Lancaster was one of the nine New Universities founded in the United Kingdom in the 1960s. They were given freedom to a much larger extent than any other new British university institutions in modern times to experiment with what was taught, how it was taught and assessed, and with the institutional structure and the physical environment in which the teaching and research were carried on. When asked why the University Grants Committee set them up, Lord Murray, the Chairman at the critical period, replied, 'It was one-third numbers and two-thirds new ideas.' Among the new ideas current in the academic world at the time the most important fall under four headings. The first, in the words of Asa Briggs, one of the founding professors of the University of Sussex and now Vice-Chancellor, was to 'redraw the map of learning' so as to get away from the early and over-specialization which was, and is, the besetting sin of English education and to provide a wider, more rounded education better suited to the needs of modern society. The second was to experiment with methods of student assessment alternative to the traditional written examination. The third was to create a new institutional structure both to serve the ideal of a university as something more than a collection of specialized departments and to allow for closer and more fertile social relationships between all members, both staff and students, of the institution. The fourth was to seize the opportunity provided by virgin sites to create a whole new physical environment of learning, in which teachers and taught, scholars paid and unpaid, could pursue their avocations, and their pleasures too, in ideal conditions.

To these four headings we may add a fifth, not so consciously bruited perhaps, but thrust on the founders by the need for rapid growth and quick results: the opportunity for new approaches to planning which the expanding demand for student places and the greater certainty in the supply of the funds gave to the nine new universities as to no others in the country before them.

The University of Lancaster was the seventh of the nine, and the last of the English ones, to be scheduled by the UGC, in November 1962. Like the other New Universities, it took most of its early tone and character from its first Vice-Chancellor. Charles Carter was a young (42-year-old) business economist and a Quaker who had become a professor by the early age of 32, with all the concern for efficiency, moral austerity and getting things done which might be expected from such a combination. He and his first colleagues procured and converted an old furniture factory into a temporary all-purpose university building, and so were able to open the doors to students in 1964, twelve months ahead of schedule.

The Vice-Chancellor was chosen by and immediately joined the Academic Planning Committee, a small group of eminent academics headed by Sir Noel Hall, Principal of Brasenose College, Oxford, and appointed by the University Grants Committee. Their task was to design, build and staff a university for the future, which would not only avoid the more undesirable features of some existing universities but would positively aim to meet the needs and conditions of higher education in the highly complex and rapidly changing technological society of modern Britain.

The New Map of Learning

The new map of learning which the Vice-Chancellor, together with the Academic Planning Committee and the first dozen professors, drew up was not, perhaps, quite so ambitious as some of the others'. It eschewed, for example, the grouping of subjects into 'schools' pioneered by Sussex and followed by East Anglia, Essex and Ulster and to a lesser extent by Warwick. Nor did it contain, like Warwick and Stirling (at first), and, most notably, Keele, one or more common courses taken by all first-year students. It was, like that of York, a map based mainly on orthodox departments, teaching traditional subjects in the traditional specialized way.

Some of the departmental subjects were, indeed, new, and designed to fill gaps in the university's service to society and particularly to the business world, notably the first departments in the country of operational research and marketing, later joined by the first departments of systems engineering, financial control, and behaviour in organizations. A feature of several of these, especially operational research and systems engineering, was their close practical involvement in the world of business, through contract and consultancy work by the staff, research projects by their mainly postgraduate students, and the provision of short-term, post-experience courses for business managers and other executives. A large part of their recurrent income, 50 per cent in the case of operational research, came from research contracts. This dependence on private business was later to be questioned by left-wing students and by non-political academics disturbed by its implications for the image of the university, but without any evidence that it affected their integrity or standards. Meanwhile, this group of new departments together with economics was to grow into a formidable school of business and organizational studies.

There was also a new department of environmental studies (now environmental sciences), a scientific kind of geography embracing geology, palaeo-botany, meteorology and, more recently, lunar and planetary astronomy (an extension of the environment into hither space). The chair of religious studies, advertised in 1967 as open to candidates 'of any religion or none', represented a new departure, away from traditional theology and towards the comparative social and intellectual study of religion. And the chair of educational research represented a swing from the traditional training of graduate teachers within the university towards a primary concern with what happened in the schools themselves.

Apart from these, the departmental subjects were strictly orthodox. The choice was deliberate and largely unavoidable, within the limits of the national need as indicated by the UGC, based on student demand and the existing provision at other universities. Many projected developments, such as architecture, medicine, German and Italian studies, were discouraged by the UGC on the grounds that sufficient provision existed elsewhere. Engineering was allowed only after convincing the UGC that the course would be of a kind, directed to educating engineering scientists rather than training traditional engineers, not easily found elsewhere.

Other new or less orthodox subjects have developed within existing departments: strategic studies within politics, linguistics within English, the history of science within history, and East European studies with emphasis on Czech within Russian studies. Even orthodox subjects not encouraged by the UGC have developed by the same device, such as German as a minor course provided by French studies, while similar proposals are being discussed for area studies of the Middle East, Southern Africa and other regions.

There are also Directors of Music and Drama, and visiting Fellows in the Fine Arts (such as sculpture, painting and ceramics), but these are financed by appeal moneys, and were originally intended to provide service to the community (including non-members of the University) rather than formal teaching. Recently, however, 'breadth subjects' of the kind described below have begun in music and in basic design, which are going in the current reorganization of the BA degree to become 'free ninth units' fully comparable with other academic courses. An appeal is now being made for funds to support a Centre for the Visual Arts, which would embrace the existing Fellows in the Fine Arts and the part-time lecturer in the history of architecture as well as two new posts, and probably cater for postgraduate research.

If based, largely though not exclusively, on orthodox departmental subjects, however, the new map of learning differed considerably from those of most traditional universities in the route which the students were to take through it. The map equally eschewed the concept of the traditional honours school, in which the 'bright' students committed them-selves before entering the university to three years' exclusive study of a single subject, and that of the ordinary general degree, for which the 'less bright' pursued a hotch-potch of unrelated arts or science subjects at a lower level. Instead, every student admitted, with whatever main interest, was to take three different but preferably related subjects in the first-year Part I course. From these, subject to satisfactory progress, he could choose to 'major' in any one (or two or three in a combined major degree) in the second- and third-year Part II. In a single major Part II he would take six courses in the major subject and also two courses in one of his other first-year subjects at 'minor' level. And in both single and double (though not triple) major degree courses he would also take, normally in the second year, a 'breadth subject' designed to give him some acquaintance with modes of thought in a subject totally unrelated to his major and minor interests (e.g. the principles of a science for arts students or the history of western architecture for scientists). At the end of three years he would be awarded a classified honours degree or, if judged not to qualify for that, a pass degree, according to his performance in all nine courses of his second- and third-year Part II.

The aims of this integrated general honours course were, first, to delay the student's final choice of specialization until he could make it with full knowledge of what the subject meant at university level; secondly, to give him a chance to try out at least one subject he had not taken at school (e.g. a social science or a different natural science) without committing himself irrevocably to specializing in it; thirdly, to enable him to see, through the breadth subject, how minds quite unlike his own operated, with a view to understanding better the role of other specialists in his future work and life; fourthly, to give him at least the foundations of a specialization of his own, so that he would know how to work in depth, not only in that sub-ject but in others which he might be called on to take up in a rapidly changing world; and, finally, to make him a specialist with a difference, by providing him with a wider base in cognate and supporting subjects than was usual in the traditional honours degree.

Ideally, perhaps, it should have gone further, and made him both a cultivated man of humane and scientific education and – that *rara avis* so much in demand in a complex world in which seeing the whole wood and dealing with new and unknown trees are invaluable capacities – a true generalist able to specialize rapidly in anything. But three years is too short a programme in which to correct the over-specialization of the English secondary school system, and this was felt to be the most that could be done in the time.

Indeed, it was felt by some participant academics to be too much, and the breadth subject in particular was to become an early casualty. It will finally disappear in the current reorganization of the degree course when it will be replaced by a 'free ninth unit' in the second or third years chosen from the full range of Part II courses, subject only to technical or linguistic qualifications for certain subjects. Its demise is no doubt an educational loss, but it has to be admitted that it has few mourners in the University of Lancaster.

The current reorganization of the undergraduate course was the result of a groundswell of discontent with the original map of learning voiced most effectively by the professor of religious studies. Ninian Smart's criticism was directed not at the aims and the spirit of the founders' model, but at the rigidity with which it was operated. He argued that the major/ minor/breadth subject conception was based on a false assumption, namely that a 'subject' was synonymous with a department. His solution was to allow much greater flexibility to the student to choose courses from different departments provided they made up a coherent, educationally sound whole, and to the teachers from different departments to co-operate in constructing jointly-taught courses which might add up to a substantial portion of a degree programme. In principle his scheme has been accepted and will come into operation from 1973. Its one drawback is that it will make an already complicated timetable, which has to allow for hundreds of different combinations of subjects, still more complicated. But that, one supposes, is the price of educational reform.

New Modes of Assessment

A striking innovation at Lancaster, as at some other New Universities, is the part played in the assessment of students by continuous or course-work assessment. Coursework marks for essays, projects, laboratory work and the rest count for a specific percentage of the student's assessment in each Part of the BA degree and in the one-year MA and MSc degrees by examination and dissertation. The percentage differs from subject to sub-ject, generally from 20 per cent to 50 per cent, but in each course the coursework mark is amalgamated with the examination mark to form a consolidated mark which helps, along with the other courses in the spread of subjects, to determine the student's final classification. The aim is to give credit for qualities not easily measured in a short examination, such as originality and perseverance in the pursuit of knowledge, and to pro-vide alternative evidence of the student's ability, especially in those cases where illness or emotional stress make the examination an unreliable test. In these aims the system has been thoroughly satisfactory.

Methods of examination have so far been mainly orthodox, although a few departments such as operational research, systems engineering, finan-cial control, and English have experimented, especially at the postgradu-ate level, with open-book examinations, advance notice question papers, and examination projects written over a short period. These experiments are being actively discussed now throughout the University, and an expectation of wider change is in the air. Student radicals and some younger staff are in favour of abolishing examinations or at least the classification of degrees altogether, but no acceptable alternatives have been offered. In particular, no one has suggested any means of avoiding the most obvious consequences of an unexamined, unclassified degree, that it would become little more than a certificate of attendance, and would put much greater and more irresponsible power into the hands of the academics who write references for students. The examination, moderated by external examiners, gives the student a chance to prove his teachers wrong, and this is a human right which many think it is important to preserve.

A Structure for Growth and Participation

Lancaster, again like the other New Universities, was designed for rapid growth, to the now generally accepted 'minimum viable size' of 3,000 students within ten years. In fact, it reached that target in its seventh year: in 1970-1 there were 2,891 full-time students (2,440 undergraduates and 451 postgraduates), and the addition of part-time graduate students brought the number to 3,029. In 1971–2 it reached 3,193. The next quinquennium should take the number of full-time students to about 5,400 in 1977. The University believes that it could grow on its present site to about 10,000 by 1981. In view of the expected doubling of demand for student places during the 1970s[1] this would be a useful contribution to national needs. Moreover, like the other New Universities and unlike the older civics, Lancaster has the advantage of ample, cost-free building land, so that expansion there is cheaper than in the urban universities or polytechnics.

The University has been designed more than most to accommodate growth without the loss of cohesion and community spirit which so often accompanies it. This innovation does not inhere in its administrative and academic structure, which is largely traditional. The most innovatory feature of the University's initial structure was the revival in modern dress of the collegiate system. From the first the University was divided between a number of colleges, groupings of staff and students which cut across the academic structure of departments and boards of studies. The intention was that, as the university grew beyond the size in which everyone could know personally everyone else, every member of staff and every student should belong to a community smaller than the whole (with some 40–80 staff members and 300–600 students) which would provide a focus for loyalty, interest and social life separate from and additional to the academic divisions. In particular, members of staff would talk to and co-operate with others outside their own departments and make contact with students other than on an academic footing, while students would organize themselves for most purposes in smaller, face-to-face organizations than the traditional, university-wide students' union. In this way opportunities for personal relationships of a meaningful, constructive kind would arise naturally, while there would be much more chance for students to take part in organizing their own affairs and less danger that the unorganized student would be lost and neglected in the large impersonal mass.

In the first two years, when the university was housed in the converted furniture factory and the first two colleges were invisible ones with no separate buildings of their own, there was great resistance to the notion, especially from student leaders who preferred the idea of the one big union. As soon as separate buildings were provided on the permanent campus, however, loyalties to the colleges began to crystallize, and the balance to even out between them and the Student Representative Council (elected, apart from the officers, by the College Junior Common Rooms). This was reinforced when the colleges became residential for most of their students and some of the staff from 1968. Each college now has residence in the form of study-bedrooms and flats for a portion of its students and staff, and – a feature unique in British universities (with the possible exception of Essex) – a quarter-share of a study for every non-residential student. This last feature is thought by the UGC to be over-generous, and has been allowed so far only because Lancaster has been very economical of buildings and capital in other ways. In future colleges the provision of a study place for each non-residential student will no longer be possible – a sad loss to the cohesion and sense of community of the collegiate body.

One of the virtues claimed for the collegiate structure is that it is an effective antidote to student and, indeed, staff, unrest. Contacts between staff and students are closer, more continuous and less artificial than in unitary institutions. The now familiar system of personal, non-academic tutors to help and advise students on personal problems is on a college basis, and can build on the common membership and face-to-face social relationships of the small community. Students and staff join together in running the affairs of the college: students have representatives on the college Syndicate, the meeting of staff members, and staff in the Junior Common Room, the assembly of students, and both elect equal numbers of representatives to a College Management Committee (or equivalent body), which controls the day-to-day affairs of the community. Students also take a full share in the disciplinary committees of the College, and indeed adjudicate all minor offences in their own committee. Both students and younger members of staff therefore have a greater chance of being elected to positions of influence and of meeting and influencing their representatives, so that the energetic and reforming are less frustrated and the gap between them and their constituents is much smaller.

This theory of small-scale, cellular democracy is borne out in practice. Lancaster, along with the other two collegiate New Universities, York and Kent, has had much less student unrest than some other, non-collegiate institutions, and what there has been has been settled swiftly and amicably. How far this has been due to the collegiate structure and how far to luck and the skill in human relations of their Vice-Chancellors it is difficult to say. Good relations are not simply a matter of good will. Genuine, practical and far-reaching reforms have been negotiated in the constitution of the university. By far the most important of these has been the admission of student representatives to the governing bodies of the university. Lancaster, along with Sussex, has pioneered full student membership of Senate, Council and Court. In doing so, ways have had to be found round the Privy Council's insistence that students shall not be involved in decisions on 'reserved matters', including examinations and assessment, staff appointments and promotions, and personal matters affecting individual staff and students. New Statutes drawn up by a Statute Revision Committee on which junior staff and students were in a majority, which have granted student representatives full membership of Senate, Council and Court, subject to the delegation of 'reserved matters' to officially appointed committees, have been accepted by the Privy Council.

Students are not generally represented at staff departmental meetings, although a few departments like French Studies and Religious Studies admit them for 'unreserved' items, but they are represented in equal numbers with staff on the departmental Staff-Student Consultative Committees, which can discuss and advise on any academic matter, including curricula and assessment, other than the personal affairs of individuals. Senate has recently voted to admit students, one elected by the student members of each Consultative Committee, to the boards of studies.

Student representation in the governing bodies of the university has been extremely successful. It has not been without cost in academics' time and trouble, at more and longer meetings, and in patiently explaining to each new generation of student representatives the meaning of and reasons for every decision and, often, each piece of existing machinery. But it has undoubtedly repaid this investment, in better-informed and more acceptable decisions, and in a greater sense of involvement in a joint endeavour.

Though not completely envisaged when the university was founded, the structure and organization of the university, with its interrelated academic and non-academic systems of representation of all interests, is designed for growth as well as for participation. The cellular structure based on the colleges allows for expansion to almost any size without loss of the advantages of the small, face-to-face community. Meanwhile, the departments, which may either be tenants of the colleges like most of the non-laboratory subjects or housed in separate buildings like the laboratory sciences, can grow to a size which affords all the desirable economies of scale and wide coverage by specialist staff. Finally, the representative system allows for a process of democratic planning whereby all members are consulted about the major decisions affecting the university's future, as we shall see in the final section. Before that, however, we must look at the fourth area of innovation, the new physical environment of learning, which itself must be designed for growth and participation.

The Integrated Pedestrian Campus

Any university designed for the future must provide accommodation for all the traditional purposes of higher education – teaching, learning, research and spontaneous intellectual contact – in a civilized environment built to human scale, with some protection against the dangers, noise and pollution of modern motor traffic. The environment, moreover, must be complete in itself at every stage of development and yet capable of continuous and undisruptive growth. All the New Universities have tried to meet the conflicting demands of this imperative specification in their different ways with more or less ambitious plans for a new, purpose-built, physical environment on a virgin site, which we may call the integrated pedestrian campus.

Lancaster's version of this is one of the more intelligent and successful. It consists of a tightly grouped, urban complex of buildings strung along a 'pedestrian spine', or half-covered footway, opening out here and there into squares and open courts. The colleges, science buildings, great hall, concert rooms, sports hall and so on front on to the pedestrian way, but can also be entered from the rear from the parking areas. There are no orthodox car parks, but the fingers of access road pushing in between the buildings from the perimeter road have aprons of tarmac on each side on which cars can park at right angles to the traffic. Grouped around the central pedestrian square are shops and banks as well as the main administrative building, the library and one college, and underneath it an underpass large enough to take double-deck buses, from which passengers emerge up the stairways. Within the complex it is possible to walk under cover from one building to any other in a few minutes.

The linear plan, created by the architect, Gabriel Epstein, enables growth to occur with the least disturbance to ongoing activities. New colleges are added as they are needed, fronting on the spine; they will never need to be extended. In between them, the administration, library and science buildings front on the spine, but can be extended outwards between and behind the colleges. Within the colleges, rooms are fairly easily interchangeable between residence, students' studies, staff offices and teaching rooms, so that different 'mixes' can be achieved from year to year.

Student residence on this plan was meant to be in the college buildings, intermingled with staff, teaching and common rooms. This enabled the same common rooms, refectories and kitchens to be used for the residential and day-time populations. The Vice-Chancellor saw that this also provided an opportunity for further economies and a new source of capital, and commissioned Haydn Smith, the architect, to prepare a scheme for a new sort of student residence. It consisted of 'flats' of ten or eleven study-bedrooms grouped round a central kitchen and bathroom, built by ordinary house-building methods. The cost per student place was £725, compared with £1,450 for traditional halls of residence, and at this price it became possible to finance them by borrowing privately from banks and insurance companies at 8 per cent on a 30-year mortgage, repaid out of student rents and conference fees. The scheme aroused great interest in the UGC and the Vice-Chancellors' Committee and was followed by some other universities. Unfortunately, at the interest rates now prevailing the scheme is less viable, and is accordingly less popular.

Student residence as a whole is probably the least satisfactory of Lancaster's innovations. Many students and resident staff and their families complain of the isolation and claustrophobia of campus life, of the unreasonable noise and disturbance made by a small minority of residents, and of the unavoidable noise emanating from the great hall when dances and pop music concerts are held. Ironically, the main reason for siting the residences so near to the other buildings, the communal use of refectories, has dwindled with the trend, common to other universities, towards self-catering by students. If the planning were to be done over again the residences might with advantage be sited at or beyond the perimeter road, out of ear-shot but still within walking distance of the central area.

Nevertheless, the advantages of the integrated pedestrian campus outweigh the disadvantages. Whether they will do so when the university grows to 10,000 students or more, and becomes a small town abandoned at night almost entirely to the volatile and abrasive student age group, has yet to be seen.

A New Approach to Planning

All the New Universities had from the start to plan for the future at a pace and with resources denied to most of their predecessors. Their objective of rapid growth forced upon them the necessity to plan and to build the planning machinery into their organizational structure. In Sussex, for example, the Deputy Registrar became the Planning Officer and built up a team specifically to collate the necessary information and advise the Planning Committee and governing bodies of the university on the choice and cost of the alternative possibilities. In doing so they evolved a system of so-called logistical planning, which related the manpower required for teaching, administration, clerical and technical assistance, maintenance, catering and domestic service to a given future number of students of varying subject 'mix'. On the basis of this formula bids could be made to the UGC for a recurrent grant in particular years, and any variation in student numbers made by the UGC rapidly translated back into manpower and costs.

Although they have not given it a new name or, perhaps, pursued it so consciously, all the rest of the New Universities have had to adopt some such system of planning. At Lancaster the Vice-Chancellor is his own logistic planner and 'does his own sums', so that he is continuously aware of the current staffing ratios and future needs of every department. These are circulated to, and can be challenged by, all departments and the Student Representative Council. They become the basis of the plans formulated by the Development Committee, a small body elected not by the boards of studies (which would tend to perpetuate existing interests) but by the whole Senate to represent present and potential subject areas. It consists of the Vice-Chancellor *ex officio* plus one natural scientist, one technologist, one social scientist, and one student of the humanities. Since all academic developments affect planning and the provision of funds, its functions have recently been extended to include a general oversight of academic policy, including the scrutiny of proposals for new courses and schemes of study.

If there is one lesson to be drawn from the Lancaster system of planning, it is not the significance of statistical model building, important as that is, but the beneficial effects of a democratic planning process, in which every member of the university, whether staff or student, has an opportunity to initiate proposals and to comment on other proposals before they are finally determined. This right to suggest and to be consulted naturally arises from the structure for growth and participation described above. Any member of any body, from the Senate or the Student Federation down to the departmental meeting or college junior common room, can put forward a proposal which will eventually find its way to the Development Committee. That Committee, in the light of all the other proposals, the general policy of the Senate and the resources available, will report its reasoned recommendations, which will then be passed back for discussion by every body in the hierarchy. Finally, after further consideration and readjustment by the Committee, the report is adopted by Senate and approved by Council as the policy of the university.

It is, admittedly, a slow process, but it has the inestimable advantage of carrying the community with it and of eliciting the willing co-operation of the planned and planned for, and so saves time in the long run. The alternative, preferred by most management consultants, of avoiding 'committee government' and giving each 'manager' in the 'chain of command' a definite responsibility for planning decisions up to a certain cost in his own area of responsibility, has the spurious efficiency of authoritarianism, and works only as long as people are willing to obey orders without question. It is doubtful whether authoritarian line-management works even in industry, where in the absence of formal or informal alternative processes of consultation it rapidly degenerates into resentment and strife. The universities in general and Lancaster in particular have something to teach business and civil service about the 'higher efficiency' of government and planning by continuous consultation. In a world in which the supreme problem is how to reconcile the ever-increasing scale of social institutions with the need of the individual to find satisfaction and fulfilment, and in which the penalty for bad human relations is frustration and discontent which can rapidly bring the largest enterprise to a standstill, this is a valuable lesson indeed.

The test of any institution designed for the future is the future itself. Whether the particular innovations of Lancaster University, in the organization of the curriculum and methods of assessment, the collegiate structure and system of participation, the integrated pedestrian campus, and the logical and democratic planning process, will succeed and survive, only time will tell. But the most significant characteristic of the future is its uncertainty, and the most essential quality for meeting and coping with the unexpected is flexibility. Up to now the University has shown itself to be more sensitive to new demands and needs and more flexible in its responses to them than I for one, with a historian's knowledge of how quickly human institutions ossify, expected at the outset. If it can retain this sensitivity and flexibility up to and beyond its planning target of 10,000 students by 1981 it will indeed have earned the right to call itself a university designed for the future.

REFERENCE

1. See Department of Education and Science, *Planning Paper No. 2: Student Numbers in Higher Education in England and Wales,* and Scottish Education Department, *Student Numbers in Higher Education in Scotland* (HMSO, 1970).

15

An Innovative University in France— Orleans–La Source: A Stocktaking

Gerald Antoine

What – viewed in perspective – is involved in the publicity, at times kindly, sometimes maladroit, at other times malicious, given to the experience we have had at Orleans University? Two things: on the one hand, in the distribution of universities in the regions of France, a crucial element of decentralization and, more precisely, the establishment of a *Université de la Couronne* called into existence to relieve pressure on the cancer of the Parisian university, that enormous and ailing monstrosity. On the other hand, in the field of educational planning: the university complex of Orleans-La Source seen as a campus which puts itself forward as a model, drawing its own inspiration from the Anglo-Saxon example. Does not one often hear of the 'French Oxford' in full flower on the banks of the Loire?

Now, if we consider only these two aspects of our plans, their achievements at this moment of time must seem disappointing. Let us be honest, if only to be realistic: a few hundred 'Parisian' students, i.e. those who would normally complete their higher education in the capital, do indeed attend the University of Orleans. But what does that represent in relation to the numbers who remain faithful to the banks of the Seine? In this respect one can only say that, at least for the present, failure is almost complete.

As for the building of a Campus conceived as offering fresh air and peace in contrast to the human furnace of the Latin Quarter, this was greeted ten years ago as a great innovatory hope and was speedily copied in several places. But fashions change swiftly, whether in the length of skirts or in the shape of universities. Today such 'Campuses' are more or less the object of execration or at least of derision. I quote, as one of the more sympathetic comments, a recent article depicting in these terms the attitudes of our students 'isolation, solitude – this is what is felt by the residents of Orleans-La Source in their bucolic "zoo", with its ambitions of becoming a "French Oxford".'

The reader should not, therefore, expect any glorious song of praise from me. How is it possible to remain indifferent to the critical murmuring, at first faint and dispersed and later insistent and orchestrated which has been beating on our ears and our walls ever since the grand climacteric – the bitter spring of 1968? But it seems no more necessary for that reason that we should deny our convictions and our early plans than defend them with blind obstinacy. What I propose to do is to describe in simple and precise terms the plans which had been drawn up with care, indicating step by step the physical and psychological obstacles encountered. It is also a matter of drawing immediate lessons from experience and of defining the means of restoring to our enterprise the direction which I, for my part, have never ceased to wish to give it: a matter of means, but also one of unity of purpose, of inflexible determination, unbending enthusiasm in the face of scepticism from some and of sarcasm from others: a matter, above all, of cohesion among all those called to work together in the establishment of an enterprise by its nature complex at the same time as it is unitary.

A Policy for University Site Planning

From the beginning of the century the map of French universities has hardly altered. This is a disturbingly static situation if one considers the movements of population, particularly the continuously increasing movement from the provinces towards Paris – often of the most enterprising and of those most ambitious that their children should undertake the long, so-called 'higher' courses of education.

In these circumstances, there was no need to be a prophet to announce that unless action was taken in a quite revolutionary way, catastrophe would speedily be upon us. All that was necessary was a little courage to confront age-old habits of thought and the Parisian privileges that, over the years, had gathered strength. It is in no sense of vanity that I repeat a statement I made in 1962 on World Town Planning Day: 'The situation of the University in Paris today is an affront to good sense. The Sorbonne and its annexes give an impression of functioning only because one student in two does not attend lectures and because eight or nine in ten abstain from attending the laboratories and libraries. That is a monstrous state of affairs in a country which claims to be civilized: but at least appearances are kept up. But, beware. It is not the Rector of a new Academy who is speaking but a professor of the Sorbonne, still attached to his Alma Mater and who continues to enjoy its inestimable privileges. Now, he is compelled to tell you that, perhaps in 1964 but certainly in 1965, the Sorbonne will no longer be able even to give the appearance of functioning. Instead of receiving a new entry of students, Paris – if left alone to face its destiny – risks seeing a revolt in that year.'

I take no credit for having sounded the alarm in those terms (moreover my pessimism was too early, for the revolt broke out three years later). What infuriates me rather is not having been listened to: Paris continued to shut its eyes and block its ears, and the very few politicians conscious of the danger and wishing to forestall it, were powerless to make their voices heard.

But what of the establishment of the Academies of Orleans and Rheims, then later those of Rouen and Amiens and the creation of the universities which were set up in those academies with the view of shaping that famous 'Couronne' around the ring of the Paris Basin? It is appropriate that I should offer an explanation in the hope of rendering a service not only to my country but to all those who are in the process of conceiving or implementing a programme to construct new universities.

It is true that the Government took the decision to create new academies, followed by new universities. But it went about it by stages, thereby losing the effects of unified purpose and of shock which are absolutely indispensable. The central administration set about their task neither with enthusiasm nor zeal. The unfortunate Rectors charged with nurturing the delicate buds of the 'Couronne' were asked first to solicit the generous support of the local and regional communities, thanks to which there arose, for example at Orleans, a miscellany of sheds to which eminent academics of Paris were pleased to attach the derisory (but justified) label of 'Municipal University'. I leave to the imagination the lack of attraction such a performance had for the minds of students in the capital. The fiasco was all the more pitiful since, simpleton that I was and believing in official promises, I had sounded a clarion call during the fair weather of plan and project making.

Another disillusion: some of us thought that the birth of a new university was a wonderful opportunity for innovation, of experiment not only in the field of architecture and site planning but also in pedagogy. This could have been another means, perhaps more viable than others, of attracting students from Paris. Alas, that hope, in its turn, was shattered by the dismal guardians of changelessness and, even more, of uniformity. We were forced to content ourselves with conjuring up in imagination a more relevant future development – which, it is true, did enable us to weather the storm of 1968 and its aftermath without major difficulties.

By a strange irony of fate, however, 1968 and its consequences were not as beneficial to us as might have been expected. In effect the 'May Revolution' was itself essentially Parisian and, once again, in the line of the French Jacobin tradition. It did, indeed, mean the complete shattering of the Sorbonne but the fragments from that explosion did not fall to enrich the provinces. They fell back, in the unlucky number of thirteen and in pitiful disorder, on Paris and its suburbs. Even worse, the most spectacular innovations with the most voracious appetite for young, dynamic academics were reserved for the capital and its surroundings – Montrouge, Dauphine, Asnières, Vincennes. Villetaneuse just escaped, the Minister of the time feeling that it was necessary at last to harness the provincial universities and not always Paris to the chariot of the imagination. But the latest information is that this plan will rise again from its ashes while the idea of an 'inner' or 'outer circle' of universities gathers strength, one which passes through Villetaneuse, Boissy-Saint-Léger, Créteil and Versailles; the other through Compiègne – and one awaits the rest.

This is not the place to pass judgment on this 'confused profusion'. Let us concentrate on a few points:

First, it is neither possible nor reasonable to furnish, with university facilities, at one and the same time, the Paris conurbation, its inner and outer circle and its 'Couronne'. A choice must be made! Now everything is happening as if it had been decided to abandon the grand initial design – that of the Universities of the Couronne – to the profit of two or three others which are capable of retaining the students – and attracting the teachers – in the infernal but, nevertheless, still fascinating circle of Paris and its inner and outer suburbs. This is, it must be plainly stated, the exact contrary of what we had wished – which may be summed up, as far as geography is concerned, as follows: rigorously to examine on the one hand all the disciplines which are, by tradition, taught in Paris and which would be better placed elsewhere (for example the vast field of agronomy and agricultural science); on the other hand, all the students who desire one thing only – to flee the capital, so long as they may be certain of finding elsewhere more pleasing forms of residence and learning; and *at the same time*, and swiftly, to build at Amiens, Rheims, Orleans-Tours, Rouen, university complexes with a double objective. For it was a matter not only, as is said too often (particularly in Paris), of creating 'Universities of Dissuasion', that is to say a defensive barrier which would halt on the Loire Front students from the Centre, or from the South and South-West, who quite inconsiderately continue to rush towards the capital. It was, and still is, a matter of persuading and of attracting in the most convincing way, those students who no longer find in the *Grand-Ville* the charms which intoxicated us in our youth and who are longing for a place where study and life are less under stress, which has more air and has a more fraternal atmosphere – where there is space and time for meeting together, for reflection, for discussion not merely between students but between young people of various origins and also, as frequently as possible, between teachers and disciples.

Carrying out such a policy presupposed a global conception carefully concerted as much at the level of the university partners as at that of those in charge of the various sectors of all the political, administrative, economic and social activities. It implied a firm determination in the execution of a design which permits neither delay nor dilution.

Unfortunately – and what a lesson for anyone whom fate leads these days to a task like ours – the co-ordination of effort and branches of the services is very foreign to our national habits and routine. Delay and administrative pettifoggery took over our project as they do any other, thereby affording arguments for the sceptical and disarming the optimistic. I can still hear the cry of one of my companions in the struggle, a Prefect of this Region: 'We have been harnessed to grandiose ambitions and now we risk falling into mediocrity and banality.' That sums up the end of a great dream – but one which deserves to rise from its ashes either at Orleans or elsewhere. It would not be out of place, therefore, to list now the elements of a strategy both of dissuasion and persuasion in university affairs.

From Town Planning to Education

Anyone looking at the plans for Orleans–La Source* would think they had come straight from Caesar's Commentaries. Here are to be descried the *Campus*, the *Forum* and the *Aula Magna* – a strange way of illustrating the topography of a university complex which is intended to follow the modern forms of town planning and pedagogy! Hardly more appropriate is the slogan tied to our project from the start: 'The French Oxford'.

Allow me, in very simple terms, to explain the misconception, which has almost become a myth, and which seems to be held around this very confused terminology. To establish at Orleans a French Oxford would seem to mean that, in the mind of the Minister who invented the formula, was the intention of giving France between the Loire and the Loiret a budding university whose brilliance might compare with that possessed, for our friends across the Channel, by Oxford at the confluence of the Thames and the Cherwell. As for the Campus, it has become the *tête noire* of the young – as of many adults for whom it is the synonym of ghetto and the final symbol of separation between the university and active life. But, please, do not judge *a priori* or without having seen first. If it is a question of the word, often accused of being *franglais*, why not relate it directly to the Latin and, indeed, to the name of the father of all campus of history, the famous Campus Martius on which the cohorts of the Praetorian Guard performed their drill exercises? In the same way today cohorts of students perform their exercises – both physical and intellectual – on the Campus of La Source. Even better, the Latin dictionary teaches us that *Campus* is the opposite of *Urbs* as Country is of Town. Now this – and it is only necessary to visit us to see – is exactly the idea behind our Campus which, to the North, backs on gardens and, to the South, on a town. There is only a street to separate – or rather link – them; the

---

* This name refers to the presence, at the heart of the park which runs along all one side of the university site, of the Loiret Spring famous for its bubbling irrepressibility.

architects even plan a footbridge across it to abolish the separation more completely.

Let us now examine the real content of the Campus of Orleans–La Source. We thought out an idea which has not always been fully understood – or which some people have not wanted to understand. Allow me to recall its charter. *Article 1*: there must be a Campus, thus a rural site, with trees, meadows and water – and not a desert of stones as is found too often elsewhere. *Article 2*: it must be a living environment, thus (and I repeat) in close contact with the town which is being built beside it. And let us hope that the town itself may become a real town, truly alive! *Article 3*: but the Campus cannot rely exclusively on the resources of the said town for its own existence – whence the important share given in its plans for sporting, social and cultural activities. *Article 4*: its chief mission must not be forgotten, which is to permit students to work: whence the grouping, on the same site, of the various centres and means of study, teaching and research.

However, this charter for a university should never limit itself to being a self-sufficient unity. It only makes sense when it is integrated into an all-embracing town plan which, moreover, is not something still to be invented but already existing and bearing a noble title: it is the celebrated charter for the town of Athens, drawn up by a team of architects inspired by Le Corbusier and promulgated in 1941. Now, as I have already said elsewhere, Article 77 of this historic document applies precisely (perhaps without its authors realizing it) and in a very particular way to the planning of a university too. It states quite simply that 'The keys for town planning lie in the four functions: accommodation; work space; recreation (or recuperation); circulation.' I should like to see these four keys featured on the coat of arms of every new university and hear them rattle on the bunch at the Chancellor's waist. I want to indicate more precisely what doors they are intended to open on the future of our students as students, for this is indeed the central point of our theme and one which it would not be absurdly pretentious to claim that the University of Orleans (as we planned it and as we hope it will become in the end) can offer as a 'Contribution to present-day Higher Education'.

First key, first function: *Accommodation*. If, once again, it expected that Orleans should help in freeing the capital of all the students from the provinces who should not be there and of the Paris students who do not feel happy there, then our University must offer them somewhere to live – and in sufficient numbers and in a more pleasant fashion. Let us examine this further. The quantitative problem is, in principle, easy to solve as soon as one decides to do so: it suffices, as far as Orleans and its sisters of the 'Couronne' are concerned, to cater for a body of students housed in accommodation clearly superior to that recognized as suitable in other universities. The qualitative problem is, naturally, more delicate. It goes without saying that, first and foremost, it is a question of finance: more spacious hostels, of a better standard of construction and more generously spaced than the Cités Universitaires of Paris, will be expensive. But one must know what is required and realize that something extra in the form of attractions is necessary. Finally – and here the experience and suggestions of the students were most valuable and led us to amend our original plans – one must take into account the variety in tastes and build some of the hostels within the boundaries of the Campus but others in the urban area for those who prefer to live in town rather than be surrounded by lawns. The crux of the problem of the triptych Town–University–Park is to combine adequately all the possibilities which can be thought of.

Second key, second function: *Work space*. This, of course, means teaching accommodation but also, and I would say almost above all, study areas, laboratories, libraries. For if at the end university level education must be little more than a corps of orientations, of stimuli in the field of documentation and methodology, it remains for the student to work according to his personal norms and aspirations. Laboratories and libraries adequately staffed with suitably qualified personnel will provide for this.

Third key, third function: *Recreation (or Recuperation)*. Here we must avoid sarcasm and ban play on words, all too easy indeed. To be twenty years old is to be at that happy age when the capacity for learning is at its height, when the facility of memory is matched by suppleness of the muscles; but it is also the age – whether blessed or cursed is for each to decide – when a kind of uncontrollable fancy makes one burst with impatience and want to kick over the traces. It is then that the Campus, in the perverted sense of the word, tends to become the worst of all ills once its residents feel themselves caged up therein, reduced to the desiccation of intellectual austerity and shut off from any opportunity of contact with cultural life be it physical, artistic or any other and, quite simply, with real life itself. The fourth key: *Circulation*, in this respect, is not separated from the third. It enables a double function to be performed – of mobility and exchanges within the Campus itself and also of relations between the Campus, the town and the rest of the world.

The fundamental importance of these two imperatives – *recreation, circulation* – is, it must be said, rarely measured. One fact, as simple as it is sad, demonstrates the proof. Heaven knows – and some people can bear witness – that O. C. Cacoub, chief architect of the project, and the writer worked from the start in close harmony of mind and intent and that they took pains to assert the priority of problems of the physical, social and cultural *animation* of the Campus and of the demands of *circulation*. I am forced to admit that, apart from a handful of far-seeing men, no one would listen to us with understanding. Far worse, we were treated as megalomaniac dreamers and one day I caught a high official of the Ministry of National Education making the kind of gesture by which one indicates that someone is suffering from DTs. I wish I had had the courage to remind him of Pascal's words: 'Ce serait être fou par un autre tour de folie, de n'être pas fou.'

The result has been the hold up referred to above: our students feel lost, shut up in a solitude vested in agrarian charm once the summer arrives (but then few students are there) and those from Paris, duly forewarned, much prefer to continue to face the bustle of the Latin Quarter: it may not be propitious for work and space may be very restricted, but one can at least escape from boredom.

Our plan was – and is – nevertheless very simple and can be stated quite briefly: at the centre of the Campus there would be a Forum and, facing the Forum, one of the refectories, the central library for general cultural subjects, a hostel with provision in particular for visitors to the University, and finally a Students' Union. The Refectory and Library are already built but the University hostel and the Students' Union are not yet. Our Campus will not accomplish what it was intended for until that is completed for it is around and through that that movement is organized. 'It is,' said the chief architect one day, struck by the absence of a common meeting place in most American or British campuses, 'the crossroads where at any moment students jostle together and get to know each other outside their work.' It should be added that this meeting-place borders on a man-made lake intended to bring into the landscape the air (and area) for reflection and peacefulness so lacking in the world today with a crucial additional benefit planned by O. C. Cacoub. 'In whichever direction the University of Orleans expands in future, the lake by its very presence will block the erection of new buildings in the heart of the complex and this wide expanse of some four hectares will stay free for ever.'

That, in very general terms, describes the elements of recreation and circulation within the university. It remains to consider the liaison between the university and the outside world – another vital problem but one too often neglected in the face of our many demands. For us it appears as a threefold problem; liaison with a town expanding alongside the Campus; with Old Orleans; and with Paris. The two areas, university and town, are, as we have pointed out, closely linked. It is still necessary that their social, sporting and cultural amenities should be complementary: and this is something which, alas, makes very slow progress. The heart of Old Orleans is about three miles from the university. Many have looked on this as a negligible distance. In fact and in many respects it is immense and the Loire is not the only obstacle to cross. What is needed is something we asked for from the earliest days: a branch of the motorway with a coach service while awaiting – and why not? – the arrival of the overhead monorail metro already being dreamed up by some inventive technologists in 1962.

As for Paris . . . when it is realized – and here we touch on pedagogical matters – that the university of Orleans-La Source has predominantly a concern with science, Paris would seem to be the point of departure (or arrival) on an axis Paris–Quai Saint Bernard–Orsay–Orleans along which could develop fruitful sharing of commitments, communication and continual exchanges. Is it necessary at this point of time to recall the hope in the mind of a Minister to whom our project owes so much? In substance this is what he said: Be certain of one thing – students, be they French or foreign, will willingly give up an overcrowded Sorbonne for a spacious Campus but only on condition of being able, without spending too much time or money, to come back at weekends from time to time to the banks of the Seine. In the same way, a student who is weary of the maelstrom of the capital should be able to return in sample, at La Source, during the weekend, the pleasures of moral and physical relaxation. And chance has arranged things very nicely: the railway is there, quite close it only requires the building of a halt 'Orleans–La Source' at the very gates of the Campus. What could be more simple, between students, than a mutual exchange of rooms? This excellent plan of a Minister who knew how to combine the art of administration with vision deserves to see itself soon translated into reality.

Some Educational Initiatives

In what measure can the 'French Oxford' boast of having 'contributed' to the present changes in university education? First, and of over-riding importance, I must stress the pioneer spirit which – consciously or unconsciously – animated the first actions of the initial team. Our firm conviction must be repeated, that we must profit from the opportunity of a new birth to make changes, and although frustrated and botched by the paralyzing sclerosis of the administrative machine in Paris and by the shortsightedness, not to say blindness, of its agents, we nevertheless succeeded in shaking up the best minds, forcing the weak to surrender and achieved some kind of a break-through, at least at the level of ideas and even sometimes at that of practical application. A first lesson may be learnt from this: innovation is not principally a matter of technique and procedure but of imagination and will.

A second fact, more original and unexpected: it will perhaps be known that one of our greatest difficulties was that of having to apportion our plans between Orleans and Tours (where there already existed some fragments of beginnings of higher education). Now from this unhappy situation grew our greatest opportunity – that of anticipating the 1968 Reform in at least two ways. On the one hand we had to assign major functions as between Tours and Orleans, an idea completely unorthodox at the time but since then hallowed by Article 6 of the French *Loi d'Orientation*. On the other hand the lame compromise imposed on us – Faculties of Science and of Law at Orleans, and of Medicine and Arts (Letters) at Tours – forced us in its turn to seek for corrective measures in the form of creating, here and there, complementary 'departments' designed to ensure a minimum of coherence to each of our two university growing-points. Thus, for example, it was agreed to develop at Tours courses in physiology appropriate for medical students and at Orleans social science courses intended to support students of economics and law. In short, this was the beginning at Orleans, as at Tours, of a broad experiment in pluri-disciplinary – even inter-disciplinary – studies.

Third initiative – and probably the one above all others which is in process of bearing the most abundant fruit: the La Source estate comprises some 700 hectares; 500 were reserved for the development of the town and 200 for our own projects. These we divided into two halves, one for the university establishments proper, the other for research laboratories. The latter are administered by the National Centre for Scientific Research (CNRS), but it was accepted from the start that the departments of science education, in particular, would work in close co-operation with the corresponding research laboratories. By a further happy chance, it has been possible to extend this liaison to the Bureau of Geological and Mining Research which had just been established in our immediate neighbourhood. So there was forged a chain linking teaching to fundamental research and then to applied research, present in its 'purest' form at Orleans. And this was not all: it has been agreed – not without a long struggle – that the policies of development of the different establishments should be correlated and that a main purpose of the whole enterprise should be defined in express terms, involving the science and technology of materials, both natural and artificial. When one considers the invincible attachment of universities, especially when they are French, to traditions of individualism and of narrow compartmentalization, such an achievement of co-operation has an air of the miraculous and, as such, deserves to be greeted as the sign of a new era.

The last two fingers of the hand are not really sufficient to indicate all the attempts at pedagogical innovation or renewal undertaken within or under the aegis of the University of Orleans. In order not to exceed the limits of the subject of this paper I will confine myself to two matters, while at the same time making reference to a Tourainian 'venture', a kind of 'literary' sister to an Orleanese scientific innovation.

From the early days of our Academy [1962] a body of earnest thinking men had conceived the idea of an 'Institute of Ligerian Studies' through which would be channelled all enquiries and research connected with the

Loire, its tributaries and the riverain regions from an analysis of the present and future evolution of the regime of the river and the whole problem of water supply and conservation to the economy and sociology of the various regions of the Loire. Thanks to the Law of Orientation, the young University of Orleans has taken on and consolidated this inheritance by organizing a department of study and especially of specific research, open not only to university students but to all experts and interested 'practitioners'.

The other scheme, which once again requires its complement at Tours, has much wider implications and which I would like to underline at some length to conclude. It bears a rather ponderous title, necessitated by its explicit nature: it involves grafting on to our university tree a 'branch of higher technological education' (*enseignement supérieur technologique long*). The Academy of Orleans, as others, includes a fairly broad network of departments of IUTs (University Institutes of Technology) which are dispersed among Orleans, Tours and even a third town, Bourges. The IUTs are designed to offer short courses of higher technical training covering two years and preparing people for employment as higher technicians or technician-engineers (as the Germans call them). For their part the UERs (Teaching and Research Units), the offspring of the old faculties, offer courses of an essentially fundamental nature not leading in any systematic way to any specific professional career other than those of teaching or research. There is therefore room for a third kind of training which would in some measure provide the benefits of the *Grande Ecole* and of the university while at the same time avoiding the disadvantages of both. This will be a higher technical education intended to produce after several years' study at three consecutive levels, the qualification necessary to become either an Engineer, or a 'Doctor of Engineering', or even, for individuals, professor in a School of Higher Technical Education.

The Orleans project is concerned with the science and technique of transport-propulsion, especially automobile and aeronautic mechanics. Its branches in the Touraine area cover the science and technology of communication media. The course of study is the same in each case: a first year in the form of a 'common core' with possibility of orientation at the end. Students who reveal gifts for 'pure' knowledge but who are not at home in the field of technology are steered towards one or other UER of the 'fundamental' kind. Those who, on the other hand, show clear aptitude for technology but lack a gift for conceptual disciplines are guided to a department of an IUT in their second year for the better ones, in their first year for the weaker. Finally those students most gifted by nature both for pure knowledge and its technological application remain (if they so wish, of course) for a third year in the technological network.

These, then, are new features that were long hampered by French tradition, still largely based on that of Jacobin centralization, but which the Law of Orientation now encourages. A great future should await them. There is nothing to prevent one from imagining that a combination of similar branches of education, diversified but co-ordinated, providing both fundamental and applied approaches, might in its turn build up an autonomous educational unity taking on the aspect of a Technological University.

Concluding Reflections

Few things created by human minds have not been confronted with difficulties and often, while working to overcome them, those in charge come to discover their true purposes and the real character of what they are attempting to create. But at the same time the obstacles must not be so many or so great that they affect the true nature of the undertaking and dishearten one from persevering. This, without doubt, is the most important psychological contribution that the experience at Orleans–La Source can offer to those who are now proposing to undertake any work of creation or renewal in the field of higher education.

If we move from the level of ideas to the level of real life, our long and harsh experience would suggest this advice to any who follow us in the career of pioneer in university work: your first duty is to the mission you have been given and to the idea behind the plan. This implies that the plan be clearly defined and accepted in structure and perspective, in its means of achievement and its timetable – and that the carrying out of the operation is left in your hands. In short, this means that, if you want to remain faithful to your task, you must obtain from those who have chosen you what is known in French political terminology (and used by Giraudoux as the title of a book) – 'Full Powers' (*Pleins Pouvoirs*). Without this, your trials, your disappointments and, indeed, your regrets and remorse will be too much for you. In the final count, that is the most concrete lesson to be drawn from ten years of struggle. It is, in essence, a matter of psychology as would be expected in any undertaking in which the mind must go before and lead the hand.

16

Directions of Development in Higher Education in Spain

Alberto Moncada

A New Education Act

In June, 1970, after eighty days of debate, the Spanish Parliament passed a comprehensive Education Act, which has been described as the most impressive turning-point in educational strategy ever reached in Spain. Following the publication of a self-critical White Paper edited by Governmental experts with the aid of foreign brains, a Parliamentary Commission examined more than 13,000 suggestions put forward in the course of a lengthy period of open discussions regarding one of the country's most controversial issues. Included among the other issues at stake were tension between government-run and private schools, the relative rights of the State, the Church and the consumer, the struggle against illiteracy and discrimination, and fundamental questions of ideology.

The Act reflects a compromise in most respects, the most important achievement being the decision to invest more money and effort in education. Politically, the Act is an important step towards greater integration in the country, aimed at breaking down the economic and social frontiers which derived in the past from a narrow and elite-styled system of education.

How and to what extent these aims will be fulfilled is another question; but the slogan, 'Better education for all', now undoubtedly represents in Spain a challenge which has been accepted by the Spanish people – whether they are of the Establishment or not – with pride and optimism.

The New Act and Higher Education

As far as higher education is concerned, the new Act adopts Anglo-Saxon criteria when deciding upon most of the questions under examination. Before this the Spanish University reflected one more application of Napoleonic centralization, and although the Act has not done away with all pre-existing patterns its aim is to strengthen the autonomy of universities while at the same time encouraging a reformatory attitude – for example in such basic matters as university government and administration, the admission of and regimes governing students, teacher status, nature of university studies, financial support, and so on. Before analysing these aspects, it is advisable to have a look at the historical background, and specially at the period immediately before the Act.

Historical Background

The history of the Spanish University up till the nineteenth century fits into the context of European evolution as described by Dr Marjorie Reeves in her work on the subject.[1] Palencia, Alcala and Salamanca were founded under the patronage of the Crown or the Church as centres of scholastic education. They trained an elite of young noblemen and children of up-and-coming bourgeois families for jobs in the Civil Service or the Church. At the time of the Reformation and the discovery of America by Columbus, the Spanish University had settled along clearly conservative lines, preferring to engage in controversy over points of the Law or Theology, rather than to play a leading role in the search for material progress.

Subsequent centuries, which witnessed the flourishing of the Sciences and the Humanities in England, France, Germany and Italy, were marked in the case of Spain by a style of higher education showing little influence of non-liberal subjects. The Spanish University defined terms of doctrine, provided a forum for training in national orthodoxy, remained a spiritual forefront of Imperial undertakings, and side-stepped the practical sciences.

The nineteenth century brought to the University the impact of European modernity. This modernity was accelerated by the Napoleonic invasion and was reflected by a series of progressive clashes with the traditional elements of the country, mainly in two fields: in the modernists' striving for material progress and in their wish to build Spanish coexistence upon the foundations of ideological pluralism. The *Institución Libre de Enseñanza* (Free Institution of Education) – an association of Spanish intellectuals influenced by European cultural trends – proved an important vehicle of modernist influence.

Within the general sphere of education, the new trends materialized in concern for the building of schools and forecasting teacher requirements in order to place culture within reach of the general public. In this context the struggle between traditionalists and modernists was particularly noticeable, above all in university circles, where reform is born, dies and is re-born, depending on the outlook of each government.

The most outstanding event was the abolition of the self-governing and private nature of the universities, causing them to be centralized, governed and financed by the State as from 1845. The teachers became civil servants, belonging to a single national body. The principal of each University, a Government appointee, was made responsible for all education in his district. A partial move towards corporative autonomy came from the

1919 and 1921 Acts, which granted legal status to the Universities and powers of deciding their internal affairs.

In the course of this period the practical sciences found their way – though very timidly – into Spanish University curricula. It was a time that saw the implanting of a pattern that is still valid today, where the University is mainly a centre for producing members of the liberal professions (doctors, lawyers, teachers), with a view to their entering government service. The separate Engineering Colleges which were founded towards the end of the nineteenth century were specially looked to as sources of top-level technicians for the State.

In 1943, after the Civil War, a new University Act was promulgated, an Act in which the principles of the new State (with an emphasis on official Catholicism and national unity) were included as governing factors in a somewhat different concept of a University, each of those recognized being given a certain degree of self-government, yet regarded very much as an instrument of spiritual and national interests. A parallel instrument was created beside it: the *Consejo Superior de Investigaciones Científicas* (Higher Scientific Research Council). In reality the situation was very impoverished. Out of the twelve Universities recognized, barely two – those of Madrid and Barcelona – had a competent teaching staff. The Civil War had caused most of the intellectuals who would not knuckle under to Franco's regime to emigrate.

Slowly but surely more funds were made available for higher education and the centres were strengthened. The Spanish Universities and Technical Colleges provided the sole training ground from which the leading-lights of present-day Spanish society were to emerge; if one judges the paths followed by these men, one is also to a certain extent judging higher education as it then was in Spain.

Forerunners of the New Act

In the fifties Spain was beginning to open up to the outside world. People were travelling, witnessing other experiences in social organization, and relinquishing the extremist attitudes of isolationism. University teachers were also travelling, and receiving more publications from abroad.

The year 1952 saw the birth of the new University of Navarre, which was to have considerable influence upon subsequent reforms. It was the first private University upon which the State granted the right to confer degrees. Its creation was the work of a group of professors belonging to the Opus Dei, a Catholic Church association. These professors set about their task with a mixture of apostolic zeal, the goal of high academic standing and candour. Their efforts, backed by the economic support of thousands of Spaniards, bore fruit as an experimental university which embodied whole-hearted devotion on the part of the teachers, included the tutorial system, the additions of new professions to the University repertoire and saw the beginnings of exploration down new pedagogical paths.

The influence of Navarre, which was at first received with misgivings and contention by the State Universities, was soon to be felt by the latter. This was also because government teachers, and the members of the University Reform movement in particular, were beginning to insist upon, and to obtain, greater autonomy in university organization and greater governmental concern with academic problems. This was also fostered by outcroppings of student rebellion, and the students' demands for not only political but also university reforms.

In the early sixties the Government took a series of part measures which marked the sprouting of reform: reorganization and economic improvements for teachers, extension of installations, increases in the number and amount of grants and other reforms of student aid, etc. With reformation in the air, however, there was a call for more far-reaching changes in the entire education system. In 1968, under Villar Palasi, the Ministry launched upon the task which was to materialize in the recently passed General Education Act. The White Paper was preceded by a nationwide survey, as well as discussions at meetings and in the press. Though the reforms introduced by the Act are probably greater in pre-university levels, yet they are accompanied, as we shall soon see, by far-reaching renovations in higher education too.

University Autonomy

Before the Act the Universities were governmental agencies where the power of decision lay mainly in the hands of the Ministry of Education itself. The extent to which the Ministry controlled the Universities was quite incredible. Centralization also spelt uniformity, because the twelve State Universities had the same Statutes and varied only in the number, but not the diversity, of their Faculties. There were Universities with five, three or even eight Faculties, but the administrative procedure and the study programmes in each Faculty were the same throughout the country.

It was the Ministry of Education – through the General Directorate of University Teaching – which approved the amount and nature of the teaching to be provided in each centre, which appointed the teaching and administrative staff, which controlled the funds and which constituted a power-platform upon whose ratifications the majority of university decisions depended. The Principal was a professor appointed by the Government and those who helped him to run the University were other professors also appointed by the Ministry. The Deans of the Faculties were in a like situation. The collegiate bodies, faculty boards and boards of governors only functioned as counsellors to the Principal and Deans.

This situation undermined the community spirit of the centres and introduced tremendous complications when it came to solving problems, since the civil servants in the Ministry were powerless to deal properly with all the questions covered by their department. Furthermore, centralization favoured a personality-slanted policy and pressure-group influence on governmental decisions. The problem of self-government was among the most important ones raised during the survey period prior to introduction of the Bill. Political objections to autonomy derived from a fear that it would favour student unrest, especially serious in the large cities.

In the first place, the new Act acknowledges freedom to set up university centres – subject to certain conditions – this being a right previously enjoyed only by the Catholic Church. As far as the State Universities are concerned, limited self-government is granted, for while the centres are allowed to draft their own Statutes, to organize teaching programmes, to appoint teachers and to draw up and administer their budgets, the majority of the key decisions still require Ministry of Education approval. Yet the creation of the National Universities Board and the Council of Principals as advisory bodies to the Ministry marks a step towards greater respect for self-government.

In each University a Trust is to be set up, its members including representatives of local interests. These Trusts may become instruments of cross-fertilization between the universities and the public, although they constitute mainly a means whereby the public can contribute economic support for education, rather than genuine participation by citizens in the running of the university. The power to appoint academic authorities remains in the hands of the Ministry, although appointments are proposed by or involve the intervention of the University. Finally there is a strengthening of the authority of the collegiate bodies, allowing for a certain amount of student involvement in decision-taking procedures. The main innovation in University administration is the creation of the post of manager, a non-professional civil servant, appointed by the Ministry after proposal by the Principal. He will be in charge of the administrative and financial machinery of the centre.

The inauguration of this post indeed may mark the beginning of the creation of University administrative staff, a vital requisite if we are to foster the business-enterprise spirit which is deficient at present, since – as we mentioned above – the machinery has previously been in the hands of teachers or civil servants. The former lacked training in administration, while the latter, as members of a national civil service, were controlled from Madrid and very much tied down by pettifogging rules and regulations. The right to draw up its own Statutes enables each University now to establish its own operational criteria and a loosening up in economic and administrative management will probably follow.

Be that as it may, the outcome of this more operative approach will depend to a great extent on the governmental machinery since the terms of the Act still leave much power of control over the Universities in the grip of the Government. This will depend, to a certain extent, on reforms already announced by the Ministry of Education, reforms which may mean a move towards genuine decentralization, in the interests of University self-government.

Curricula – Teaching and Research

The Spanish higher education system, as we have said, has in the past served basically as a training ground for members of the professions (doctors, lawyers, engineers), many of whom tended subsequently to enter Government service. Some centres, such as certain Engineering Colleges, were in actual fact mainly places for training civil servants.

Unlike its Anglo-Saxon counterparts, the University did not aim at training students to develop an intellectual or scientific outlook; rather it drew up its narrow curricula on the basis of the idea that a lad at sixteen would have already made up his mind that he wanted to be a lawyer and that his five years at university should be devoted almost solely to turning him out as one. Over and above that, and as an outcome of his five years of university life, he would also acquire general knowledge, but this would be thanks more to his own interest and efforts than to programmed encouragement exerted by his university. The same could also be said of chemists or engineers.

The teaching given was highly theoretical, both as an outcome of the traditional speculative nature of science and the Spanish disposition, and also because of the scanty opportunities offered for experimental work, especially in the practical sciences. It followed that graduates launched upon their professional careers with excessive theoretical specialization and insufficient practical experience, even though these deficiencies may have been partly remedied by the well-known versatility and intuitive gifts of the Latin. Indeed, foreign companies which had been setting up branches on a growing scale in Spain frequently praised this end-product, for the Spanish graduate, despite deficiencies in training, does show great capacity for adapting to present-day cultural and technological evolution.

The less practical studies (Philosophy, Literature, Pure Sciences), affecting a minority of students, have produced intellectuals and scientists who hold positions which favourably compare with those of their European and American contemporaries, and have supplied reasonably competent teachers for Spanish secondary and higher education centres.

One of the consequences of centralization was that the study programme for each subject and faculty was common to the whole of Spain. Hence a student of Law in Madrid would study the same items in the same period of time as his fellow in Barcelona or Santiago. While this made it easier for a student to move from one University to another, it hindered diversification of scientific or regional approach.

To a certain extent this was a consequence of the as yet standing criterion governing the awarding of degrees. Academic degrees in Spain are given by the State, not the University, and an academic degree or diploma is all that is needed for exercising a profession, to the extent that the professional corporations are unable to control the quality of the new graduates. For this the State appeared to need a uniform criterion as to the contents of each academic degree. This explains the uniformity of the study programmes.

Certain changes began to occur after the mid-fifties: Navarre University was the first to explore three lines of development: first the extension of university teaching to include new professions and leanings (business administration, journalism, etc.) which had no place in the traditional schemes: secondly, the creation – subject to legal conditions – of new degrees (in Liberal Arts) and experimenting with existing ones (the Post-Graduate School of Medicine); and finally, integration of the Industrial Engineering College and the College of Architecture into a university context, this being less narrow than the traditional type of engineering college.

The Ministry of Education began to move along these same lines, allowing some Universities to introduce experimental study programmes, and creating three so-called Self-Governing Universities in Madrid, Barcelona and Bilbao, where experiment was to be the rule rather than the exception. The new Act endorses the principle of freedom in teaching organization, albeit subject to governmental approval when it comes to important measures and to respect for the general guidelines laid down by the Act itself.

Among these new general guide-lines the most outstanding are:

(a) The extension of university courses to include subjects or professions previously only covered in vocational or professional institutes of higher or lower standing. At present engineering, teacher-training, commerce and journalism figure as subjects taught in the university.

(b) The division of university studies into three cycles, each of which is concluded with a degree, rather as in the American system (Bachelor, Master, PhD). The difference lies in the fact that parallel to the first cycle there is another, of a more practical nature, covering most of the short vocational courses previously followed outside the University (second-grade engineering, commerce, nursing, etc.), although the possibility exists for students of the latter to subsequently go on into the second ordinary cycle.

(c) The basically departmental structure of the University. This unit –

the Department – is the forum for teaching of the main sciences and for research into them. It is related on the one hand to the Faculties and to the centres responsible for the academic degrees, and on the other to the Institutes, the centres responsible for applied research and professional specialization.

(*d*) The setting up of an Education Science Institute in each University as a teacher-training centre covering all levels of education, as well as for pedagogical research and assessment.

These reforms mark a sharp break from the earlier situation and may well take time to settle down, in view of the strong traditions binding us to the previous system. In the first place, it is difficult for the Universities rapidly to absorb – either administratively or academically speaking – all the centres in their districts teaching the subjects listed in paragraph (*a*). Calculations carried out at Santiago University show that there are ten such centres scattered over the 30,000 sq. kilometres of the area for which it is now responsible. Their incorporation will involve many organizational problems unless a pattern of considerable decentralization is adopted. While geographical dispersion is advantageous from the point of view of maintaining human dimensions in the centres, its inconveniences derive from the genuine and positive contribution that the university spirit ought to make in such centres, which have in the past been renowned for their pragmatism. This problem is made even more serious by the fact that regional rail and road communications in Spain are not good.

In theory the ideal might be for short-course students to be able to benefit from the University teachers and resources so that nurses, for example, would become by-products of the Faculty of Medicine, and technicians by-products of that of Engineering, but for the time being this does not seem to be feasible, except in the large cities. One interesting line of evolution is the possibility of setting up University Colleges in cities and towns which previously had no University. These colleges would provide courses only in the first basic cycle of university teaching.

The new formula of university cycles presupposes acceptance of the criterion of initial basic training, where specialization is postponed to the second cycle, although the picture is complicated by the short-course cycle, the nature of which has yet to be defined in practical terms. In the case of the incorporation of the Engineering Colleges into the University, the Act makes an exception by allowing the setting up of Polytechnic Colleges, with a status similar to that of the Universities. Plans are afoot for one in Madrid and another in Valencia, combining all the technological instruction previously provided in each city.

As far as research is concerned, the new Act introduces greater co-ordination between university research and that sponsored by the Higher

Council for Scientific Research, thus bridging a gap which had led to problems in the past.

The Act also fosters collaboration between other public and private activities, although there is still a deficiency of research in the country, both pure and applied. At present, the Spanish Government is preparing another White Paper on Research, because of its concern over the way the economic development of the country is so heavily dependent on foreign patents.

Institutionally, universities have kept themselves quite cut off from national development, since they have neither done research work for firms nor acted in an advisory capacity; they have participated even less in programmes of community development. It may be said, in this respect, that Spanish higher education has been and continues to be essentially a system of teaching. One of the intentions of the new Act is to slant the tendency towards the interests of research and services, but this will call for considerable investments in universities and also a certain change in the mentality of the nation. While it may be easy for the individual university research worker to be accepted by the economic world, it is not customary for the university as such to be used, nor is it sufficiently prepared for being used in this way. It may well be that the suitability of distributing means of research and teams of experts more rationally throughout the country should be analysed for this purpose, in the interests of functional concentration.

Teaching Staff

Spain is no exception to the world university situation as far as shortage of teachers in face of a growing demand is concerned.

The teaching staff at the 15 State Universities number 1,252 top-ranking professors, 625 second-grade professors and lecturers, 2,149 third-grade lecturers and 4,000 young assistant lecturers. In the Higher Technical Colleges there are 540 top-ranking professors, 532 second-grade professors and lecturers and 660 young assistant lecturers.

The first and second categories were appointed by the Government, on the basis of the findings of a board of high-level professors, to fill vacancies, and were members of a national corporation of civil servants. Universities had no right to select, rule or dismiss them and their careers (change of post, etc.) depended on decisions at the centre.

The third and fourth categories were more closely handled by the Universities but the system as a whole did not encourage people to wait long enough to obtain a tenure. In fact there did not exist in Spain any post which an academic could obtain and in which he would be paid properly and progressively and enjoy promotion. When tenure was obtained, however, the professor's personal status was high, well paid and independent. A professor's duties, which had been almost negligible in the past, were clarified some years ago, under the establishment of various grades with corresponding salaries, though control of these proved hard to maintain. In recent years, it is true, a limited amount of progress has been achieved, with Government scholarships and grants provided for young people aiming at an academic career.

The new Act represents a compromise between the previous situation and the direct relationship which is desirable between the professor or teacher and the University. The curious situation of the professor or teacher as a civil servant belonging to a national body was to a certain extent due to the need to ensure against arbitrary bias on the part of the academic authorities. Nowadays, with the tremendous demand for teaching staff, this would appear to be no longer necessary, although the Act endorses a system which continues to uphold the national bodies, despite the fact that the Universities are granted greater influence in the appointment and management of their teaching staff.

The nation-wide shortage of teaching staff, exacerbated by sociological changes in the country and new opportunities for graduates in industry and the services, may grow even more serious when the reorganization referred to under the new Act is implemented. This will call for added organizational and financing efforts in an attempt to attract skilled youngsters to the teaching profession, and away from other jobs being offered on the national market, including teaching and research jobs abroad, where the attractive conditions are producing a serious brain drain.

Students

On the eve of the Education Act there were 170,000 students enrolled in the Universities, including the Higher Technical Colleges. After the promulgation of the Act, as a result of the above-mentioned absorption of medium-level professional studies by the Universities, this figure will have immediately risen to about 500,000. In fact only the lower vocational training schools – where admission does not depend on the student's having passed his *bachillerato* – or school-leaving examination – will remain outside the University. This is bound to introduce more complications in the already serious staff shortage, a shortage which is especially outstanding in the first courses, where student congestion is at its greatest.

The first courses always offer most problems. It would seem obvious, at least theoretically, that the youngster straight from secondary school full of hopes and expectations as he enters the University, should need more care and attention than the old-hand in his third or fourth year. Yet the universal practice in Spain so far has been quite the contrary. It is the final years of undergraduate studies and the graduate schools that receive preferential attention from the professors and teachers. There is a lack of devoted teachers ready to accept the undeniably more selfless task of introducing students to their subject, and this is a job which is falling more and more to the younger lecturers, producing a situation which only offers the advantage of the optimistic devotion of the latter. A real tutorial system of the kind that the terms of the new Act envisage, however, calls for experienced teachers and they do not seem to be available as things are at present.

The Act introduces a preparatory course involving collaboration between the secondary and higher education centres, where the stress will be laid on general background and on working out the student's preferences and promise. This may well prove to be an ancillary formula whereby to solve the problem, although it also has the defect of lengthening university life precisely at a time when there is talk of shortening it.

Like most countries, Spain has witnessed a rapid increase in its university population. In 1950 there were 54,605 students; twenty years later, as indicated above, the total had jumped to 170,000 and the figure will continue to grow, especially under the influence of a parallel increase in secondary school student figures, which likewise grew from 334,316 in 1950 to over 1,500,000 in 1970. The motivating force behind this growth was an Act passed in 1960 whereby Income Tax funds were allocated to scholarships and other aids so as to provide extensive schooling at all levels. This Act remains in force, thus making education available to many young people who had been previously deprived for economic reasons. Moreover, academic fees are low, to the extent that University students pay the University less than 20 per cent of the actual cost of their education. Under the terms of the new Law the Universities, which had so far been forced to accept all secondary school students who had passed their finals, may now introduce their own prior selection system, a necessary but not obviously popular requirement.

Student life varies considerably, depending on whether it is in Universities in the large cities like Madrid or Barcelona or those in the provinces. While it is true that the former have better professors and teachers as well as means, the latter offer more of an academic atmosphere. Some Universities, like Santiago and Salamanca, have a predominant influence over the towns to which they are set, and produce something of an Oxbridge situation. A Halls of Residence tradition of long-standing exists in Spain. The Halls provide accommodation for about 16,000 students; some belong to the Universities and others to various public or private bodies. It is becoming more and more usual, however, for students not living at home to live in flats or lodgings.

Only Madrid and Barcelona, where the Universities have their own specialized Departments, cater for appreciable numbers of students from other regions. So far Spain lacks a social and economic regime which would allow such free student circulation throughout the country. Some 15,000 foreign students, hailing above all from Latin America, are in the Spanish Universities. The latter benefit from the low cost of living in Spain and constitute a cultural bond between Spain and South America when they return to exercise their professions in their homelands. The number of students from Arab countries is at present increasing noticeably.

Student participation in running their universities has always been on a small scale. After the Civil War student associations were introduced as State controlled unions of which membership was compulsory. They engaged in good aid-provision work, but failed to allow ideological pluralism. Following upon a complicated stage, during which student's rights of association were successively granted and hamstrung, the new Act has established them once more, on a fairly broad footing, and also allows student representation in the government of the Universities.

Spain is no exception to the rule of world-wide university or campus rebellion, although it speaks mainly in terms of reaction against the political structures, which the students consider to be old-fashioned.

Economics

In 1970 the money spent on (public and private) education in Spain amounted to around 55 per cent of the national income. With regard to governmental investments, education received 42,500 million pesetas (£255 million), standing second only in relative importance to the armed forces. In the same year the university system received 8,000 million pesetas (£48 million) of the above sum. This was principally invested in government-run centres; only a small amount – 106 million pesetas – were in aid to privately-run teaching centres. Of this figure 60 per cent is absorbed in staff costs, so tangible investments as such are small. The Government, along with other public and private entities, grants large sums of student aid. An official long-term, low interest-rate credit scheme likewise facilitates the building of private university premises and residences.

Prior to the new Act the Universities had practically no power to plan and allocate their budgets. Where economic matters were concerned they were merely subsidiary offices to the Ministry of Education. Investments in buildings or installations were planned and directed at Ministry level, students' fees all went into a Central Fund and even the teaching staff were paid from Madrid. Such a policy made it impossible to carry out a conscientious survey of university finances, a task which can only now be tackled.

The Universities have very gradually begun to receive some non-earmarked grants. At the same time the teaching staff are also beginning to receive a little more money for research directly from the Government.

The new Act endorses the principle of economic autonomy, although restricting it in two important aspects: Government approval is required for the budget; and the universities' economic dependence on governmental grants, which continue to be their main source of income. One interesting innovation is that distribution of grants among the Universities must be carried out after a report by the 'Junta Nacional de Universidades', or National Universities Board, a body rather like the British University Grants Committee.

Conclusion

Summing up, we can say that the Spanish Universities are facing the future under a double question mark: Will their centres be up to the challenge of the new Act? Will the Government be ready enough to fulfil its promise to grant the Universities greater autonomy and more money?

This has still to be seen. In the meanwhile there are clearly two credibility gaps to be bridged. Spanish society is not all that satisfied with its Universities; it accuses them of social isolationism and lack of efficiency. A fair proportion of the Establishment nowadays also looks at them with fear, seeing them as forums from which Society and the Government may be criticized.

Furthermore, there is a highly generalized tendency which prefers to devote greater attention to the big problems facing the infra-structure of education (such as primary schooling, the fight against illiteracy, and so on), rather than to those of the higher levels. Nor is the Spanish economy - which has other urgent calls upon its purse-strings - in a position to spend a great deal. There is no easy answer to difficult problems, and the question of University Reform is no exception.

NOTE

1. See Marjorie Reeves: 'The European University from Medieval Times' in W. R. Niblett (ed.) *Higher Education: Demand and Response* (London, 1969; San Francisco, 1970).

17

La Trobe—A Case Study of a New Australian University

Ronald Goldman and A. W. Martin

In an article outlining for the 1959 *Year Book of Education* the development of Australia's universities, W. F. Connell listed ten foundations, the first in 1850, the last in 1949, and all but three before 1930.[1] It is some measure of the revolution through which Australian tertiary education has passed in the last decade that to bring this list up to date Connell would now have to add another seven universities, three of them pre-existing colleges which have achieved independent status, the other four entirely new foundations. This growth has reflected a lively national reaction to the shock of discovering in 1957 how serious a crisis Australia's universities were then facing. The Prime Minister's Murray Committee in that year pointed up the burdens being carried by universities suffering from the cumulative effects of interwar neglect, post-war pressure of student numbers and uncertain finances, and warned of an impending avalanche of enrolments which could be expected to double the country's university population within eight years. The Committee urged emergency grants to aid existing universities and found new ones, and it recommended that an Australian Universities Commission be set up to advise the Commonwealth on universities' financial requirements and to help promote rational and coherent development. Substantial government acceptance of the Committee's report heralded a 'new deal' for university education in Australia.

The Establishment of La Trobe

La Trobe is one of the academic communities founded during the expansive period that followed. Its establishment – like that of its sister institution, Monash – was part of a vigorous effort by Victoria, Australia's second most populous state, to remedy the neglect of the past and to catch up with the increasing demand of an expanding and diversified community for highly trained graduates. Both Universities were, at the same time, significant instances of the immediate fruitfulness of Commonwealth assistance and advice, effected through the new Universities Commission, to State authorities hampered in the exercise of their constitutional responsibilities in the field of education by limited budgetary resources. Monash, founded in 1958 and opened to students in 1961, promised a first measure of relief to the old-established University of Melbourne, which had catered single-handed for Victoria's university needs since 1854. The Australian Universities Commission was soon to note (in its second report) the still-growing numbers of Victorian students vainly seeking places and to urge the need for yet another university. The State government responded in May 1964 by setting up a 'Third Victorian University Committee' whose recommendations led to the establishment of the university late in 1964. La Trobe opened its doors to an initial intake of 500 students in 1967, envisaging rapid expansion to cater for 10,000 by 1977. It is a measure of the pressures of the period in which the University has come to birth that despite the speed of its planned growth as well as that of Monash, and despite simultaneous development in other fields of tertiary education the State government felt it necessary to establish in 1970 a planning committee for a fourth university.

Although – in common with all other Australian universities – La Trobe is a government foundation, its planners inherited a jealously guarded liberal tradition which in this country has within the limits of financial appropriation always accorded a high degree of independence to universities in shaping their own structures and managing their own affairs. The tradition is British, strengthened, sadly enough, by public apathy – the legacy, no doubt, of a recent colonial past – towards many aspects of higher learning. The new university had to be developed in the light of the Australian Universities Commission's overview of national needs and its assessment of likely funding from state and federal authorities; advice from the Commission and from local expert sources, particularly the other Victorian universities, would obviously create a conception of what areas of learning La Trobe should cover. But beyond that successive planning bodies could hope freely to shape the new institution according to those assumptions upon which principle and experience led them to agree.

The Third University Committee, established under the chairmanship of Mr J. R. A. Glenn (subsequently Sir Archibald, and Chancellor of the University), gave place in December 1964 to an Interim Council which, with the advice of an Academic Planning Board it at once established, supervised the development of the University over the next year. Considerable continuity of membership between Mr Glenn's committee and the Interim Council facilitated an early consistency of policy; the original committee had in any case incorporated in the university Act the broad essentials of the University's structure. Within these limits, both Committee and Council were anxious to leave purely academic decisions to the Academic Planning Board, a body composed of distinguished scholars, mostly practising academics from other universities. For its part, the Board insisted that, as far as possible, decisions about academic structure should be left to the University's first professors and teaching staff. The Vice-Chancellor, Dr David Myers, was appointed in March 1965 and took up his post in the following September. A Chief Librarian had already assumed duty and eighteen foundation professors arrived at various times during 1966. From the time of appointment (in the majority of cases late in 1965) the professors were engaged in sometimes frenzied planning for the beginning of teaching in 1967, and vital principles were in the process laid down regarding the University's future work. Equally, however, the professors found on arrival that a number of structural decisions already made had profound academic implications: with the best will in the world the earlier planning bodies had found it impossible neatly to separate the academic from the non-academic.

Problems of Planning and their Solution

La Trobe was the child of its time; the planners' freedom, great as it ostensibly was, was subtly tempered by the circumstances and the climate of opinion within which they worked. For one thing, the urgent demand for university places in Victoria created a crisis atmosphere which forced the pace of development, and it became the *sine qua non* of all early planning that the first students had to be accommodated in 1967. As a consequence there was not time for the academic staff, whose role it would be to give life to the new institution, to be appointed early enough to take part in determining its broad shape or to engage with their new colleagues in those long exploratory discussions which (as, say, David Daiches' account of the evolution of the structure of studies at Sussex clearly shows)[2] were essential for the generation of really adventurous ideas. One eminent member of the Academic Planning Board, Professor Hugh Stretton, pleaded urgently, in July 1965, that in planning for Schools in the Humanities and Social Sciences it was imperative that organizational decisions should follow after educational ones. The whole point of 'Schools' organization, he wrote,

> is to try to make each School co-extensive with one student's permitted range of study. Only when you have decided which integrated three- or four-year courses you will offer can you name and delimit the Schools intelligently. To name the Schools first, then seek their Deans, then hire the working staff, *and then* plan the curriculum is to preempt precisely those complex educational decisions which the founding academics themselves ought to work out.[3]

But time was not available for so leisurely — if academically desirable — a procedure. In September 1965, at the moment when it was acting on the first selection committees' recommendations for foundation chairs, the Academic Planning Board decided to advise the Interim Council that the four initial Schools should be Humanities, Social Sciences, Biological Sciences and Physical Sciences. Stretton's warning notwithstanding, time forced the organizational decision first, and the door was closed to one whole series of academic possibilities.

It was nevertheless a notable fact that Glenn's original committee – a mixed lay and academic body – had evinced sharp sensitivity to current Australian and overseas discontents with the traditional forms of university organization. The committee was aware of the fruitful experimentation that other new universities seemed to suggest might follow from the organization of studies by Schools 'intermediate in size between traditional faculties and departments', each of them (as the Academic Planning Board came later to put it more grandiosely) 'a functionally effective unit for teaching and research covering a group of related disciplines'. It deplored the tendency in large universities for the traditional Professorial Board to become 'large and unwieldy'. It was alert to the problem of counteracting that student anonymity and alienation which in large institutions, particularly in North America, were being taken at the time to be the explanation for deep stirrings of undergraduate discontent. The committee in fact wrote into the Act its preference for Schools rather than Faculties: full details were left to be worked out, but it made clear its view that each School should be 'headed by a Dean with a Board of Studies representative of the professors and the academic staff of the School'. The Committee likewise recommended the substitution, for the traditional Professorial Board, of an 'Academic Board of about twenty', of which the Vice-Chancellor, Deans and Chief Librarian would be *ex officio* members and the remainder elected from the academic staff. An unquestioned assumption was that a mixed lay and academic council, including student representation, should, in conformity with normal Australian practice, stand at the apex of the university. The blueprint was thus drawn up for a three-tiered structure of government: Council, presided over by the Chancellor; Academic Board, under the Vice-Chancellor; School Boards, headed by the Deans. Limitation of the size of Boards promised effective despatch of business; the inclusion on Boards of grades of staff other than professor at once democratized the university's key academic bodies and gave them direct access to opinion at all levels of the academic community.[4]

The College Concept

Size and its effects on student morale and welfare was the theme of one chain of discussions in Planning Committee, Planning Board and Interim Council: the outcome was a college system which in its early days became the special hallmark of La Trobe. As it had evolved by early 1965, the plan was to make a series of colleges the social centres of the university, to provide in effect a number of sub-communities of approximately 1,000 members each, which might offer staff and students at least some of that sense of 'belonging' believed to be common in smaller universities. Some members of colleges were to be in residence (40 per cent of all enrolled students was the first hope); beyond that, all students and members of staff were to belong to colleges, in which were to be located those facilities provided conventionally in Australia in central unions and staff clubs.

The 'college concept' was undoubtedly the original planners' most carefully considered attempt to meet a fundamental problem at that time troubling thoughtful university teachers and administrators everywhere. Together with the search for a more effective academic and administrative structure it matched the spirit of innovation being displayed by the planners of other new Australian universities (particularly Macquarie in Sydney and Bedford Park in Adelaide), and it was appropriate at a time when educationists were pleading for the provision in Australia of types of university experience varying from the standard patterns of the old state universities.[5] The Interim Council gave it weight and authority by deciding that an initial college (Glenn) should be set up at once, its necessary buildings to take precedence, with the Library, over those which would house the Schools. The latter were in any case best delayed until the first academic staff had been appointed and were able to take part in their planning: initial staff and administrative offices could meantime be temporarily located in Glenn, where planned lecture theatres and tutorial rooms ensured that facilities would be available to teach the initial intake of students. The main buildings of Glenn were completed by March 1967, and for this first year of operation the university in many senses *was* Glenn College. Its students, teachers and many of its administrative staff formally belonged to the college, which became in effect a small and varied community of perhaps six hundred people: a community, so it was sometimes thought, which offered a foretaste of the intimacy and variety which would characterize every future college.

But the planning and foundation by 1968 of a second college (Menzies) quickly suggested weaknesses in this analogy, for much of Glenn's cohesion grew from the artificial wedding there, thanks to the exigencies of necessarily staggered building construction, of the social and the academic. Inevitably, a new college could not reproduce the circumstances which gave Glenn its special flavour, especially when a fast-moving building programme quickly gave body to the clear wish of the majority both of lay planners and first academics that teaching be located in the Schools and not the colleges. In any case, by the end of 1967 many of the University's staff and students were voicing strong criticism of the college system as a whole and an intense internal debate as to its future was under way.

Forces Making for Centralization

The university has proved notably responsive to this debate, though to move with the current of opinion has meant severe modification of the founders' college scheme. Early in 1969 the Council organized seminar discussion of the colleges and solicited the views of all sections of the university community; from a short visit to the United Kingdom and North America, the Vice-Chancellor brought back special observations on collegiate universities; students, anxious for first-hand knowledge of practice elsewhere, sent two of their number on a brief but extensive visit to colleges in overseas universities. Debate and investigation of these kinds led the Council late in 1969 to decide on substantial modifications in the management of colleges, hitherto organized on the traditional British pattern of control by Masters and Boards of Governing Fellows. A high degree of self-government by committees, marked by heavy student and staff representation, has largely met the demand for democratization of college government, while new means have been adopted to give due weight to the different and sometimes conflicting interests of resident and non-resident members.

New colleges, it seems to be understood, will develop according to a variety of patterns which will be determined by the changing needs for student accommodation and the views of planning committees and governing bodies, on which ample staff and student representation exists. What is at present ambiguous is how far colleges can fulfil their union function to the satisfaction of all elements in the university community. The foundation of a staff club is planned within the coming triennium, and it has always been a student complaint that the absence of a central union robs the student body of a self-governing, financially profitable and politically powerful institution such as is enjoyed by their fellows in most other Australian universities. Whether this last complaint will be satisfied by the high degree of participation allowed for in the revised government of colleges remains to be seen. But given the general temper of student opinion it can be expected that at La Trobe, as in other universities everywhere, the chief thrust will be towards the centralization that gives power rather than the decentralization that attacks anonymity. In this matter, as in others, general opinion has undergone a marked change in the short time since the first shaping of the university began.

Counteracting the Tendency to Centralize

Anonymity has come, however, to be implicitly countered by other developments and ideals. The student body itself, for example, though initially small in number, quickly developed an active group life; at the end of the university's first year (1967) the interim Students' Representative

Council had over twenty clubs and societies as affiliates, while the Sports Union Council co-ordinated the work of 17 active sports clubs. Two years later, when the university had just over 2,000 enrolled students, miscellaneous clubs and societies had increased to 40 and there were 28 sports clubs. Even allowing for the fact that these societies were sometimes small and intermittent in their operation, their formation did reflect a remarkable degree of group activity for a new body of students most of whom (about 80 per cent) lived off campus, many of whom travelled considerable distances to the university, and some of whom were part-timers.

Again, the teaching method most strongly advocated by the early academic staff and subsequently woven into most coursework is prized as a further counter to student anonymity. Where appropriate, tutorial discussion in groups of between five and seven students has been accepted as the basic method of teaching and maintained – despite financial strains – from the beginning of classes in 1967. This system, with its emphasis on the face-to-face relationship between student and teacher, is commonly agreed to have done much to extend the range and flexibility of undergraduate instruction. It also lies behind the relative ease with which some departments have been able to enter fruitful discussion with their students on a wide range of matters concerning academic course structure, examining and teaching methods. La Trobe is still a long way from being the kind of total and creative academic community envisaged by theorists like Harold Taylor.[6] It is, however, a university whose sociology department could happily accept during 1970 their students' invitation to jointly sponsor a weekend seminar on the teaching of sociology in the University, or in whose Schools of Humanities and Education staff-student consultative committees regularly meet to discuss matters of importance to their Schools with a view to passing on recommendations for consideration by their respective Boards. While at a general policy level the University has begun somewhat belatedly to examine rationally the broad question of student representation on academic boards and committees, the effects that such representation might be expected to produce are already operating in various departments and Schools thanks to the enthusiasm, good feeling and good sense of many teachers and their students.

Schools and Departments

The four original Schools took academic shape as a result of discussions among the foundation professors in 1966; the teaching that began in the following year brought further staff and the first steps in a process of continuing self-evaluation, proper to a new and expanding university. Government pressure was an important factor in the formation in 1968 and 1970 of two new Schools – Agriculture and Education – to fill inadequately served public needs. Both differed from their predecessors, which at the beginning opted for rotating Deanships, in that they were initially formed and shaped by Deans appointed as such. In the original Schools the spirit of innovation was not strong enough to overcome those administrative exigencies and that concern for establishing disciplines which pointed towards organization by department. Pressure of time accentuated the tendency: foundation professors had to find staff and organize courses at a rate which inhibited the full and leisurely exploration of possibilities which real experimentation often requires. Departments thus developed at once in all Schools except Biological Sciences. A subsequent tendency in the university to look for euphemisms to describe the reality and yet avoid the word 'department' briefly and amusingly reflected what can only be thought of as a species of communal guilt at the drift, organizationally, towards conventional faculty structure.

In the Schools of Humanities and Social Sciences discussion came rapidly to assume the primacy of established disciplines: innovation centred around their arrangement in relation to each other and the degree to which, by varying the pattern of concentration already evident in the other Victorian universities, La Trobe might meet a need not elsewhere catered for. The Interim Council had already decided on the establishment of chairs in economics, politics and sociology in Social Sciences, and modern languages, English, history and philosophy in the Humanities. Agreement among the foundation professors varied this pattern to the extent that history and philosophy, though formally located in Humanities, were in fact to operate also as full members of Social Sciences. In each School it was decided that the ordinary undergraduate course should consist of ten units and that five of these should be in the student's major discipline. The aim was to strike some balance between traditional Australian 'pass' and 'honours' courses, to give all students an opportunity of gaining from their undergraduate studies a firm grounding in one discipline and an appreciation of its bearing upon a selected group of others. In Social Sciences the latter object suggested course patterns which restricted students to disciplines offered within the School – wholly social science studies, in other words, focused in various ways around a chosen specialty. Inter-connexion was to be implicit in the arrangement of courses by the different departments, but in addition a small selection of frankly interdisciplinary courses were planned: as models, it was hoped, for studies later to be developed on the initiative of interested staff. The Humanities School took perforce a more flexible position which would allow course combinations including some subjects taught in the other Schools; it was possible, indeed, soon to envisage 'area majors' in which, by judicious selection from ordinary departmental offerings in the humanities and social sciences and the promotion where appropriate of special ancillary courses, students could be offered the opportunity of taking as the central core of their studies five units focused more particularly on an area or a series of related problems than on a discipline as such. Hence, for example, language, literature, history, politics and sociology might in various ways be drawn upon in a special major centred around the study of North America or Latin America, or – to spread the net more widely – the history and philosophy of science might offer the kind of focus which could draw upon the resources of some of the university's other Schools. The anxiety to look to the relatedness of different fields of study, expressed in these and other ways, was accompanied by a concern to offer students an early feeling that they were members of a School community devoted in the wider sense to a common intellectual endeavour. In each School it was thought that one first year unit taken in common by all students might help achieve this end, especially if taught in such a way as to involve close contact between staff and students. Thus developed 'Social Sciences I' and 'Humanities I'. The former had two parts: an introduction to statistical methods for social scientists, and a study of a series of books of general significance for all students of society and social processes. The latter similarly centred on a booklist, drawn up with an eye to the main interests of the School's departments and to be supported by a lecture course in which representatives of all relevant disciplines would participate. In each School the book 'course' was to be taught by way of a series of one-to-one tutorials, in which all members of staff would be asked to participate.

Four years' teaching experience has inevitably tested and modified these original plans. Incoming staff, whose numbers rapidly increased (by 1970 there were almost 150 teachers in the two Schools), inevitably brought new ideas and in some instances did not share the same ideals as the founders. The challenge of a new university attracted enthusiastic and predominantly young teachers who in many cases imparted a lively sense of experimentation to the work of their departments. But if anything the trend of opinion has been away from a 'School' and towards a discipline-oriented approach to development. The history and sociology departments have succeeded in establishing joint courses at first and second year level, and in the School of Social Sciences a limited number of inter-disciplinary subjects have been devised. But a large number – perhaps the majority – of students now pass through these Schools without undertaking any formal interdisciplinary courses.* And, to the wistful regret of many foundation staff members, Humanities I has been abolished and Social Sciences I so modified as to have lost its original shape and rationale. These were changes made after long debate and in the light of two years'

---

* The exception are students studying in the School of Social Sciences for the BEc degree, the rules for which require that one interdisciplinary unit be taken at third year level.

experience. They reflected with particular sharpness the strength of feeling against what some thought to be arrangements likely to compromise the integrity of the Schools' basic disciplines. The growth of this feeling underlines the fact that in the Humanities and Social Sciences La Trobe's most distinctive work seems certain in future to centre around departments, which are already capitalizing on the special opportunities offered by the five-unit major to develop interesting and sometimes adventurous sequences of studies to consolidate and integrate work within individual disciplines.

The foundation disciplines in the Schools of Physical and Biological Sciences were, respectively, chemistry, mathematics and physics, and botany, zoology and genetics. Subsequent discussion has led to the decision to add, in the near future, geology in the Physical Sciences and biochemistry in Biological Sciences. A vigorous research programme developed at once in both Schools, and plans rapidly matured for the reception of undergraduate students from 1967 onwards, on a scale dictated by the speed at which laboratory and other specialized teaching facilities could be developed. In devising course structures, both Schools were concerned to match rigorousness of scientific training in the conventional sense with the cultivation of some awareness of the preoccupations of scholars in other fields.

One result was the early decision that undergraduates should be encouraged to take a subject from the offerings of the Schools of Humanities and Social Sciences, and in special areas – the biology of human populations is one example – the possibility was fruitfully explored of devising joint courses with social scientists. The School of Physical Sciences thus arranged with economists a course leading to a BSc degree which included a substantial economics component: on a broader scale the hope for new co-operation with the social sciences is reflected in a project at present under discussion for developing a future school of Behavioural Sciences in whose work existing departments, like sociology and biology, will second the offerings of new disciplines, primarily psychology. At the same time, in the physical sciences proper, plans are in train for the development of a postgraduate engineering course which will build on the existing undergraduate degree, and for a variety of special research centres focusing on such matters as environmental studies.

The Schools of Agriculture and Education

The more recent Schools of Agriculture and Education have a somewhat different record. The Academic Board's special committees which handled their establishment took great care not to impose organization or course structures in advance of the coming of the first foundation professors, who were to be appointed as the initial deans. The professional orientation of the Schools meant, moreover, that each would have a cohesive potential not evident among their predecessors. And the presence of a dean likely to be in office for some time promised the opportunity for a purposive follow-through in implementing policy.

Initial proposals by the dean for developing courses in Agriculture quickly illustrated the point. These proposals stressed the need to present Agriculture as an integrated study rather than to emphasize the many individual disciplines involved. Difficulties were recognized: staff sympathetic to this approach had to be recruited, and there was the problem of providing sufficient study in depth within such an integration of subjects. But the first years of experience suggested that such difficulties need not be too formidable.

Basic courses are mounted in chemistry, botany, mathematics and physics leading on to subjects concerned essentially with the reaction of animals and plants to their nutritional and physical environment. The School of Agriculture, although possessing specialists including veterinarians, physicists and economists, has about 40 per cent of its teaching conducted by the Schools of Biological Sciences, Physical Sciences and Social Sciences and has not so far developed an internal departmental structure. Courses are geared to produce agricultural biologists, not soil scientists, plant pathologists and other specialists. This kind of specialism is left to postgraduate studies and research. The initial integrative emphasis is upon the farm as a biological and an economic unit and academically at least such an approach has already proved viable. Whether or not it will have appropriate vocational effects cannot be known for a considerable time. In agricultural research it is not what the graduate knows at graduation which is of ultimate importance, but how and often whether he thinks. The integration of courses is more marked in agriculture than in other Schools, due to several factors such as the nature of the deanship, the professional and vocational purpose of the School and the small compact numbers of staff and students.

The school of Education was conceived and born in a 'crisis' climate arising from the pressure to provide more 'places' for students. By 1968 it was evident that large numbers of La Trobe students would wish to become teachers. Indeed, many were obliged to do so under the prevailing studentship scheme of the Victorian Education Department. Stress was therefore evident from the beginning: 126 students – new graduates of the university – had to be catered for in 1970 with a one-year course Diploma in Education.

Awaiting the new dean's appointment was, in addition, a recommendation that concurrent courses for the Diploma in Education be provided for undergraduates, so that a degree and a diploma could be awarded at the end of an integrated four-year course. Only one course of a similar kind was taught in a Victorian university: a science-education concurrent course at the University of Melbourne. Attempts to mount a concurrent education course at the new Monash University had failed, largely because of the opposition of other departments not wishing to see the 'unity' of their courses affected by professional courses.

Despite the strains on a new staff of setting up two major Diploma courses, one-year and concurrent, concurrency was offered from the beginning (1970). This was not achieved without opposition, considerable debate, involving requests to delay and re-examine the concept of concurrency, taking place in late 1969. The first courses were limited to undergraduates in the Schools of Humanities and Social Sciences, later extending to Agriculture, but Physical and Biological Sciences remained outside the offerings and certain restrictions were placed by some departments on their potential honours students.

The major innovation, consistent with the early aims of La Trobe, was to be seen in the organizational structure within the School of Education. The multi-disciplinary nature of Education, both for teaching and research, was conceived as a basic concept which if not built into the School structure from the beginning would give way, as in other Schools, to a discipline-based series of departments, whether called such or not. The 'functionally effective unit for teaching and research covering a group of related disciplines' was conceived as a Centre for Study, taking a major area in Australian education not worked in depth elsewhere, in which staff, headed by one or more professors, could generate courses, research and development with increasing postgraduate numbers. Over a period of time such Centres would produce a concentration of skill and a corpus of specialized knowledge of value to the educational systems of Australia. The first Centres founded were Comparative and International Studies; Educational Communication and Media; Innovation in Education; Teachers and Teaching; and Urban Education. To each Centre a psychologist, philosopher, sociologist and other specialized staff members have been appointed. Currently a joint appointment with the department of Philosophy has been made and similar joint appointments with economics, English, history, mathematics, politics and sociology, as well as the range of science departments, are being explored. Courses and research in such areas as the politics and sociology of education, the economics of education and mathematical and science education might well emerge. It is still problematical whether the concept of multi-disciplinary teams will work, since it requires a considerable mixture of freedom and organization, and an awareness by the specialist staff involved that by their specialisms they are part of the disease they seek to cure.

Education has followed the characteristic La Trobe pattern of small group teaching, the tutorial being the basis of all courses at Diploma and

BEd levels (the BEd is a further one-year qualification beyond the Diploma).

Central Services in the University

School and course structures, the College system and innovations in administration have been reviewed, but opportunities for innovation are also present at a university's beginnings by the provision of central services. Firmly established in the early years have been medical and counselling facilities for students and an audio-visual unit to facilitate the use of teaching aids in the central lecture theatre complex. This latter, two years after its birth, is currently under discussion as to whether it will remain a purely technical hardware service run by technicians or whether, in addition, it should be under academics who would stimulate fellow academics to innovate new methods of teaching. Linked with this is the possibility of a professional advisory service for academic staff to help improve standards of teaching in the university, and an Educational Research Unit to research into the university itself. Some resistance to these has been encountered for both ideological and financial reasons. Some senior academics argue that these matters are properly the concern of individual staff and that finances are better used for teaching and research purposes in the Schools.

Conclusion

A university, like any other social institution, is a creation both of its time and of the complex of skills, ideals and prejudices of the individuals who give it life. La Trobe has been no exception. At the beginning it had, theoretically, freedom at its disposal, but time placed constraints on experimentation, and human fallibility conjoined with the force of tradition to limit the range of possibilities which might have been imagined to flow from the initial planners' vision. Time tyrannized in a double sense: on the one hand structures had to be evolved and staff appointed at a speed which closed some options from the start; on the other, it was the University's fate to be born in a period of extraordinary change, so that much of what seemed in the early 1960s to be academically and organizationally radical was within less than a decade overtaken by the march of events. Thus administrative exigencies combined with the discipline-oriented views of a rapidly swelling teaching staff to limit the academic meaningfulness of the 'Schools' concept and interdisciplinary work, though existent, developed a weak and unpromising life. The concept of rotating deanships, though on many tests vital as a safeguard against academic and administrative tyranny, weakened School cohesion and augmented the influence of departmental interests and specialisms. Developments in Agriculture and Education hint at the innovatory potential that could flow from unity and consistency of policy at the deanship level, though it might certainly be questioned whether in the non-professional areas of the traditional Arts and Sciences such unitary planning would even in the most favourable circumstances be viable, or indeed, desirable.

Time also overtook the collegiate system: it flourished at the beginning but staff and student pressure alike came in the end to call into question decentralization of facilities and sometimes even to attribute to the university's founders a sinister set of objectives they had never had: most notably, a wish to contain student reformism through a policy of 'divide and rule'. The debate on the college system reflects with particular sharpness how rapidly the external climate of opinion has been changing during the university's brief life. Universally regarded in 1965 as farseeing, the scheme had by 1970 become for many a symbol of traditionalism. Student views in particular were clearly affected by sentiment and experience elsewhere: the fast-growing demand, for example, in Europe and North America for variety and freedom in the forms of student accommodation, or, more important, the world-wide thrust for student power and for the organizational structures (the central student unions on most Australian campuses are often seen in this light) which would facilitate its growth. But while to a few members of the university community the modification of the college system may inevitably be a cause of sadness, most others see it as a necessary and healthy response to real needs and sentiments, and accept in good faith the challenge of trying to hammer out a modified collegiate system which will embody a viable compromise between the demand for centralism and the joint perils of student anonymity and the mass action which overrides minority needs and rights.

The mode of university government developed at La Trobe, with its small Academic Board including non-professorial staff and its matching Boards of Studies in the Schools, has manifestly worked well and may be counted as one of the University's more successful experiments. It of course has its critics. Some academics (especially in the professorial ranks) complain at not being involved enough in decision-making, and student activists express varying degrees of dissatisfaction at limitations set by the present system on their role in the exercise of power. The former complaint is perhaps less serious than the latter. Wide circulation of Board and Council agendas and minutes offer all staff and students the means of keeping abreast of discussions and decisions, and open channels exist for the expression of opinion or the exertion of pressure through School meetings, Board members and Deans. The students' position, at least by standards that have recently come to be accepted elsewhere (and even in Victoria), is less clearcut. Informal consultation has beeen established by convention and a Students' Representative Council operates as a pressure group and a forum of debate on matters of student concern, but the question of student participation in the work of university bodies other than Council, such as the Academic Board and its committees and the School Boards of Studies (students already sit on Council and Council committees), is a live issue in the university. At the time of writing, this is under investigation by a Commission appointed by the Academic Board.

On balance, development at La Trobe might be said to exemplify the dictum that in explaining the shape taken by a new institution the assumptions of the founders are often less important than the structures set up to implement those assumptions. The structures are not always appropriate for achieving the aims that give them birth; in addition they take on a life of their own which can become an independent factor in shaping the course of development. At La Trobe some ancillary objectives achievable through common consent under any general system – the small tutorial ideal is a good example – survive to give a particular flavour to the university's teaching. But structure, time and tradition have tyrannized over foundation dreams in other respects to produce a university which fits the traditional British mould in most essential respects. Its experience may hold lessons for other new foundations in whose conception the drive for innovation is strong. For La Trobe's community of teachers and scholars there is perhaps consolation in reflecting that innovation for its own sake can be a shallow aim and that the most dynamic element in a young university's life is the drive for the achievement of excellence in that academic work for which the university exists. In its four years of life La Trobe has lost none of the enthusiasm with which, in this respect, it began. It may not be unreasonable to hope that there will be resilience – even in some of the existing structures – to facilitate adaptation to the shifting demands that the pursuit of excellence imposes.

REFERENCES

1. W. F. Connell, 'The Development of Universities in Australia', in G. Z. F. Bereday and J. A. Lauwerys (eds.) *Year Book of Education 1959* (London: Evans, 1959), pp. 95–107.
2. D. Daiches (ed.), *The Idea of a New University* (London: Deutsch, 1964).
3. La Trobe University, Academic Planning Board Paper APB/9 of 5 July, 1965.
4. Victorian Parliamentary Debates, Session 1964–5, vol. 275, p. 524.
5. See, e.g. P. H. Partridge, 'The University System', in E. L. French (ed.), *Melbourne Studies in Education, 1960–1961* (Melbourne: Melbourne University Press, 1962), pp. 57–71.
6. Harold Taylor, *Students Without Teachers: The Crisis in the University* (New York: Avon Press, 1969).

18

Flinders University and the Pressure to Conform

Richard J. Blandy

Introduction

Flinders University occupies a 370-acre site in the southern suburban fringe of Adelaide, a city of some 800,000 people and the capital of the State of South Australia. Adelaide has been described as a 'backwater within a backwater' (meaning Australia itself). It is a place the international flights pass over. The great mineral discoveries of the 1960s in Australia were in other States. With few exceptions the headquarters of industry and commerce in Australia lie elsewhere. To sustain Adelaide's population, water must now be pumped from the River Murray some 40 miles away to supplement the storage system in the surrounding hills.

What Adelaide has to offer is charm. The city is trapped on a plain between the sea and a horseshoe of hills, amongst which two thirds of Australia's wine is produced. The climate is superbly Mediterranean. The State's politics have become the most liberal and stylish in Australia. Good restaurants abound and a Festival Theatre complex is under construction as a focal point for the biennial Festival of the Arts. There are signs that the future shape of the city's life may be bound up with research activities of one kind or another and with intellectual and cultural pursuits generally. Such is the background to Flinders University.

Originally conceived (in 1961) as an extension of the existing University of Adelaide, Flinders University achieved full autonomy by Act of Parliament in 1966, the year in which its first students were enrolled. It now has more than 2,000 students (of whom 90 per cent are undergraduates) and over 200 academic staff. Fifteen million dollars have been spent on developing the site, and on a buildings complex which has won an Australian architectural award.

How has this young, growing institution used its freedom? Does Flinders make any difference?

What Flinders illustrates is the classic battle between conformity and difference in the Australian culture. And with predictable results. Planned to be different, Flinders is reverting to pre-existing university patterns slowly but surely. There are two main strands to the story: external limitations on difference imposed by the way universities are financed in Australia, and by public conservatism; and, much more important, the internal disintegration of the credibility of the founding vision, an erosion of faith brought about largely by the university's growth and the loss of power by the committed foundation faculty to less committed new-comers. Gradually, by degrees, the founding fathers have foundered.

External Limitations

Like all Australian universities, Flinders is overwhelmingly Government-financed. Private endowment and gifts are negligible, while students' fees amount to about 15 per cent of recurrent expenditure. Governmental decisions on finance for universities are the *sine qua non* of their development, therefore.

Finance for each university effectively depends on recommendations made by a Commonwealth-appointed, but independent, body, the Australian Universities Commission (AUC). Each university comes under the direct financial control of the State in which it is located, but the Commonwealth provides matching grants up to amounts based on re-commendations of the AUC, which are in turn based on consideration of submissions made by each of the universities. The one exception to this rule is the Australian National University (located in the Australian Capital Territory) which is financed *directly* by the Commonwealth Government, on recommendations of the AUC. These recommendations, and the grants, are made for triennial periods, so as to permit more orderly planning to take place. Capital grants are shared equally between the Commonwealth and State Governments; recurrent grants are shared in the ratio of 1 : 1·85, the larger share of which comprises fees as well as the State grant. These financial arrangements have meant that the development of Flinders University has depended and will continue to depend on the acceptability of its plans to the AUC.

Following time-honoured Australian tradition, the AUC must have due regard to equity in the distribution of funds between the States and between universities. The finance made available to each university depends largely on projections of its enrolments. Within its grant, each university may balance off expensive developments against less expensive, so that the planned student numbers are catered for. Since an unusually expensive development, or expensive distribution of students between fields of study would imply that student/staff ratios would be forced higher than in other universities, or library acquisitions reduced below comparable levels elsewhere, or some such financially compensating development, the AUC has tended to be a conservative force in the development of the new universities, like Flinders. The norms of expenditure per student tend to be heavily affected by the weight of the enrolment patterns of, and services provided by, existing (older) universities. It is difficult, financially, for the newer universities to deviate from this pattern, certainly in so far as the distribution between expensive fields (Science, Engineering, Medicine) and inexpensive (Arts, Economics, Law) is concerned.

By the same token, however, the AUC has prevented the new universities from becoming cut-price institutions absorbing large numbers of less able students in low-cost facilities, while the cream of students and resources were directed to the established universities. Indeed, the AUC has, if anything, tended to load its financial recommendations in favour of the new universities. Finally, there can be little doubt that without the AUC, all Australian universities, and the new universities especially, would today not be as prosperous as they are, because the scale of Commonwealth financial support would be much less.

The AUC is, of course, aware of the tendency to conformity and duplication in Australian universities and is interested in considering steps which might reverse the tendency. The AUC's non-approval of some specific developments in the past, may represent attempts at such steps. Unfortunately, however laudatory this aim, growth in the power of the AUC to influence developments of the universities in particular (unique?) directions may be at the expense of the autonomy of each institution to experiment in its own fashion, and may sap the very spontaneity from which creativity and excellence (as well as disaster) spring. It remains, however, that the AUC has wielded a conservative, if supportive, role in the development of the new universities, because the Commission's immediate base of reference has been what already existed, and because it has tried to be fair.

The way in which universities are financed in Australia is by no means the only external limitation placed on the capacity of the universities to develop differently. In a sense, the financial limitations are superficial reflections of more fundamental attitudes embedded in Australian society itself. Australians are highly conservative as well as conformist, although their conservatism is about a system of values and way of life which is different from that in the United States, for example. Australian conservatism is based on radical nineteenth-century philosophy, a utilitarian outlook with a measure of egalitarianism, a belief in positive government intervention and lack of faith in the beneficence of competition. It has been said that Australia is the country least likely to spawn a revolution. All institutions are measured in terms of their acceptability to the prevailing conservative ethic and the universities are no exception. There are strong pressures exerted by employers, press and public for university activities which yield a product that is recognizable by the standards of existing institutions. New-left suggestions to restructure universities along 'participatory' lines meet the utmost hostility, as do suggestions that the universities should become politically committed in the cause of social justice. Because the new-left student movements have been strongest in the new universities like Flinders (although they have not, in fact, been very strong) public opposition has been focused on the new institutions. This has undoubtedly had the effect of eroding confidence in those things in which the new universities differed most significantly from the old.

Flinders has not escaped these pressures. Indeed, since the external pressures have come at a time when internal pressures have been mounting in the same direction, a rapid erosion in the founding conception of Flinders has occurred.

Internal Disintegration

The conflict between conformity and difference at Flinders can be most clearly seen in the basic organization of the University. From the outset, Flinders made a departure from the established Faculty organization of the older universities and adopted a so-called, School system. The Schools attempted to group connected fields of study under School Boards which controlled academic developments within the group. Thus, economics, geography, psychology, politics, sociology, history, education, American and Asian studies and social administration are grouped in the School of Social Sciences. Languages, philosophy and drama are grouped into the School of Humanities, and so on. Within each school, major fields of knowledge are demarcated as Disciplines, viz. the Economics Discipline, each headed by a professor. Sub-professorial staff are responsible to the Professor of the Discipline to which they are assigned, and the professors are responsible to the University Council. The Council is also advised by the School Boards, however, which comprise not only the professors, but all sub-professorial staff and some student representatives.

The power of the professors and of individual Disciplines is tempered by the power of the School Boards. The more powerful the School becomes, the less scope for individual manoeuvre is left to the Disciplines. The more autonomy the Disciplines get, the more like collections of Faculties do the Schools become.

It is widely felt at Flinders that the School system is in a process of disintegration, and that the university is reverting to a *de facto*, if not yet *de jure*, Faculty system. The reasons for this are complex but at the root lies an inability to make the formal connections between Disciplines in each School *real* connexions, that is, academically meaningful.★ There are very few interdisciplinary courses and those that do exist are largely reassemblies of pre-existing parts from other more specialized fields. Furthermore,

---

★ In some of the Schools, disintegration is minimal or non-existent. This would apply to Biological Sciences and Mathematical Sciences, which have managed to integrate their course offerings to a high degree and which are small. In other Schools, such as Humanities and Social Sciences (which is very large) disintegration has gone some distance. Hence, the problems which are dealt with here apply with particular force to these latter Schools.

although students carry two majors for their entire three year ordinary bachelor's programme, virtually no explicit integration is attempted. A politics and geography major remains just that, a creature with legs in two camps, but perhaps no body connecting the legs.

Against the often forced togetherness of the Schools thrusts the desire of some Disciplines for greater specialization by their students in their own fields, and the desire of other Disciplines for a less restricted range of courses for their own students than those offered within the School. On the one hand, there is a real fear that the psychology/economics graduates from Flinders may be recognized neither as psychologists nor as economists, because their workload in each field is less than elsewhere. This might be welcomed if the joint product could be perceived as possessing a discernibly different and valuable outlook or *modus operandi* compared with his peers from other universities. Regrettably, there is no strong evidence to suppose that this is so. On the other hand, there is a feeling that students in History or Politics, say, should be permitted a more liberal range of choice in the other fields they study, as they would in other universities. Both tendencies attack the middle-way concentration of studies on connected fields which is the *raison d'être* of the School system.

This is not to denigrate the idea of the School system, which offers the prospect of a radical reorientation in university education in Australia. But without a switch *throughout* Australian higher education towards middle-way generalist undergraduate degrees followed by specialization at the graduate level, or without a massive collective effort at intellectual integration *by the faculty*, the Schools are destined to become shells. The conservative forces have become too strong; the problems of integration are too difficult. Curiously enough, amongst the faculty, the proponents of the School system have sometimes been called the conservatives and yet, in truth, it is they who are radical in the context of Australian higher education. By and large, the faculty want to retain their identification with particular specialist fields, partly for academic reasons, partly for mobility and promotion prospects. These are strong and valid reasons, and against them stands only an exciting but unproven idea which may be a chimera. As with financing techniques and public pressures, so with the faculty. Flinders increasingly promises not to be different, but to be more of the same.

In this context, there is one committee at Flinders which might possibly have stemmed the tide running against the School system. This is the Academic Committee of the University Council which is responsible for co-ordinating all academic developments in the University. All the Schools are represented on the Academic Committee, the Vice-Chancellor is its Chairman, and its decisions carry great weight with the University

Council. In retrospect, perhaps the Committee's most fateful decision affecting the Schools was its decision to allow the School of Humanities to permit its students an open choice of non-major course combinations from its own and other School's offerings, a 'liberalizing' change which attacked the very rationale of the Schools. By acceding to this development, the Academic Committee set a precedent which has facilitated the disintegration of the Schools.

Another important area of innovation at Flinders, which has already been touched upon, is the limitation of professorial power. Professors in Australian universities have generally held the reins of power tightly. They have been referred to as the 'God-Professors'. At Flinders, power is more widely dispersed through the faculty, with sub-professorial staff having more influence than at most Australian universities. The political superstructure of Flinders includes explicit provision for much more than token representation of junior staff. So much so, that student pressure for increased student representation has garnered very little support amongst the sub-professorial staff, who find their influence in the University to be considerable, who are on good terms with the professors as a result, and who therefore need no allies to establish themselves. Increased, but still limited, student representation in University government has, however, been accepted, and it remains to be seen whether this will enhance or diminish professorial authority.

Perhaps equally important, the explicit diffusion of power between faculty members in a host of committees, has considerably increased the influence of the administration, and especially its head, the Vice-Chancellor. The Vice-Chancellor of Flinders, since its inception, and until his elevation to the Chairmanship of the Australian Universities Commission in 1971, was Professor P. H. Karmel, a remarkably gifted man who would have wielded great influence in any event. The diffusion of power in the University produced a complex committee structure which greatly increased the influence such a capable man could bring to bear. Proposals from lower-level committees could be reviewed by many committees of which the Vice-Chancellor was *ex officio* member. Wearing any of a multitude of different hats, he was favourably placed to influence the nature and timing of proposals for change in the University, by referal backwards, forwards and sideways. Furthermore, in a complex situation, knowledge is power. Few men, other than the Vice-Chancellor, *could* know all the angles. His was one of the few voices which was completely well-informed. Hence, his counsel was given even greater weight than his great natural talents would have accorded him in any event.

The future of Flinders University is, therefore, more intimately tied up with the personality and vision of its Vice-Chancellor than most Australian universities. With the departure of the founding Vice-Chancellor, the

University may develop in new and unexpected directions. It may revert even faster towards a Faculty system. It may emphasize the development of more professional schools, such as engineering, law, architecture and so on. (The only such school at Flinders at present is medicine.) What the incoming Vice-Chancellor thinks about such matters will more materially affect the outcome at Flinders than at many other Australian universities, where power is not so diffused and, where a professorial oligarchy often holds *de facto* power.

Conclusion

The proof of the pudding is in the eating. Have the differences at Flinders produced, or are they likely to produce, intellectual endeavour on a higher or different plane than would otherwise be the case? One can mention pioneering developments like the creation of Chairs in Drama, Meteorology and Spanish. Philosophy has developed a strong applied flavour – courses in Marxism/Leninism and the US–Australian involvement in Vietnam, for example. Biology has a strong position in cancer research, and economics in labour economics. There is a flourishing Institute of Oceanographical Research, and the Mathematics School is outstanding. Sins of omission will undoubtedly be visited on my head by irate colleagues, but the point is that in none of these cases can the counterfactual proposition be dismissed. There does not appear to be any unique set of circumstances about Flinders which alone permitted, or even materially assisted, these developments. Regardless of the structure and organization of the University, these developments could have taken place. There does not seem to be any particular 'Flinders' flavour about the activities being conducted at the University. It is easily conceivable that they could have occurred elsewhere in Australia.

Even if Flinders has not developed any particularly distinctive brand of thinking, how is the quality of intellectual activity likely to develop in the years ahead at Flinders? This really amounts to trying to assess changes in intellectual quality in Australia as a whole, because Flinders is, overwhelmingly and increasingly, simply a part of the Australian whole, a cutdown replica of other universities elsewhere.

Australian universities are becoming stronger. Both the status and pay of academics have risen very greatly in Australia during the 1960s. Australian academics must now rate amongst the most fortunate in the world in relative status and pay when viewed in their own national context. Financial provisions for study leave, travel and research are excellent, although not so lavish as in some American institutions. Universities are politically hot and big news. These developments have injected a new sense of confidence into the academic community. This, together with the growth of Australian nationalism in the 1960s, offers the prospect that, during the 1970s, the beginnings of a distinctively *Australian* intellectual touch may emerge from the Universities. If this happens, Flinders is likely to be in the van, partly because Adelaide is likely to be increasingly a city whose economy is based on intellectual pursuits, and partly because, being young and chameleon-like, Flinders is well placed to respond to such a trend in the academic mood. The collective loss of nerve signalling the collapse of the School system at Flinders may yet yield dividends through a more rapid acceptance of such a new, Australia-wide reference pattern, therefore.

19

The University of Wisconsin-Green Bay: Man and His Environment

Edward W. Weidner

The University of Wisconsin-Green Bay focuses all of its activities on an urgent problem of the future, man and his environment. Therein lies its distinctiveness.

Values, Self, and Society

To be human is to have and assert individuality but it is also to relate this individuality to other men and to the planet earth. A consideration of man and his environment leads to an emphasis on man in society. Environmental education provides an excellent framework for students to consider conflicts between self and society and priorities of values. It highlights what is meant by being responsibly human. In this respect, it is closely allied with the great religions of the world. All of them have moved toward a greater concern for this world and its future. They identify peace and love as cardinal virtues, and are concerned about the conditions sufficient for their attainment. It is evident that there no longer can be peace or love without a substantial measure of environmental quality. Man is morally compelled to take action to assure environmental quality for the future, even for generations yet unborn.

Environmental education flows from such value premises. At the University of Wisconsin-Green Bay, freshman students begin their Liberal Education Seminar work by grappling with value conflicts and priorities in regard to environmental problems. Emphasis on them continues throughout their education.

The Emphasis on Problems

Environmental education is problem-focused education, as contrasted to education focused on the idea of the well-rounded renaissance man. Centuries ago, it was possible for a student to cover exhaustively many if not most areas of knowledge during a few years of higher education. Nearly all courses were compulsory. But by the middle of the nineteenth century, it was obvious that the explosion of knowledge prohibited such practices from being continued. In the United States, new courses were introduced. While many required courses continued, students were granted choices or electives within certain guidelines. Confining university study to classical subjects was replaced by sampling knowledge in many fields. But the predominant goal of the well-rounded renaissance man remained. The substitution was an accommodation, within this goal, to new subjects and new vocations.

The whole liberal education movement has been deeply influenced by the idea of the well-rounded renaissance man. For example, almost all universities in the United States have distribution requirements, under which a student is compelled to select courses from a number of different groups of disciplines. Another typical requirement is that of various tool subjects, such as mathematics and foreign languages. The justification for these requirements is that every educated person should have knowledge and skills of this kind. The liberal arts major, in which a student selects courses from many different fields, is rather explicitly based on such a concept. The liberal arts major was particularly promoted during the 1930s. Twenty years later, the general education movement had its zenith in the United States. Here the aim was to make available samples of knowledge from many different fields. Students sometimes could pick and choose among general education courses, though most frequently such courses were on a required basis. The well-rounded renaissance man idea in higher education originally was developed to give a classical education to gentlemen and ladies. It has remained something for the upper middle class and upper class. It tends to be passive and aloof in terms of society, and backward looking in terms of concern. It fastens the educational objectives of the few on the many. It assumes the melting pot theory of society.

In contrast, problem-oriented education is fundamentally involved with the values, knowledge, and instrumental abilities of students in relation to problem solving in the years ahead. It does not assume a singleness of culture or educational needs. Problem-oriented education is based on the assumption that the first priority of society and of education is to assure a future for generations yet to come.

Problem-focused education is theme-related. One example of such a theme is environmental quality. There are many other examples, such as human conflict and co-operation, human rights, and empathy, understanding and love. Problem-focused education is concerned with the major problems confronting a society and the entire world today, and in the future. It approaches the liberal arts and sciences and general education with a set of values that rejects the validity of *random* sampling of knowledge. A new set of criteria for selecting courses and sampling knowledge emerges, based upon what is related to the problem at hand. At the University of Wisconsin-Green Bay it is man and his environment. Both by inclusion and exclusion, as well as by emphasis, the courses at UWGB reflect this choice of problem. In brief, problem-oriented education is education for all classes, all races, and based upon the brotherhood of man and a sense of responsibility for the future of mankind flowing from such brotherhood.

Environmental education, in common with other problem-focused education, requires a future time orientation. Young people have been demanding more relevant education. They have not always been able to define the term relevance precisely, but it is apparent that they point to the urgent problems facing the world, and they point to the present, and especially to the future, rather than to the past.

There are two issues here. First, there are many persons in higher education who suggest that what a scholar does is his own business, and not the business of society. They insist that students should return to the library, and sample the stored knowledge. Universities should continue to do what they have been doing for centuries, it is said. The defect of this approach is that it overlooks the value judgment underlying the accumulation of knowledge and wisdom. What books in the library should one select for reading and study? What problems should a scholar consider? What is significant to the life and learning of student and professor? And what measure of social responsibility should an individual and an institution of higher education exhibit? The search for all knowledge is based upon a value judgment, stated or unstated. It is no criticism of problem-focused, environmental education that the knowledge it organizes is selected on the basis of a value judgment. All knowledge selection is so based. In fact, in the case of environmental education the explicit nature of this value judgment is an advantage.

A second issue in the future time orientation of environmental education lies in the enjoyment of things of value. It is said, and properly so, that a painting by a master, a symphony by Beethoven, or a sonnet by Shakespeare is a thing of beauty. Beauty is one of the underlying values of life. Therefore, goes the argument, a future time orientation to a university is inconsistent with the main purpose of life. Beauty is an important value. But it is important to distinguish between the kind of beauty traditionally associated with the upper class, and the lack of beauty so frequently associated with the mass of people. The urgent imperative is that all mankind proceed to a new level of beauty, and the full enjoyment of life. Education should take the leadership in such a struggle, rather than just being the principal custodian of the culture of courts and kings. The future and an adequate quality of life for everyone need to be assured before the values associated with the few can have their proper place in the scheme of things.

Changing the time orientation in learning does not mean that history, the humanities and the fine arts are ignored. However, it does require a new approach to history and the humanities, just as it requires a new approach to other subjects. History must be studied not alone, and not, primarily, from the antiquarian point of view, but with the future in mind. Similarly, philosophy and the great books must be studied not primarily from a past orientation, but from a now and future orientation. All subjects, including history, literature, philosophy, and the fine arts are related to environmental education. But they are related to environmental education only to the extent that the subject is oriented to the future. The fine arts and the humanities can be future time-oriented in a very meaningful fashion. Not to do so restricts these fundamental and exciting areas of knowledge to a few persons of the upper class, and removes them from the mainstream of human action and thought.

At the University of Wisconsin-Green Bay, education for the future is emphasized in all parts of the curriculum. One example is a capstone senior-level Liberal Education Seminar. Each small group of students selects an environmental problem and explores its dimensions and possible solutions in the distant future – perhaps thirty or forty years hence. Education for the future liberates universities from slavish devotion to what was, and frees them to concern themselves with what may be. However valuable well-rounded individuals may be, the times cry for men for whom the past is, at best, signposts for the future.

Transdisciplinary Courses

Problems are by their very nature interdisciplinary and even transdisciplinary. All parts of the university need to be called upon to contribute to environmental education. Every discipline, every subject matter, and every profession is an important contributor.

The University of Wisconsin-Green Bay is divided into four theme colleges. Each of these colleges is authorized to study a particular set of environmental problems. One college is devoted to the biophysical environment, another to the social environment, a third to human adaptability to different environmental conditions, and a fourth to human identity and the attempt to change environmental conditions. Each college is subdivided into two or three concentrations. There are eleven concentrations all told, each concerned with a specific transdisciplinary environmental problem area. Transdisciplinary and interdisciplinary courses at the University of Wisconsin-Green Bay are college or concentration courses, and only transdisciplinary and interdisciplinary courses are found at the college and concentration levels. The aim is to have each concentration offer about a dozen transdisciplinary courses at the undergraduate level. In the future, graduate work will add to this number.

Under traditional educational theory and practice, citizenship education, often considered synonymous with liberal or general education, has been viewed as basically different from education that was job oriented. Those concerned with social problems have been strong supporters of liberal education. If a student sampled many different areas of knowledge, he would presumably be a more effective citizen. In the United States, the movement for citizenship education developed special strength after World War II. It was thought of as a kind of education that contrasted with specialized majors or professions. It became intertwined with liberal education, the liberal arts major, and general education; citizenship education brought some unusual courses into the curriculum of colleges and universities. American studies, international studies, and courses in effective communication, interpersonal relations, and family living were among the items introduced under its rationale. Since citizenship education was thought to be different from education for future employment, there was no impact on the disciplines or professions as a result of this movement.

True citizenship education needs to be related to the future positions that persons will hold on an employment basis, as well as to the roles that each person will play as a citizen quite removed from his occupation. In fact, if the focus be on environmental quality, it is obvious that every discipline and every profession is important, as well as most non-vocational activities that persons perform from time to time. Problem-focused environmental education thus provides a way of relating one discipline to another, one profession to another, and the specialized disciplines and professions, as a whole, to liberal education and general education. It provides a framework within which the biologists can co-operate with the artists, the sociologists can co-operate with the chemists, and the political scientists can interchange with those in business administration or teacher education. And all can co-operate with all concerned students and other citizens.

In addition to transdisciplinary, problem-oriented courses, it is, of course, necessary to offer disciplinary and professional courses. Thus courses in biology, chemistry, sociology, economics, literature, art, music, and mathematics as well as courses in teacher education, business and public administration, social work, and other areas are an important part of a university. The normal university is organized around such courses, with disciplinary and professional departments or schools. At the University of Wisconsin-Green Bay, however, disciplinary courses are grouped together in subordinate organizational units called options. Professional courses are grouped in still other organizational units. Thus a full range of transdisciplinary, interdisciplinary, disciplinary, and professional courses is available to students. All transdisciplinary and interdisciplinary courses are focused on the environmental theme. Disciplinary and professional courses are of two kinds: basic or general courses that are not particularly environment-related, and environment-related courses. UWGB seeks to be adequate in the number of basic or general courses in disciplines and professions, but it aims at unusual depth in regard to environment-related courses in these same disciplines and professions.

A student selects one of the concentrations. He has the additional option of choosing one of the disciplines and/or one of the professions. In other words, a student must choose an environmental problem area, or concentration, but it is up to him whether he chooses a disciplinary and/or a professional area of study in addition. If he makes the second choice as well as the first choice, his programme provides for specially relating the discipline or profession to the environmental problem represented in the concentration.

It is in this manner that the University of Wisconsin-Green Bay has tried to make citizenship education compatible with employment education, and to make transdisciplinary education compatible with disciplinary and professional education. There is little purpose in developing an undergraduate transdisciplinary programme if a student cannot continue his education in a graduate or professional school, or if he cannot use the knowledge gained to obtain employment after he leaves the university. Yet a transdisciplinary, problem-oriented approach can actually improve disciplinary and professional education. The programme of the University of Wisconsin-Green Bay is predicated on the belief that students making the second choice, that is, a choice of emphasizing a discipline and/or a profession *in addition* to concentrating on an environmental problem, will increase their understanding, motivation, and retention concerning the discipline or profession far more than if they had taken a conventional course of studies at another university. UWGB seeks to make the profession or discipline 'come alive' through relating it to other disciplines and professions, and through relating the whole to environmental problems of the present and the future in a transdisciplinary setting. Environmental education at UWGB meets the test of relevance and social applicability; at the same time it is integrally related to the world of knowledge, and to future employment.

Community Action

Environmental quality cannot be attained without strong community action. Therefore, environmental education is of necessity associated with a community action approach to education, focused on environmental problems. Such an approach obviously is consistent with the basic ideas of John Dewey. While there are many admirers of John Dewey, higher education has really not extended the 'to do' idea outside the confines of the classroom. Higher education has not concerned itself with the subject matter of community action and its techniques to any great extent. Had it done so, students would not be insisting that higher education is irrelevant. It is time their message was received.

A community action approach to higher education does not mean that the role of the university is direct community action. Rather, the teaching role of the university is to help students learn the importance of community action and to help them improve their skills in taking effective community action in the future. Universities need to be concerned with improving the abilities of students in regard to decision-making, problem-solving, and group action. Skills in these areas are undoubtedly far more important than skills in some of the traditional tool subject areas. Yet most universities do not even have a course in the techniques of community action. Many do not have courses specifically geared to decision-making and problem-solving. Their curriculum is simply not instrumentally oriented.

The case for environmental education rests upon two considerations: the educational values of a problem-focused academic plan and the community values associated with environmental quality. The role of the university is not to indoctrinate but to focus attention on, and reflect about, the values of environmental quality and associated and competing values. Its function is not to take direct action itself, but to prepare its students to be capable of taking such action in the future. The role of the university is not to direct community change in regard to environmental quality, but to consult and work with communities on an invitational basis in regard to such objectives, lending its special resources and expertise. Environmental education encompasses several facets such as an environmental ethic, environmental awareness, technical knowledge, and plans, ways, and means for effective community undertakings. The goal of the well-rounded renaissance man is a value-laden goal. The goal of an environmentally oriented and instrumentally equipped man is no more and no less value-laden.

A community action approach is integral to the academic plan of the University of Wisconsin-Green Bay. There are many courses that specifically relate to decision-making, problem-solving, and group action. Many other courses use live community environmental projects as a major source of reference and data.

Environmental education must of necessity be experiential education in large degree. In no other way can a student – or professor – gain an adequate amount of insight, knowledge, and experience. Students cannot receive a complete education in the classroom or in the library and laboratory.

Experiential education requires a university to engage in a melding of the teaching, research, and community outreach functions. At many of the universities in the United States, undergraduate teaching is quite separate from basic research and graduate teaching. Each of these, in turn, is rather separate from community outreach or extension functions. In the United States, a hundred years of the land-grant philosophy in practice has failed to unite these three activities. Environmental education sees each of them as integrally related and provides a rationale and basis for doing so. In fact, in environmental education it is often difficult to discover if a given activity of a professor relates to teaching, applied research, or community implementation. The three are often very closely intertwined. Of course, if the three are going to be integrally related, professors must be attracted who are happy with this kind of approach. A professor who wants to isolate himself in his laboratory, quite removed from any social application of what he is undertaking, is not one who is likely to make a substantial contribution to environmental education. Similarly, an extension professor who is removed from applied research and teaching will have a very limited role and impact. The teacher who does not go outside the classroom, or the library, will likewise have limited results to show. What is needed is a professor who sees the entire society as his classroom, and understands the close connexion between teaching, applied research, and community action.

In addition, experiential education requires a university-community relationship of a kind different from that found in the great majority of campuses around the world. What is necessary is a kind of co-operation with the immediate community that permits student and professor to be associated with the community in environmental quality undertakings. This is a two-way process. There must be a basis for students and professors going off campus and observing, studying, and working directly in the field or with community groups. There also must be a basis for lay citizens to come to the campus and participate with students and professors in courses and other university affairs.

As a consequence, the University of Wisconsin-Green Bay relates to its nearby community in a number of distinctive ways. First of all, the university makes extensive use of community advisory committees. This stems from the first days of UWGB in the fall of 1966, when local citizens were asked to volunteer to help the new Chancellor plan and develop the university. Six committees were established that year. Gradually the number of committees has expanded, so at the present time there are more than fifteen with more than two hundred members. A general university advisory committee serves as a monitoring body for the entire advisory committee system and relates directly to the Chancellor. Each of the four theme colleges has its own citizen's advisory committee. There are two professional advisory committees – one in the area of business and public administration, and another in the area of teacher training. Advisory committees are very helpful in making experiential education possible.

Another way of relating to the community has been the appointment of a number of community lecturers. Currently, approximately fifty lay citizens serve in such a capacity each semester. They bring their experience and insights into the classroom, often combining with a professor to form a panel. Typically, they help plan the course with the professor, and have responsibility for one or more sessions during the semester.

A third way of relating to the community so that the town gown relationship is close and mutually supporting lies in the development of communiversity projects. Communiversity projects are projects that involve teaching, applied research and community implementation. They must be numerous enough so that all themes, all transdisciplinary efforts, and all disciplinary and professional areas at the university can have their classroom, laboratory, and studio efforts supplemented with opportunities for participant observation in live community undertakings.

In the short course of its existence, UWGB has engaged in fifteen or twenty communiversity projects of some substantial nature. One of the largest of these involves a lake that has some problems of water quality. A combination of university resources, assistance from the national government, and support from the county government has permitted an intensive study of the lake, aiming toward community action to eliminate the difficulties. Undergraduate students receive credit for working on the project, and professors use the lake and the data collected about it as illustrative material in courses in several different disciplines. It is truly a cooperative effort, with people trained in political science, law, economics, sociology, chemistry, biology, limnology and other fields participating. It is an example of many students profiting from an applied research and community outreach project. A single communiversity project may enhance the value of many kinds of courses – the liberal education seminars, concentration courses, independent study, and discipline or professional courses.

Experiential education ideally begins at home. A student and a professor should not leave their university and surrounding communities unless they have looked at them in regard to the same problems that they intend to explore in some distant community. Otherwise, the basis of comparison is not at hand, and in particular the student and the professor cannot appreciate the kinds of pressures and community relations that are involved in environmental problems. Comparison in the field is built into the UWGB academic plan. For example, in the Liberal Education Seminar during the sophomore year a student is exposed to environmental problems in the Upper Great Lakes region of the United States, and during his junior year he is exposed to similar problems in another cultural setting.

The University of Wisconsin-Green Bay is actively considering the establishment of formal field stations or observation points. Of course, the communities closest to Green Bay serve this role already. The effort is to develop such opportunities at some distance from the campus, and under markedly different cultural conditions.

It is often suggested that a university that focuses on man and his environment will get into some kind of trouble with its nearby community. Those who are concerned about this matter frequently assume a simplistic devil-angel theory of environmental deterioration, with a few polluters being the devils and the many citizens being the angels. This is a tragically incorrect reading of the environmental crisis. Everyone is a polluter. Everyone encourages pollution by others. Everyone has a responsibility to see that governmental controls and policies are established that will minimize pollution by everyone, the 'heavy' polluters and the 'lighter' polluters alike.

Force against polluters is required from time to time. The exercise of such force is a function of governmental and community action, not universities. Educational institutions must be themselves. They must examine all kinds of strategies for environmental quality, ranging from the most forceful to the most educational, and determine which seem to be most effective under what circumstances. In relating to communities, universities as institutions are confined to observational, consultative, and cooperative approaches. Experiential education is impossible on any other basis.

The Student and Professor

An environmental education approach to higher education requires a close student-professor relationship. A whole undergraduate generation has been turned off just on this one point. In the worst instances, professors are seldom around; the teaching assistant may be present, now and then, but not the professor. Professors pride themselves on the extent to which they do not teach undergraduates. The overwhelming focus of the classroom is a teacher-student relationship, with the student taking notes and largely in a passive role. It is not possible to have an effective problem-solving approach on environmental topics under such circumstances.

Environmental education places the emphasis on problem-solving, and problem-solving requires collaboration of many persons. The professor becomes the number one learner as both the professor and student explore community priorities and possible community action in regard to a variety of environmental problems. Every community is different, every problem has some distinctive aspects. Therefore, in each case a different group of concerned people must be melded together if proper community action is to be secured. Professors have substantial opportunities to assume a leadership role in learning when so much of the learning involves the exploration of problems that have not yet been fully identified, let alone fully solved.

In sum, the mode of instruction should be learning rather than teaching. The student should be front and centre, aiming to develop his potential. The professor is normally an authority in regard to the abstract portion of a subject matter. He is the authority within the confines of a classroom lecture. He is the number one learner as professor and student consider community problems of an emergent and urgent nature.

There is much encouragement through official UWGB channels for professors to relate to students outside of the classroom, and even in their homes. Joint field experiences are numerous. Close student-professor relationships depend in part upon favourable physical arrangements. Through the design of university buildings, UWGB has tried to foster such relationships, particularly emphasizing informal physical spaces in which small groups of students and faculty members can be accommodated.

An environmental education approach to higher education requires student initiative education. This concept goes beyond the usual liberal education emphasis of developing the communicative, critical, and analytical abilities of each person. Problems such as those of the environment cannot be identified, understood, or moved closer to solution by routine lectures engendering passivity and rote learning. Nor is a detailed syllabus, teaching outline, or list of readings adequate. The objective is to develop the capacity of young persons to solve complex problems. This requires that the learners gain experience in taking the initiative, in addition to mastering subject matter. Community problem-solving requires initiative by the many, not just by the few. If students are to be effective in later life as community leaders or even as intelligent community followers, they must have some experience as participant-observers in taking the initiative relative to the urgent requirements of society.

It is not an easy matter to go from a traditionally structured curriculum or course to a flexible and open curriculum or course. Students do not automatically know how to take initiative in their own learning. Universities must therefore develop learning modules that help teach the student how to take such initiative. A number of courses a student selects during his years in higher education must use this approach, if much lasting impact is to be obtained. In other words, student initiative education cannot come about just by immersion; it must come about by planned development of a student's capabilities. The University of Wisconsin-Green Bay has developed certain learning modules with this objective in mind. In addition, student initiative education is reflected in the curriculum. Requirements are minimal and flexible. If a student does not like any one of the University's concentrations, or the supplementary opportunities to specialize, he may propose his own concentration. A number of students take advantage of this opportunity. In addition, all honours students are exempt from all course and curricular requirements.

Conclusion

We are living in a time when national and world-wide priorities are being questioned and reordered. Inevitably, higher education is a part of such questioning and reordering. Central to national and world-wide priorities are human survival and survival at a humane level. Universities are being asked to orient themselves to the future of mankind. This is a reasonable and justifiable request. It requires the universities to give up their heavy preoccupation with the past on a disciplinary basis, and look to the future with a problem focus and on a transdiciplinary basis. Environmental education is a part of this sobering and exciting challenge. It is based on a firm ethical and value foundation, a foundation that places self in society. Environmental education calls for a philosophy of personal responsibility and involvement in this world.

20

The State University of Novosibirsk: Experience and Problems

S. T. Belyaev and Taukoed Golenpolsky

In the heart of Siberia, four hours' flight away from Moscow in the midst of picturesque pines and snow-white birches, some 20 miles outside of Novosibirsk proper, stands Akademgorodok – the Academytown campus of the now famous Siberian Branch of the USSR Academy of Sciences, with a score of research institutes including mathematics, hydrodynamics, computer centre, theoretical and applied mechanics, nuclear physics, physics of semiconductors, automation and electrometrics, chemical kinetics and combustion, inorganic chemistry, organic chemistry, catalysis, cytology and genetics, geology and geophysics, economics, history, philosophy and philology. Today in the large Siberian Science Centre there are about 7,500 scientists including 1,500 full and associate professors. It was here that the campus of the State University of Novosibirsk – the SUN, appeared in 1959.

Twelve years is not quite a long enough period to speak of Experience with a capital letter. The creation of the University here in unusually favourable conditions was not only a necessity but an experiment as well. Some of the accumulated results that are being constantly studied by a combined group of sociologists and educationists provide us with certain observations. As for problems – as anyone in touch with academic life very well knows – twelve years is a space of time more than enough to be forced to tackle a score per year.

It was Sir Eric Ashby who quoted from a statement published by the University of Witwatersrand: 'Every civilized society tends to develop institutions which will enable it to acquire, digest and advance knowledge relevant to the tasks which, it is thought, will confront it in the future. Of these institutions the University is the most important.' The rapidity of progress so typical of the twentieth century makes such problems as the development of science and the training of highly skilled specialists especially acute. In tackling these, one of the key positions belongs to the universities. Appearing as a response action to the corresponding demands of society, the universities contribute their effort to its further development. In each case the character of the contribution is determined by the specificity of the demands of society and by the manner in which these demands are met within a given university.

Traditionally it has been considered that the efforts of universities are directed towards two main problems: the development of fundamental knowledge and training of future specialists. The experience of universities throughout the world has proved that this is no longer sufficient.

The task standing before universities today, as we see it, combine science and the training of highly skilled specialists with the development of a feeling of responsibility in young members of society. Some who will be professors in the early twenty-first century are already university graduates and many citizens of the coming century are attending high schools today. We are, therefore, to a very great extent responsible for what the twenty-first century will be.

Universities Within the Framework of a Higher Education System

The main task of any higher educational system is the training of highly skilled specialists in the field and quantity dictated by current needs and by the perspectives of the development of the country's national economy and culture. In the Soviet higher educational system, universities quantitatively are only a small fraction of the more specialized higher educational institutions: technical, medical, pedagogical, etc. The peculiarity of the universities lies in the fact that they train specialists in fundamental fields of knowledge, for staff research institutes as well as other higher educational institutions and high schools. This stresses the very special and significant social role assigned to the universities not only in the development of scientific institutions, but in the whole system of education.

The main influence extended by universities to higher educational institutions is realized through the training of research and teaching cadres as well as through a system of refresher courses. There also exist channels of influence – the writing of textbooks and teaching aids, scientific seminars and conferences, consultations, joint research in science. Sending groups of university graduates who are liable to develop into worthy researchers to other higher educational institutions is also fruitful. This is liable to strengthen the links between those higher educational institutions and universities and help the integration of research carried out by the staff of higher educational institutions.

Thus by influencing the activity of other higher educational institutions, the university defines, to a certain extent, the level of skilled labour in the country as a whole. The social function of the universities in this aspect depends upon the extent of its influence and significance in the development and activities of other higher institutions, whether or not they, the universities, have managed to become the leading force in the national system of higher education.

The Character and Content of the Education Given in the University

The ever-accumulating amount of human knowledge has a definite tendency towards becoming obsolete. That is why society is in need of specialists who have not only acquired a definite level of knowledge, but who are also constantly able to enrich their knowledge, perceive new ideas and participate actively in their further development. Here is the reason why a modern specialist hardly exists without a broad scientific outlook and contemporary research techniques. This functional borderline (i.e. the separation of research activity from that of teaching) influences the higher education institutes negatively and could in the long run become a shortcoming in the normal activities of the institutions in which the specialists are being trained.

That is why in the training of future specialists close contacts between universities and scientific and industrial institutes are of great importance today. This problem is solved in a variety of ways.

At the University of Novosibirsk this goal is achieved by means of a full University-Research Institute integration, by means of (*a*) inviting scientists from research institutes to hold, in addition, posts as part-time professors at the university; (*b*) an obligatory participation of all the undergraduates in research carried out at the institutes; and (*c*) an organized, far-and-wide search and competitive selection of applicants willing to enter the University from all those residing in Siberia.

What is the advantage of such an integration? First of all there is a practically unlimited source for selecting highly skilled specialists to teach at the University. Today there are some 4,000 graduate and undergraduate students studying at the University of Novosibirsk. The Faculty consists of about 900 people engaged in lecturing, conducting seminars and laboratory work, the majority being from research institutes. There are 100 full professors and 300 associate professors. Besides that, a significant group of research specialists are directly guiding students' research in laboratories outside the University. There is indeed a significantly larger number of specialists here involved in training undergraduates than under the conditions of a 'classical university'. This also provides Faculty members with a more flexible time distribution between teaching and research. The University, moreover, never lacks those willing to participate in the training of students. Today every serious scientist understands that teaching makes the teacher extend, broaden and systematize his knowledge – which is the best countermeasure against the inevitable narrowness of specialization.

Using research institutes as a base for teaching also provides for a constant improvement of the University curriculum and the content of the courses taught. The content of all the specializations here tends to be widely based upon mathematics. Physics and physical methods are strongly emphasized for those specializing in natural sciences.

Thus it has become possible to concentrate and modernize the general courses in sciences without the need for over-specializing the training of students. Besides the normative courses there is a choice of over 200 special courses offered to the student, covering all the basic trends of scientific research. As a rule, these courses reflect not only the latest achievements in the given fields of science but also those obtained by the lecturer, being a kind of generalization of his recent work.

At the lower stage of university education where general science education is concentrated, contacts between students and active scientists are especially fruitful and have a great educational impact, stimulating and directing the scientific interests of undergraduates. Simultaneously, contacts of this kind give a chance for capable undergraduates to be noticed at an early stage of their activity and to involve them in seminars designed for a significantly higher level. A variety of supplementary courses and seminars as well as the annual conferences sponsored by the Student Scientific Society give real help in adapting and training undergraduates in science research. The possibility of participating in diverse conferences, symposiums and seminars, very often on an international scale, organized in Akademgorodok as well as in the various routine seminars carried on into research institutes provide, beyond any doubt, strong impetus for the students.

The fact that the University campus is situated in direct contiguity with the research institutes provides for a possibility not only of having the students come to institutes but also to introduce, starting with the fifth semester, from one to five research days per week during which the students are exempted from University lectures. Thus active student-research institute contacts cover the period of the last two to two-and-a-half years spent at the University.

Practically all the research institutes of Akademgorodok are used as a base for the training of undergraduates. At present there are about 1,500 students working at the institutes where they brush up their general and special training, do their annual research and write their diploma theses.

Working with research bodies provides them with the possibility of acquiring knowledge in their narrow field and the technique of research work. At the same time it is a serious psychological and educational factor. The specific character of research bodies develops in the student a critical perception of the studied material, self-dependent thinking and creative activity. In its turn a constant inflow of students into the various laboratories of research institutes has a stimulating effect upon their work and undoubtedly compensates for the additional worries connected with it. The efficiency of the system adopted by the University is proved by the fact that by the time the student graduates he has accomplished research of his own. About a third of the graduates take up work at the research institutes of Akademgorodok.

The activities of the University of Novosibirsk are carried on under very exceptional conditions and its experience (in training specialists of a narrow range) cannot exactly be repeated in other institutions. But the advantages of this system of training future specialists are evident and some of its elements may be utilized in places where more or less similar conditions arise.

The tendency for science to break away from the universities is obvious. For science gets more and more industrialized and there is a constant need of large-scale financial investments. These investments cannot usually be provided by the universities.

Moreover, the university is clearly not the best place in which to carry out many types of research, for research demands large investments and deprives the university of its flexibility in guiding the directions of specialization.

The experience accumulated from the interaction of the University of Novosibirsk and the Institutes of the Siberian Department of the Academy of Sciences demonstrates an alternative possibility: that research should be done in the institutes and the training of researchers at the University. But the links between the two must be flexible enough to make it easy to carry over the emphasis from one scientific trend to another as required, and hence from one research institute to another.

The SUN and its Departments

The State University of Novosibirsk has a five-year course of undergraduate studies. Those admitted must be under the age of thirty-five, have had a high school education and have passed a competitive entrance examination. This examination makes the University of Novosibirsk along with Moscow and Leningrad Universities one of the three hardest to enter.

There is no tuition fee. More than 70 per cent of the students receive state grants and practically all the students (with the exception of residents of Akademgorodok) get dormitory accommodation.

There are six departments at the University. The Mathematical Department trains students in pure and applied mathematics with the following specializations: differential equations and equations of mathematical physics; functional theory and functional analysis; mathematical logic; programming; algebra; geometry and topology; probability theory; mathematical economics; computer mathematics. Students taking applied mathematics and mechanics may specialize in hydrodynamics, gas dynamics, theory of elasticity and plasticity, dynamic meteorology, mathematical geophysics or theoretical cybernetics.

The Department of Physics offers specialties in nuclear physics, in plasma physics and charged particles accelerators, in semiconductor physics, thermal physics, physical hydrodynamics, automation and electrometry, gas dynamics and quantum radiophysics.

The Department of Natural Sciences offers specialization in chemistry or biology. Those taking chemistry may specialize in inorganic chemistry; analytical chemistry; organic chemistry and biochemistry; physical chemistry catalysis; crystal chemistry; radiochemistry. Those in biology are broadly educated in general theoretical and experimental biology. They are trained enough in the foundations of mathematics, physics and chemistry to be able to apply precision methods in solving problems of modern biology. They may specialize in cytology, genetics, physiology or biochemistry.

There are three specializations in the Department of Geology: geophysics, geochemistry and geology. With the development of an oil industry in Western Siberia a need has appeared for specialists in the geochemistry of oil. The students both in the Departments of Natural Sciences and Geology take part in annual expeditions to remote parts of Siberia, the Pacific Ocean Maritime zone, Sakhalin, the Kurils and Kamchatka.

In the recently organized Department of Economics students specialize in economic cybernetics, sociology and political economy. Special attention is given to the level of mathematical knowledge.

The Humanities and Their Place

The significance of the humanities in this technological age is widely discussed throughout the world. Since our University tends to specialize in the sciences, it has tackled the problem of 'physicists vs. lyricists' by organizing a Department of Humanities which is very dependent on mathematics. The high school students have to go through a stiff written examination in mathematics in order to enter the Department.

The Department of Humanities offers its undergraduate and graduate students the following specialties: linguistics, literature, languages and history. Studies in these specialties contain a two-year obligatory course of mathematics – even traditional linguistics does so.

In linguistics the students may specialize in modern Russian, stylistics, English literature, the history of Russian, comparative linguistics, Siberian dialectology and folklore as well as the languages of the Siberian aborigines.

Applied linguistics is a new subject. Its aim is to work out precise methods of language analysis with the aid of modern mathematics and computers. Besides giving the student knowledge in general, linguistic courses also include a course of mathematics very close to the level required in the Department of Mathematics. Languages are taught with special care. Those graduating may also work as translators and interpreters in two foreign languages.

Students of history may specialize in the history of the Communist Party of the Soviet Union, history of the USSR, archaeology, or Siberian and Far Eastern ethnography. As in all other Departments specialization here begins in the third year, the first two being devoted to an all-round education in general history, general archaeology, general ethnography etc. Here too, the students from their first year go upon expeditions to the various archaeological sites of Siberia, Mongolia and the Soviet Far East.

The presence of the Department of Humanities has a very special impact upon students of Sciences. Discussions and lectures in problems of arts, literature – Soviet and foreign – history, international relations, are constantly organized by the faculty and the students of Humanities for all the other Departments.

Developing a Sense of Social Responsibility in the Universities
Today more and more people throughout the world understand that it is no longer enough to look upon the university only as a place of professional training and one where scientific knowledge is obtained. Important as these goals are it is still more vital both for young men and women and for society to put the knowledge obtained to good use, to lead future scientist and humanitarians to live useful and rewarding lives.

Very often today we hear from foreign educators that the explosion in the student population, a good thing in itself, is paralleled by an unpleasant fact: that undergraduate life lacks focus and meaning. We in Russia see an answer to these problems in bringing up a generation of socially committed students. The poet Yeats once wrote: 'In dreams begins responsibility'. One of the most important functions of a higher educational institution is making responsibility a reality.

Society needs specialists, but more than that it needs specialists with a humanistic outlook, with a strong commitment to social responsibility, specialists who actively participate in social life. This function of a higher educational institution has, we believe, three main aspects: the forging of a materialistic outlook, an all-round development of the personality of the student and the formation of an active character as a member of society.

Studying modern achievements in science, direct involvement of students in research, and everyday contacts with active scientists create favourable conditions for the forging of a materialistic outlook. Of great importance in the course of social and political studies is the interrelation between the philosophical and the practical sides of the fundamental science in which a particular student has specialized. Such interrelation is especially stressed.

Seminars at the University of Novosibirsk are organized in the form of discussions on crucial problems. Students, even those specializing in sciences, present papers of serious interest in the more complex and most vital problems of social sciences. Students are also offered a number of courses in various fields of knowledge and arts. The University organizes get-togethers with outstanding Soviet and foreign scientists, writers, actors, painters, statesmen, university student groups and delegations from all over the world.

Very considerable numbers of students are active members of the University's team of lecturers. By lecturing to large public audiences and school children in social and political problems and problems of modern students, they not only broaden their own outlook, but also learn the art of lecturing and making contact with the listener. They acquire the corresponding knowledge actively, not merely as passive consumers. They use it as an instrument in the process of disseminating knowledge among the vast masses of population. Thus, most of the information acquired inside the University is kept in a mobile and active state.

A significant role in forming the student as an active and responsible member of society belongs to the organizations of students through which they participate in the various sides of university life. Through their organizations – Komsomol, trade union, Departmental Academic Boards of Students, the Student Science Society, Boards of Departmental Dormitories (each Department has its own dormitory) and University and Department newspapers, the organization and work of the curriculum, everyday life and recreation is influenced. Such problems as the distribution of state grants and scholarships, financial aid, rooming and life in the Department Houses, Club work etc. are fully in their competence. Representatives of student bodies are members of the Department Councils, where in accordance with the University status, Deans of Departments, Heads of Chairs and members of the professional staff tackle the various sides of University life.

The traditions of Akademgorodok have influenced student-staff relations. Thus faculty members are available to and are with the students not only during lectures, contact hours and consultations – but with the students in their extra-curricular work.

There is great activity of a variety of clubs – sport clubs, drama clubs, classical music clubs, jazz clubs, amateur poet, writer and translator clubs. There is a broad spectrum of International Friendship clubs including American, Cuban, Czech, English, French, German, Polish, and others. These clubs produce wall-newspapers, conduct meetings on the problems, traditions, literature and arts of a given nation, exchange students with foreign countries, carry on group and individual correspondence.

Student construction teams are of no less importance in forming the personality of a future specialist. These teams, self-organized and self-governed, are formed out of students who wish to spend their summer holidays as construction workers in the remote areas of the Soviet Union. Team work, team earnings, team responsibility introduce a feeling of friendship and collectivism, give experience in self-government, make people more communicative and active in life. Besides construction work they lecture in clubs and schools to the local population. The popularity of the builders' teams can be elucidated by the fact that in the summer of 1969 every fourth student of the Novosibirsk University joined them and worked in the various remote areas of Siberia.

The Impact of the SUN upon High Schools

It is no secret that the mobility of orientation of a modern specialist in any field of activity depends today on his preparation in the field of fundamental knowledge – be it science or the humanities. The foundations of these are laid in school. It is here that the student acquires the knowledge in mathematics, physics, chemistry, biology and the humanities which are necessary for his future education in any specialty or even just for the sake of his own cultural development.

In the Soviet Union the high school system operates on the basis of a centralized curriculum and uniform textbooks for all the schools of the country. As for content, it is based upon the foundations of knowledge in the fields of science and the humanities. When speaking of the activities of the university in modernizing high school education one may mention two dominating trends: the modernization of the high school system itself and the direct work with high school students.

The first trend includes the participation of the university in defining the content of high school education, experiments in school education, the making and the publication of teaching aids for teachers and students, the preparation of the future teaching staff and the refresher courses for them. Of special importance is the transfer of the necessary sections of fundamental knowledge which will be required in future from the university to the school curriculum. The need to be on the lookout for corresponding tendencies, the finding of the ways and means of transferring this or that part of knowledge to the stage or level the school children have reached, is one of the very complicated and painstaking tasks. Such processes as the normal functioning of the whole system of higher education depend to a large extent upon how this is done.

The second trend achieves its goals through the so-called 'Science

Olympics' – contests among school students from the whole of the territory of Siberia, the publication of popular science series and so on. It is noteworthy that direct work with high school students influences the whole high school system indirectly by pulling it up to the level of the up-to-date needs of society.

The participation of the university in modernizing the high school system has also a social aspect. Investigations showed us that the possibility of achieving higher education depends to a significant extent upon the cultural environment of the teenager and the level of the high school he attended. Altering the cultural level of an environment is an enduring problem which must be solved, together with the general culture growth of the population. But the modernization of the system of education, the possibility of bringing it closer to the necessary level can be achieved in a significantly shorter period. This is one of the keys for widening the range of possibilities for youth to acquire higher education.

The university-high school contacts take various forms. Though the University of Novosibirsk specializes in the training of research workers and does not prepare teachers *en masse*, it does not overlook the needs of high schools. For a number of years already our University has run a refresher course for school teachers. Over 2,000 teachers from various parts of Siberia, the Soviet Far East and Central Asian Republics have already attended them. These courses aim at raising the school teachers' level of knowledge and broaden their information on the latest achievements in the sciences. For the high school students showing special interest towards either science or humanities, our University has organized a network of extramural and Sunday schools. Thus high school students from Novosibirsk may come and work in the Sunday school of our University. Here they may attend lectures in sciences and attempt to solve problems with the help of advanced University students.

Extramural schools, or as they are called here 'schools by correspondence', are especially promising in Siberian conditions. Those accepted into these schools are given special tasks and assignments as well as test papers. A few words ought to be said about the specialized Boarding High School of Physics and Mathematics under the University of Novosibirsk. It includes three senior high-school years and it is designed for the teaching of those interested in sciences and residing in Siberia, especially in remote country regions. A proportion of the students are selected from those attending the top two grades of high schools, who gain good results in the physics, mathematics or chemistry 'All-Siberian Olympics', sponsored jointly by the University and the local Boards of Education. Several thousand students annually participate in the traditional three rounds. In addition the 8th grade students (in Soviet schools there are 10 grades in all) are taken in from country schools on school recommendations. All necessary conditions are created for the various groups of the school to encourage successful graduation and satisfaction of their scientific interests. Among those teaching at the school are a number of full professors and other lecturers from the University. For the especially gifted students there is a more elaborate programme, of above high school level, especially in the sciences. Students are allowed to concentrate their attention on the various parts of a subject and those in advanced groups may choose either the experimental laboratories of scientific seminars at the University or the Research Institutes. The existence of a school of the kind under the aegis of the University permits able students from far-off corners of Siberia to get a good high school training and to continue their studies at the University. The University in its turn gains by knowing that it is admitting well-trained students. But it is not only that. The existence of this school provides a possibility for conducting experimental work in the contests and methods of high school teaching. The results of this 'teaching laboratory' may serve as the foundation for future changes in the national high school system.

Conclusion

In fulfilment of the needs of a developing society, universities have become large scientific and educational institutions, custodians of the traditions of fundamental science. The main social function of universities, as educational institutions, is the preparation of future specialists in the field, the number being defined by the needs of society today and tomorrow. The preparation of specialists at the universities includes an all-round development of the personality, their education in the spirit of civil responsibility, their understanding of the role of an active citizen of a socialist country.

The development of science apart from educational institutions requires, under modern conditions, a search for ways of amalgamating the efforts of the universities and scientific institutions in educating the future specialist. Being centres of fundamental science and of the preparation of specialists for various institutions of education, the universities are called to exert a decisive influence upon the development of the whole system of education in accordance with contemporary needs of the society.

But that is not all. We, the citizens of today, are not and cannot be indifferent as to the face of the future. Educators throughout the world are aware that whatever it will be will depend to a very great extent upon education. Hence the key-word today and tomorrow: Education.

Section IV

Binary Policies

Introduction

W. Roy Niblett

For a hundred years and more many countries have had – and still have – vocational colleges designed to prepare, either by full-time or part-time courses, those who have left school for a wide range of jobs. It is only in the past twenty years or so that there has been a marked tendency for some of these to be recognized as themselves institutions of higher and technological rather than of technical and further education. One reason for this has been a vast expansion of the demand for highly trained men and women to carry on responsibility in an increasingly complex society, dependent upon a supply of experts to run it: computers, transport, the health and social services, catering, marketing and a hundred other careers are needing people of graduate qualifications to staff them.

With such an emphasis upon the production of professionals are not universities likely to be too academic in the type of education they offer, too theoretical, even too research minded? And not merely this, would it not be too expensive to expand them in numbers or size or both to meet the situation?

These are among the reasons for the upgrading in a number of industrialized countries of what in a previous era might have been technical institutions only but now quite clearly are inadequately described as such. The chapters by Mr Fowler and Professor Wright about the 'binary' developments in England and Ontario respectively are authoritative. It is all the more significant therefore that both, while recognizing what Mr Fowler calls 'the historic justification' for the advocacy in the 1960s of a binary policy, have doubts whether the present extent of the separation between the two systems of higher education can continue indefinitely. If such separation is not to continue, however, one suspects that changes in outlook and understanding may be very necessary in universities as well as in the 'other part' of a state's or a nation's system of higher education. As Tyrell Burgess and John Pratt have recently pointed out,* some of the impetus towards producing any such alteration in the outlook of the universities is likely to come from the other part of the binary system.

---

* *Technical Education in the United Kingdom*, Paris, OECD, 1971.

267

21

The Binary Policy in England and Wales

Gerald T. Fowler

The phrase 'binary system' is now conventionally used to describe the English and Welsh* organization of higher education in which the universities, financed by central government through the University Grants Committee, stand apart from the polytechnics, other Further Education colleges, and most Colleges of Education, which are maintained by individual local authorities, or by two or more local authorities together. It is not an all-embracing categorization of higher education establishments, since it covers neither the voluntary Colleges of Education, nor those few institutions financed directly by the Department of Education and Science.† Further, the statement that a college is 'maintained' by a local authority may mislead those ignorant of the system of pooling costs through the Teacher Training and Advanced Further Education Pools, whereby all local authorities, contributing according to set formulae, share the burden of a college's expenditure. It may also conceal, by suggesting a clear division, close similarities in the academic character of some universities and some polytechnics. Nevertheless, the phrase is either accurate or evocative enough to raise passions, some seeing in 'binary' the root cause of whatever is or is believed to be amiss in particular establishments – a poor library or excessive vocational emphasis in one, lack of contemporary social relevance in the courses of another – while others argue that any effective system of higher education must have an institutional split between the vocational and the critical or contemplative.

The 1960s and the Binary System

The split in English higher education is not of recent origin, although the use of the word 'binary' to refer to it is. The education of most intending teachers in monotechnic colleges outside the university system, though linked to it, has long been our practice. Nor is the possibility new of reading for a degree or for an advanced, though sub-degree, technical

---

* In Scotland, the issue is complicated by the Central Institutions, non-university colleges financed from central government.
† e.g. the Royal College of Art.

qualification outside the walls of a university. It is however plausible to speak of the binary system as a recent development because of three major changes in the 1960s.

The first has been the unexpectedly rapid increase in the number of students pursuing full-time or sandwich advanced courses in non-university colleges. In 1963 the Robbins Committee[1] forecast that there would be 51,000 such students in Advanced Further Education by 1973/4. By 1966[2] the official estimate had risen to 70,000 by 1969/70. In fact, the figure for that academic year was probably just over 100,000. (Part-time students on advanced courses were always numerous. There were some 50,000 on HNC courses in 1963; but here there has not been comparable growth.) Numbers in Colleges of Education have also increased rapidly. The growth rate in universities over the past decade has been some 6 per cent per annum, while in Colleges of Education it has been about 11 per cent, and in Advanced FE about 13 per cent. Today, rather more than 6 per cent of the age-group attend universities, and a little less than 6 per cent are on full-time or sandwich courses in other establishments of higher education. The non-autonomous or maintained sector has thus become numerically as important as the university sector.

Secondly, both academic and institutional arrangements in Advanced Further Education have been systematized in the course of the past decade. It is arguable that when we speak of the 'binary system' as new, we should emphasize the second word. In accordance with a recommendation of the Robbins Committee, the National Council for Technological Awards was replaced by a new Council for National Academic Awards.[3] For the first time there was a body empowered to validate degree and postgraduate awards across the whole spectrum of academic disciplines, for colleges without a Royal Charter and hence the power of self-validation. Unlike London University external degrees, such awards are based on syllabuses internally devised and examinations internally set and marked (although with some external assessment to maintain parity of standards). In 1966, the then Government announced in a White Paper[4] the establishment of some 30 new institutions, to be known generically as Polytechnics, which would be formed from existing Colleges of Technology, or Commerce, or Art (later two Colleges of Education were added), and in which advanced full-time and sandwich courses in the local authority sector, except those leading to a teacher's certificate, would be concentrated. By the end of 1970, 27 of the 30 had been designated. Finally, changes in the government of local authority colleges following the Weaver Report[5] and the Education (No. 2) Act 1968 based upon it have ensured them a greater measure of autonomy and academic freedom in their future development, hitherto thought to be perquisites of the universities alone.

Finally, the word 'binary' came into official usage, and an at least super-ficially coherent policy of separate but equal development was created around it. The first public statement of the government's intention to develop a distinctive sector of higher education within the FE system was the speech made at Woolwich Polytechnic in 1965 by C. A. R. Crosland, then the Secretary of State. At the same time, his Minister of State, Reg Prentice, was chairing an informal advisory group of people from further education and industry, and the National Advisory Council on Education for Industry and Commerce prepared a report which stressed the need for the effective use of resources in FE through a concentration of advanced courses. All of these strands met in the 1966 White Paper,[6] of which the sub-title, 'Higher Education in the Further Education System' reveals most clearly the content, and which remains the basic text on the develop-ment, of the binary system. Despite this, it is reasonable to suspect that the thinking behind the policy, at least within the Department of Education and Science, goes back beyond the Labour victory in the General Election of October 1964, and that even the word 'binary' may first have been applied to higher education in the internal policy debates following the presentation of the Report of Robbins Committee.[7]

The Aftermath of the Robbins Report

Both the Conservative Government then in power, and the successor Labour administration, accepted the bulk of the Robbins recommenda-tions, including the grant of university status to the Colleges of Advanced Technology. These had already been taken out of the local authority sector in 1962, and made dependent on direct grant from central govern-ment: the change of name and status was therefore inevitable. It is how-ever important to see that if there had ever hitherto been a long term plan for the development in the local authority sector of a viable form of higher education alternative to that found in the universities, neither the 1962 change nor the acceptance of the Robbins recommendation could have taken place. The 'promotion' of the CATs lopped off the top of the Further Education system.

It was the Robbins Report itself which strengthened the hand of those opposed to such developments, and drove them to formulate a detailed alternative policy. Robbins recommended[8] that Colleges of Education should be absorbed into new university Schools of Education, and that despite the maintenance of some local links, they should be financed through the university grants machinery. The recommendation was not accepted by Government. If it had been, the local authority sector would have lost the majority of its full-time advanced students. Less well re-membered are the sections of the Report[9] dealing with the Technical Colleges. Here Robbins suggested that some of the then Regional Colleges might become constituent parts of universities, with a period of direct grant from central government as a transitional phase.[10] While first degree work, under the aegis of the new CNAA, should be developed in the Regional Colleges and some Area Colleges, students wishing to undertake postgraduate study should transfer to a university.[11] This section of the Report is ignored by the 1966 White Paper, which embodies the antithesis of the Robbins philosophy.

There are, it is true, superficial similarities between the two policies. Thus, Robbins suggested[12] that some Regional Colleges might 'profit from federation with another technical college or with a College of Education, or both'. The White Paper[13] recommends such federations as an alternative to the merger of existing colleges. (In fact, this suggestion was then tacitly ignored: all Polytechnics formed from more than one precursor college have been formed by merger, not by federation.) The Robbins philosophy was, however, essentially a rationalization of what had always happened in English higher education: institutions with their origins in local need or initiative should, when their academic achievements justified it, be accepted into the national university system, by the grant of a Charter, by merger, or by affiliation. Outside the university sector was a league table of institutions, where effort might earn promotion, bringing university status nearer. This philosophy was already explicit in the 1956 division of local authority technical colleges into four groups – CATs and Regional, Area, and Local Colleges. Once it is accepted, then all establishments of higher education must be judged by the degree to which their academic and educational aims and achievements approximate to the university model – assuming, as we have generally done in England, that such a model exists and can be clearly defined. Thus, Colleges of Education, affiliated to universities by the establishment of Institutes of Education following the McNair Report of 1944,[14] were now, on the Robbins system, to come much further into the 'university orbit', with degree work validated by the universities. The Committee rejected the suggestion that they might instead be given greater autonomy, with an independent degree-validating mechanism, in order to preserve their 'characteristic approach to their work'.[15] Yet this approach, with its strong vocational emphasis, might be thought to be alien to the English university tradition, and closer to that of the FE system. The Report, in its fundamental discussion of the aims of higher education,[16] recognizes that there will be differences in the way each of the principles it identifies will be incorporated in different types of institution – but gives no systematic analysis of those differences.

Reasons for a Binary Policy

The early advocates of the binary policy were thus seeking, not to create a depressed, second-class, and under-financed sector of higher education, as their opponents sometimes contend, but to give recognition to the possibility that there might be more than one valid philosophy of higher education, or such differences of emphasis within a philosophy as to require more than one institutional model. They wished less to create a new pecking order of colleges than to question the right of all universities to be above all non-university establishments in the order. They hoped to encourage educational innovation in a separate system strong enough to resist the temptation of assimilation to what was thought to be the university pattern.[17] To achieve these aims, no immediate action was thought to be necessary in the case of the Colleges of Education, beyond changes in the system of government. (The Robbins proposal that the new degree in Education should be validated by the universities and not by a new national body was however implemented, so that it is impossible to claim that the advocates of either opposing philosophy won a clear victory.) Advanced further education, on the other hand, would have to be rationalized in any event: here was the opportunity to test the new policy.

Theoreticians in Government must also be practical men. Advanced courses in FE were proliferating in a large number and range of colleges.[18] As the 1966 White Paper[19] diplomatically put it: 'By their foresight and vigour in recent years [the colleges] have expanded provision in anticipation of the growing demand and simultaneously improved standards.' In order to make the most effective use of resources, higher education must be further concentrated. 'The effect of distributing it as widely as at present is that many departments and colleges are too small to sustain high academic standards and to provide a satisfactory corporate life. This also involves an uneconomical use of resources, not least of teachers qualified to undertake the higher levels of work.'[20] The Paper therefore looked to the establishment of a 'limited number of strong centres with the staff, buildings, and equipment needed both to achieve and maintain high standards and to provide the right setting for an active community of staff and students'.[21] These centres would be formed from one or more existing colleges, and would be designated by the Secretary of State after consultation with interested bodies, regionally and locally, when he was satisfied with the academic and administrative arrangements made for the new institutions.

The creation of the Polytechnics was thus determined not least by economic and educational arguments about the use and spread of resources. Nevertheless, the White Paper showed marks of the debate about the philosophy of higher education which had followed the Robbins Report. It was emphatic[22] that higher education included students following sub-degree courses, and part-time students. The Polytechnics should

therefore be 'comprehensive' in the sense that they included these categories as well as those on full-time and sandwich degree courses. It was
this 'comprehensive range and character' of work which would 'broadly
distinguish' them from other kinds of higher education institution. Their
development on 'polytechnic lines', containing a wide variety of disciplines,[23] implicitly marked off the new institutions as clearly from the
old CATs as from the Colleges of Education. (This point has not always
been taken by those who complain that some Polytechnics are developing
more rapidly in the social sciences and the arts than in science and technology.) Students would be 'wholly or largely' of 18 and over;[24] but
even this left open the possibility of a wider age-range than is normally
found in the universities. The economic viability and educational strength
of the new Polytechnics would be ensured by the requirement that they
should plan for growth to at least 2,000 full-time students, plus part-
timers from surrounding areas,[25] and, once the list of Polytechnics was
settled, there would be no additions to it for about ten years, so as to give
the designated colleges a firm foundation for their development, with adequate resources.[26] Clear in this is the Department's determination to
give a fair and extended test to what was seen as a new form of higher
education.

The Nature of Polytechnics

Subsequent Ministerial pronouncements, too numerous to cite individually, further developed the Polytechnic philosophy. Continued local
authority involvement in the financing and control of colleges, many of
whose students would be recruited nationally, was justified by the need to
ensure the continued provision of part-time education in the Polytechnics,
and by the service it was hoped they would provide to local industry,
commerce, social services, and the community as a whole. To this end,
research in the colleges would, it was expected, be geared to the solution
of practical problems and would be sponsored by industry or local
authorities. The volume of research would in any event be less than was
normal in universities, since the Polytechnics would be primarily teaching
institutions. The thinking behind this policy was partly that the close connection found in British universities between higher education and the
type of research which was designed to push back the frontiers of knowledge was fortuitous. The two activities were separable: if research could
be conducted in institutes with no educational function, so too could
students be educated at least to first degree level in colleges where little or
no pure research was conducted. Postgraduate research oriented to the
solution of practical problems might enhance the student's vocational
prospects and value. In part, however, such arguments, valid though they
might be, were a veneer to conceal hard economic reality: no government

could contemplate the increase in public expenditure on research which would be necessary if the polytechnics were to follow the university pattern.

Courses offered in the polytechnics might also be expected often to have a vocational or practical orientation. There were already traces of this philosophy in the Robbins Report, in its discussion of the Regional Colleges.[27] In the course of the 1960s, as the proportion of the age-group in higher education increased, so did concern that many students, following courses with no vocational element, might be being educated for unemployment. Unwilling to contemplate the type of job they might have taken at 16 or 18, graduates might lack any qualification specifically fitting them for higher-level work. So far there is little evidence to support such a view: the proportion of new graduates remaining unemployed for a significant period has risen, but remains very small. Nevertheless, unease about the future has undoubtedly strengthened the belief that the polytechnics should retain the traditional vocational bias of the FE system. Some even argue that such institutions should be the major part of the higher education system, educating those who will work in the wider society, while the universities fulfil a monitoring or critical role, refining rather than simply transmitting the common culture, advancing learning, and educating those who will advance it further. If we could begin with a *tabula rasa*, it might be desirable to devise such a system: but at a time when the demand for higher education is growing more rapidly than the total number of places available in all types of institution, it is quite impracticable.

Over the past three years Ministers have frequently stressed the autonomy of the new polytechnics. Under the Education (No. 2) Act 1968, their Articles of Government require the approval of the Secretary of State. Thus, it has been possible, prior to designation, to ensure that academic control rests firmly with the Academic Board of each polytechnic, which will normally contain representatives of the junior staff and of the students, as well as Heads of Departments. While this is now also common practice in university Senates, the polytechnics are the first British institutions of higher education in which students and significant numbers of junior staff have been involved in forward academic planning right from the outset. It is too early to judge what effect this, and student membership of most other polytechnic committees, will have. Most important of all, staff and students are also represented on the Governing Bodies of the colleges, as well as local industry, trades unions, and educational establishments. Thus, the Governors are not dominated by the appointees of the maintaining authority; nor are they a sub-committee of that authority. While its approval of the annual estimates, and consent to particular forms of expenditure, are still required, the polytechnics and the academic community within them enjoy greater self-determination than local authority colleges ever did in the past, not least because of the power of the Governors to exercise virement within broad heads of expenditure once the estimates have been approved. Even here, however, the precise degree of freedom enjoyed depends upon the financial regulations made by the maintaining authority and the spirit in which they are operated. The Weaver Report[28] made a strong plea for liberalism here, but practice varies widely.

The 'pooling' arrangements for Advanced Further Education guarantee that most polytechnics cannot become an excessive burden on local rates, so that maintaining authorities have less incentive to prune educationally desirable expenditure. What counts as excessive is however relative to the size of the authority: what is a trivial sum to the Inner London Education Authority may bulk large in the estimates of Kingston-upon-Thames or Oxford. Thus polytechnics in the smaller boroughs may be tempted to stop or to transfer to other colleges courses expenditure on which cannot be charged to the pool, even when educational advantage lies with their continuance. In any event, it is hard to believe that the pooling system will long continue without some restrictive change, since it is inflationary by its nature; everyone spends what everyone else pays. While it does, however, the polytechnics may be thought to enjoy greater financial freedom, at least in respect of revenue expenditure,* than do the universities, who must operate within a grant fixed quinquennially by the UGC.

The Polytechnics and other Institutions of Advanced Education

Ministers have also developed the theme, already outlined in the White Paper,[29] that polytechnics should co-operate wherever possible with other maintained colleges engaged in higher education, and with universities. There are already several examples of the academic sponsorship by a polytechnic of advanced courses, full- and part-time, at other colleges within the region; such an arrangement ensures the maintenance of academic standards, permits the provision of specialist courses where demand for them exists, and may allow fuller utilization of costly equipment than would otherwise have been possible. Co-operation with universities has however proved more difficult. The White Paper mentioned sharing of staff, and the joint use of communal and other facilities. Such joint use can be established only when one institution has spare capacity, which is not often, and when suitable financial arrangements can be made, which the different systems of university and polytechnic financing inhibit. The best example of inter-sector collaboration, between the University of Aston and some of the precursor colleges of the Birmingham Polytechnic, now

---

* The Department of Education and Science exercises central control over capital expenditure on some equipment and on buildings.

seems unlikely long to continue. Further, while a member of the staff of a university or of a polytechnic can easily give *ad hoc* instruction in the other institution, joint appointment of specialists is precluded by the different salary scales, pension arrangements, and conditions of service. If then a tenet of the binary philosophy was that the gulf between the two sectors might be bridged where it was educationally or economically desirable, the systematic character of the separation has so far frustrated the realization of the hope.

The polytechnics were, then, to be centres of higher education in a wide range of disciplines, offering courses at sub-degree as well as first degree and postgraduate level, often or usually with a vocational bias. They would cater for full-time, sandwich, and part-time students, some of them possibly below the normal higher education age-range. They would be more closely integrated into the local community than were most universities, and some of their courses and much of their research would be geared to local needs. They would in any event be mainly concerned with teaching rather than research. Local authority control would remain, but the colleges would enjoy a wide measure of autonomy and of academic self-determination, and would exercise academic oversight of some advanced courses located elsewhere within their regions. Time and money would be given them to allow them to develop and test their own form of higher education.

The Robbins Committee[30] identified four objectives for a system of higher education. They seemed to rank highest the cultivation of the general powers of the mind, and the advancement of learning, followed by the transmission of a common culture and common standards of citizenship, and finally by the inculcation of vocational skills. This might in general be taken to represent the university scale of values. Some might in the past have argued for the inclusion in the list of the moulding of the future leaders of society; but this is an aim logically subordinate to the development of the general powers of the mind. The polytechnic philosophy accepts all of these objectives, but sets much greater value on vocational instruction (as well as broadening the range of vocations covered), lays less weight on the advancement of learning, is beamed at the education of the led as much as of the leaders in society, aims at a broad service to as well as the promotion of the general cultural life of the local and regional community, and extends the notion of transmitting common standards of citizenship to include a direct acquaintance with and an understanding of a wider section of society.

These are high ideals, and difficult objectives to achieve. It is much too early to estimate the likely degree of success of the polytechnics. They have already been subject to excessive scrutiny. Nevertheless, certain problems, and weaknesses in the philosophy, can be identified.

Present and Future Problems for the Polytechnics

The integration of part-time students with full-time into a coherent academic community, where each group benefits from contact with the other, is valuable in theory, but hard to realize in practice. Day release students have little time to socialize while in their college, block release students are birds of passage, and evening students are not in the college at the times when full-timers are normally there. Further, as the polytechnics grow, the proportion of full-time students must increase rapidly, and that of part-timers decline, even if their absolute number rises. So far few polytechnics show any inclination to follow the CATs in shedding their part-time degree work. But here they are now in competition with the Open University, and in most areas the pent-up demand created by the past inadequacies of the higher education system will be satisfied in much less than a decade. While, therefore, the polytechnics must seek to develop their part-time courses, there is little to suggest that this work will materially affect the character of the education received by their other students – although constant contact with students in other kinds of employment may be salutary for some teachers. This argument assumes that the Government will not seek to compensate for a shortfall of full-time places in higher education by further development of part-time degree work; such a decision would ignore the relative difficulty of achieving high-level qualifications by the part-time route.

More fundamentally, the description of the polytechnics as 'comprehensive' institutions is valid only in the narrow meaning given to the word in the White Paper. In consequence, the point at which polytechnic work should split from that appropriate to the local College of Further Education is not always obvious. Thus, it is often argued that the fifth year of a full Technological Certificate course should be in a polytechnic where this is possible: but it is not obvious that the institutional separation of the last from the earlier years of a course is educationally desirable. In a few disciplines any split is difficult; in Music, for example, instrumental work does not necessarily run parallel to academic, and the same instrumental teacher may often profitably guide a pupil from the age of sixteen to the completion of a degree. In other disciplines the high cost of the machinery and equipment necessary to education at any level precludes its duplication within the same municipality, and in consequence two departments of two separate colleges, handling work at different levels, may have to co-exist and co-operate within the same building. All of this may be thought to point forward to a more genuinely comprehensive reorganization of further and higher education at some future time; but it is not the purpose of this chapter to discuss such a possibility.

It is often argued that present deficiencies in facilities or plant will prevent the polytechnics achieving parity of esteem with the universities. Certainly library provision, for example, is often woefully inadequate. But this is not inherent in polytechnic status: to remedy such weaknesses requires only the injection of resources, and there is as yet no sign that these will not be provided.

A much more serious impediment to polytechnic development is the external course approval procedure, the complexity and rigidity of which destroys much of the value of the academic freedom ensured to colleges by the Weaver arrangements. The Regional Advisory Councils for Further Education, which have a proper role in the consideration of part-time provision and of some other courses with a mainly local recruitment, also examine proposals for full-time degree courses. Thus, a local authority is now precluded from interfering in the academic arrangements of its own polytechnic, but may, through the RAC, meddle in those of another. Worst of all, the RACs, the Inspectorate, the Department of Education and Science, and the CNAA, by the nature of the tasks given them, all concentrate their attention on individual courses rather than on a poly-technic's academic development plan, thereby inevitably making both the production of such a plan and adherence to it doubly difficult.

The recruitment of high quality academic staff in competition with the universities is hampered by the Burnham salary scale which applies to the polytechnics as to the rest of the FE system. Despite the thesis that they will be primarily teaching institutions, professorial salaries can be achieved in the polytechnics only by those who have ceased to teach at all and de-voted themselves wholly to administration. The pointing system by which departments are graded is a non-academic restraint on academic organiza-tion. By relating financial reward to the level of work handled, it directly contradicts the comprehensive principle.

There are other complaints. A polytechnic may find difficulty in keep-ing together a powerful academic team in a particular field if no private organization is willing to sponsor its research work, and support from public funds is excluded on principle. The creation of a genuine com-munity of staff and students is less easy where there is little or no residential accommodation. The system of discretionary grants applying to students on sub-degree courses creates divisive tension and resentment.

Such weaknesses can however be eradicated if central Government has the necessary understanding and will. Despite them, the polytechnics can translate into practice much of the philosophy implicit in their creation. While it would be wrong to suggest that there is a sharp distinction be-tween all polytechnics and all universities, there are clear generic differ-ences. Several polytechnic degree courses, inherited from precursor colleges, have not only a vocational orientation, but a specifically local significance; examples are Textile Marketing (Huddersfield), Ceramic

Technology (Staffordshire), and Nautical Studies (Liverpool and Plymouth). There are several courses in applied biology and in business law, clearly beamed towards a different objective from that of their less vocational university counterparts.

Most polytechnics are seeking conscientiously to develop their sub-degree as well as their higher level work. In some disciplines HND courses provide a valuable fall-back position for students who, having embarked upon study for a degree, find it beyond them. Conversely, the CNAA permits a limited measure of promotion from HND to degree courses. Since there is no wholly reliable way of fitting a student to the right course at 18-plus, the polytechnics have here a clear advantage over less 'comprehensive' establishments.

The rapid increase in demand for places in higher education during the 1970s, which all projections show, assures the polytechnics of enough good students to achieve institutional viability. If they are adequately funded, and do not lose sight of the philosophy behind their creation, they will make an original and valuable contribution to British higher education. To doubt whether we have yet evolved the best institutional arrangements for the approach to mass higher education is not to question the historic justification for the advocacy in the 1960s of the binary policy.

REFERENCES

1. Report of the Committee on Higher Education, under the Chairmanship of Lord Robbins, Cmnd 2154 (HMSO, 1963).
2. *A Plan for Polytechnics and other Colleges*, Cmnd 3006 (HMSO, 1966), para. 9.
3. op. cit., para. 433.
4. Cmnd 3006, n. 2 above.
5. Report of the Study Group on the Government of Colleges of Education, under the chairmanship of T. R. Weaver (HMSO, 1966).
6. See n. 2 above.
7. See n. 1 above.
8. op. cit., paras. 351–60.
9. op. cit., para. 415 ff.
10. ibid, para. 419–20.
11. ibid, para. 432.
12. ibid, para. 419.
13. Cmnd 3006, para. 13.
14. *Teachers and Youth Leaders* (HMSO, 1944).
15. op. cit., para. 312.
16. ibid, Chap. II.
17. For the development of the CATs to university status, see T. Burgess and J. Pratt, *Policy and Practice* (London: Allen Lane Press, 1970).
18. See Robbins, op. cit., paras. 83–98, and tables 14 and 15, for the 1962/3 figures.

19. op. cit., para. 5.
20. ibid, para. 10.
21. ibid, para. 3.
22. ibid, para. 4.
23. ibid, para. 3.
24. ibid, para. 16.
25. ibid, para. 17.
26. ibid, para. 14.
27. See, for example, para. 414, on practical foreign language courses.
28. op. cit., n. 5 above, para. 57.
29. op. cit., para. 26.
30. op. cit., Chap. II, paras. 22–9.

22

Hatfield Polytechnic Today

Norman Lindop

Anyone who has been at the Hatfield College in Hertfordshire, England, during its comparatively brief yet hectic existence might be forgiven if, when asked 'What is going on, and where do you go from here?' he begs to be allowed to pass the question. So much has happened in less than twenty years of growth, and so much is still happening, that it is difficult to know how or where to begin to describe the College today. No institution of higher education can be in a state of rest: it must change or it will atrophy, and no one at Hatfield would acquiesce in that. In trying to describe it as it is today I must refer not only to the past but to our hopes for the future – and here we are likely to be beset by hazards yet unknown and probably beyond our control.

Retrospect

The history of the College is straightforward; it began in 1952 as a small local technical college, with 55 full-time and 1,683 part-time and evening students. In those days most of the courses were of the technician and higher technician type, and many of them related in one way or another to the aircraft industry, which was dominant in the immediate locality. From the first, the staff were prepared to work hard to achieve good results and progressively to expand the range of courses; simultaneously Hertfordshire County Council was establishing a number of Colleges of Further Education in the main population centres in the county, each designed to take on a considerable load of work for the 16–18 age group in addition to serving as community colleges for non-vocational courses. Hatfield was therefore able, as more advanced work grew, to shed the courses for that age group, so that within ten years of its formation it had practically eliminated all work for students under 18 years of age and of an academic level below the Advanced General Certificate of Education, or, for part-time technician students, the Higher National Certificate. At about this time the Hatfield College was designated a Regional College, serving a wide area of the north-eastern home counties and East Anglia; Regional Colleges were 'second rank' institutions on the national scene at that time, second only to the Colleges of Advanced Technology and many Hatfield eyes were fixed on that status as an aim.

Here history took a confused turn. The Colleges of Advanced Technology were recommended for university status in the Robbins Report of 1963, and the public sector of higher education seemed to have been decapitated. The idea of a University of Hertfordshire was mooted, in which Hatfield would play a part – or rather, some part of Hatfield would play a part, for it was not expected that the University would be based at Hatfield nor would it have included the whole of the College. A change of Government produced a change of policy, and all dalliance between the public sector and the so-called autonomous university sector was abruptly terminated. Hatfield was therefore thrown back on its own resources academically: it had been a narrow escape, regretted by some, by others regarded as a danger avoided just in time. When I came to the College in 1966 a Government statement of intent was expected daily, and in May of that year it appeared – 'A Plan for Polytechnics and other Colleges'. Thirty polytechnics were to be created, and Hatfield was to be one of them – one of the very few in the list, incidentally, which were not required to merge with other institutions to form a polytechnic. We have therefore had the minimum of organizational upset in our transition to polytechnic status, which has been so smooth as to have been almost imperceptible. The cynic would no doubt ask whether there had been any significant change at all; any weight there might be in such a query would derive from the rather exceptional nature of the pre-designation College, for there was no doubt that we were well prepared for the transition.

The College as it is

So here we are in 1971, a two-year-old Polytechnic (having been among the first to be so designated in January 1969); before we guess where we may go from here, let us attempt a self-portrait. Polytechnics are all derived at least in part from Technical Colleges and we are no exception – that half our students are engineers of various kinds is a direct reflection of our origins. But ten years ago the proportion was far higher – since then, although engineering numbers have gone up steadily, the scientists, mathematicians and social scientists have increased more rapidly. Our 1,800 full-time students can be classified in various ways: they are all over the age of 18 and all have reached GCE A-level or its equivalent in one or more subjects. 1,400 of them are studying for degrees of the Council for National Academic Awards, the rest for diplomas of various kinds or professional qualifications. There are 40 full-time and 10 part-time postgraduate students following supervised research programmes for degrees of MPhil and PhD. Only about 30 per cent of our full-time students come from Hertfordshire, the rest come from all over Britain (about 6 per cent come from overseas). This means that most of them are living away from home, yet we have only 300 residential places (and we have only had those for a year); so for the typical Hatfield student there is a daily journey to and from College which is complicated by the fact that we are in a semi-rural environment, with poor and failing public transport. This suggests that, even in the unlikely event of a national decision to enforce or encourage attendance at a College near the student's home, residential accommodation would still be important for us.

The inclusion of sub degree courses in our programme of work has been a feature of Hatfield throughout its growth and we are anxious to extend such non-degree work in the future. There is undoubtedly a continuing demand for the products of these courses, many of whom obtain posts in competition with graduates, often at the same or higher salaries. There are other reasons for our attachment to this type of education. The greater diversity of types of course means that the inherent uncertainty of the selection process at first entry into higher education can be mitigated by the possibility of subsequent transfer, for example from a degree course to a diploma course for those for whom a degree turns out to be beyond their capacity. Alternatively a student whose performance before joining us was indifferent and who could not therefore be placed on a degree course, but who subsequently shows promise, has the possibility of promotion to the degree course and thereby retrieves an earlier failure. This broad spectrum of work is particularly characteristic of a polytechnic and is not likely to be emulated by the universities. It is a function which we alone can perform and which we must at all costs continue to perform.

We currently have 1,000 part-time students, 250 of whom are preparing for Bachelors or Masters degrees, the rest for higher technician or professional qualifications. The tradition of part-time study is well established in British further education, but with the rapid expansion of full-time opportunities in the last decade there have been suggestions that it may well be that the part-time route would wither and die, there being none left of sufficient calibre to profit from it. Our experience at Hatfield does not bear this out. It is true that some of the traditional courses, for example for Higher National Certificates, are less well supported than formerly, but in the belief that there might well be mature students anxious and able to study for degrees we have instituted a number of degree courses specially designed for part-time students, and these have found a gratifying response. The longest established of these is the Mathematics course, which is now in its fourth year. There are about a hundred students enrolled on this course altogether, and the first graduates have been produced. One of those graduates had travelled on one day every week for three and a half years a distance of sixty miles each way to attend the course. Half the members of the course are serving teachers and we feel that we are making a not inconsiderable contribution to upgrading the calibre of the teachers of Mathematics in the schools by this kind of provision. The example of the Mathematics course has encouraged us to develop others in Chemistry, Biology, Physics and most recently in English. We hope to extend our range of part-time courses, not all of them at degree level, and in this way to spread the influence of the Polytechnic widely over the region and to demonstrate that we are indeed an institution without walls. Some of these courses might well be held physically at other institutions, the academic responsibility remaining with us but the physical and some of the teaching provision being provided locally. This would make the courses available to a wider area of population and we are actively looking into the possibilities. As our Bachelors degree courses, both full-time and part-time, have developed it has been natural for staff to look to the development of Masters degree courses. The Academic Board has decided that in the absence of any real evidence of need for more full-time Masters degree courses in the country as a whole, we should concentrate on part-time courses which are demonstrably filling a local need, and in this way we have developed MSc courses in Control Engineering and Computer Science, in each case in close collaboration with industry, which has been able to ensure a steady supply of students for these courses.

The provision of part-time courses of all kinds, including short courses and refresher courses for adults, we regard as an essential part of our programme, one that we wish to see develop and diversify. Here again is a peculiarly polytechnic type of responsibility, which we are well suited to perform.

If one seeks to identify areas in which the contribution of Hatfield has been notable, one naturally starts with aeronautical engineering, which was by way of being a foundation study and which gave Hatfield its first degree course; now we are one of the very few specialist centres outside the university system. It clearly sprang from our symbiotic relationship in our early days with the aircraft industry, just as, a few years later, our development of one of the first degree courses in Computer Science in the country paralleled the growth of the computer industry in Hertfordshire. The particular slants given to the traditional disciplines of chemistry and biology at Hatfield are directly related to industrial developments in plastics, pharmaceuticals, biocides and in the food and beverage industries; no trace of the conventional litmus or dogfish approach to these subjects survives. Mathematics is treated in a way which emphasises statistics and their applications in, for example, the social and life sciences, at the expense of the more conventional formal aspects of the subject. Our business studies degree course was one of the first of what is now a very large number of such courses; it is an amalgam of economics, accountancy, law and sociology especially designed for commerce and industry, and allowing specializations such as marketing, personnel management and operational research. The applied social studies course aims to produce, not graduates in sociological theory, but qualified and trained social workers. Completing the cycle back to engineering we have an almost unique course in industrial engineering which combines management with the principles of production and, for good measure, a thorough study of a European language; all set for Europe, in fact!

Part-Time Courses and College Unity

All the above are sandwich degree or diploma courses. Hatfield has been the most active polytechnic in the development of specially designed part-time degree courses for adults; one of these, the MSc in Control Engineering, was the result of a team effort involving staff from no less than five departments of the Polytechnic and three industrial organizations.

A recurrent theme in our recent thinking has been the necessity to formalize to some extent and bring together the considerable effort which is being made in the Polytechnic in the provision of short and refresher courses for adults; what will probably emerge will be a Polytechnic Institute for Adult Studies providing an organized extra-mural service in addition to an all-the-year-round programme of courses at the Polytechnic. This would probably include the present programme of specialist management studies courses together with a wide range of courses for professional specialists, housewives and married women, teachers and social workers.

A feature of all our sandwich and full-time courses is that at some time during the first or second year of the course the whole student group goes on a residential five day course at some centre remote from Hatfield, together with the staff associated with the main course. A programme of lectures, visits, seminars and discussions is arranged on a topic bearing some relation to the main course, and a relaxed informal attitude is encouraged. More is contributed than just the novelty of being in residence together – an experience not otherwise available to most of our students; the student-staff relationship is invariably transformed and improved beyond recognition by this brief translation to a more leisured intimate kind of existence, and the effect lasts for the rest of the students' life at the Polytechnic. As we grow larger it is more difficult, yet more important, to devise means of fostering closer day-to-day contacts between students and staff; even apparently trivial procedures can help, such as the weekly Director's tea parties to which groups of first-year students are invited, together with new, and some old, staff members.

The Future: Teachers and Students

We have at present about 300 teaching staff who live over a wide area of Hertfordshire and North London; they are organized in twelve Departments, each of which is responsible for one or more major courses. The main areas of academic endeavour are Applied Biology, Applied Chemistry, Business Studies, Computer Science, Aeronautical, Electrical, Mechanical, Civil and Industrial Engineering, English, Management Studies, Mathematics, Psychology, and Social Work: we also have special interests in Astronomy (based on a small but well equipped observatory), Applied Physics, Control Engineering and Modern Languages. Notable absentees from the list, which we would like to include eventually, are Education, Fine and Applied Art, Architecture and Music.

For a single and comparatively small College, this is an unusually wide range of courses and in spite of its relative youth the College has rapidly gained a national reputation. It has to be said at once that further developments are completely dependent on fulfilment of major building plans: without further accommodation we can do little more. Already we are severely restricting entry to most courses and this means that many of them are less than ideally economic – more students could be handled by the staff we have. We have come to the end of expedient and making-do, with annexes miles from the centre and all the irritations and inefficiencies that means; we have many ideas for the future, but all depend on this one physical factor.

We shall continue to be, first and foremost, a teaching institution: we shall be student-based. Not only have we gone to great lengths to include students in our decision-making machinery, we are at pains to ensure that we recruit staff who share our view of the primacy of teaching. Those who join the staff without training or previous experience as teachers, whatever their grade, are required to attend an in-service training course of about 250 hours in their first year; this includes observed lectures and supervised projects. At the moment this does not lead to any formal qualification, but it may be that, in collaboration with other Colleges in Hertfordshire which have similar schemes, some more formal course may develop. Certainly we feel we have a real and immediate interest in the training of teachers – our own and other people's – and we would hope to extend this interest.

Our concern with students will not end with the training of the teachers; we have a well-established student counselling service which includes vocational guidance and a professional medical and psychiatric service in its activities. Eventually we expect to have a student health service based at Hatfield. We have appointed a Principal Tutor to organize and co-ordinate such student based services, together with responsibility for an appointments service, physical recreation and short residential courses for non-residential students. The Students Union, a vigorous and independent body will shortly be taking over its own building – the first time we shall have been able to give it this simple degree of autonomy. The Union is very active in investigating ways of providing student housing and is collaborating with the Polytechnic and the Hatfield Rural District Council in promoting housing schemes.

The Future: Planning and Decision Making

One of the innovations at the time of designation was the Polytechnic Council. This makes a trinity with the Governing Body and the Academic Board of representative bodies involved in the government of the College. It is the only one of the three on which staff, students and 'lay' Governors have roughly equal numerical representation, and its job is to review continually the communal life of the College and exert pressure to ensure that in all the planning for the academic and physical development of Hatfield the human and community factors are given full weight. We would expect the Council to become more important as the scale of our operation grows: already it is acting as a watch-dog, not only on health and welfare matters, but on refectory services and physical and cultural recreation; it has recently discussed the smoking habit and has called on all members of the Polytechnic to join in determining which rooms and areas shall be 'no smoking' zones.

When we come to discuss the role and position of a staff member at Hatfield in the next decade we are at the nub of all our current questions. How will the teaching be organized? How will the staff responsibilities be allocated? How will initiative be fostered and encouraged? Who will decide who teaches what? Where in the scheme of things is the individual teacher who wishes to do research? There is a whole complex of such interrelated problems, some of which we are only just beginning to sort out. This must, therefore, be a report of work in progress: no finality is in sight.

To an outsider we are at present organized on a conventional Departmental pattern, the division into Departments following the usual boundaries between disciplines. In reality the boundaries are deliberately diffused, and many staff work in two or more Departments and serve on Boards of Studies and Course Committees other than those in their own Department. These Boards and Committees are run democratically and include student as well as staff members. Nevertheless there are signs that the present system may change. We have avoided a formal Faculty structure for a number of reasons; there are always problems of allocation and demarcation, the new boundaries could prove to be more troublesome than the old, and the tradition of permanent hierarchy, so deeply ingrained in British technical education, would be further strengthened by the appointment of permanent heads of faculties. Yet there are areas in which the interests of cognate departments so overlap that a fusion of function, at least in part, can greatly benefit teaching and the organization of courses. We shall probably see the appearance of Schools formed by the voluntary grouping of departments, with the Chairmanship of the School rotating periodically. More significantly, from the point of view of the quality of the teaching, there are likely to be progressive changes in the recognition awarded to teaching groups; there is an increasing awareness that much subject teaching is essentially a group or team activity. Members of a group of teachers engaged on teaching a particular discipline or sub-discipline have much to gain from each other and have more to contribute to the whole if they are encouraged to think of themselves as a group with shared responsibility to work together on curriculum development and the servicing of courses. We are looking for ways of giving greater recognition to subject leaders and teaching team leaders without following the traditional rule in further education in Britain that to obtain career advancement a teacher must be prepared to do less teaching and more paper work.

The point at once arises – what about professorships? Would it not be appropriate to nominate the subject team leaders in this way? Without excluding such possibilities altogether (and there is no statutory reason why such titles should not be conferred straight away) I would offer some reasons for caution. Within the highly co-ordinated system of the British universities, in which the title of Professor has a definite and fairly well known connotation, there is a national system of salary scales or ranges attaching to these posts; in the further education sector our salary system is totally different and not only does not include such a titled grade but does not permit of payments to teachers of anything like the same magnitude; any professors nominated at a polytechnic would receive salaries far less than those obtaining in universities, and this fact would be well known. Such a move would give support to those who wish to merge the polytechnics with the universities; I do not favour such a blurring of outlines. Moreover any conceivable criteria applicable in polytechnics to the entitlement of a 'chair' would necessarily be different from but would be interpreted as inferior to those traditionally accepted in universities.

As an illustration of the confusion which titles can cause one recalls that a title very much associated with universities, that of Reader, has already been applied to polytechnics; this was done somewhat deviously, and its application has been rather uneven. The reason for this has been the uncertainty which, at least at national level, surrounded the question of research in polytechnics. The Department of Education and Science, in its anxiety to discourage polytechnics from emulating universities has been at pains to emphasize that research is something extra, an important adjunct to the teaching no doubt, but extra all the same. The result is an emphasis on the nature of the research (it should be so far as possible 'applied') and on the financing of it (not from public funds) which is not usual in discussing readerships at universities. The title is therefore being used in two quite different ways and confusion is inevitable. At Hatfield we have not sought to appoint many Readers: two are in post, in departments in which a large volume of sponsored research was already being carried out, and two more are to be appointed soon. In most departments the balance between research and teaching has been struck without too much difficulty: bearing in mind that there is a negligible number of full-time senior research posts, most of it is conducted or supervised by teachers and we expect this pattern to continue. What is likely to happen is that there will emerge a polytechnic-wide organization to co-ordinate and develop the consultancy, research and development effort of the staff, so that the work of qualified people is concentrated where it can be most effective, and an organization can be built up to organize the marketing and financial aspects.

I have a feeling that there is about discussion of this topic of research in polytechnics an air of unreality, almost myth. The myth is that a teacher cannot teach at Honours degree level if he is not engaged on research; I believe this to be an overstatement. I am sure that, unless he maintains a vigorous and active interest in the development of his subject, by being in day-to-day contact with current research, he will not teach effectively at Honours level: but this does not mean he must be actively engaged on research himself. Nor does it mean that we should only promote to senior teaching positions those who have successfully prosecuted research projects. 'Publish or perish' does not apply at Hatfield.

Although the Polytechnic does not seek aggressively to assert its independence of the university system or its determination to be distinct from it, it is important to emphasize that we see our aims to be different. We aim to be a teaching institution first and foremost, and we expect the main preoccupation of our members of staff to be the teaching of students. We expect them also to be of a calibre and disposition to seek every way of developing their grasp of their subject and in particular of developing their knowledge of the applications of their subject, so that their courses will be informed by a systematic study of the role which the students might play on successful completion of the courses. This is sometimes summarized as being a concern with the vocational bias of the courses, but it is not quite as narrow as that. It is more a philosophy of approach to the academic work, an attitude of mind, a concern for the realities of life. Thus we try to ensure that, as far as possible, those we take onto the staff as teachers are not only well qualified academically, but have had experience in the outside world. This is in any case desirable because they are not only teachers of full-time students, they have to face the classes of part-time students, among whom are many with several years' experience in the practice of their chosen profession or technique, who are rightly critical of teachers who are not up to date in their knowledge of current practice, and who are even less tolerant of academic poses than full-time students.

The Future: Courses

What of our courses, how are they likely to develop in the future? Beginning as we did as an institution responding to local needs it is natural that many of our courses should reflect a concern with the kind of product we aim to produce – a student who can take his place at once in society and the world of work, with knowledge, expertise, confidence and, we hope, enthusiasm. Our courses tend to be product-oriented rather than discipline- or subject-oriented. I would expect this type of course to remain in our programme for some time to come, modified and adapted from time to time as the type of product needed changes; it seems to fulfil a social and industrial need – it certainly satisfies a readily identifiable category of student. The strongly vocationally oriented student is often attracted to Hatfield precisely because the courses are product-oriented. The full-time courses are almost all sandwich in pattern – e.g. the usual three-year degree course occupies four years, the additional time being spent under Polytechnic supervision in industry or commerce acquiring first hand practical, on-the-job experience. The Polytechnic accepts the responsibility for the industrial placement of students, and the Polytechnic staff become involved in regular visits to the students during their industrial periods, and in collaboration with industrial supervisors ensure that the experience gained by the students during these periods is relevant to, and as far as possible supportive to, their academic studies. The organization of sandwich courses is more complicated and onerous than full-time courses, and the responsibility of the industrial supervision of students is one which makes heavy demands on the staff of the Polytechnic, but this is a principle to which we attach great importance. There are dark clouds on the horizon at the moment because of the inability of industry to fulfil its promises in relation to the provision of training places in all cases. Inherently, a sandwich course system must depend upon some degree of assurance that industry can fulfil its promises and provide the places for the students at the time they reach their industrial training period. British industry does not seem very good at long range planning and no doubt it would say that it is at the mercy of forces beyond its control which militate against the long-term view. Education is however a long-term process, and it is simply not possible for us to change the pattern of our courses overnight because a cold wind has passed through industry. We have the responsibility of the whole higher education and career expectation of our students and we cannot let them down. We are relying on industry to fulfil its part in the bargain however difficult it may be. It is particularly galling for us to find the difficulties appearing in our path at a time when academically the success of the sandwich course seems assured, and when industry has frequently paid the kind of compliment that matters to the graduates from our sandwich courses i.e. by taking them in preference to those trained on full-time courses, and in some cases paying them more. But there will always be those who feel that sandwich courses are too difficult to organize, and who will advocate falling back on to the traditional full-time course; it is for industry to support those of us who believe in the sandwich principle. There is no doubt that the output from these courses is significantly different from those from full-time courses. Clearly, they are on the whole one year older, and one year more mature, particularly since that one year has been spent in the outside world in the practice of their profession. Perhaps this contributes to a greater degree of stability in the student body at Hatfield compared with many other places. The fact that at any one time a high proportion of the student body has had experience of working in the outside world means that there are always plenty of cool heads and moderating voices to discourage excess. We have our excitements, of course, but they are usually about things that genuinely concern the students and their conditions of work. It would be a sad day indeed if the student body of the Polytechnic, simply because it was considered to be a strongly vocational institution, was thought to be for that reason inarticulate or insensitive about broader issues. I would rather have some lively expressions of dissent than dull acquiescence. But better than either is constructive contribution to the constant debate which should inform and vitalize all our work.

I have said that we tend to attract the strongly vocationally oriented student; this is one of the few generalizations we can make with any confidence about our student population, because we have not had time or resources to study it. Entry to polytechnics is not yet co-ordinated as it is to universities; students make individual applications to each polytechnic in which they are interested, and often apply for university entrance as well. Some regard us as a second chance, others, and their numbers grow, make us their first choice. Whatever their motive they are all considered carefully, usually interviewed and offers made in accordance with the market situation in each particular subject. The factors which influence student choice and tutor choice are so little known that we have little idea what produces our annual intake, but I suspect that if analysed it would not be very markedly different from that of many universities. The average

academic attainment of our intake, in terms of school examination performance, would be slightly lower, but this is known to have little correlation with performance in degree courses anyway. There would be some
high flyers in our group, if only because of the inefficiency of the university
selection methods; there would be a stronger vocational motivation, and
we find that this can often more than compensate for lack of academic
brilliance. Certainly, whatever deficiencies our students may have on admission they are well regarded as graduates when they leave and our
external examiner colleagues regularly comment on this. In terms of the
social origin of our students, I suspect that we would find it difficult to
argue that we are catering for a materially different section of society from
the universities; much though I regret it, I do not think we are yet making
much headway in providing a new avenue for the socially deprived,
though we are taking this problem seriously. One aspect of it is the problem of articulacy in writing and speaking, so much at a premium in all our
academic assessment systems. We have a team of staff working on ways of
encouraging the less articulate to express themselves, not by psycho-
analysis but by the application of common sense and logic to everyday
language and statement.

In its rapid academic growth Hatfield has developed a range of relatively specialized courses; these were initiated separately and at different
times and arose naturally from the demands of particular industries and
professions. They are not narrow in content or outlook; in fact they all
include systematic studies in non-specialist areas, yet if the course pattern
had been planned as a whole a greater degree of rationalization would
probably have been introduced; for example, there might have been a
greater commonality of first-year studies and a more conscious planning of
generalized foundation courses, perhaps with a choice of specialist final
options to follow. The problem now is to effect a transition from our
range of separate specialist courses to a more flexibly based system which
would give students a greater possibility of change of direction or orientation. We are actively investigating the possibilities of reconstructing all
our courses on a module system to facilitate a greater degree of student
choice, though with due safeguards to ensure a rational pattern of options
and to reduce the number of possible combinations. Such a system will
only be achieved by surrendering some of the precious autonomies and
independence which have become built in to the present system.

An even more fundamental challenge comes from the apparent conflict
between the concept of generalist courses now widely advocated and the
kind of vocational course which has become traditional at Hatfield. Although a vocational course is not necessarily narrow and indeed some of
the most carefully designed vocational courses are deliberately broad, e.g.
the Business Studies courses, it is nevertheless true that on the whole

vocationally oriented courses tend to be specialized. They are therefore particularly vulnerable to the criticism that in preparing students according to a specialized concept of a particular discipline at a particular time, we are educating for obsolescence, because what we feel may be important today will almost certainly not be important ten years hence, and in any case graduates hardly ever follow a straight line career pattern. A characteristic of a graduate should be that he is able and prepared to undertake a diversity of jobs and apply the qualities of mind trained and brought to the surface by his degree studies to a wide range of problems, far wider than studies in any single degree scheme. On the other hand, there is strong resistance in some quarters at Hatfield to the idea that we should take on students who wish to do general courses because they are completely unmotivated vocationally and have no idea what they want to do eventually. Those of us who favour the development of generalist courses feel that it should be possible for a polytechnic to offer a distinctive contribution in this field as it has in others. In adding generalist courses to our spectrum we are not seeking to encourage aimless students, but merely to accommodate those who genuinely wish to avoid specialization at the undergraduate stage; there is surely a place in polytechnics for these, as well as the highly vocationally motivated, some of whom become far too narrow in their interests; a deliberate broadening of courses may be in their long term interests too, however vigorously they may oppose the idea at the time. In designing generalist courses in a polytechnic, all the traditions of an outward looking philosophy, a reliance on knowledge related to its real-life significance and application, and of commitment to a positive social role will influence the result; they are hardly likely to be aimless studies in tranquil academic backwaters.

The Problem of Autonomy

The other great debates of the future will no doubt revolve around the questions of the degree of autonomy of such institutions as Hatfield. This Polytechnic has evolved in conditions which were peculiarly favourable to our development, and with the consistent and enlightened support of the Hertfordshire County Council. One of the most significant features in our development has been the part played by the Council for National Academic Awards (CNAA). This uniquely British body, which combines a concern with the establishment and maintenance of standards with a determination to place the responsibility for the maintenance of standards on the Colleges themselves, has provided the opportunity for Colleges like Hatfield to serve their apprenticeship and come of age in the academic sense. Until the advent of the CNAA, we could only participate in degree-level work by offering courses for the External degrees of the University of London. Now a virtually Internal system has replaced the necessarily impersonal External one, with great gains all round. In particular the staff of the College have realized that the future and reputation of the institution were in their hands and they have undergone the transmutation which occurs when full academic responsibility is placed upon professionally competent individuals. They accept the positive responsibility for the quality of their work instead of negatively seeking the approval of an external examiner. There is no other experience which can produce so productive and fertile an amalgam of experience and initiative.

The inevitable question arises for the future – how long will we continue to operate under this scheme? How long before the voices which say we are now an adult institution and should accept complete responsibility for setting our own standards and for awarding our own qualifications will become overwhelmingly persuasive? Until recently only universities had the power to confer their own degrees, but there are precedents now for institutions in Britain receiving charters to award degrees although they are not and do not intend to become universities. To many of us acceptance of the idea that our only future lay in joining the university system would be a betrayal of all that we have striven for. The greater breadth of our work including non-degree as well as degree work, part-time as well as full-time students, a diversity of courses of all kinds, and an outward looking, 'no walls' philosophy, would be at risk if we were asked to conform to the patterns of the universities. This is not antagonism for antagonism's sake, but a determination to retain individuality. Inevitably as the Polytechnic develops, its links with the CNAA will change in character, the strict monitoring of early days giving way to a broader relationship of mutual respect and trust. In the very long run there would seem to be a prospect of a natural transition to complete independence.

The last question of all concerns the ultimate responsibility for running and paying for such institutions as Hatfield Polytechnic. The polytechnics were conceived and designated by the Department of Education and Science, but they remain firmly within the further education sector of the local education authorities. Leaving aside all questions of high policy and national politics for a moment, Hatfield is, and would wish to continue to be, an integral part of the Hertfordshire further education service, although with considerable national responsibilities; the Hertfordshire authority has a good name for educational progress and is sufficiently large to be able to take in its stride the problems of comparative complexity and scale which a polytechnic creates in an education service. Moreover Hatfield has in many ways set out to serve the rest of the county and we aim to make it something of a centre-piece, not only geographically, which it is inescapably, but educationally.

We operate joint courses with a number of other Colleges in the county and aim to extend this provision. In other ways, for example in Library and Computer services we are providing a central facility which is widely available and of higher quality than would otherwise be possible. Very early in the development of the Hatfield College the County Education Committee established the Hertfordshire Technical Information Service and the County Technical Library Service; both these are based at Hatfield and serve the whole county. In this way the Polytechnic Library serves not only the students and staff of the Polytechnic, but it augments the libraries of the fourteen other Colleges in Hertfordshire, and it also provides an industrial information service with over a hundred subscribing members. The book stock of all the libraries is centrally acquired, catalogued and processed so that a member of any of the Colleges has access to the whole stock; a courier system ensures that the books are available quickly. By the time of designation the place of the Library in the Polytechnic was so well established that it was the unanimous decision of the Academic Board that the first allocation of major building capital which became available after the designation of Hatfield as a Polytechnic should be spent on a new purpose-built Library block which would constitute the first phase of the ultimate central Library complex. This is now open and in use. It is more than a collection of books and journals; it is a multi-media resources centre, including study carrels equipped with audio-visual media, microfilmed information storage and quiet study areas staffed by professional librarians, information officers and tutor librarians to help students and staff to make maximum use of the facilities.

With the development of the Computer Centre it is natural that a similar pattern is being followed. A large multi-access installation was acquired in 1970 and this is already capable of dealing with fifty users simultaneously, each calling up his individual file. Twelve of these users can be at remote terminals placed in schools and Colleges in the county far from Hatfield; the rest of the terminals are scattered over the Polytechnic sites. In this way the Hatfield computer is available to school children and students at a variety of institutions throughout Hertfordshire, all of whom can gain 'hands on' practical experience on a sophisticated powerful computer; again Hatfield is making a direct contribution to the educational development of the county as a whole. Whatever future changes there might be we would not wish these links to be broken or weakened in any way.

When in 1966 we at Hatfield had the temerity to produce, on admittedly very tenuous foundations, a Development Plan for the Polytechnic, it was not well received in some quarters. It was not in the tradition of the English further education service that any college should seek to map out its own future; colleges had always, like Topsy, 'just growed' and were expected to go on doing so and not indulge in presumptuous speculation. One detects more respect these days for the idea of rational planning, however difficult it may be. Unfortunately, we are no more able to plan realistically for the future now than we were in 1966. The annual financial review which is inherent in all local government financing continually frustrates and limits our horizons; yet it is free from some of the irksome restraints of long-term programmes which are overtaken by inflation. Some compromise is needed by which polytechnics will be enabled to see further ahead; some planning should emerge which is not simply dictated by a desire to cut costs but which carries credibility from the academic point of view.

At all costs let us in the polytechnics stick to our brief; at Hatfield there is one polytechnic which is not preoccupied by seeking the title and status of a university: we are united in a determination to demonstrate that the ethos of the polytechnic is identifiable and distinctive. It is developing all the time and changing, but is not being transmuted into a different ethos altogether. All the signs are that in the higher education system of the later seventies the polytechnics, if they stick to their principles and win their battle for acceptance and social respectability, will wield considerable influence; they may well become the model towards which others will aspire. It is my hope that Hatfield will then be seen to have been a prototype.

23

Recent Developments in Higher Education in Ontario

Douglas T. Wright

Introduction

In 1970 the Province of Ontario had a population of 7·5 million, representing about 36 per cent of the population of Canada, with a Gross Product of $35·0 billions, representing some 41 per cent of the total Canadian GNP. Although covering a total land area of 363,000 square miles, Ontario is highly industrialized and urbanized with most population concentrations along or close to the Great Lakes and St Lawrence. The social, political and cultural features of Ontario reflect a combination of British and American influences (some 65 per cent of the population of Ontario lives within direct range of American television broadcasting stations). Just under 10 per cent of the population of Ontario is French speaking, and the remainder, once mostly British, now reflects many backgrounds following high rates of immigration in the years after the Second World War.

The trend to industrialization in Ontario since 1940 coupled with the waves of post-war immigration and the high birth rates of the late 40s and 50s set the stage for an educational explosion which developed first at the elementary and secondary level in the 50s, and proceeded to the post-secondary level in the 1960s.

Table 1 shows the dramatic increase in the scale and scope of post-secondary educational endeavour in Ontario in recent times. By 1969 the total freshman enrolment in all post-secondary educational institutions in Ontario was 55,400 corresponding to over 45 per cent of the population of 19-year-olds.

The late 60s saw the development of a fairly loosely-structured system of post-secondary education in Ontario with a number of interesting features. While the number of universities, and particularly the number of students enrolled in the universities, increased greatly, the traditional role of universities was maintained with remarkably little change. The Ontario universities offer undergraduate programmes in the professional faculties along with traditional liberal arts and science programmes. An interesting anomaly in Ontario (as against the rest of North American

297

TABLE 1
SUMMARY DATA ON HIGHER EDUCATION IN ONTARIO

	1949–50	1959–60	1969–70
Universities			
Institutions	6	9	16
Enrolment	16,380[4]	21,638	108,750
Grants[3] (in millions)	4·3	24·2	456·7
Technological Institutes			
Institutions	4	6	21
Enrolment	736	5,492	30,742
Grants[3]	0·8	2·9	117·9
Other Post-Secondary Institutions[1]			
Institutions	over 75	74	75
Enrolment	7,327	14,882	19,484
Grants[2, 3]	3·6	11·4	12·4
TOTAL ENROLMENT	24,443	42,012	158,976
TOTAL GRANTS[3]	8·7	38·5	587·0

[1] Including Teachers' Colleges, Agricultural Colleges and Schools of Nursing.

[2] Not including amounts applicable to Schools of Nursing.

[3] Grants represent total amount provided by the Government of Ontario, not including student aid. Total ordinary institutional revenues would include, as well, endowment and gift income (about $2·5 million to universities in 1969–70), income from tuition fees (averaging about $200 per student per year in 1949–50; averaging about $400 per student per year by 1969–70).

[4] Not including 4,483 ex-servicemen.

practice) is a thirteen-year elementary and secondary system, with three-year university programmes leading to general degrees, and with four-year programmes leading to Honours degrees and most professional degrees. Until well into the 1960s very few postgraduate degrees had been awarded in Canada, and Canadian university faculties were dependent for staffing on Canadians who had gone (usually) to the US or Britain for advanced studies, and the immigration of qualified people. As in so many other jurisdictions, the 1960s saw an intense preoccupation in Ontario universities with graduate studies and research.

Non-university institutions include teachers' colleges, nursing schools, and the new colleges of applied arts and technology. Until the late 1960s, teacher training in Ontario for elementary schools was provided in one-year programmes in teachers' colleges operated directly by the Department of Education. Secondary school teachers took a one-year postgraduate programme after completing conventional programmes in arts or science. By 1968, changes were well in hand to transfer the teachers' colleges to the universities, to strengthen and lengthen programmes in anticipation of requirements for degree status for all school teachers. The 1960s also saw a fundamental change in the structure of nursing education, with a general move from three-year hospital-operated schools, with a strong traditional component of training and practice to regional schools operating two-year programmes with a relatively strong academic content, in close liaison with local hospitals where training opportunities continue to be provided.

Although Ontario had a handful of institutes of technology and the Ryerson Polytechnical Institute at the start of the 1960s, the combined enrolment of all of these institutions was small, and Ontario relied heavily on immigration for skilled technical manpower. The perception of a need for much broader opportunities for post-secondary education for many young people for whom traditional university courses were simply not appropriate led to the creation of a network of twenty colleges of applied arts and technology operating one-, two- and three-year programmes in a great variety of subject areas. Programmes have been designed to be strongly orientated towards community needs and the development of skills that were directly related to opportunities for employment. In most colleges studies in general arts and science were developed either as majors in their own right, or minors for vocational programmes. The Ontario CAATs can be said to constitute, with the universities, a binary system in that the two kinds of institutions stand side by side with different roles and activities without either serving consciously as a feeder for the other. Questions of transfer (and advanced credits) naturally do arise. Up to the present, no very formalized processes for transfer have been developed and judgments are made on individual cases: it seems likely that more formalized processes of some sort will become essential.

Organization of the System

The rapid growth described could not have developed, of course, without a major financial commitment from Government. This in turn led the Provincial Government into the development of organizations and processes for planning and decision making related to post-secondary education. (It should be noted that what still passes as a Canadian Constitution, the British North America Act of 1867, identifies education as a provincial responsibility.)★

Because of the traditional autonomy of the universities, with their roots

---

★ In Canada, the Federal Government makes direct grants to universities for research. While certain federal-provincial tax sharing agreements are related to expenditures on post-secondary education, the whole of the ordinary direct responsibility for financing post-secondary education is borne by provincial governments.

as private institutions, the Government of Ontario established a separate department to deal with university affairs in 1964. In its dealings with universities the Provincial Government had long sought external advice, and this process was formalized with the establishment of a Committee on University Affairs which was substantially re-organized in 1964 when the Department was established. The Committee comprises a dozen members, of whom about half are members of the academic community, and the others are drawn from the general public (business, labour and so forth), the Committee having a full-time Chairman. The Department of University Affairs serves as secretariat for the Committee and the Committee is advisory to Government through the Minister of University Affairs. The Committee receives briefs from the individual universities and on the basis of these and its own studies advises Government on, 'matters concerning the establishment, development, operation, expansion and financing of universities in Ontario', to quote from the Committee's terms of reference. Some of the most important work of the Committee has been the development of general policies for planning and finance (outlined more fully later in this paper).

While the universities individually make representations to Government and to the advisory committee, the Ontario universities have a 'collectivity' in the form of a committee of presidents (actually comprising the President and an academic representative of the Senate from each university, and recently renamed the Council of Ontario Universities), supported by its own secretariat.

A somewhat similar system exists for the colleges of applied arts and technology in their relationship with the Department of Education and the Council of Regents. Reflecting the Government initiatives that caused the CAATs to come into existence, the style and character of the relationships between the colleges and Government and its agencies are different from those relating to the universities with their autonomous tradition in being somewhat more centralized.

One of the most interesting questions for the future is, of course, the extent to which university dependence on government assistance will lead to greater centralization, as against the development of institutional strength and diversity in the college system which may lead that system to become somewhat less centralized. Both universities and colleges presently have their own boards of governors with, of course, considerable scope for local decision making.

Operating Grants Formula

Formula financing as used in Ontario resulted from an attempt to devise an objective procedure for distributing provincial operating grants to universities that would apply in the same fashion to all provinciallyassisted universities. The formula, which was established in 1967, determines grants as a function of (1) enrolment in various categories, (2) weighting numbers reflecting average costs/expenditures faculty by faculty, and (3) a dollar multiplier or unit value which once fixed determines all grants and expenditures. Table 2 shows the weights and categories, as well as grants per student and payments made in 1969–70. Formula income in any year is simply the sum of weighted enrolment (enrolment in each category times weight for that category) multiplied by the unit value established. Actual grants are equal to formula income less tuition fees. (Annual tuition fees have been virtually constant since 1964 at about $500.)

Formula income is defined to cover costs of maintenance, book purchases for libraries, and all purchases of equipment (except initial equipping of new buildings), as well as ordinary costs of operation. Most importantly, this system, while acknowledging average levels of cost in different parts of the university, does not in fact constrain the apportioning of the university budgets to various faculties and departments. Extra-formula grants are made to offset higher unit costs in new universities and in starting major new professional faculties. Most special grants are on a declining scale and provided only for a fixed number of years. It is of interest to note that grants for part-time and co-operative (sandwich) course enrolments are on a simple pro rata basis.

The advantages claimed for the formula system when introduced were that (1) The resulting grants would be demonstrably equitable. (2) University autonomy would be preserved. (3) Government would be provided with a means of foreseeing and controlling on a consistent basis the general magnitude of university and college grants. (4) There would be a maximum incentive for universities to be efficient and to manage their affairs well; any notion that improvement in efficiency would lead to a corresponding reduction in support would be offset. Long-range planning of university operations would be greatly facilitated. (5) Rather than limiting initiative or imposing any 'dead hand of uniformity' the formula system would give freedom to the individual institution to order priorities and take necessary decisions. (6) Private donors would be assured that gifts for operating purposes were an added resource to the university and not a substitute for public support.

Four years of experience suggest that the formula has fully lived up to these expectations. A number of criticisms have arisen: the formula encourages growth; it pays for process rather than product; it discriminates in favour of or against this or that interest. No alternative as generally acceptable to politicians, the provincial treasury, the universities and their faculties seems to be in sight, however.

In 1970, a similar formula system was developed for Ryerson

TABLE 2

OPERATING GRANT ALLOCATIONS ACCORDING TO FORMULA CATEGORIES
FOR FISCAL YEAR 1969–70
PER FULL-TIME EQUIVALENT STUDENT

Category	Formula Weight	Form Inco
1	1·0[1]	1,5
General Arts and Science,[1] Journalism, Social Work		
2	1·5[1]	2,2
Honours Arts, Commerce, Law, etc.		
3	2·0[1]	3,0
Undergraduate professional programmes, Engineering, Agriculture, etc.		
4	5·0[1]	7,
Medicine, Dentistry and Veterinary Medicine		
5	2·0[1]	3,0
Master's level – Professional programmes without thesis requirements		
6	3·0[2]	4,
Master's level – Humanities and Social Sciences		
7	4·0[2]	6,
Master's level – Applied Sciences		
8	6·0[2]	9,
All PhD (except 1st year PhD direct from Baccalaureate)		
Sub-total	—	-
Medical interns and residents	2·5	3,
Theology graduates at 50 per cent	1·0	1,
TOTAL	—	-

[1] Applied to conventional 2-term academic year.
[2] Applied to trimester year-round operation; only two-thirds paid for conventional 2-term academic year.

Polytechnic Institute and the Colleges of Applied Arts and Technology, at the urging of the Ontario Treasury.

Capital Formula

By early 1969 the need to induce effective use of physical resources and to plan new capital development led to the development of a capital funding formula paralleling the operating grants formula.

The intent of the capital formula was quite simple. Provision of funds for capital should reflect the extent and quality of existing physical resources (and their intensity of use), should reflect certain general standards

Grant	Total F.T.E. Enrolment	Weighted Total Enrolment	Basic Operating Income	Percentage Distribution of B.O.I.
1,045	59,484	62,131·8	$95,061,654	31·2
1,815	18,078	27,117·2	41,489,316	13·7
2,550	20,948	41,895·8	64,100,574	21·0
7,000	2,480	12,400·8	18,973,224	6·2
2,600	2,045	4,090·0	6,257,700	2·1
4,190	4,846	14,539·0	22,244,670	7·3
5,720	5,898	23,592·0	36,095,760	11·9
8,780	1,428	8,568·0	13,109,040	4·3
—	115,207	194,334·6	297,331,938	97·7
3,825	1,737	4,342·5	6,644,025	2·2
930	129	129·2	197,676	0·1
—	117,073	198,806·3	304,173,639	100·0

applied uniformly to all institutions, should primarily control dollars rather than details of construction, should leave the universities free to undertake priority and resource allocation decisions on their own, and should give clear indication that private support would complement rather than substitute for public support.

Financing/Planning

The combination of formula structures for operating and capital support and the co-ordinating/planning function performed by the Committee on University Affairs, all on a rolling five-year planning base, may be identified as a disciplined but highly decentralized planning/decision-making structure. It seems already evident that the use of formula financing for operating and capital support is fostering better management and more effective use of resources. Given the size of the Ontario university system, such a pattern has appeared most appropriate. The Committee on University Affairs has argued that decision-making power and related responsibilities should be left as close as possible to the arena of action. While the increasing dependency of the universities on government support might tend to lead to the transfer of more and more decision-making power to central authorities, it appears to be in the public interest instead to cultivate competency and confidence in decentralized institutional decision-making structures with a minimum of central control.

Since the formulae relate support to enrolment, there is a fairly clear and simple inhibition against unnecessary duplication of academic programmes. Proliferation of academic courses and programmes is virtually an infinite sink for resources applied to universities and colleges. Under the formulae, an institution must be able to anticipate sufficient enrolment, on average, before inaugurating new programmes, or even to decide on continuing existing courses and programmes. This is a kind of market regulation which seems to be working with some effect. In the four years (1967–71) since the operating formula was introduced the number of new courses/programmes introduced has been much less than in the previous four years (1963–7).

While the cost of supporting university education continues to rise very rapidly, the largest part of the increase is seen to be associated with the increasing number of students. Rates of increase of unit costs of university education in Ontario are considerably below rates of increase of unit costs for other social services such as primary and secondary education and health care. This would seem to suggest that the formula system provides more effective general control than traditional budgeting systems which may involve scrutiny and even control of line item expenditures, and so offer the illusion of control, but in fact lead only to control of some components with the total remaining effectively uncontrolled.

System planning is based primarily on social demand. While guarantees are not offered as to the availability of places in particular programmes or particular institutions, the Government of Ontario has for some years pursued a policy of providing places in universities and colleges for qualified students wishing to attend.

In detail, planning initiatives lie primarily with individual institutions, both in respect to determining enrolment growth and in determining the development of new programmes and courses. Such developments take the form of proposals which are reviewed by the appropriate governmental advisory committees as a prerequisite for funding.

The assumptions on which notions of planning are based and the nature of 'social demand' are being studied by the Commission on Post-Secondary Education, as outlined under that heading below.

Student Awards

Before 1960 only minimal student assistance was provided in any part of Canada, and the principal criteria had to do with academic excellence, with only a fraction of the available assistance applied to bursaries. Total student assistance in 1960 was approximately $1·8 million. By 1970, total student assistance had been transformed and increased to $29·4 million, in bursaries, $32·7 million in loans, and $7·4 million in graduate fellowships and other special awards, for a total of $69·5 million. The programme is fairly complex in detail, and confused further by the involvement of both Federal and Provincial Governments. The Federal Government provides the Canada Student Loans Plan which is means tested. Loans are carried interest free until after graduation, and experience with repayment has been excellent. The Ontario Government provides supplementary assistance in the form of free grants to individual students when assessed needs exceed a $600 loan limit. Total indebtedness is thus carefully limited. It is to be noted that the same programme applies to students in all post-secondary institutions in the Province. The result of introducing this new programme appears to have been to remove, to a large extent, financial barriers to students seeking post-secondary education. Removing financial barriers is, of course, not the same as removing social barriers.

A number of studies have been completed over the past two years in Ontario relating to accessibility, student finance, and the economics of education generally. There have been developed notions which are now being studied in further detail for a contingent loan system which might replace the present loan/bursary mix. The new proposals suggest that necessary funds would be advanced to students (still means tested, however), with an obligation for repayment that would be indexed to future income so that payments in any given year after graduation would not exceed a certain proportion of ordinary taxable income. The proposals further suggest that after a certain predetermined number of years (perhaps fifteen) any unpaid residual would be simply forgiven. The sense of this is, of course, to redistribute costs and benefits, burdening those who realize significantly higher incomes following graduation with an obligation to repay some substantial part of the assistance they received, while at the same time limiting liability so that the burden of long or disproportionately heavy repayment as a future prospect would not serve as a disincentive. Whereas the present system combines loans and grants on a concurrent basis, the proposed system would provide for loans in the shorter term, with the 'grant' made at the end in the forgiving of any unpaid balance. It is argued that such a scheme would be much more attractive than the educational opportunity bank proposals discussed in the United States in recent years which have a locked-in pari-mutuel effect in which repayments could exceed the amount borrowed.

Students and Faculty in Decision-making

There have been substantial changes in processes of governance in Canadian universities and colleges during the 1960s. Until well into the 60s traditional patterns prevailed in which university boards of governors composed entirely of laymen had full authority and responsibility for financial affairs, while university senates in happy isolation deliberated and determined on academic affairs. That system operated often as a kind of benevolent despotism which, given the small scale and rather intimate character of individual institutions, as well as their fairly elitist flavour, did not seem to cause undue pain.

As rapid growth commenced in the early 60s, the increasing scale of management problems, the special burdens placed upon university presidents as mediators between boards and senates, and concerns for 'democratization' of governance led to a study of the government of universities by Duff and Berdahl[1] which has had major influence. As Sir Eric Ashby noted in his review of the report,[2] 'It should be required reading for all who are entering for the first time into the corridors of academic power. . . . Beneath its disarming simplicity and its urbanity there are to be found some of the subtle secrets which distinguish a well-governed university from one which is misgoverned.' Major changes and reforms followed the publication of the Duff–Berdahl Report, leading to much stronger faculty participation in all aspects of governance, and leading to much more complete consultative processes within the institutions and such other changes as term appointments for academic department heads, deans (who in Canada hold substantial administrative responsibility), and even presidents.

Interestingly, for all its impact and for all its concern with democratization, the Duff–Berdahl Report did not anticipate the demands for student participation in the same processes which came to be voiced very soon after the report had been published. In many institutions the ordinary responses and changes resulting from the Duff–Berdahl study came, fairly naturally, to embrace significant participation by students, as well, in councils, senates and boards. Not to say that all such changes occurred smoothly: but by and large in Canadian universities, and certainly in Ontario, there has been a reasoned approach to the problems of government, accountability and participation which have led to substantial changes without disruption. Most conspicuously, there has been revealed through long and careful deliberations a substantial willingness on the part of all participants to consider reasoned argument and change.

At about the same time as the disturbances arose in the art colleges in Britain in 1968, some problems arose in the Ontario College of Art. A subsequent investigation[3] led to proposals for a simple, unicameral governing council comprising roughly equal parts of external or lay members and internal members, including administrative officials, teaching staff, and students. The proposals were accepted and the necessary legislation passed in 1969. The success of this experiment, and other considerations, have led to considerable interest in so-called unicameral government in which the functions and responsibilities of boards of governors are merged with those of academic senates.

The arguments, put most simply, are that few decisions on financial matters can be taken in the university without influencing academic affairs, and vice versa. Prompted partly by the Duff–Berdahl Report, the University of Toronto established an internal Commission on University Government which spent a little over a year in its studies and deliberations. Its report[4] came down strongly in favour of unicameral government. While generally supported within the University, the University's Board of Governors was not so enthusiastic. Just as this is being written, the Government of Ontario has announced that it intends to proceed with the necessary legislation, replacing the present Board and Senate with a new governing council somewhat larger than, but similar in make-up to, that established for the College of Art.

Beyond all these concerns with senior structures of authority, important changes have developed at departmental and faculty working levels in most universities providing fairly generally for student and faculty participation in decision making, with debate continuing over the proportioning of power to the various groups.

Commission on Post-Secondary Education

As the 60s drew to a close the Government of Ontario as well as many people concerned with the universities and colleges in the Province came to realize that some general overview should be undertaken relating to the accomplishments and growth of the 1960s and the needs for the 70s and 80s.

Towards the middle of 1969, then, a Commission on Post-Secondary Education was established with quite broad terms of reference to study the whole sphere of post-secondary education in Ontario. Although the Commission was composed largely of people who were involved in and in the main committed to the present system of universities and colleges, it determined, fairly early in its work, to try to consider and analyse the inner logic and usual assumptions of the educational system as a basis for its recommendations.

The Commission has engaged in some extensive research and studies.

In usual fashion, the Commission was required to hold public hearings and advertise for briefs and submissions. As a preface to the hearings, and following upon its own initial deliberations, the Commission published, 'A Statement of Issues', which discussed some of the assumptions and problems relating to the social functions of post-secondary education, problems of economics and finance, and problems of organization and authority. Some of the more provocative of these were carried on the covers of the document:

> One of the impressions that the Commission has formed about post-secondary education is that there is abroad an air of genuine doubt about current efforts in post-secondary education. It is not only that the government is unhappy about the costs, that the students rebel, and that the public is bewildered by it all. For the first time in a long while – perhaps for the first time ever, and definitely for the first time in memory of all living – the very foundations of our education, and especially of our educational structure, are being questioned. Perhaps it is not even the questions themselves that are new: What is new, rather, is the earnest sense in which they are being asked. The Commission shares many of these doubts and, in particular, is struck by the relevance of the following questions:
>
> 1. Why do we keep piling one year of schooling after another upon our students? Why is it necessary to have up to twenty years of *continuous* schooling. Why not break it up and, if necessary, space the years over a lifetime? What, indeed, are the emotional and social costs we are imposing upon our youth and ourselves when we, in fact, 'conscript' them into our educational institutions (or, as some observers have it, 'minimum security prisons') for so many years? By tolerating and encouraging forms of master-apprentice and officer-cadet types of relationships for young men and women in our educational institutions, are we not doing something to our social fibre as well?
>
> 2. Why is it necessary to assume that 'learning' must take place only when institutionalized? Why would it not be possible to have, in place of segregated and fragmented institutions, a plethora of educational services available to all, at any age? Is going to X number of theatre performances less 'academic', less for 'credit', than attending one course in English offered by a university or a college teacher? Is 'research' possible only at the graduate level?
>
> 3. Why should professional associations be allowed to stipulate formal educational requirements instead of administering tests regardless of educational backgrounds? Why should there be any formal links between educational requirements and occupations? Why, indeed, do we use degrees and diplomas for certification purposes? And if we must, why not issue such degrees and diplomas for only a limited period – say for five or ten years? After all, why should *one* certification last for a whole lifetime?
>
> 4. Is there any justification for the 'academic year'? Do we still believe that students must go back to the farms to help with the harvest – hence the need for free summers? Why is the trimester the only alternative? Why not two six-month periods of schooling?
>
> 5. What are the true implications of universality for post-secondary educa-

tion? Even if it is assumed that universality does not mean attendance by all but merely an equal opportunity of access for all, how 'far up' – for how many years – should this be? All the way to the PhD? Why should society invest this kind of money in one person and not in another? Merely because one is being 'educated'?

6. Do our post-secondary institutions really contribute to a better, fuller, life? Or should we, perhaps, be asking the same questions about 'more' education as are beginning to be asked about 'greater' economic growth?

It is dubious whether the Commission will ever arrive at answers to these questions; it is equally questionable whether any reasonable and realistic answers can be found by considering merely the financial and organizational issues, important though they may be. But if we are to have a debate over post-secondary education, it should be on issues that are fundamental to the quality of life in Ontario. Only after a basic appreciation of the present reality and beliefs can we be prepared not only to anticipate the inevitable but also to facilitate the desirable.

Finally, it is clear that if the Commission is to be at all successful in its task, it must have the help of the people of Ontario. It is our hope that via briefs, public hearings and other fact finding, Ontario citizens will engage in a fruitful public debate with the Commission. Our Interim Statement is meant as an invitation to such a debate.

The Commission indicated that it intended to publish its final report and recommendations in *draft form* in the autumn of 1971, and then to hold additional public hearings to determine public response before making final recommendations to the Government of Ontario early in 1972.

REFERENCES

1. *University Government in Canada*, Sir James Duff and Robert O. Berdahl, Toronto, University of Toronto Press, 1966.
2. Review of: University Government in Canada, Sir Eric Ashby, *Universities Quarterly*, v. 21, n. 1, pp. 110–15, December, 1966.
3. *Report on the Ontario College of Art*, Douglas T. Wright, Department of University Affairs, Toronto, September, 1968.
4. *Toward Community in University Government*; Report of the Commission on University Government, University of Toronto Press, 1970.

NOTE

More detailed information can be found in the annual Reports of the Committee on University Affairs and the Minister of University Affairs, both published by the Department of University Affairs, Toronto, and in the annual reports of the Council of Ontario Universities (formerly the Committee of Presidents of Universities of Ontario).

Section V

The Comprehensive Principle at Work

Introduction

W. Roy Niblett

The idea is now widely spread that tertiary education should follow secondary as a natural thing for very many young people. The proportion who go on from school to college or university is increasing in most countries despite growth of population and despite the financial burden. In the USA mass higher education seems likely to become universal higher education by the end of the century or soon after the beginning of the next.

The scale upon which most countries are providing higher education brings enormous problems with it. The two main types of problem are of structuring and of content. How can the institutions offering higher education be interrelated in a sensible way? How can the studies they offer be made and kept relevant to social and personal needs?

Problems of Structure

Roughly speaking, there are three main methods of structuring a higher education system, each method providing a number of variants. In some countries all three methods are used.

Structure One provides for very large intakes of students into an initial one or two years of full-time higher education, followed by selection in some form before a continuance of full-time education to first degree level.

Structure Two allows a diversity of institutions to offer full-time courses of three or more years up to the first degree stage, the choice of which institution a student should enter being made on grounds of high ability, or special vocational interest, or personal preference, or a combination of two or all three of these.

Structure Three provides for part-time higher education at least to the first degree and for this to be completed in stages, admission to each stage being dependent upon success in the previous one.

The tendency in almost all advanced countries is to develop a more flexible, inter-connected system of tertiary education, initial entry being made less restrictive, passage between the sectors less difficult, barriers between the subjects of study being lowered. But the need for preserving as final goals the achievement of rigorous intellectual standards is still implicitly accepted almost everywhere – the place of honour being given to research (pure or applied), to scholarship and the ability to reason.

The natural result overall is the evolution of a university that is more comprehensive in type. It may not see itself as yet in any such role; its connexions with other institutions of higher education may still be tenuous or even sub-conscious; it may pride itself on being 'not as other men are'. All the same it is likely to find itself more and more in the coming half century indissolubly linked with other institutions of tertiary education.

In this Section the American Community College exemplifies Structure One; and Trinity and All Saints College, Leeds, Structure Two. For in England every college of education for teachers is a constituent part of the institute of education of the university of its region. It has entered its students for qualifications, and since 1968 or so for degrees, that are internal to that university while preserving a considerable measure of freedom to have its students work to syllabuses it thinks suitable. Structure Three is exemplified by the Open University in Britain, but in many countries the principle that people should be able to make up academically later in life what they missed earlier, or have come to need, is increasingly accepted.

The *Gesamthochschulen* now developing in the Federal Republic of Western Germany are thus a logical step in the sequence. Their title declares their awareness of their own function. But it will not be easy all the same for them to fulfil it – in a country where universities have traditionally been concerned with the production of professionals for a relatively narrow range of occupations. Changes of orientation and attitude are called for if even comprehensive universities are really to play an emancipatory role in society. The aim must not be to train theoreticians and practitioners under one label, conferring the same degree on them, but to cross-fertilize them.

Problems of Content

By and large more consideration has been given so far to the structural than to the curricular changes encouraging institutions of higher education to face the future. The curriculum remains predominantly cognitive and predominantly specialist in almost all universities and colleges. Well equipped experts are essential to the very existence of a modern type of state. Many more graduates are called for and the proportion of these coming from technological types of university is rising. In Holland for example it has changed from the 1 : 2 of a few years back to the 1 : 1 it is now, and it seems likely a little later to become 2 : 1.

Is there still a place in universities and colleges for the general education of the inquiring mind? Where should a young man or woman expect to get this – from inside his place of higher education or outside? What is the place of interdisciplinary studies in the comprehensive university of the future? Has the concept of the residential college a part to play *educationally* as well as in providing roofs over heads? Some of these points are touched on in the final chapter of the book.

But many questions remain. If universities in many countries are to become more comprehensive the motivation for the change must be very powerful – a deep moving current not to be denied. 'Melting the mould' takes heat and heat takes energy. It looks in 1972–3 as if this might well be the way in which they should face the future. But what may the position be in 2072–3?

24

The American Community College:
Its Contribution to Higher Education

Leland L. Medsker

Throughout the United States and to a lesser extent in Canada, a new type of post-secondary school is serving an impressive number of youth and adults. Known as the junior college, the community college, or the two-year college, this twentieth century institution is attempting to meet the particular educational needs of a changing western culture.

The widespread use of the term, 'community college', as applied to public two-year colleges, implies that they are designed to provide a variety of community services. Certainly the public has accepted this concept of its function. In 1968, of the 1,072 two-year colleges of various types in the United States, 584 were public community colleges, attended by nearly 85 per cent of the 2,000,000 students enrolled in all two-year colleges. It is unofficially estimated that in fall, 1970, total enrolment in two-year colleges had increased to 2,400,000 students.[1]

The Fundamental Role

It seems fair to assume that the community college has risen to prominence in the United States because of its pervasive purpose, evolved over the years. To be sure, it performs the variety of services discussed here later, but these are merely the means by which it fulfils its overriding goal – to provide greater access to postsecondary education. Providing 'access', however, encompasses more than the admittedly extremely important notion of placing postsecondary institutions within commuting distance of both high school graduates and older persons who desire to re-enter the educational stream. It includes awareness of the necessity for refraining from setting up barriers to admission, and also the conviction, translated into action, that its curriculum, its educational policies, and the attitudes of its staff must be geared to serving a heterogeneous student population well. This not only means that the institution offers a diversity of programmes, but that it is willing to accommodate many students with lower than average ability and motivational patterns, particularly those from homes in which education beyond high school has heretofore been the exception rather than the rule.

Originally conceived of as a means by which university-bound students would appropriately pursue their first two years of work in a local institution before transferring as 'mature university students', the early community college in effect served the university rather than the general population. But over the years, with egalitarianism spreading to almost every aspect of American life, the idea that education beyond the secondary school is a right became increasingly entrenched. As a consequence, the emphasis on community colleges increased, and they were invested with expectations which led not only to their universal growth, but to their open-door policy, their multi-faceted curriculum, and their general concern about how best to accommodate a broad spectrum of diverse students. Thus, access has come to equate with the theory that real opportunity depends as much on accommodation to need as upon ease of admission and the physical proximity of institutions.

There is consensus that the community colleges have gone far in democratizing postsecondary education in the United States. Nationally, they now account for nearly 30 per cent of all undergraduates and 25 per cent of all students in higher education, and there are ten states in which the national average is exceeded. In California, for example, more than 90 community colleges enrol well over 60 per cent of all undergraduate students. The Carnegie Commission on Higher Education has estimated that by 1980 as many as 4·3 million students may be enrolled in community colleges, and it projects the need for 230–280 new institutions of this type by then.[2]

While growth in the number of institutions and enrolments does not of itself necessarily attest to real democratization, many studies indicate that the community colleges have promoted 'access' in its broadest sense. One of the most comprehensive of the studies[3] documented the extent to which the community college is removing geographical, financial, racial, and sex barriers to further education, and is providing appropriate educational programmes for a diverse student population. The author concluded that in general, 'There is cause for optimism regarding the capacity and spirit of the two-year college in providing postsecondary education for all.'

Characteristics of the Community College

Of the numerous distinctive features which the community college has developed to enable it to discharge its responsibility to the larger community, a few can be noted briefly. The colleges are characterized by a diversified curriculum which provides students with the opportunity either to prepare for a job at the end of their community college experience or to transfer to a four-year college or university to work toward a baccalaureate degree. The terminal occupational training programmes are ordinarily geared to the preparation of technicians and semi-professional workers in such fields as engineering, health, and business, although in some of the community colleges there is increasing attention to the preparation of workers for certain service occupations and for skilled work that does not require higher level technical training. Increasingly, too, occupational programmes serve a re-training function; both older youth and adults use them – most typically during evening hours – to upgrade their skills or to change occupational direction. Not all of the many thousands of adults who enrol in the community college on a part-time basis do so to improve a specific work skill, however. A high percentage take academic programmes for self-improvement, which naturally may enhance their competence on a job, but only incidentally to their immediate goal of developing themselves; others acquire credits toward an Associate degree, given at the end of a two-year programme; and many expect to use the credits toward a higher degree.

A related feature of the community college is its effort to serve students in need of remedial work. Since the open-door principle admits increasing numbers of students with deficiencies in knowledge and learning skills, special programmes are needed to help bring such students up to a level where they can master the course material related to their educational and vocational goals. Such remedial courses take many forms, bear a variety of names, and are the subject of some controversy about their purpose, methodology, and success. They must nevertheless be considered an indispensable part of any effort to give students a second chance at a period in their lives when the motivation to succeed has increased with maturity.

Closely allied with curricular offerings is the perceived need for the community college to help students make good educational and vocational decisions and gain social skills. To these ends most community colleges place a high premium on guidance programmes and other forms of service activities for students. Many educational leaders believe that unless the community college succeeds in this part of its programme, it will not be able to fulfil its overall responsibility for serving a highly diverse spectrum of students and channelling them into realistic pursuits after they leave the community college.

But over and beyond admissions policy and programme there is, at least by popular consensus, one core feature of the community college which is central to any consideration of its role in the American system. This is its staff's respect for the students and dedication to teaching. Much of the folklore of the community college is that it is a 'teaching institution', meaning that a premium is placed on teaching instead of on research and the other functions that most often characterize four-year institutions. Staff members in community colleges generally devote full time to teaching or to other services to students, such as counselling. Since the college and university practice of using teaching assistants is not followed, the only faculty contacts students have is with the regular staff. Moreover, partly because historically community colleges were small, legend still has it that there is an unusually close relationship between students and staff. Although the attribute of small size is becoming less prevalent, this fact alone does not necessarily inhibit the formation of close relationships between faculty and students. During the last several years of wide-spread unrest in American colleges, there has been much less dissension in community colleges than in the four-year institutions and universities. The reasons for this relative calm are indeterminate; it may spring from the students' greater sense of satisfaction with the institution, or it may be that students attracted by the community college tend to be less critical.

The Impact of the Community College on the American Educational System

Descriptions of the status, role, and nature of the community college are helpful in establishing the reality of this institution on the American scene, but leave unanswered the question of what influence this two-year institution exerts on the system of postsecondary education. That it creates an opportunity for many youths and adults to continue their education is evident from the review of its growth and present size, but it is interesting to speculate on what postsecondary education would be like today if there were no community colleges. What distinctive functions, in effect, do the community colleges render, and why?

Generally speaking, the advent of the community college has added greatly to the diversity of higher education in the United States. Its presence in a majority of the states has enabled the four-year institutions not only to become more selective in the students they admit, but to restrict the variety of programmes they offer. Thus, by maintaining an open door and thus including in the college population young people from lower ability levels, the community college has widened both the spec-trum of institutions and the diversity of student characteristics in post-secondary education. Of the 2,551 institutions in higher education listed in the 1969–70 US Office of Education Directory for Higher Education, 903 (35 per cent) were classified as two-year institutions. And although there is a great overlap in the types of students who attend two-year and four-year colleges, the former do attract a larger number who fall below the median in terms of economic level, academic aptitude, and previous achievement.*

Within the last two years much has been said in the United States about

---

* It should be noted, however, that while most community colleges operate under the open-door policy, and thus admit students from low levels of ability, motivation, and achieve-ment, they also attract almost as many students from the other end of the scale.

the principle of 'open admission', which in essence suggests that four-year colleges and universities may become less selective than heretofore and that students who do not meet conventional admissions criteria will be given an opportunity to pursue a college programme. During the 1970–1 academic year, a number of four-year institutions have begun either to experiment with this principle or to consider its adoption. Among the most notable of the experiments is that found in the City University of New York, a system of colleges and universities in which the open admissions policy became effective in fall, 1970.* It is estimated that at that point more than 9,000 students who would not have been admitted in prior years entered these hitherto highly selective institutions. While it is much too early to evaluate the experiment, the university is in the process of doing so as it works at the challenge of serving its new clientele. Meanwhile, the country awaits the outcome and ponders the merit of having open admissions in all types of institutions. Many observers suspect that the principle will be adopted as far as systems of higher education go, but that it will never become universally applied to all individual institutions. If this proves to be true, the community colleges will play an increasingly important role in implementing the principle.

Just as the community college has greatly expanded higher education and in so doing has opened the system to most high school graduates, so also has it increased the variety of educational programmes that now exist under the 'college' umbrella. It is for this reason that in the United States the term 'postsecondary' education is often used as a substitute for 'higher education'. Nonetheless, the inclusion of the great variety of one- and two-year occupational programmes ranging in scope from machine shop to engineering technology and from cosmetology to professional nursing – usually with a general education component – is testimony to the variety of educational programmes in institutions which include the word 'college' in their official title. The breadth and variety of offerings have come a long way since the days when college attendance had for its sole occupational goal the preparation for a profession.

About one-third of the students in the community colleges are enrolled in occupational programmes designed to lead directly to employment, and an appreciable percentage of students not enrolled in such programmes also enter the labour market after their community college experience. But even the career programmes are increasingly being viewed as open-ended in the sense that they not only make students immediately employable, but that many of the credits earned in them can be transferred to four-year institutions and used as a base for more advanced occupational training.

---

* See Chapter 28.

Still another element of diversity provided by the community college lies in its role in continuing education. For more than a decade, one of the country's perceived needs has been some provision of opportunity for people of all ages to continue their education on a part-time basis. As is true in other developed countries, this need springs from many factors, among them the changing technology which affects manpower needs. Approximately one-half of all community college students are enrolled on a part-time basis, and a large percentage of these are well beyond the 18–24 'college age' category. While other types of colleges also offer a variety of opportunities for part-time education, it is the community colleges which offer the special advantage of being near the homes of potential part-time students. These institutions will thus increasingly come to be regarded as 'education centres', accommodating most of those in the community who feel the need to go back to school.

Community colleges may also come to play a critical role in facilitating a new and developing pattern of college attendance. Two major bodies in the United States have recently made significant statements about the time span over which individuals should logically be enrolled in college. The Carnegie Commission on Higher Education recommended that many students might well interrupt their college experience from time to time, alternating their experience there with employment and other life activities. The Commission further proposed that the time required for earning the baccalaureate degree be substantially reduced.[4] Essentially the same suggestions were made early in 1971 by The Assembly on University Goals and Governance.[5]

Within the last year the idea of awarding college credit for non-traditional educational experiences also has received widespread attention in the United States. For the first time in the country's history, the awarding of external degrees, 'colleges without walls', and credit by examinations are being seriously discussed. Two major foundations have made grants to institutions and agencies to help them initiate new programmes along such lines. Although it is too early to determine the exact role of the community college in implementing the suggestion that people continue their college experience over time or have their educational experiences validated by appropriate examinations or a short-term residency, many believe that the community college will inevitably become exceedingly important in the process.

It is generally conceded that the community college has exerted still another major influence on American higher education. Its emphasis on teaching by regular faculty instead of by teaching assistants and its concern for students who lack the skills to carry on conventional college work are cases in point. Most community colleges also strongly emphasize individual and group guidance as a means of assisting students in making vocational, educational, and personal decisions. It is widely believed that this general institutional concern for students has set an example for personalizing higher education that may well be considered by the staffs in four-year institutions. So vital do community college administrators consider the close relationships between students and faculty, that with the growth of enrolment in individual community colleges, many concerned administrators are now seeking new organizational arrangements which will preserve the historical emphasis on concern for individual students.

Over the last several years, one of the complaints of disaffected American college students on one campus after another has been that higher education is depersonalized. The students, with cause, have pointed to the lack of meaningful contact with faculty and to the fact that campus size and the mechanization of record-keeping have reduced student identity to sheer 'IBM numbers'. Those responsible for colleges and universities are concerned; whether sufficiently to correct the situation remains to be seen. But the higher education community – particularly in the large state institutions – is mindful of the example already set by the community colleges. Moreover, with an ever-increasing percentage of lower division students going first to a community college, the total problem is potentially lessened provided, of course, the community colleges are able to continue their emphasis on personalized education.

Initiative and Constraints

Implicit in the preceding discussion is the general idea that the eyes of the country are on the community colleges. In a sense this is the case, for as state after state moves in the direction of strengthening its community college system, a set of public expectations emerges. For example, the rationale expressed for the expansion of the system is usually quite pragmatically oriented; often arguments for the move have been based more on the need to relieve the four-year institutions or to reduce overall costs than on the means by which community colleges can improve undergraduate education or render educational services not previously available. To be sure, other arguments are also advanced – about the merit of the multiple purpose nature of the community college, as well as other of its attributes mentioned above – and although these arguments may be secondary in actually effecting legislation leading to additional community colleges, they nonetheless become implanted in the minds of potential students and their parents. Thus, the general public comes to look upon the community college as an agency that can do innumerable things for innumerable people, while the legislators and educational planners often regard it primarily as a means of restructuring postsecondary education.

By and large, administrators and other staff in the community colleges subscribe to the various expectations held by the public. There is, in fact, so prevailing an orthodoxy among community college leaders that they are widely regarded as cultists who make impossible claims for the institutions. Yet it is unfair to question the motives of leaders who strongly believe in an institution to which they are dedicated. They see the community college as an institution which bridges many gaps for many people and meets needs unmet by any other postsecondary institution. Seeing the necessity both for greater democratization of higher education and for an institution that continues to serve people who are long past the normal college age, by and large they take the initiative in making good on their claims. It is not that these leaders reject the role of four-year institutions, but that they believe the country will be better served by a new structure which places heavy reliance on an 'in between' institution – often referred to as a distributing agency – which accepts the majority of high school graduates and helps them to their next level of pursuit, whether in the four-year institutions or elsewhere.

Unfortunately, however, both external and internal constraints make it difficult to achieve the ideal of the community college. The external difficulties are due primarily to a pecking order of prestige among institutions and to the public's tendency to be clearer about the role of the four-year college and university than that of the community college. As a result, the community college has had difficulty in building a distinct and viable identity of its own, just as within the colleges themselves certain programmes have had difficulty establishing themselves as attractive and worthwhile. The more socially prestigious programme leading to transfer dominates the community college scene for too many students. About two-thirds of all entering community college students assert unrealistically that they plan to transfer, whereas only about one-half of them move immediately beyond the community college. Similarly, regardless of the students' aptitudes and practical goals, much greater percentages of them take courses leading to the more exalted technicians' jobs rather than those leading to lower skilled and service jobs.

Internally, the community college suffers most from the faculty's lack of agreement on its purposes. While a good percentage of faculty members are certainly in sympathy with the goals of the comprehensive institution, there are many who do not subscribe to all of its purposes and programmes.

A study[6] of attitudes held by more than 4,000 staff members in 57 randomly selected community colleges revealed some startling facts. While 53·8 per cent of respondents indicated their preference for being employed in a community college, 26·7 per cent preferred a four-year college, and 17·7 per cent a university. That so many staff members would prefer to teach elsewhere raises at least a question about the fabled institutional commitment of community college staffs.

The staff members surveyed were also asked whether they believed that certain types of educational programmes were 'essential', 'optional', or 'inappropriate' for the community college. The responses revealed a tendency to favour the more traditional aspects of college and to question many of the special services which the community colleges are presumed to render. Most of the staff said it was essential for the college to offer both a transfer programme and standard two-year technical curricula, but when less conventional programmes were under consideration, the responses were not nearly so universal. Only one-half of the group felt that occupational curricula for skilled and semi-skilled trades were essential, and only about one-fifth thought the college should be concerned with occupational programmes of less than two years' duration. Only about one-half of the respondents thought that remedial courses were essential, about one-third thought remedial courses should be optional, and almost 16 per cent said they were inappropriate. Questions about other offerings and services unique to the community college revealed the same tendency for many of the staff to question what was either new or different from conventional college curricula. Almost one-half of the respondents thought that too much stress is placed on the *quantity* of students and not enough on *quality*.

The faculties surveyed were also almost equally divided on the question of whether the community college should be open to all high school graduates. In response to a statement that, 'The junior college should offer a flexible programme, unhampered by conventional notions of what constitutes higher education,' more than one-fourth of the staff said they disagreed. As might be expected, the responses varied with institutional responsibility and background. Counsellors and administrators were generally more flexible than teachers in their attitudes toward the programme, and teachers of academic subjects were more traditional in their points of view than were those who taught in applied fields. Those who preferred to teach in a four-year college or university were more likely to oppose occupational and remedial programmes.

The problem reflected by such staff attitudes is serious because an institution staffed by members not in harmony with the expectations held for the community college is less likely to realize those expectations. It may be, of course, that a study of attitudes in any type of educational institution would reveal no greater degree of harmony. But since the functions, programmes, and services of the community college are so diverse, it is particularly essential that those who work in it accept the goals which society in general sees for the institution.

One may hypothesize that one reason for faculty disagreement with institutional goals at the community college level is that many faculty, recruited directly out of graduate school, continue to identify with the more prestigious institutions from which they just came, rather than with a new institution with different goals about which they know relatively little. Theoretically, the problem will be overcome in time as the community college becomes better known and understood and as it accelerates its orientation programme for new as well as existing faculty. However, the current oversupply of recent doctoral graduates who are finding it difficult to obtain positions in industry and four-year college teaching could constitute a danger if an inordinate number of them were suddenly to take jobs in community colleges as a last resort.

Obviously, over-emphasis on lack of harmony on the part of either students or faculty could do the community college a grave injustice. Great numbers of students and faculty are affiliated with these two-year colleges for good reasons and with excitement at the opportunity to try the new and different. Other types of colleges can also be presumed to have some students whose ambitions are unrealistic and some faculty who would, if they could, reconstitute their institutions.

An Assessment

Those whose business it is to evaluate the overall functioning of the community college in American education are generally agreed on the high quality of both its promise and performance. It already has had a profound impact on postsecondary education, although many call attention to its failure to make good on all its claims. They cite the lack of comprehensiveness in the programmes of many colleges, the inadequacy of many guidance and other student personnel services, the increasing size of institutions and the danger that attention to individual students will be minimized, and the fact that in the light of their future activities, too few students enrol in occupational programmes. The critics also express concern over the high attrition rate in community colleges and suggest that when second-year enrolments drop to one-half of what they were the first year, the holding power of the institution is inadequate.

These same criticisms have frequently been voiced by the author of this chapter. But no institution is ever perfect, and the relative newness of the community college suggests that its lifespan to date has been too short for it possibly to have attained perfection. This new experiment in postsecondary education can and will be improved, and it bids fair to exert dramatic changes in the education people pursue after high school, and in when and how they do it.

REFERENCES

1. The Carnegie Commission on Higher Education. *The open-door colleges: Policies for community colleges* (New York: McGraw-Hill, 1970).
2. The Carnegie Commission on Higher Education. *The open-door colleges: Policies for community colleges* (New York: McGraw-Hill, 1970).
3. Cross, K. P., *The role of the junior colleges in providing postsecondary education for all*. Office of Education, Department of Health, Education and Welfare (Washington, D.C.: Government Printing Office, 1971).
4. Carnegie Commission on Higher Education. *Less time, more options: Education beyond the high school* (New York: McGraw-Hill, 1971).
5. The Assembly on University Goals and Governance. *A first report* (Cambridge: The American Academy of Arts and Sciences, 1971).
6. Medsker, L. L., Study of community colleges. Unpublished manuscript, Center for Research and Development in Higher Education, University of California, Berkeley, 1967.

25

Towards the Comprehensive University in Germany

Hildegard Hamm-Bruecher

German Universities from 1800 to 1919

Those who wish to understand the German system of higher education in its present-day state must first look back to the beginning of the nineteenth century – which was the beginning of the 'era of the bourgeoisie'. Since the end of the eighteenth century, more than half of the forty-two universities in the German-speaking area had had to close their doors. Those remaining were academic vocational and specialized schools. The reform which began at that time did not, however, grow directly out of this crisis, but from the new Berlin University, which had been founded by the philosophers of German idealism and enlightened, liberally-minded Prussian civil servants. The founding of the Berlin University was completed by Wilhelm von Humboldt in 1809–10. Within the space of a few years, universities similar to it were founded at Breslau and Bonn.

The establishment of this new type of university was inspired by the idea of 'education by academic learning' – not influenced by utilitarian considerations, but dedicated to the unfolding of individuality, to a way of living embracing the entire man, in 'seclusion and freedom' (*Einsamkeit und Freiheit*) both for teachers and students. Its highest goal was to encourage a philosophy, which should reflect critically on experiences of the world as it was, and seek to discover a meaning by which they would be drawn together. The principle of the 'unity of research and teaching' is derived from the character of this 'pure academic learning' – a learning which should concern itself not only with established knowledge, but also with unsolved problems requiring further research. This principle has had a momentous influence on further university development, as has also the principle of freedom of study, which has united professors and students and led to the rejection by professors in academic institutions of the idea that practical training should be their responsibility. Humboldt's concept of academic learning consciously and deliberately separated academic learning, as expressed in research and teaching, from its application in life. This new type of university broke up the class distinctions of feudal times with the consequence of a dualism in higher education – namely, academic 'education' (*Bildung*) and lower-level 'training' (*Ausbildung*). This dualism established a basis for the demands of a new elite.

From the institutional point of view, Berlin University, too, was – as were all the other German universities before it – a state institution, and economically dependent on it. The University received the right of self-administration in academic matters – e.g. the outward representation on the part of the elected rector, or the awarding of honours to university students by conferring on them graduation degrees and lectureships. Within the framework of this 'autonomy', state administration was confined to ensuring the lawfulness of the decisions made and measures taken by the universities.

This new model for a university constitution encouraged similar efforts outside the boundaries of Prussia. Within a few decades, Humboldt's basic ideas had been adopted at all the German universities. The numbers involved at these universities ranged from 30 to 60 professors and 300 to 2,000 students who constituted in each case a 'body of teachers and those receiving instruction' at the universities.

In the course of the nineteenth century, immense progress was achieved in the sciences – particularly in natural science and, later on, also in engineering science. New branches and disciplines were constantly being established, which then developed into independent faculties. The classical faculties expanded. Professors and students sought more permanent organizational forms for research, teaching and studies. New training requirements came in the wake of the accelerated transition from an agrarian to an industrialized society, and thus the range of educational establishments offering subject-oriented education, e.g. mining colleges and agricultural schools, was expanded after 1870 to include commercial colleges and technical colleges of higher education, which strove hard to receive the standing and legal status accorded to universities.

Universities from 1919 Onwards

The introduction of the first German republican democracy marked a decisive turning-point in the development of the universities after 1919. Article 142 of the Weimar Constitution laid down that: 'Art and science and their teaching shall be free. The state shall guarantee their protection and help to foster them.' This provision was interpreted as the 'basic right of the university'. The same Constitution introduced general compulsory schooling of at least eight years' duration, and made provision for the 'training of teachers according to uniform principles'. During the 1920s, new institutions were therefore established for training primary school teachers. In Prussia, under C. H. Becker, the liberal minister of education, these were called *Pädagogische Akademien*. In their regulations governing admission, in their internal structure and in their status, they differed from the universities. Nonetheless, since World War II, they have developed step by step in such a way as to become institutions of higher education almost equal in status to the universities from the academic point of view. Endeavours are being made to achieve their full integration into the 'comprehensive universities' planned today.

In the history of the German higher education system, too, the years from 1933 to 1945 constitute a humiliating era. In many places, professors and students readily opened the door to national socialism, and the ideology of racialism led to a blood-letting among German scholars which is still felt today. Resistance to the expulsion of Jewish scholars was far too isolated.

After World War II and the downfall of the Third Reich, the German universities lay in ruins in 1945. The first postwar decade was therefore characterized by extremely laborious rebuilding operations. Nonetheless, three new universities were established: Saarbrücken, Mainz and the Free University of Berlin. After the partition of Germany into an Eastern and a Western area, both parts of the country received their own differing constitutions at the end of the 1940s. Since then, both political systems have continued to take increasingly divergent paths in almost all fields, including the university sector.

In the remarks which follow I shall confine myself to describing university development in the Federal Republic of Germany. The West German Basic Law includes in Article 5 the guarantee of 'freedom for research and teaching' as a basic democratic right. The eleven Länder – as member states of the Federal Republic – received the main competences for the educational sector. It was therefore the exclusive task of the Länder to develop and expand the universities, to finance them and attend to their legal structure. The universities themselves attempted, as a reaction to twelve years of the centralistic 'Führer state' and academic bondage, to fend off wherever possible the influences exercised by the state on their internal affairs. Venerable traditions were reintroduced and embedded themselves without being critically examined by the universities. At the same time, the 'classical' universities clearly defined the boundaries between themselves and other institutions of higher education such as teachers' training colleges, and colleges of art, music and sports. Up to the middle of the 1960s, the universities' own idealized and retrospective understanding of their tasks in science and education predominated.

This phase of the development was – and still is – critically defined by progressive thinkers as a 'restoration'. Nonetheless, during the first twenty years after the war, serious endeavours have been made in the cause of 'university reform'. Today there is a vast mass of written material on the subject. Nonetheless, all the attempts to redefine the intellectual position of the university largely failed to produce practical consequences. The so-called 'Honnef Scheme' for study assistance was an exception which, from 1957 onwards, has made possible for the first time assistance for a considerable number of students – about 20 per cent – by way of scholarships and grants.

Apart from this progress, the inner structure of the universities, their conception of their function, and their prestige, remained unchanged. As before, the holders of chairs (professors in ordinary) constituted in themselves the unity of research and teaching, and made the decisions with regard to all academic matters in the faculties, assemblies and senates. Every form of co-operation, or even co-determination, on the part of other members of the universities was, and remained, out of the question.

The public, too, had relatively little interest in the universities during those years. The Länder, intent on exercising their independence, endeavoured to cope with the steadily growing financial requirements necessary to deal with the universities' problems, caused by the steadily growing number of students (1950: 110,000 students, 1960: 206,000 students, 1968: 288,000 students) and the needs of modern research. However, the rapidly increasing requirements exceeded their financial resources. For this reason, the Federal Government participated for the first time in 1958 in bearing the investment costs for university construction. Its first contribution amounted to 34 million marks. This was increased over the years up to 1970 to over 1,000 million marks.

A further new factor in the development of higher education policy was the 'Science Council' established in 1957, in which the Federal and Länder governments worked out expert opinions and recommendations together with experts from the field of education. These recommendations included detailed statements on the necessary expansion of universities from the point of view of new buildings, additional staff and extra equipment. Thus they influenced the increase of expenditure on universities in the Federal Länder and the voluntary contributions on the part of the Federal Government.

The Crisis of the mid-1960s

In spite of all the efforts to expand the universities, conditions of those in Western Germany visibly deteriorated during the 1960s. Observed at first by only a few, the concept, aims and tasks of the traditional German university had, as a result of the rapid changes in the sciences and as a result of the development in society, been caught up in a serious crisis. Despite all the protestations from official sources: the German university no longer had a sound core! Even with considerably greater funds and a rapid increase in academic staff, the critical situation could no longer be mastered.

The recommendations of the Science Council with regard to the founding and structure of new universities therefore received great support in several of the Länder. Six universities and three schools of medicine were to be built, with a structure in accordance with progressive principles. 40,000 new study places were thus to be provided and the university sector was to be expanded by about 20 per cent within a few years.

These plans too, however, were swallowed up by the growing avalanche of students advancing on the universities. This increase in numbers was a consequence not only of the greater number of qualified grammar school-leavers seeking admission at the universities, but resulted from the fact that university students needed more and more time in which to complete their studies, on account of the steady deterioration of study conditions, particularly in the most popular disciplines with the greatest number of students.

In the mid 1960s, the crisis in the universities became apparent to everyone. The external causes have already been described. The internal causes were as follows: in 1963, the sociologist Schelsky defined the change in modern learning with the terms 'work character' and 'resemblance to a business enterprise'. Thus the work of a professor, which has come to be a profession, is characterized by devotion to the logic of the 'matter' he studies, the specialization of knowledge, the mechanization of the processes involved in the production of new knowledge, the compulsion to practise co-operation in his work, and the didactic imparting of knowledge, coupled with the organization of instruction on the pattern used in schools. The new requirements in teaching and research work involved in such fundamental changes necessarily led to tensions – which could not be relaxed – within the traditional university, and called into question the principle of the unity of research and teaching which had been effective since Humboldt's day. Last but not least, the extremely complex organization of the university – which had assumed gigantic proportions with a budget equal to that of a medium-sized town – overtaxed the traditional self-governing system of university administration.

In the mid 1960s, students also intensified their activity in the sector of general policy and higher education policy. Already in 1961 and 1962, two reports published by students – 'The University in the Democratic System' and 'Students and the New University' – provided the beginnings for this movement. The 'political awareness' of the university, first and foremost on the part of the students, made rapid progress after the 'long, hot summer' of 1963 in Berkeley. Particularly in Berlin and Frankfurt, students increasingly made basic aspects of German and international policy the central issues of public discussions and campaigns (e.g. recognition of the German Democratic Republic, emergency laws, the war in Vietnam, etc.).

In addition, their basic social commitment was fired by the constitutional principles of social democracy. Both the genuine and the false privileges within and without the university were called into question. The education ideology of an elite was replaced by the 'citizens' right to education'. The social make-up of the students, which revealed an obvious over-representation of the children of educated citizens, whereas the children from working-class and farming families were noticeably under-represented, caused increasing offence. In some places, students organized campaigns in rural areas and in working-class families, in order to win listeners over to attending secondary schools.

After 1965, the neglected factors and shortcomings of the development became increasingly obvious to the public. Not only the material needs, but also the position of the university and of the sciences in society, became the subject of public political controversies in associations, political parties and parliaments. The pivotal point of the discussion can be summarized in the formula of 'the democratization of the education system'. Students and teaching assistants – and also a number of professors – sought for a new understanding of democracy as their way of life, and developed numerous models for the democratic university. They did not succeed, however, in achieving unity on the structural questions of university reform on the one hand, and the extent of co-determination on the part of the members of the university on the other hand. During the years 1967 to 1969, this led constantly to new controversies, demonstrations, strikes and disturbances in the West German universities on widely differing occasions. The subjects of student protests were *inter alia*: the outdated university structure as ostensibly a community of teachers and students, the hierarchy of the teaching staff (which was no longer capable of functioning properly), the lack of orientation to social policy on the part of the university and its tasks, the increasing enrolment restrictions and proposals for the rigid systematization of studies, aud topical issues of domestic and foreign policy. New methods of protesting were introduced: 'sit-in', 'go-in' and the organized heckling and bringing to a standstill of lectures. In 1967, nothing short of a 'non-parliamentary opposition' (APO) group was formed, whose organized protests partly degenerated into brawls aimed at 'provoking the Establishment'.

Faced with this situation – a series of neglected reforms and disappointed hopes, all cleverly exploited by declared opponents of parliamentary democracy – several Länder tried to restore 'law and order' with the aid of new university legislation. However, despite some attempts at reform, still no comprehensive concept of the reform had been agreed upon – a fact which prompted Professor Kurt Sontheimer, the political scientist, to make this oft-quoted remark: 'Reforms can be carried out, but nothing must change.'

In 1968, the West German Rectors' Conference elaborated a declaration for a common university reform. At about the same time, university teaching assistants established the Federal Conference of Assistants, which soon afterwards stepped into the public arena with noteworthy concepts of higher education policy. Finally, the eleven Länder agreed upon joint guiding principles with regard to university reform. Nonetheless, the trend towards radicalism on the part of organized students could no longer be warded off. The German Students' Association (*Verband Deutscher Studentenschaften*) took on the shape of an extremist left-wing militant association aiming at 'overcoming the system', and student representative bodies at the individual universities were ruled mainly by rival leftist groups.

It is difficult to trace in detail the development in the universities since 1970. The first signs of a *détente* in higher education policy are becoming apparent, but there are also new setbacks giving rise to concern.

Towards Root and Branch Reform

The criticism over a number of years of the outdated and undemocratic ideologies of education, particularly in the higher education sector, had led to the recognition that no more progress was to be expected from individual and partial reforms, but only from a comprehensive overall concept for the higher education system of a society bearing the stamp of a scientific and technological civilization, and which intends to make social democracy a reality.

The new Federal Government established in the autumn of 1969 has made this 'root and branch' education reform one of its objectives, and has discussed it in the 'Report on Education' submitted to the German parliament in June, 1970. The reform of the higher education system is to be effected in accordance with the following basic principles:

1. Efficiency and, at the same time, adaptability on the part of the institutions of higher education, whose 'freedom of research and teaching' will be guaranteed;
2. Equality of educational opportunities for all students by integrating institutions of higher education, hitherto functioning independently of each other, and by differentiating the content of study courses;
3. The introduction of a democratic structure for the institutions, and the democratization of their self-administrative system by way of co-determination and co-responsibility on the part of those working within them.

For the implementation of these principles in legislation and administration, the Federal Government has only limited constitutional competence, first established in 1969. This competence comprises the joint responsibility of both the Federal Government and the Länder for the 'co-operative task' of planning and financing the extension of existing universities and the construction of new ones, and, in addition, educational planning and the promotion of research (Art. 91a and 91b of the Basic Law). Finally, and most important, the Federal Government was given competence to pass 'skeleton provisions on the general principles of the higher education system' (Art. 75, para. I, No. 1a of the Basic Law).

The efforts on the part of the Federal Government to bring about a comprehensive reform in the sector of higher education are made and supplemented in three sectors.

As the first important step, a 'law to promote university construction' was passed in 1969. The law provides for the continued planning over a number of years of all building projects in the university sector, and the bearing of 50 per cent of the higher education investment costs by the Federal Government. Thus systematic and longer-term planning of the extension of all institutions of higher education is made possible for the first time, and their financing is ensured.

The Federal Government's second important step in the sector of higher education policy is the drafting of a so-called 'skeleton law on higher education'. The Federal Government's draft is at present being discussed in the German parliament. The constitutional problem of this law lies in the restriction of the Federal Government's only being permitted to lay down a 'framework of general principles'. The clothing of this framework is an exclusive task for the legislation of the Federal Länder. This is where the problems – but also the possibilities – for a reform of the higher education system in the Federal Republic are to be found. The necessary comprehensive and inter-locking reform of the higher education system in the Federal Republic depends on whether agreement is reached between the Federal Government and the Länder on all basic aspects of the function, structure and organization of the higher education system. Once such agreement is attained, the chances for the success of the reform will be greater than if a uniform law were to be passed 'by those at the top'.

Before the principles of this 'skeleton law on higher education' are described in detail, three further initiatives for the reform of the higher education system must be named for the sake of completeness. For the systematic training and promotion of young scientists a 'law for the promotion of graduates' is envisaged, which will make legal provision for financial assistance over a period of two years to candidates for a doctor's degree. A 'university statistics law' will be passed in order to obtain sufficient objective data for university planning, and a 'Federal law for the promotion of training' will be passed for financing the studies of less well-to-do students.

Of the five reform laws mentioned, the 'skeleton law on higher education' is the most significant for the future development and re-structuring of the West German higher education system. The law includes the following five priorities:

1. The transition from separate institutions of higher education to 'the integrated *comprehensive university*'. With this aim in mind, institutional barriers and outdated differences in status among the types of higher education establishments existing hitherto are to be removed. Individual institutions of higher education in any one region are to be functionally and organizationally merged into the new type of 'comprehensive university'. The comprehensive university will combine research and teaching in a majority of academic disciplines, though variations in the study content of the disciplines, in the establishment of priorities and in capacity are, of course, conceivable. The comprehensive university is to cater for differentiated, but nonetheless related, study courses and examinations, enabling the student to plan his course of study in the best possible way and, if necessary, to make changes during his studies at the university.

2. *The reform of study courses* by way of the re-establishment of study objectives and study curricula. The academically oriented training to be provided in future in all study courses is to lead to a wide range of professional fields of activity, instead of to individual professions. In so doing, a specialized branch of training can include several training courses differing in duration and with differing emphasis on theoretical and practical training – thus resulting in differentiated final examinations. The interweaving of these study courses, i.e. the integration of their content, is important. The type and extent of the integration of study courses can vary in the individual branches of study, especially since it is hoped that, within the next few years, correspondence courses using multi-media approaches will also be introduced in the comprehensive university.

   The manifold permanent and problematical tasks in connexion with study reform should be attended to by special commissions, whose members come from university circles. Government agencies and vocational organizations should co-operate in an advisory capacity.

3. *The reorganization of the staff structure* Up to now, there has been a large number of groups of persons in West German universities whose work has been concerned with research and teaching. As a result of the hierarchical order in which these groups were arranged, dependent relationships have arisen which impede academic team-work and thus have a certain paralyzing effect on scientific productivity. According to the generally accepted view, this outdated staff structure must be simplified, and access to the profession of university teacher

must be objectified. Therefore, in the comprehensive university in future there are to be only professors and assistant professors on an equal footing, and scientific and artistic co-workers, bound by directives and all working full-time at the university. The 'all-powerful' professor in ordinary will no longer decide on the respective projects and objectives in research and teaching, and on the participation of the individual persons in them, but the competent collegial body.

4. *The 'democratization' of the university* This objective is probably the most controversial, and therefore requires interpretation. In the opinion of the legislator, it is important for the German universities that all members share responsibility in connexion with the tasks of self-administration, that transparency (openness and rationality in decision-making processes) be ensured, thus discarding unjustified privileges. The principles for the type and extent of co-determination in university bodies are laid down in the skeleton law. They guarantee the 'freedom of research and teaching' and are intended to avoid an extremely one-sided political development in the universities. With this aim in mind, distinct solutions are planned, providing for differing powers of co-determination in different areas of decision-making for the member groups in the university. This will in particular be obvious for the student group, which is to be accorded the full right to vote and make decisions with regard to questions involving studies, whereas in the case of questions concerning research and the engagement of university teachers, students will be able to participate in the decisions made, but their votes will not be counted when calculating the majority. Where individual research projects are concerned, however, all those working on them will have equal rights in decision-making.

5. *The modernization and strengthening of the self-administration of universities* The organization, administration and operation of universities have become far too complex and extensive during the past few years for them to be dealt with by the system of self-administration in an honorary capacity, as has been the case up to now. Therefore it is generally agreed that the competence of the university to practise self-administration should be intensified and that that of the state should be confined to supervising legal matters. In future, therefore, the university will as a rule be headed by a president elected for a period of several years, who will exercise this function in a full-time capacity. The comprehensive university, which is composed of various specialized fields of study, will not only decide its research and teaching programme itself, but will also draw up its own budget and elaborate its plans for further development.

The five most important principles of a reform of the higher education sector in the Federal Republic described above show clearly that we really do want to say goodbye to Humboldt's conception of the university. Its place will be taken by the concept described above of a democratic comprehensive university, both efficient and adaptable. Even this new concept must not become rigidly established, for even after the completion of a reform, the problem will arise repeatedly of ensuring that the institution of the university remains unbiased towards the change in social tasks and towards the adaption of its functions, structures and organizational forms to fit in with these changes.

Higher Education in the Education System as a Whole

In the Federal Republic of Germany, the reform of the higher education sector is merely a part – frequently overestimated in importance in public discussion – of the overdue reform of the entire German education system, from elementary education to further education. The objective of the overall reform is the realization of 'the citizen's right to education'. A far greater number of people than up to now are to attend educational establishments at all levels. (For example, the number of students today (approx. 350,000) will increase to approximately 680,000 in 1975 and in 1980 to approximately 1,000,000.)

This extraordinary quantitative expansion poses very difficult problems for all those participating and responsible. The 'Overall Education Plan' up to 1985, including an 'education budget', at present being elaborated by the Federal and Länder Governments, is to constitute a major prerequisite for the solution of these problems. This education plan is to put the objective aims of the education reform into the shape of a continuous and coherent plan, providing for concrete legal or administrative measures, determining the chronological order of these measures and setting out the necessary financial outlay in each case. Governments, parliaments and the public, who have recognized the priority of education policy, will endeavour to reach a consensus where far-reaching decisions are concerned, in order that the Federal Republic of Germany can catch up on the education standards of other states. This applies also, and in particular, to the content of the educational processes, which should also contribute to the more civilized co-existence of men and nations.

26

The Free University of Berlin: Case Study of an Experimental Seminar (1968–69)*

Ingrid N. Sommerkorn

1. *Student Unrest in Berlin and the Movement for University Reform*

Student demands for reform of the German university during the 1960s were based on specific grievances. Students charged that conditions within institutions of higher learning were unsatisfactory because: the traditional notion of a scholarly community of teachers and students had become obsolete owing to overcrowding. The number of students entering universities rose from about 25,000 in 1950 to almost 65,000 in 1970 – from 3·5 per cent to just over 8·5 per cent of the relevant age group. The universities were organized as hierarchical, authoritarian structures in which full professors were all-powerful. An average faculty-student ratio of 1 : 60 made personal contact between the student and his professor impractical.[1] The teaching-learning situation was becoming increasingly depersonalized while the examination structure remained subjective and personal. 'Knowledge' was not evaluation according to certain objective or formal criteria, but was assessed impressionistically by the professor. Certain course structures and curricula were deemed 'irrelevant' and the amount of time necessary to finish course requirements was considered unduly long. These and other negative aspects of university education were leading to high dropout rates, one-third of the men and one-half of the women students.

Students themselves made serious efforts to improve the situation. As early as 1961 and 1962 some student groups drafted substantial blueprints for reform aimed at democratizing the university.[2] Administrative responses to their proposals were viewed by the students as merely being rhetorical. The students responded by becoming more activist. Renouncing diplomatic negotiations with university authorities through proper channels, students invented new tactics and exerted pressure in various unorthodox ways. Their unexpected degree of belligerence must be attributed to cumulative frustration with the universities' unyielding attitude.

---

* This chapter was written in 1970 and allowance for subsequent events should be made (Editors).

A detailed account of the students' responses and activities cannot be given in the context of this chapter. What is pertinent here is the development of the Critical University as a liberating counter-university to the established Free University of Berlin. It was created by some students and young faculty members as a response to actual political experiences in society and at their place of 'work' in the university. These experiences highlighted the connexions between the university and society and reinforced the view prevailing among this group that the concept of an a-political neutral university is a myth.

The Critical University was conceived as a socio-political institution in the sense that its objective was to establish solid and specific relationships with the non-academic community; it was designed to be a university administered by students for students and other social groups, such as workers, employees, high school students. The credo of the Critical University was to make the societal implications of scientific knowledge an integral part of the teaching-learning process by stressing the interdependency of science and society. Its aim was to dismantle the ideological ivory tower of the traditional German university and to transform science into an agent for social reform, even social revolution.

In effect, the students' campaign for university reform and change was based on a specific critical notion of science. This concept of science and scientific education incorporated the organization of the university, work and 'life-styles' within the university, the application of technology, and the structure of society as a whole. It decrees that there should be no segmentation of an individual's roles as scientist, public citizen and private person. Democratic co-operation between teacher and pupil, between employer and employee – the democratization of the university and society – is fundamental to this critical concept of science. The student activists critically reanimated and adopted Wilhelm von Humboldt's notion of 'emancipation through scholarship' by relating academic concerns to social reality. Thus, education as a 'practical experience' (W. v. Humboldt) can become a vehicle for social liberation.

In this context the main objectives of the Critical University were as follows:

1. To change the structure of the university and to reform the curriculum and learning procedures;
2. To prepare students to evaluate scientific and political actions – to inform action by reason;
3. To prepare students to exercise socio-political judgments in their future vocations and to support the role of the critical intelligentsia in society.

A central postulate of the German student movement is that educational reform is not possible without structural changes in an advanced capitalistic society.[3] In this sense all improvements within the university which came about through student initiative must be viewed from a political perspective.

2. *The Experimental Seminar in Sociology at the Free University in Berlin, 1968–9*

In the spring of 1968 an experimental seminar in sociology was initiated at the Free University of Berlin. Interest in the project was generated by the critical atmosphere of the times and by the example of the Critical University in which twenty to thirty work groups had been operating since the summer of 1967. The topic of the seminar – socialization and compensatory education – seemed to lend itself admirably to integrating reform ideas into a regular course because it was a socio-politically relevant study area and because it also established a link with the then current practical educational-political activities of the Campaign for Education.

The Campaign for Education was a large scale attempt by students, teachers and educationists to provide working class children in Berlin with tangible help in the form of after-school study centres. Its aim was not merely to tutor weak pupils but to offer learning experiences which were qualitatively different from the authoritarian style of the children's morning classes. To achieve this objective the organization needed empirical and theoretical information on the relationship between class-specific rearing techniques and language codes on the one hand, and motivations, aspirations and school performance on the other. It also needed access to material on personality development and anti-authoritarian educational methods. The Campaign for Education received funds from the Berlin School Authorities to pay the student leaders of the after-school study groups. However it had no financial backing for an in-service training programme or for evaluation of its compensatory educational services. Therefore it was logical to seek an official tie with the 'knowledge factory' – the university – in order to inform action by reason.

The emotional and socio-political climate of Berlin at the time made this a viable connexion. Furthermore the innovative premise of the seminar at the Free University reflected the demands of the critical students, namely: 1. that discussions about the necessary reforms and changes in the university and society were to be made part of the student's learning process at the university itself, and 2. that students be given the right to participate in the decision-making process with respect to their curriculum, course structure and methods of learning and teaching.

We resolved to run a seminar in which the formal structures would be conducive to learning freely through participation. Our previous experience suggested that traditional lectures and seminars conditioned students to be merely receptive 'consumers'. Professors usually lectured to students or assigned topics for lengthy papers (to be read aloud by students in class). Discussions which followed were regularly chaired by the professor. We wanted to abandon all traditional modes which bred student passivity and to create new instructional strategies which would encourage more demanding and more productive ways of learning. Our intent was to change the seminar from a teacher-centred to a student- or possibly research-centred undertaking.

The aims of our experiment can be summarized under two major headings: 1. establishing a model of participatory democracy; 2. facilitating an experience in social reality by: (a) choosing a relevant sociopolitical topic, (b) providing the sociology students with an opportunity to participate in an empirical research project, according to John Dewey's concept of 'learning by doing'.

Although at the outset the idea of social action referred to participation in empirical research activities, it came to signify political action, i.e. working toward changing the power structure of German society. This transformed interpretation became the most explosive factor in the seminar, especially since we were not aware of its potential force at the time and thus did not incorporate it into our classroom learning procedures.

The seminar was scheduled as part of the regular sociology curriculum at the Free University for two consecutive semesters, the summer semester of 1968 and the winter semester of 1968–9. Since before the introduction of the experimental programme no group of students existed to formulate the project (an unavoidable problem in a transitional phase), the general topic and the reform component had to be suggested in the traditional way to the participants.

Since our experimental seminar was part of the overall university structure, we could not altogether eliminate giving credits. Thus we made it part of the reform proposal that all active participants should receive the same grade. Through this device we hoped to divert the emotional and intellectual energy normally spent in earning conventional marks into more fruitful learning experiences which would foster engagement, commitment, and a feeling of well-being. We also hoped the quality of the seminar papers would improve since it would no longer be adequate for a student simply to quote authoritative sources without attempting an analysis and interpretation of his own.

By emphasizing democratic procedures and small group work, we tried to bring about a greater degree of student participation. We ruled out the traditional individual long research paper and introduced the team paper instead. Every student participated in one of the five study groups, each of which produced a joint paper which was then mimeographed and sent to all seminar members. All students were expected to read the papers in advance so that they could be discussed at the plenary seminar sessions where progress reports of the various sections were also exchanged. In keeping with the notion of reform we abolished all *ex-officio* authority; neither the professor nor his assistant had the automatic right to chair the plenary sessions. Since our aim was to increase the involvement and the responsibility of the students, the study group in charge of a session either nominated its own spokesman as chairman or, most frequently, a group of students presented their paper co-operatively to the seminar.

Another organizational feature of the seminar was the *ad hoc* 'initiating group' which was designed to co-ordinate matters generally and to be the 'in-house' centre of critique and evaluation. Any interested student could be a member of this group. It met briefly at the end of each plenary session and convened occasionally whenever anyone thought crucial organizational and substantive issues called for decisions. On the average only about a dozen students turned up at these meetings. We probably did not sufficiently appreciate the necessity for this initiating and co-ordinating function. For example, we were not particularly conscientious or skilful in establishing systematic feedback mechanisms between the different study groups and the plenum.

Since every student was awarded the same grade, competition for academic rank was no longer necessary. However, new qualitative pressures for achievement seemed to develop. Our new learning structure which repudiated the 'consumer attitude' gave rise to different expectations in which the role of the reticent student was no longer acceptable. It became clear that changing the formal teaching-learning situation in an effort to implement valid democratic objectives did not automatically create a liberating productive group atmosphere. We neglected to consider the impact of emotional factors and the resulting group dynamics. Although, as compared to traditional seminars, we had fewer silent or passive students, there were still a number of seminar members who remained largely uninvolved in the plenary sessions.

Among the errors we made was that of ignoring the political and social fragmentation resulting from the events at the Free University and in the community at large. The introduction of the Emergency Laws, dismissal of left-wing research assistants, cancellation of scholarships, disciplinary actions against political activists and the counter-actions of the students – the strike, the occupation of various university institutes and the President's office, the organization of students in autonomous sections and project groups – all of these manifestly affected our 'action-oriented' seminar. Although we talked about these issues in the study sections and in the plenary sessions, we did not recognize that in the context of this particular seminar which strove to integrate educational processes, science, and social reality, the differential notions of 'social action' amounted, in effect, to 'social dynamite'. These factors contributed to the disintegration of the seminar in the second half of the second semester.

Whereas during the first (summer) semester the students worked diligently on papers and seminar affairs, the enthusiasm for such 'pure' academic work diminished noticeably in the course of the winter semester when political events gained momentum and demanded response through action. Many seminar participants were deeply involved in the strike and in other political activities at the Free University and in West Berlin during the turmoil. They lacked the time and inclination to immerse themselves in academic matters to the same extent as they had done previously.

The infiltration of political concerns tended to divide the seminar in the sense that the participants broke apart into 'reformers' and 'revolutionaries'. The 'reform group' was in favour of continuing to work towards social change within the framework of the Campaign for Education which was backed by public money. The 'revolutionary group' claimed that within this official context only short-term goals could be achieved, and furthermore, that the Berlin School Authorities were supplied by our programme with an alibi which excused them from making basic improvements in the school system. We were not fully aware of the interplay of social, political and psychological forces in our discussions of compensatory education as a political concept and as a practical model and since we did not deal with these dynamics, the situation began to deteriorate. The 'reformers' went on working with and for the after-school study centres, and the 'revolutionaries' became increasingly involved in overt counter-activities.

In concluding this description of our experimental attempt to integrate education and social reality within the learning process, emphasis must be laid on the fact that there are indeed times when political actions should take precedence over scholarly pursuits. Granted that the Berlin seminar chose an explicitly socio-political topic, it must be acknowledged that the issues which engage social scientists are rarely neutral – they are *societal* problems. Since academic learning is part of a wider social process, the connexion between education and social reality has to be strengthened if the gap between living and learning is to be bridged.

3. *General Considerations of the Democratization Process in Higher Learning*

Understandably, educational structures are not directly 'transplantable' from one country to another; nevertheless, we believe that some aspects of the Berlin educational experiment are of more than parochial relevance, especially the following.

In undertaking educational reform and given the problems inherent in its implementation, it is obviously not sufficient to change or improve only certain formal structures. The emotional and informal problems accompanying change must be dealt with in the new situation. How should we cope with certain internalized norms and expectations which act as a 'countervailing force' in new learning environments, i.e. how do we contend with latent functions? What are the prerequisites which ensure a successful interaction between the social structure and the individual? How can we overcome the handicaps which are the result of contradictory norms and values? On the one hand, the traditional school and university system forces the student to pursue a competitive self-interest and to work as an isolated individual; on the other hand, in reality situations, ideals and necessity demand collaboration, team work, and mutual assistance.

A Lengthy, Slow Procedure

We learned from our endeavour in Berlin that experimentation takes time and patience. We do not claim that with this one experiment in educational innovation a 'formula' has been developed which can prescribe how to achieve such educational objectives as problem-solving skills, critical awareness, independence and autonomy, decision-making maturity, etc. These 'achievements' should be the educational outcome of any successful learning experience. It takes time to un-learn authoritarian, basically cognitive learning and socialization patterns of long standing. Since academic learning is part of a wider social process, we should be aware of the broad range of human and intellectual problems involved in educational experimentation.

Unity of Institutional Reforms

We also discovered that piecemeal improvement is futile without a comprehensive programme. Basically we had changed only two areas of variables in the traditional seminar structure:

(a) we provided various instructional strategies to increase the students' participation and responsibility;

(b) we provided a mechanism for learning by experience. It is quite likely that the innovative variables were not sufficiently powerful to produce the desired results.

Any innovative change can be only partially successful as long as it remains an isolated attempt – as long as it remains 'embedded' within the regular course and reward structure of the educational institution. Educational experimenters who, for various administrative and socio-political reasons, are obliged to proceed on a fragmentary basis should be aware of these inherent constraints.

This in turn means that we must think more critically about the educational objectives of universities, the functions of the course structure, the content of the formal curriculum and its connexions with indirect support structures such as the residential system, the teacher-pupil relationship, etc. Our Berlin experience and other evidence suggest that one or even a few innovative programmes within an otherwise unchanged educational setting will not be effective. As indicated previously, the reform seminar required so much time and work that basically only those participants who could adapt their schedules and focus their energies on 'socialization and compensatory education' profited from the experience.

A democratically-organized seminar demands a greater investment of effort from faculty as well as from students. In the final analysis, educational reform implies a redistribution of the teacher's time and value system; increased student participation and responsibility does not mean less faculty involvement. Although the instructor gives up his role as an *ex officio* authority figure and becomes an egalitarian resource adviser, he must be thoroughly informed in the subject matter and be continually available to the students.

The organizational and technical requirements are another feature of this kind of educational experimentation and should not be underestimated. When team papers and memos have to be mailed weekly to a large number of participants, secretarial assistance is indispensable and overall institutional support is essential in providing services.

Authority Structures

One of our major innovative aims was to do away with formal official authority figures.[4] Since it can be assumed 'that the major supports for learning come from the norms of a peer group in which one has status and acceptance',[5] we probably should not have been surprised to discover that informal authority figures developed among the more vocal students, especially among those who were actively involved in political events at the Free University and in West Berlin. However, we did not give adequate consideration to the unprecedented and unusual obligations of democratic learning and socialization and thus did not anticipate the emergence of a new informal hierarchy based on differences of sophistication. A new gap opened up between those students who were able, willing and motivated to make a greater commitment to the seminar – who read and worked harder and had an informational advantage – and those who were not and did not. This created many anxieties which hampered us.

To the same extent that formal authorities can have a supportive function because they provide certain role expectations and behaviour patterns, informal latent authorities can have a somewhat disruptive effect because they lack a legitimate base: students as reference groups are supposed to be equal. When radical authorities or opinion leaders emerge, additional strains and tensions tend to build up. In our seminar the gulf between the claim of democratic equality and the hierarchic reality was particularly significant because the abolition of all authority was a crucial aspect of the anti-authoritarian student movement.

This touches on a central issue in any teaching-learning situation: to what extent is the abdication of authority (*a*) possible and (*b*) beneficial? How can a learning environment be created in which the socio-emotional climate fosters the non-authoritarian transmission of legitimate forms of authority?

Cognition and Feeling in Educational Processes

The traditional emphasis in education has been on the cognitive and intellectual aspects of learning, as reflected in the formal curriculum. Academic learning, however, cannot be separated from a continuum of personal and emotional processes. Recently, there has been a revival of interest in the informal, affective aspects of learning. In fact, the popularity of this 'reawakening' to the importance of feelings and emotions – understandable as a reaction to traditional preoccupations with irrelevant, often alienating, academic matters – tends to make self-analysis, self-actualization, human growth an educational end in itself, to the neglect of content and socio-political or historical contexts. 'Navel-watching . . . is (indeed) no substitute for education'[6] but, nevertheless, it has to be an acknowledged part of any educational experience.

'The tasks of "academic learning" and "human relations learning" are interdependent processes and . . . achieving the ability to diagnose interpersonal process in the *work* situation is an important aspect of achieving optimal learning conditions.'[7] We should have built a mechanism into our Berlin experiment for registering the psychological and social forces operating within the group. An enlightened consciousness of the nature of group processes (and their connexions with social and political events in the world outside the classroom) seems to be necessary in order to understand learning itself. Education has not yet solved the problem – which for us became a trap – of determining how, optimally, to give due regard to group dynamics without making self-awareness the sole concern. What is the route for progressing from *naïveté* to self-awareness without becoming saturated by the abstractions of self-consciousness?

Whether it would have been wise for us to rely on outside professional help in the form of either an education-oriented psychiatrist or psychoanalyst or a psychoanalytically-oriented educationist or social scientist (provided such a resourceful person had been available) is debatable.

Bringing in special service personnel to facilitate our dealing or non-dealing with the evolving group dynamics and interpersonal stresses might have had an adverse effect on our effort to create an emancipatory learning environment. In any case, to give up one kind of authority – the professor – and replace him by another – a group dynamic specialist – might well have compromised our objectives. This raises a cautionary question: how can a new authority be integrated for resource purposes into the operation of this kind of experiment without defeating the democratization process?

To recapitulate, it seems evident that a consideration of pedagogical aspects of higher learning (*Hochschuldidaktik*) must involve the relationship between education, science, and social reality within the context of specific disciplines. An educational experiment which is concerned only with the effectiveness of technical improvements in methods of instruction does not contribute to democratizing the university and society but rather to cementing the *status quo*. Alterations in the formal external structures do not automatically bring about more liberated learning experiences. Such changes must be accompanied by new educational processes which modify the attitudes, norms and expectations of all participants.

NOTES

1. The ratio of *full* professors to students shows a wider gap: 1 : 87 in the Arts (Philosophical) Faculties; 1 : 97 in Law, and 1 : 113 in Economics and Social Sciences. (See W. Baumeister, 1970.)
2. *SDS-Hochschuldenkschrift, Hochschule in der Demokratie, 1961* ('The University in a Democratic Society'). [Later extensively elaborated and published in book form: W. Nitsch *et al.*, Hochschule in der Demokratie (Neuwied: Luchterhand Verlag, 1965)]; *Verband Deutscher Studentenschaften, Studenten und die Neue Universitat, 1962* ('Students and the New University').
3. Only passing reference can be made here to the historical and theoretical roots of German student protest. Without the socio-critical impetus of the *Frankfurter Schule* (Max Horkheimer, Theodor W. Adorno, Herbert Marcuse, Jürgen Habermas, Wolfgang Abendroth), and without the theoretical work of the German SDS in the 1950s and the early 1960s, this particular interpretation and perception of societal, political and university events and structures would not have been possible. The *Frankfurter Schule* was a catalyst for student action, for social development and political change.
4. In our experimental design we did not include participant observers or researchers to analyse and evaluate group processes. Therefore, we could not check on how the abolition of authority was perceived and internalized by the students. Hence, we did not find out whether or to what degree we were successful with the manifest structures.
5. R. Lippitt and R. S. Fox, p. 1.
6. S. McCracken, 1970, p. 54.
7. R. S. Fox and R. Lippitt, 1968, p. 2 (emphasis added).

REFERENCES

W. Baumeister, *Die berufliche Lage der Nichtordinarien*: Untersuchung über Arbeitsbedingungen und Rechtsstellung der habilitierten Hochschullehrer ohne Lehrstuhl. Göttingen, 1970.

Robert S. Fox and Ronald Lippitt, *The Human Relations School*, mimeographed paper. University of Michigan: Centre for Research on Utilization of Scientific Knowledge, April 1968.

Dietrich Goldschmidt and Ingrid N. Sommerkorn, 'Some University Problems Today: Transmission from School to University in the Federal Republic of Germany', *The University within the Education System*, Proceedings of the Comparative Education Society, Ghent 1967; 1968, pp. 59–75.

Stephan Leibfried (ed.), *Wider die Untertanenfabrik*: Handbuch zur Demokratisierung der Hochschule (Köln: Pahl-Rugenstein Verlag, 1967).

Ronald Lippitt and Robert S. Fox, *The Development and Maintenance of Effective Classroom Learning*, mimeographed paper, University of Michigan: Centre for Research on the Utilization of Scientific Knowledge, no date.

Samuel McCracken, 'Quackery in the Classroom', *Commentary*, Vol. 49, 6 (1970), 45–58.

Ingrid N. Sommerkorn, 'The Campaign for Education in Berlin', *Western European Education*, I, 2–3 (1969), 117–24.

Sozialisation und kompensatorische Erziehung: Ein soziologisches Seminar an der Freien Universität Berlin als hochschuldidaktisches Experiment, SS 1968 und WS 1968–9. Berlin, June 1969; 243 pp.

27

Trinity and All Saints' Colleges, Leeds, England

Andrew M. Kean

Introduction

The purpose of this paper is to give a personal account of the organization of study developed by a new institution for the education of teachers in England over the first five years of its existence.

Trinity and All Saints' Colleges are Roman Catholic Colleges, the first for women and the second for men. They are of separate foundation but fully integrated for academic, administrative and social purposes. They are member institutions of the University of Leeds Institute of Education and prepare students for the Certificate of Education of that Institute (a full-time course lasting three years) and for the degree of the Bachelor of Education with honours of the University of Leeds, which involves an additional year of full-time study. The 900 student members of the Colleges take a full part in the work of the Colleges. Although this paper does not deal with the religious life of the Colleges, nor with the different forms of religious study involved, it would be improper not to refer to the influence of a common Christian ethos in the development of social and academic structures. There is a close and highly informal association between students, academic and administrative staff and principals, which helps the solution of problems through public discussion and prevents undue concern being paid to institutional structures or academic stereotypes.

General Principles of Organization and Framework of Study

The common ethos of the Colleges, their relatively small size, the concentration of their facilities in a restricted space, the proximity of campus residences to teaching and study areas, the general acceptance by staff and students of a common professional purpose, all encourage conscious participation in a community. There is no need, therefore, for complex institutional structures or for formal regulative codes. Such structures (whether administrative or scholastic) as have been developed are regarded pragmatically; their operation is flexible rather than directive; they are to be interpreted as serving individual and group initiative.

The basic structure of the Colleges is that of the Class, identified by the year of entry and remaining as a constituent unit throughout the course. It is through the Class that professional study is conducted. A senior member of the academic staff acts as Director of Studies for each Class with the responsibility of supporting it and its individual members throughout the years of their study. Since each entry class will number about 250, it is possible for the Director of Studies of each Class to know personally each student in it. It is accepted that every student has a right of direct access to his or her Director of Studies and that this will be made available with immediacy. Each class tends to develop an individual mode of academic, professional and social conduct. As a new class comes into existence and sets about living and working in the Colleges, there is a new impulse in the community, a new set of disturbing experiments. It is College policy and practice to give encouragement to this individuality, rather than to restrain it.

The second major structural feature of the Colleges is that of the Division, each Division representing a pragmatically defined area of human knowledge which is of concern to the Colleges. There are six Divisions at present: Divinity and Philosophy; Language and Literature; Social Sciences; Mathematics and Natural Science; Creative Arts; Media. Each Division includes a number of Elective Course Areas. Within the Division as a whole and within each Elective Course Area, academic courses are planned and conducted. In contrast to a Class, a Division includes all students from all years of study who are following an academic course of a similar nature. Each Division also provides specialist services to the Colleges as a whole.

The major time structures in College organization are: the division of the overall course of study into two periods of two years each; the periodic absence of students from the Colleges on professional exercises; the structure of the year; the various types of weekly timetable. The overall course of study in the Colleges tends more and more to break into two periods of two years each, identified as Parts I and II. The distinction is more marked in professional than in academic study. At the beginning of their third year, students undertake a term (of about 12 weeks) of full-time responsible teaching in schools. The effect of this is to divide the Colleges into two groups of classes: those in Years 1 and 2 who are still concerned with preparatory work and those in Years 3 and 4 who regard themselves as now professionally engaged and as having enjoyed the first fruits of practical competence.*

---

* At the moment of writing, the Colleges offer officially a three-year course leading to the award of the Certificate of Education of the University of Leeds Institute of Education and to recognition as a qualified teacher. This is followed by a one-year course leading to the degree of Bachelor of Education with Honours of the University of Leeds. Entrance to this latter

During the greater part of each year about a quarter of the students are absent from the Colleges on professional exercises. At the moment these are confined to preparation for teaching. Each student spends rather less than one-sixth of his time on professional exercises, a proportion which, it is felt in the Colleges, could with advantage be increased. Exercises of this kind involve a close co-operation with schools which, of course, work on a different yearly time-table from the Colleges. This has led to the development of a yearly structure which permits of flexible arrangements with co-operating schools.

The College year lasts for about 38 weeks. Within the year two types of weekly programme are available: those of a Closed and an Open Week. In a Closed Week for a given Class a standard timetable is used. This specifies the periods of time within which arrangements may be made for face-to-face meetings of staff and groups of students, whether in the form of lectures, seminars or workshops. Individual tutorials or group meetings conducted by the students themselves are not included in the Closed Week timetable. It is not mandatory that all the slots thus provided in the Closed Week timetable should be used. For a given Class about 21 hours of meetings is thus made available in each week. Closed Weeks are normally gathered in collections of five or six, known as Closed Periods, these aggregations having been found to permit flexible arrangements for professional exercises and to offer a useful modular system for conducting work in the Colleges. In an Open Week, in contrast, a full week is kept clear for a given Class, either in the field of professional work or in that of academic study, so that for this period of time work can be organized in a specially appropriate way and in greater freedom than would be the case in a Closed Week. An Open Week often takes the form of a conference; intensive use is made of visiting lecturers; field-work away from the College may be undertaken; cross-disciplinary themes may be treated. The overall pattern of the year is therefore determined by professional exercises and by the sequence of Closed Periods, with an Open Week intercalated wherever possible.

The General Framework of Professional and Academic Study

Within the structures of the Class and the Division and of the temporal sequences and periods described above, courses of study and activity are organized as follows: *Pre-professional Studies*, conducted through the Class and covering the period of the first two years. Although these are designed to provide a preparation for the later professional study of teaching,

---

course is based on grades achieved in the final Certificate examination. The qualification of the Certificate is seen more and more by students as a supplementary and incomplete one. There is a very general agreement to regard the second two years as a unit, broken and disturbed by the departure of those students who take the Certificate only.

they are capable of ready adjustment to the needs of a number of other professions. *Professional Studies*, conducted through the Class and covering the period of the second two years. These are specifically designed for teaching. *Elective Course Areas*, conducted through the Divisions and now showing a tendency to divide into two periods of two years each. These are courses of an academic nature but in some ways are different from traditional courses of subject study. *Collegial Studies*, a very wide collection of studies and activities, planned by the Colleges centrally with the co-operation of students and open to all Classes and Divisions throughout the four years of study. The general purpose of Collegial Studies is to provide facilities for personal and group interests which cannot readily be accommodated in other forms of study. *Exercises*, practical work of a professional or of an academic nature, taking place at periods throughout the whole course.

There is naturally a close concordance or 'fit' between pre-professional and professional studies, between the two sections of the Elective Course Areas and between each of these groups and the appropriate exercises. Within each of the two year periods designated as Part I and Part II a further correlation is being developed, that, in each case, between professional and academic study, the exercises and Collegial Studies. This will always be rather loosely planned but it has already reached a sufficient level of correlation for the Colleges to be able to refer to Part I as a General and Liberal Studies curriculum and to Part II as a Specialist and Operational one. The complex structure of study and activity thus formed is illustrated in the figure on page 351.

The form of the planning of these studies is that of defining objectives by listing the means judged appropriate for attaining them; then treating these means as objectives themselves and finally their clarification by the listing of quite specific means of carrying them out. This involves the working out of a vertical structure in which an element at each level of analysis will stand as a means to that immediately above and as the end to those immediately below. This structure is systematic in that each element, at whatever level of specification, is held to be capable of being related to any other in the overall system, whether or not that relationship will actually be investigated in detail. To the analytical and vertical organization, therefore, a collocative and horizontal one is added.★ The system is

---

★ A very simple example might be the following. Suppose the main objective of the system to be defined by the listing of two subordinate objectives *b* and *c*. Then the process of analysis might be represented as follows:

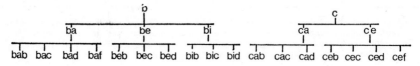

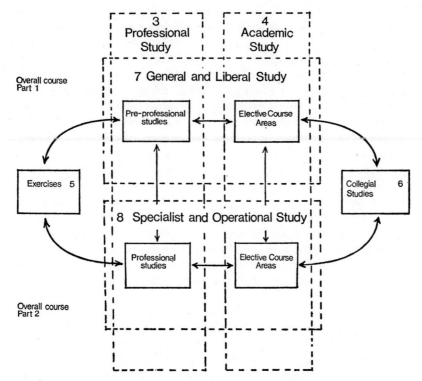

Fig. 1. The framework of study: co-ordination.
(Arrowed lines are lines of co-ordination. Numbers refer to sections in this paper.)

publicly presented and open to criticism and discussion. Its defects are public and shameless; they are there to be forgiven and retrieved. The system therefore has to be capable of modification, excision and extension; its organization and extension is an ongoing process and no formal and conclusive elaboration is sought.

In the course of his pre-professional and of professional studies over a period of two years, each student will normally have available twelve Closed Periods and four Open Weeks. Each of these sixteen periods is regarded as a module of the overall course. Each module will involve the presentation of a subordinate College pathway or pathways within the contextual map of objectives, an analytical development to various degrees of specificity of one of the vertical areas of purpose, an exercise or exercises. Each module is in itself systematic, modifiable and public. In relation to the pathway selected and justified, each module will include a set of

Systematization involves the assumption that *bac* and *ced* may be related and that *bib* and *ca* may be related. The decision as to whether such a relationship should be investigated is (as we shall show) a personal and pragmatic one.

College services or offerings. The most important of these will be the pathway itself and the library and materials resources centre. In addition to these there will be a range of College offerings of many different kinds: general mass meetings to offer introductory or methodological assistance, papers analysing common-places and other general questions, lists of references to materials of different kinds, the presentation of materials through film, television or graphical devices, workshops, small group seminars, a question and answer service and exhibitions. As a mandatory matter of planning the last week at least of each module is reserved for a programme of studies arranged by students. During the module opportunities for individual tutorial consultation are available on demand by students.

The number of students in any one Class who are undertaking pre-professional and professional studies will at any one time be very large (about a quarter of the College enrolment), in comparison with the relatively small groups in each Elective Course Area. After considerable experiment the Colleges have come to the conclusion that the only effective solution to this problem is to be found in radical individualization of study. This involves the provision of a structure within which individual study may proceed (the contextual map) and the provision of a wealth of supporting facilities (the College services and offerings). It further involves the creation of a system of assessment and evaluation of a very wide diversity of work, with all the tutorial concern which this involves. The experimental beginnings of such a system are described below.

From a professional point of view knowledge and information is sought in the prosecution of an objective. It is not, as in Elective Course Areas, pursued mainly for its own sake. A very wide range of considerations is relevant to a full and reflective professional activity. Many of these have to be handled in a manner which might be called (without any pejorative implication) vulgarization. By vulgarization is meant acquaintance with knowledge and information at other than a specialist level, acquaintance in which there is no pressing concern to validate the sources of information or to examine the criteria applied in producing it, acquaintance in which commonplaces and stereotypes usually find an unchallenged place. Obviously vulgarization can exist at various levels, from the most gross kind of irreflective generalization to what might be called 'high' vulgarization, of a considerable intellectual though not academic order. Indeed the level of precision to be pursued will tend to depend on the nature of the operation, it being understood that at certain extreme levels of conventional generalization, the information available is worse than useless. Much professional activity depends on the search for materials relevant to that activity and on the determination of the level of specificity at which these materials are to be employed. Search calls for a strategy of surveys of materials; the determination of levels calls for some plan of specification; both of these are to be found in a contextual map of objectives. There is therefore no need for a serious student to cover all that might be conceived to be possibly relevant but rather (through the experience of exemplary study) to be able to deal, when necessary, with what is relevant in a given situation, and to do so with speed and with individual responsibility.

Within the complex but practically viable organization sketched above, the general objective of pre-professional studies is to provide a basis of experience and of knowledge upon which later professional study may be based. The major subsidiary activities through which such an aim is to be achieved and which therefore act as a definition of this general purpose include the development of skills of study; the use and manipulation of various modes of communication; a general and elementary consideration of sources, motivations and modes of human behaviour and action including interpersonal relations; a study of group, institutional and associational structures in our society; the cultural history of the lifetime of the majority of student members of the Colleges, particularly the last ten years; a study of the generalizing concepts, assumptions, procedures and languages involved in the description and interpretation of human behaviour and action, both individual and social, in our culture; some study of the physical environment, particularly those aspects of it which are conventionally or can be directly related to human behaviour and action, both individual and social; selected aspects of an Elective Course Area.

The major aim of professional studies is to permit the student to prepare himself for the conduct of the first years of his professional life in a way permitting him to learn from the experience of these years, and enabling him to undertake further professional study. This he does:

(a) Through the study of professional ideology and ethos: a set of accepted generalizations and assumptions which provides a secure context within which membership of that profession can be sustained and within which professional discourse, debate and dissent can safely take place; this will include standardized information, general beliefs, the identification of 'problems', all of these at various levels of comprehension and precision. This area of study is formalized in the study of 'Education', particularly in the examination papers for the Certificate of Education.

(b) Through the performance of a set of operations and routines; activities institutionally defined, prescribed and ratified; operations and activities which are accepted as professional means, which are assumed to be permanently available and effective and which are therefore unchallenged. In the professional preparation of teachers, this area of activity is that described variously as 'practical teaching', 'basic competence' and so on.

(c) Through the study of, and practice in, planning, decision-making and evaluation, including the cost-effectiveness of the activities of the individual professional person and involving not only the development of proximate purposes but also the establishment of criteria of their effectiveness. In the practice of teaching such work includes curricular planning, 'schemes of work', the diversification of long-term plans for immediate purposes, the manipulation of ends and means, the establishment of procedures of individual and group evaluation.

(d) Through the handling and manipulation of the varied social contexts within which and very often through which the profession is conducted. In an educational setting this refers not only to the school and the class but to the complex personal relationships which occur therein and to the ethical questions involved.

(e) Through an acceptance of personal and group responsibility within certain defined areas of activity, including legal as well as ethical responsibility and also professional protection. The educational implications of this are obvious.

The keynote of the complex system presented above is that of personal, self-directed activity. In very many professional situations, in teaching particularly and above all in the preparation of future teachers, one is dealing with purposes, both general and specific, which are realizable only in the activities of persons, as distinguished from mass groupings or types. The system of study, the Colleges believe, must not only account for this but also foster it. An open and personal system of this kind has its advantages and disadvantages. The system creates difficulties for many students in their first year in that they have to break away from the conventions with which they successfully coped in school. A graded approach to pre-professional studies is therefore necessary. For slower-moving students and for those who seek the security of conformity, difficulties tend to be more lasting. It is felt in the Colleges that a student who has not given evidence during pre-professional studies of capacity to deal with this system should not proceed to further professional study, whatever his success in other areas of work or his personal commitment. Stresses of this kind gave pre-professional studies a propaedeutic character and call for much personal counselling. In a similar way we should expect certain students to fail progressively to cope with the demands of professional studies, no matter how gently these are introduced. The need for a planned approach and for an evaluation of personal competence calls for the creation of an instrument of general judgment. At the time of writing the following one is being used experimentally:

1. The level of conformity, of adequate integration into commonly accepted patterns, of correspondence with common prescriptions.

2. The level of individuality and of personal style within an overall

conformity, the level of partial emergence from some of the compulsions of accepted patterns, the level of different emphases and colourings within these patterns.

3. The level of analysis, modification and manipulation of commonly accepted patterns, the level of rational change, experiment and originality (as distinct from incompetence, hazard or irreflective guess).

4. The level of mastery in which conformity, individuality and the practice of analysis can be shaped into an operative whole.

The stages of this instrument of progression are not presented as if movement from one to another was final or as if there was no possibility of regression. Nor is it suggested that a student will at any particular moment reach the same stage in all areas of his activity. It is assumed, however, that competence at stage 1 alone is unsatisfactory and indeed disturbing.

Academic Study

Academic study is arranged through the various Divisions and takes the form of Elective Course Areas, a descriptive phrase used to indicate emphases different from some of those traditionally associated with the word 'subject'. The list of Elective Course Areas conducted in the Colleges at the time of writing is as follows:

Division of Divinity and Philosophy: Divinity

Division of Languages: English Language and Literature, French Language and Literature, Spanish Language and Literature, Language and Linguistics

Division of Social Sciences: History, Geography, Economics, Sociology, Psychology, Home Economics

Division of Mathematics and Natural Science: Mathematics, Physical Science, Biological Science

Division of Creative Arts: Art and Design, Music, Drama, Human Movement (including Physical Education)

Division of Media: Communication Arts.

All of these Elective Course Areas are offered at the level of Certification (three year course) and at the level of the degree of Bachelor of Education (four year course). Student numbers in each Elective Course Area are small; teaching is therefore largely individual and tutorial.

The purpose of each Elective Course Area is to provide a personal and general education through a discipline, an organized and defined body of study which has its own skills and procedures of study, its own specialist language and forms of communication, its own important if restricted view of the universe of human concern, which has its own history, its own generalizing concepts, models and basic assumptions. It is not only a form of knowledge but an art* to be practised, one which necessarily involves the production of materials in conformity with its own standards and procedures. Thus academic study differs from professional study in that it seeks a general end through one intensive and restricted study, which the student has elected to undertake and within which he will progressively be able, if he has the interest and capacity, to undertake from time to time more intensive and restrictive studies. Since the aim will be a general and personal one, this work in the Elective Course Area will always have an exemplary character and be distinguished by concern for basic structures.

As has been noted there is a tendency for the Elective Course Area to be considered in two sections of two years each. This is partly caused by the strongly marked division between pre-professional and professional studies, with the consequent change in student outlook. The first two years of study of an Elective Course Area tend to be more general and wide-ranging while the latter two years tend to be more concerned with restrictive and defined tasks, the aim of each section being that of encouraging the student towards a creative independence. This personal development will be adequately estimated in terms of the instrument of progression mentioned above: conformity, individual style, rational organization and mastery.

At present the great majority of Elective Course Areas are based on a single discipline. The choice of an Elective Course Area by students is often an irreflective one, and based solely on school experience. The first two years of College life often involve basic changes of attitude and of interest. The Colleges are therefore considering the possibility of permitting as a standard arrangement transfer from one Elective Course Area to another at the end of the second year of study, so that some students will complete an overall course embodying the study of two disciplines, both at a general and preparatory level. It is strongly felt that the provision of an initial general course on some topic such as 'European Civilization', from which Elective Course Areas might devolve, is no solution to the problem, since the conduct of such a course at any acceptable academic level involves special pre-existent competences. An arrangement for transfer of the kind suggested above would help to solve an additional problem, that of the academic study appropriate to teachers of young children. The Elective Course Area is designed for personal education. But it must also have some relationship to the needs of the professional person, and (in the particular context of education) to schools. It is usual for a student who is preparing for teaching to have made (by the end of Part I of his overall course) a considered choice of one of a number of age-

---

* We should go so far as to speak of the 'art of physical science'.

ranges of children for more specialized study and practice. It is a common and not unreasonable assumption that teachers of younger children would benefit from having a wide range of study. The possibility of transferring (without any lowering of standards) to another Elective Course Area at the end of the second year would, in association with some of the activities mentioned in Collegial Studies, allow this.

If personal and academic standards are to be maintained, the content, sequence and conduct of Elective Course Areas cannot be pre-shaped to conform to school practice or to fit in with the ideology of the serving teacher. Since, however, many students will eventually be engaged to teach a 'subject', the conduct of an Elective Course Area will have important implications for their future professional activity.

The colleges assume that anyone teaching in school is above all engaged in general education and that as far as his professional practice goes he is not engaged in 'specialization'. He must therefore be conscious and critical of the processes by which he received a general education in the Colleges through the medium of his Elective Course Area. This involves the application of principles of a professional nature to experience of his Elective Course Area and will tend to take place during Part II of the overall course. In planning school work he will above all be interested in structures and general principles and will have undertaken the study of a Course Area in which these have been given an important place. The Colleges take as a general guide-line that the successful teacher must have considered the elementary aspects of his study from an advanced viewpoint. Professionally this is perhaps his greatest skill.

It follows from all of this that Part I of an Elective Course Area will be concerned (as the distinction develops more fully) with a rather wider ranging study than Part II and one in which the relationship of the Elective Course Area to wider human concerns is dealt with by using this as a constituent major mean. In Part II of the Elective Course Area, with its emphasis on more restrictive study, there will be a recursive and reflective consideration of work in Part I from a professional point of view and an ongoing attention to a fuller understanding of the elementary aspects of the course area. It may perhaps be mentioned that each of these will be intellectually demanding.

Exercises

While in overall planning the term Exercise is used to mean an activity within some predetermined structure, in these notes special attention will be given to Exercises of a pre-professional and professional nature. We are concerned at the moment with Exercises which relate to the profession of teaching, though the same procedures could be applied to other vocations. Exercises in this sense are arranged as follows:

Year 1: a period of five or six weeks concerned with the personal experience of social and institutional organizations. While this takes place in schools at the moment, it need not necessarily do so. The Exercise is conducted in conformity with the sequence of work in pre-professional studies and with another Exercise which involves the study of a geographical area.

Year 2: a period of six weeks concerned with the planning of flexible programmes of work within an institution and with the adjustment of aims and means as these programmes proceed. This is also undertaken in schools and usually involves the planning of a project in association with the school. This is undertaken in concordance with a set of modular pathways in professional studies.

Year 3: a period of twelve weeks' full professional work in which the student takes an individual teaching responsibility in a school. This experience is planned as the basis of later professional work. It is also carefully and cautiously underprepared so that the student may be confronted with the need to plan and to make decisions rather than to carry out a predetermined scheme of work devised by the Colleges. The co-operation of schools, not only in receiving students, but in encouraging them to take initiatives, is essential.

Year 4: there is no exercise in this year. It is the wish of the College to be able to arrange a further exercise which will involve activity of a nature described in grade 3 of the instrument of progression.

All exercises except the first involve the experience of planning and the preparation of materials. All exercises create some emotional stress and demand tutorial support and guidance.

Collegial Studies
This refers to a very wide range of work of a personal nature which is not readily accommodated in other areas of activity and study and which is open to all students, whatever their Class and whatever their Elective Course Area. Collegial Studies (while subject to periodic trends) will normally include the following: Activities in the creative arts, such as instrumental music and painting; activities in Modern Languages, often with an emphasis on oral mastery and covering a number of languages in addition to those catered for in the Elective Course Areas; discussions and studies of matters of current debate, often mounted with great speed; the multidisciplinary treatment of specific topics such as the question of pollution or the study of the culture of a given year, say 1810; opportunities in the coaching of certain sports and games; the description of matters of contemporary interest to staff, such as projects in educational research; specialist study of matters treated in pre-professional or professional studies which have created a strong but restricted interest.

Collegial Studies are planned in modules and may last from one Closed Period to a whole academic year. They take place outside the normal daily timetable (in the early evening) or at week-ends. Considerable use is made of part-time and visiting staff. The style of study and of teaching varies widely. It is far from unusual for a student member of the Colleges to conduct one of these courses. In association with Collegial Studies mention must be made of a group of Basic Studies, involving English and Mathematics, which are undertaken in the first two years of the overall course and in which a certain standard is mandatory for all students. With these is further associated a course in Divinity which moves from more general questions of religion to matters concerned with the religious education of children over the first three years of the course.

Part I: A General and Liberal Curriculum

The association in the first two years of the course of the first part of the Elective Course Area, of pre-professional studies, of various Exercises and of Collegial Studies creates what might be described as a general and liberal curriculum. The Elective Course Area provides an opportunity of understanding something of the co-operative creation of knowledge within limited fields of human endeavour, an experience of fairly narrow and academically demanding studies, a chance to apply some aspects of the Course Area to matters of more general human concern. Pre-professional studies provides an introduction to methods of independent, selective and exemplary study of the modern world. Practical Exercises give an experience of having to work within the context of actual human relationships and of gaining a personal awareness of the tensions and ambiguities often involved. Collegial Studies offer a range of activities and of studies of a more personally adventurous kind than would otherwise be possible and make a place for what might be called the creatively irrelevant. These different aspects of a liberal and general curriculum are loosely co-ordinated and have their active support in the close relationships within a year Class. At the same time Part I is designed finally to sever bonds with an earlier school education, to permit a more fully reflective choice of vocation and to allow the student to select some aspects of that vocation to which he wishes to devote particular though not exclusive attention.

Part II: A Specialist and Operational Curriculum

Part II is specialist in that a final professional decision has been made and now informs the whole curriculum, in that more specific studies are now possible in the Elective Course Area, and in that Collegial Studies tends to be used with very special purposes in mind. It is operational in that the general trend is towards a type of activity which has been planned towards a certain end, in that theory and practice can now be more fully interwoven.

The complex and highly contrastive programme of studies described in these pages is one designed to offer a personal, professional and academic education to the individual student, whose freedom is to be respected and whose responsibility is to be assumed, within the close and highly informal community of the Colleges.

28

The City University of New York

Timothy S. Healy, S.J.

The City University of New York (CUNY) is a federation of 20 collegiate institutions, all of them lying within the geographical boundaries of New York City. One is a medical school (Mount Sinai), one is a graduate school (the Graduate Center), and one is an upper division college admitting only transfer students in their third year (Richmond College). Two of CUNY's colleges opened in September 1971, Medgar Evers in Brooklyn and LaGuardia in Queens. All of the other 15 colleges are currently involved in the first year of 'Open Admissions'.* The word federation is used advisedly, since the individual colleges enjoy a real autonomy under the public Board of Higher Education and CUNY's Chancellor. The system has frequently been described as an autocracy whose harshness is made liveable by the consistent insubordination of all of its elements. Two other introductory remarks are in order. The 15 colleges include eight senior colleges and seven community colleges. CUNY has 200,000 students, 12,000 faculty members and a budget of approximately $400,000,000 a year.

Although free public higher education in New York City has been a goal since the establishment of the Free Academy (later the City College) in 1847, the demand for college places has long since outstripped the University's capacity to enrol the growing number of qualified students. New York City is without a doubt one of the greater pools of academic talent in the Western world. Thus although an Open Admissions policy was actually in effect for approximately two decades at the turn of the century, the need to determine which high school graduates would fill a limited number of college seats led to the growing use of objective measures for admission, specifically high school grade averages and a variety of standardized test scores. An example of how the net gradually

---

* Bernard M. Baruch College (1919); Brooklyn College (1930); The City College (1847); Hunter College (1870); John Jay College of Criminal Justice (1964); Herbert H. Lehman College (1931); Queens College (1937); York College (1966); Borough of Manhattan Community College (1963); Bronx Community College (1957); Kingsborough Community College (1963); New York City Community College (1946); Queensborough Community College (1958); Staten Island Community College (1955); Eugenio Maria De Hostos Community College (1968).

tightened can be seen from the statistics for the City College. In 1924 a high school graduate could gain admission with an average of 72 per cent. By 1936 he would have had to have 78 per cent; by 1962 that figure had climbed to 82 per cent; by the end of the decade it had reached approximately 85 per cent.

An Open Admissions Policy

Given the chronic seat shortage and the rising demand both for regular admissions as well as for access to the University's large number of special programmes, the Board of Higher Education and the University administration anticipated an almost inevitable confrontation. In the spring of 1969 it came. Aided almost certainly by the wave of student unrest then sweeping the nation, violence broke out on several CUNY campuses. High among every set of grievances was the demand for increased black and Puerto Rican enrolment. The pace of change demonstrably was out of step with the drum beat of the times. The University had already decided that by 1975 its physical plant and its financing would be in good enough shape for it to begin a cautious Open Admissions policy. However, after the set of confrontations, strikes, and meetings of the spring of 1969, the Board of Higher Education unanimously concluded that the comfort of a 1975 target date for Open Admissions would have to give way to the certainty that immediate Open Admissions was the only course available open to the University. The Board then created a special University Commission on Admissions, to be made up of 10 members named by the Faculty Senate, 10 appointed by the Student Senate, 10 by the Council of College Presidents, four alumni and four representatives of outside public organizations which had demonstrated their concern for the University. After two months of strenuous discussion the Commission arrived at one major conclusion:

> The best way of determining whether a potential student is capable of college work is to admit him to college and evaluate his performance there. Within the pool of 10,000 students rejected each year by the 'traditional system' . . . there are thousands of students who, if given a chance at college, would do satisfactory and even outstanding work. When all the students who never apply to college because they have been told through twelve years of previous education that they are not 'college material' are added to this pool, the great loss in human potential generated by an exclusionary policy becomes evident. This city and this society cannot afford such a loss.

The Board of Higher Education ultimately composed both a series of guidelines for Open Admissions and an admissions structure. Open Admissions at CUNY the Board declared must not only offer a place to all June 1970 secondary school graduates, but it must also:

— provide for remedial and other supportive services for all students requiring them so that open admissions does not become the illusion of an open door to higher education which in reality is only a revolving door, admitting everyone but leading to a high proportion of student failure after one semester;

— result in the ethnic integration of the colleges (significant in this language was the Board's deliberate avoidance of the phrase 'ethnic integration of the University', a directive that could well lead to de facto segregated institutions within CUNY);

— maintain and enhance the standards of academic excellence of the colleges of the University;

— guarantee admission to specific community and senior colleges to those students who would have been admitted under previous criteria;

— provide for student mobility among various programmes and units of CUNY.

The Choice of Who Should Enter

All June 1970 high school graduates were distributed over two scales, each scale made up of ten groups. The first scale grouped applicants by the rank they held in their individual high school graduating class; the second grouped them by their overall high school grade averages. Each student was given placement priority according to the scale on which he stood highest. For example, an applicant with an 80 per cent average (thus in the fifth group on one scale) who graduated in the second tenth of his class (thus in the second group on the other scale) was given a second group priority. Each applicant thus stood on his own best ground.

Thus for all the public furore that attended its inception Open Admissions was emphatically a metaphor. The two most obvious and immediate restrictions were that it was limited to students from one high school class (1970) and that in order to qualify for the Open Admissions programme a student had to have a high school diploma. Some 70,000 high school graduates received diplomas in New York City in 1970 (this figure includes both public and private high schools). Only 55,000 of them applied to the City University. Thus 15,000 students were either not interested, or not involved, and in any case not making application. Of the 55,000 who did apply, 20,000 either went elsewhere or did not go to college at all. CUNY's freshman class was 35,000, so that even under Open Admissions, the actual number admitted was only half of the possible high school class. Nor does this touch the larger social fact which looms behind all discussions of University admissions in New York City. The 70,000 who graduate are approximately half of those who begin the high school process. Fully 50 per cent of those who start high school do not graduate.

One of the great fears of those who opposed the Open Admissions plan, was that the colleges would be inundated with black and Puerto Rican students, and that effectively the CUNY system (or at least elements of it) would turn into minority colleges. The facts did not justify this fear. For the school year 1970–1 the City University of New York had approximately 16·7 per cent of its student body who were black and approximately 4·9 per cent who were Puerto Rican. Taking its freshman class alone the same two figures came out to 17·9 per cent black and 8·1 per cent Puerto Rican. That statistic, of course, points out one of the great psychological realities of Open Admissions. It is perfectly clear that the black and Puerto Rican community simply did not believe the University meant what it said, or perhaps rather more sharply, did not believe that the University could deliver on what it promised. Neither of the two major minority groups in the City entered the year's freshman class in any numbers near their totals in the high schools. The gap of alienation, of fear and of distrust their absence reveals is perhaps one of the most significant things that Open Admissions has already brought to light.

One major miscalculation should be cleared up. The City University in the fall of 1969 admitted 21,000 freshmen. According to its own plans, made years ago and long before Open Admissions was an issue, in the fall of 1970 it was scheduled to admit 28,000 students. In fact it admitted 35,000 students. Thus it is not true to say that the University was admitting a majority of its freshman class under any kind of open rubric. Fully 80 per cent of the students admitted that year would have been admitted under normal academic canons. As soon as this is said, however, another set of figures must be added. Of the 35,000 freshmen admitted in September 1970, approximately 50 per cent were in need of remedial work in mathematics or in English. Ten per cent of that total were in need of serious remedial work. Thus while 7,000 of the students admitted under Open Admissions in a freshman class of 35,000 were in need of remedial help, another 10,000 who would have qualified under the normal admissions canons were also in need of the same help. What this says about the high school preparation which the City of New York provides for its citizens is mercifully not our topic here.

These figures and the problems they represent lead to the conclusion that Open Admissions for City University is only a stopgap measure. By this I do not mean any temporary commitment to the students involved, or any diminishing of the impact that these students will have upon the University's process, its structure, and its vision of itself. But effectively the University cannot encompass, and the public will refuse to pay for any extended commitment to remedial work on the college level. Grammar school and high school work should be done in grammar schools and high schools. The principle is so simple that it sounds revolutionary. Unfortunately in New York it is. What the University can accomplish by Open Admissions is the purchase of time.

This time has to be used in two ways. The first of these is a restructuring and rethinking of its teacher education programmes. One of the senior and best of New York's educational theorists, Dean Harry Rivlin of Fordham, has remarked that for too long we have trained teachers both for Manhattan, Kansas and Manhattan, New York in exactly the same way. The difference between the two communities would appear obvious even to a child. It seems to have been profoundly mysterious to most of our trainers of teachers. In saying that Open Admissions buys time for the reform of teacher training, one must note how little time it buys. But that is something over which the University has no choice. The job has to be done within five to six years, or there may be no University left to do it.

The second aspect of this same problem to which Open Admissions addresses itself is that it should help to diversify the racial mix on the faculty of the City's schools. The Board of Education employs approximately 10 per cent black teachers and administrators and 2 per cent Puerto Rican teachers and administrators. Even to approach a satisfactory working distribution there ought to be 30 to 40 per cent black and 10 to 15 per cent Puerto Rican teachers and administrators in the system. There is no question that here the City University of New York is simply and squarely at fault. The school system cannot hire teachers if the University does not train them, and the University has not in the past trained anywhere near this number. Even though Open Admissions is perhaps the long way around, it is a way around, and it can work. This change in distribution of percentages is not a panacea, nor will it work immediately. But from everything that the sociologists tell us, it is a clear *sine qua non* to beginning.

Problems to be Solved

I should now like to turn to a consideration of the problems which Open Admissions will present. This is perhaps an area where little further public statement is necessary, since the scenario for the tragedy has been well drawn, with heat and eloquence, by many private and public figures including the Vice President of the United States. The scenario runs something like this: first of all there will be the substitution of remediation for regular college courses, and in this way the high school curriculum will creep upward and the colleges will no longer be dealing with 'college level' work. As soon as enough of these high school courses have been collected the student will then move to an automatic degree. This will put the City University in the same position that the City high schools are in. But instead of a diploma awarded for time served, the City University will be giving a Bachelor's degree. Such a process is, of course, the destruction and the denial of all standards, and this will mean a precipitous flight of good students out of the City University into the more placid and serene atmosphere of the State University, or the various pinnacles of private excellence in and around the City. Along with the students will of course go the good faculty members. As if all this weren't enough, it is perfectly clear that hordes of ill-prepared students will not be content with a community college education, but will all opt for the straight liberal arts presentation which is the speciality of the senior colleges, and thus the senior colleges will be swamped and the community colleges empty.

This scenario, so often stated and so brilliantly summarized by *Fortune* magazine as 'the high schoolization' of colleges is indeed a tempting intellectual construct. It is very neat and very simple, and meets most people's prejudices. It is the kind of thing one can live with quite easily. The only problem is that there is no evidence available yet that the process so described is happening. What then are the facts?

No college in the CUNY system is giving credit for strictly remedial work. This means that while the high school curriculum is physically present in the college, it has yet to get under the hide of the college curriculum and consequently cannot be said to pose a serious threat so far. That there is here a clear and evident pressure point, is something the University had best admit. But the University has had success in holding off the pressure or in diverting it into sensible arrangements. One such sensible arrangement is the awarding of college credit for college material, taken, however, at a pace which no college would normally envisage. For example, remedial reading can be taught out of a series of texts which are on the high school level or below. Remedial reading can also be taught, using texts (principally and appropriately sociological ones) or works of art (principally poetry) which are in themselves distinctly on a college level. In more formal terms this process can be described as the effort to work on a conceptual level which is in advance of the student's instrumental level of preparation. Given the fact that the remedial courses principally involve both reading and writing, and that reading and writing are not necessarily developed in tandem, this is a clear possibility.

The City University has had for six years a variety of special programmes in both its senior and community colleges. It has thus been able to generate a body of experience for dealing with the pressures inadequately prepared students bring upon their college, in order to justify their existence as men and women, in order to support their pride in their race and heritage, or simply in order to translate their natural impatience at being 19 or 20. In all of these six years the University has never awarded an automatic degree, nor is there any evidence that this is what students in the special programmes wanted it to do.

The predicted flight of students and the faculty members is a more complex problem. It is a matter of established fact that elements of the City University have, for the past several years, been losing their appeal to many traditionally qualified students. It is also a matter of fact that other elements of CUNY have gained in that appeal. The college most under threat would be the City College, and the principal gainers would appear to be Queens and Brooklyn Colleges. The reasons for this shift are not directly associated with Open Admissions, nor is there any serious evidence that Open Admissions has substantially increased the rhythm either of loss or of gain. What is actually at work here is the impact of the physical setting of the college and the shift of boroughs in the City from benign to dangerous; in other words the enormous complex of social problems that centre in Harlem, and that are somewhat surrealistically absent in Bayside.

Much the same statement can be made about the predicted flight of good faculty members. Aside from deaths and retirements, the City University has a 3 per cent annual turnover rate on its faculty. This is largely due to the fact that its salaries are good, and also to the fact that the market for faculty talent has very sharply and suddenly contracted. As long as the market holds in this condition there can be little serious loss of faculty personnel. In addition, even raising the question in a sense begs it. The University has as yet received no evidence that if it put the question of Open Admissions to a vote of its entire faculty, that the policy would not carry the vote. It would fly in the face of several decades worth of evidence to claim that the social conscience of the University's students stands in any way in advance of that of its faculty.

The final prediction remains to be commented on. This is perhaps the most interesting precisely because those who wrote the scenario reveal in it their absolute lack of trust in any kind of common sense among students. CUNY's community colleges are not threatened by a lack of applicants. The University's Open Admissions policy placed primacy of assignment to colleges upon the student's own choice, thus allowing the student to select his own programme and his own college (and meeting well over 67 per cent of these first choices). As a result the University enrolled 19,000 in its senior colleges and 17,000 in its community colleges. This is precisely what it had hoped to do, and corresponds almost exactly to the rhythm of enrolments in the two branches of the University over the past four years. This distribution reveals that the students are quite capable of self selection, and shows that their self selection was both rational and modest. The vast majority of the students with the weakest averages in reading and in mathematics opted themselves into programmes where, although both weaknesses were major problems, they were less seriou s and likely to have less long lasting consequences than they would have had in senior colleges. There is something to be said, as usual, for giving the other fellow, even if he is a student, some credit for brains.

Open Admissions and Open Process

Just as it is relatively simple to sit down and foresee tragedies in the Open Admissions process of the City University, one can also sit down and foresee some changes. The first of these will be changes in structure. All of them can be quite simply summed up in the statement that Open Admissions should, in order to make sense, lead to open process.

The first opening up of process occurs in the admissions office itself. If the 'handicappers' were worried at the announcement of an open admissions programme they had every right to be. It was in effect their death knell. Along with them goes the hosts of tests, barriers, 'descriptive instruments' and 'predictive instruments' with which we have so successfully harassed class after class of freshman applicants. If this means that fewer of our admissions directors will act like our best athletic coaches, as one academic who has taught generations of freshman classes, I cannot shed many tears. They had no business barring the gates as effectively as they did in the first place. The notion that universities and colleges ought to be rated principally on the selectivity of their admissions process is a curiously modern one. Like the more stringent of the Catholic positions on birth control, it dates from the beginning of the century. It has no application to 750 years of the English speaking university's existence, and as such can well be regarded as a passing disease. That it may have passed is good news. That is not said with any sense of pique. Effectively the screening to which applicants were submitted was in itself a vast falsification. First of all the screening was aimed at one colour, one class, and only one kind of preparation. It was probably every bit as effective in excluding genius as it was in excluding poverty and it seems a strange posture for universities to admit that they accepted easily the exclusion of either.

Out with the barriers at the gate of the university should go another hurdle which is even more curious: the notion that students come in four sizes, 18, 19, 20 and 21, and cannot rationally be conceived in any other way. For a long time our major urban universities have not really been honouring this idea in anything except the extraordinary difficulty they pose to re-registrants and re-entering dropouts. One of the first things that an open admissions process does, once it gets out of the metaphorical stage where CUNY's is unfortunately lodged for the moment, is declare a moratorium on judging students by their age. There is nothing to prevent a 25 or a 35 or a 45-year-old from registering, and if he is interested, cares to work, and wants to share in what the college or university offers, he ought to be registered without more ado.

Another structural change will be the opening up of the time lock once a student is admitted. The four-year undergraduate curriculum has for too long been confused with the laws of nature. If it errs at all for the traditional run of students it errs on the side of length. For the poorer student it obviously errs on the side of shortness. The City University special programmes have proved that students who care to get a Bachelor's degree (and are also interested in the education which by profession should accompany it) are quite willing to spend more than four years if need be. On the other hand, half of the average freshman class could do the course we propose to them in three years, probably with considerably more profit than they derive from the four which is imposed upon them.

A further structural change which is clearly coming, thanks to Open Admissions, is a re-accent on professional training. Most of the students who do not qualify in classic ways for college admission will have a strong vocational orientation. New York is about to repeat the wave of immigrant students which swept through the urban colleges and universities in the first half of the twentieth century. These will not be the classically oriented or classically prepared students. But they will be students with a hard edge on them. They will come from families with a touchingly total faith in the ability of education to raise a man's status, and they will have a clear goal in mind. This goal may differ from the classic academic goals in that it will not be useless. One of the great ironies of those of us who process the 'liberal arts' is that we feel their essential dignity has been tied to their radical uselessness. The original university was founded to provide society with four classes of professional specialists. In undergraduate education we have now focused our attention for almost two centuries on only one of those four faculties, and since it no longer has any meaning as a prep school for clerks and secretaries, we have decided that uselessness is a sign of superior virtue.

The students who come to us through Open Admissions are going to have very little tolerance for the kind of aristocratic ideal that the liberal arts currently hold up to the young. It is not that they will disapprove of people spending their time on such studies, and they will exercise towards their elders the tolerance at which the young are adept. (If they do it a little more patronizingly now than in the past, this can be put down to a general decline of manners, ours as well as theirs.) But they will have sharper axes to grind and will insist on having them ground. Thus over the next few years it is perfectly clear that major complex university systems are going to have to face an enormous increase in demand for technical professional and pre-professional programmes. This will have several good results.

The first of these results will be that we may stop teaching all students as though they were pre-PhD candidates. The conviction that rules in so many undergraduate classrooms that the PhD is all, and the devil and the draft can take those who are not interested in pursuing it, is one we could well be rid of. One would be hard put to say whether or not the canonization of one peculiar academic destination has wrought more havoc on the students or on their teachers. I would hazard the guess that the latter have been more damaged; while we may have more substance to corrode, corrosion is likely to have a more lasting impact.

A second healthy change will be the reduction of pressure on departments of history, English, language and the other liberal arts. Perhaps getting them out of the pressure cooker might be a very good idea. They never were designed for masses of students, and have never at any period in western history worked very well for masses of students. In order to accommodate the masses their practitioners were only too willing to prostitute their style and much of their content by pretending that these disciplines were 'scientific' or, worse, 'objective'. Both of these deviations may now cease, and those who practise the liberal arts may get back to their trade in full freedom of conscience to deal with values, with human reality, and with the multiple capacities of human beings to learn by ways other than rational analysis. It is not beyond the bounds of probability that if enough pressure were removed, the liberal arts could once again discover their civilizing souls.

Educating for Citizenship

That last change in structure leads quickly and easily into the significant changes of style and of mind that Open Admissions is likely to beget. If at the one time the University is consciously facing the social problems which surround it, and is striving in so far as it can to solve them, it might conceivably get back to educating its students for citizenship. Part of the falsification of values and standards imposed upon us over the last 40 years has come from the fact that we claim to do something absolutely useless. Since it was useless, society had no right to influence it, to comment upon it, or to interfere with it in any way. We had a whole array of weapons in defence of this position, the principal one being the gossamer web of academic freedom. This, we discovered in the 60s, could be stretched to cover inanity or impropriety, even those that were strictly illegal, if only we shouted loudly enough. There was no question that society would not long tolerate a cuckoo in its midst with such solemnly and speciously destructive habits. It will not and has not. The gentlest way it can impose its will upon us is through our own students.

The restoration of 'education for citizenship' is likely to be the greatest restorative that the liberal arts professors on our faculties have ever received. This was after all in happier times our specific business, and if we were only honest enough to remember that, and stop pretending that every imaginable subdivision of us makes up something called a 'profession', we might get around to doing it superbly well. It is just those intangible value areas associated with citizenship in a democracy that the liberal arts can handle and handle with distinction. It is precisely the forcing of these same liberal arts into a professional strait-jacket, with its focus upon the arcane inanities of many PhD degrees, that has distorted us out of all recognition.

By returning ourselves to education for citizenship, by admitting our serious and varied professional obligations to the society which surrounds us, by dropping the objectivist pretences under which we have shielded both our incompetence and our incapacity to grasp our own purpose, we in the universities might get back to the teaching style described in Whitehead's *Essays on Education*. Our society badly needs remaking, and the most immediate laboratory in which it can be remade is still the undergraduate classroom. Out of its shocks and confrontations, where many of our faults may come back to haunt us, but most of our insights can still be brought to play, in this controlled chaos, a new republic can be created.

So much will happen within universities as the result of opening their doors again to the society which supports them that it seems almost otiose here to talk about the impact their academic programmes may have on that society. Still, I do not think we should close without touching briefly on at least one major possibility. Open admissions can achieve a degree of racial integration under a common purpose which our cities have not known for well over a century. I do not think that the current mood for separatist black studies and black departments will long continue. My reason for this is neither theoretical nor emotional, but quite simply financial. It is quite possible for a black community to support its own grammar schools. It may be possible for a black or any other community bent upon separation to support its own high schools. But nothing in our national economic stance gives any hope for the long survival of separatist colleges and universities. The clear and manifest trend in the nation is exactly in the opposite direction, and this may or may not be a good thing. All I am saying here is that it is an obvious tendency.

Consequently, Open Admissions can achieve a level of integration in our colleges and universities which can be achieved no place else. The people of both races involved are caught at their most important and impressionable age, and they are caught in a clear and relatively structured set of purposes. Putting different races and creeds and cultures together in some kind of social sack will not produce either a melting pot or a pluralistic society. It is much more likely to produce a bag of warring cats. But putting these same people together with a common purpose, in a common place, with common structures, common experiences, and even with some common enemies, is a totally different process. There is no question of integrating the races completely or fully. But they will be together for a few hours of each day of each week. They will be together for a purpose as well as a process which they share. These mutual sharings of time and end and process could ultimately lead them to share each other.

And just for completeness there is perhaps one last comment that should be made and this is the simplest of all. By its policy of Open Admissions the City University is striking at least one blow at a major deviation of our time, the notion that in some ways the University is a church, that the college is a kind of blessed community, and that entrance to either somehow implies salvation. There are many who feel this way, and perhaps their feeling is explained either by the over credentialization of American society or the decline of formal religion in the same society, or by both. If, however, the University is in the business of granting salvation, this means that University faculties (and rather more spectacularly University admissions offices) are in the business of granting admission to that salvation. There is no question but that many academics find it easy to play this god-like role. On the other hand, it is a very bad idea. It is demeaning to our students, it is pompous and counterproductive in the eyes of the public which supports us, and it is ultimately destructive of us ourselves. Open Admissions means that the City University says to its prospective students, 'We are doing a good thing, come and join us.' Once we drop the innumerable barriers at the entrance gate, we may also drop the notion that it is we who select the truly blessed. If we do, we academics certainly will profit more than anyone. We do not after all make good substitutes for the Lord God.

29

The Open University in Britain

John Ferguson

January 1971 saw the first students of the Open University starting their courses. With this the latest and most original of our universities is off the ground, and, in a variety of senses, into the air. The year 1971 will see how far the optimists are vindicated, how far the sceptics are triumphant. Both will in measure happen. There is little doubt that the Open University is doing some extremely exciting things; there is also little doubt that some of its approaches will be less successful than others. This chapter has to be written before the pattern is clear; by the time it is published the facts will be much clearer. Prophecy would expose itself to hindsight. It will be wiser to concentrate on current facts and impressions. In a pioneering enterprise there is constant flow. There will be change. Current facts and impressions are at least part of the record.

The Origin and Development of the Concept

The initial concept of the Open University came to Mr Harold Wilson while touring America before he became leader of the Labour Party. Robbins[*] – and all that – was in the air. It was clear that Britain could use more graduates; it was clear that the high selectivity of the British universities excluded many who could profit from university education. Mr Wilson saw this. He saw also that the answer did not lie in the large intake and 50 per cent dropout of the American university. He saw in America the proliferation of television, and the small extent to which it was put to constructive use. He conceived then of a university which should be founded on three principles. First, it should draw its students from those who had missed out on the conventional system of education. Second, it should provide them with some kind of in-service training; they would retain their normal work while pursuing university studies in their spare time. Third, it should use the modern media, and television especially, for communication with students in the most effective ways possible.

When Labour came to power Mr Wilson handed responsibility for this

---

[*] Report of the Committee on Higher Education, under the Chairmanship of Lord Robbins (Cmnd 2154, London, HMSO, 1963).

area to Miss Jennie Lee (as she then was). February 1966 saw the White Paper 'A University of the Air'. September 1967 saw the appointment of a Planning Committee under the chairmanship of Sir Peter Venables, then Vice-Chancellor of the University of Aston. It is worth recalling the composition of the Planning Committee: six Vice-Chancellors or former Vice-Chancellors, and a College Principal; two Professors of Education; the General Secretary of the Association of Education Committees; the Chairman of the Arts Council; the Deputy Education Officer of the ILEA (Inner London Education Authority); senior officials from the educational side of BBC and ITA; and five other senior academics. There were no politicians on the Planning Committee; and it would be hard to imagine a weightier or better balanced group of educationists. This must be said. The initiative came from politicians, but the planning was done by academics, and some of the scepticism expressed in the conventional universities showed a singular lack of confidence in their own best representatives.

The Planning Committee presented its report on the last day of 1968. It was already clear that the concept of a University of the Air was too narrow, and the title adopted was the Open University. Meantime initial steps had already been taken. A Vice-Chancellor had been found in Professor Walter Perry, Deputy Vice-Chancellor of the University of Edinburgh, and four Deans (or, as they were then called, Directors of Studies) appointed. The university needed proximity to London because of its relationship to the BBC, but the sort of accommodation required would have been prohibitively expensive in London itself. Walton Hall offered a stately façade, grounds adequate for expansion, easy communication with London by road or rail, and reasonable accessibility (especially with the foreseeable completion of the M6–M1 motorway link) to and from most of the country. It was also firmly in the centre of the projected new city of Milton Keynes. The Milton Keynes Development Corporation hospitably welcomed this Ugly Duckling; the university felt that in its somewhat anomalous position of lacking the usual contacts with students there was something to be said for having cultural connexions with a local community; and Lord Crowther saw a happy omen in the link with two great names of English history. Architects Maxwell Fry and Jane Drew were appointed towards the end of February, and, astonishingly, in the glory of the 1969 summer, the faculty block with its two double-storey wings was partially occupied by September and wholly by October. By then the university had its charter, its Chancellor (Lord Crowther), its Council, Senate and Academic Advisory Committee, its working agreement with the BBC for the production of radio and television programmes, and its first complement of academic and administrative staff.

The period from mid-1969 to January 1971 has been dominated by the preparation and production of the four original foundation courses. The Social Sciences course is entitled 'Understanding Society'; the Arts course 'Humanities: a foundation course'; the others are in Mathematics and Science. Buildings have been rising, to house the computer which will keep the student records, the machine for packaging and despatch of material to students, the science laboratories, and all the other accoutrements common to all universities or peculiar to this one. So much for skeletal facts.

Basic Principles (I): Openness to Students

The originality of the Open University consists in three things.

First, it is open as to students. The Planning Committee wrote: 'We took it as axiomatic that no formal academic qualifications would be required for registration as a student. Anyone could try his or her hand, and only failure to progress adequately would be a bar to continuation of studies.' Those who shaped the university had from the first in mind a widely varied clientele of students: the lad who went to a poor school where he was never inspired to learn, left at 15 because his family needed his income, went into industry and has shown himself bright, intelligent and eager to learn; the girl who did reasonably at school, but got married at 18, is now in her thirties, as her family grows has time for study, and sees the opportunity and need to take a full-time job in a year or two's time; the long-term prisoner, whose whole future may depend on his having something constructive to do when he comes out; the teacher, with a certificate but without a degree, who is enthusiastic to learn more of his subject and become more highly proficient in it, and who indeed, with present trends, may require a degree for his future within the profession; the civil servant who finds himself in a similar position; the retiring, or shortly retiring, soldier, who would like to obtain a fresh qualification; the person who wants to change his job but cannot afford three years off work to obtain a degree; the man or woman in retirement looking for a new interest in life and wanting to keep their minds sharp; the shepherd on the island of Mull (one of our favourite notional figures), who, being a Scot, has a good basic education and can floor visiting clerics with his theological questionings, who would like to try his hand at higher education. Add to these – and many others – those who are qualified but who need post-experience courses to update their qualifications, say in statistics or computer science.

In fact there had to be some selectivity. In the first place the Open University was not established in rivalry to existing universities but as complementary to them. It seemed desirable to establish an age-limit of 21, *below* which students would not be accepted unless they could show reason of physical handicap preventing them from attending a conventional university. In the second place there were financial and organizational constraints on the number it would be possible to take initially; the figure was settled at 25,000 (it is in fact just under that) and they had to be chosen from some 43,000 applicants. Applicants who showed no sign that they were ready to take a university course were interviewed by a counsellor. If the counsellor felt that they were unready he advised them to try some other course first, but if the applicants wished their application to stand they had every right to insist on this. Parameters were discussed using motivation and preparedness as criteria, but they were not in fact used.

The basic principle of the admissions policy was 'First come first served' but three other parameters were used. One was based on the principle that the four foundation courses should have approximately equal numbers of students. There was an appreciably heavier demand for Social Sciences and Arts; national need was arguably stronger in Science and Mathematics. In the event we decided to aim at 8,000 for each of the first two, and 7,000 for each of the others: the discrepancy between that total of 30,000 and the figure of 25,000 is explained by the University's decision to allow about 20 per cent of students to take two courses simultaneously; it was not possible to allow all who wanted this to do so. The final figures are not at present available.

The second parameter was based on the regional organization. The country was divided into twelve regions for the organization of tutorial work, each with its own regional office, regional director and staff. It would plainly be wrong if all students came from London and none from Scotland – or vice versa. It was decided to admit students on a regional basis in a ratio which struck a balance between the demand from each region and the proportion of the total population of the country in each region. Here the figures are available up to January 1st, 1971. In the event, in only one region does the proportion of students admitted vary by more than 1 per cent from the proportion of the total population in that region, and in six of the twelve regions the figure is within 0·3 per cent.

The third parameter was based on occupation. Here the figures are available only for the original 25,000 students who were offered places. Something like a fifth refused the offer, presumably either for financial reasons or because they felt they could not give the time to the work; their places were offered to others and the final analysis is not available as I write. The major question was what proportion of teachers to accept. They form 1·6 per cent of the adult population; they formed 36 per cent of applications received. We fixed on a figure of 30 per cent for the first year, though other constraints raised this to 35 per cent. Some sections of the press made strange comments that the university was serving the middle-class housewife. There are no grounds for this assertion. House-wives form 27 per cent of the total population, but only 10 per cent of the admitted applicants are housewives, and neither we nor anyone else knows whether they are middle-class or not. We would agree that we did not do sufficient to get through to the industrial worker. Still, of the 25,000 offered places, 8 per cent were draughtsmen, laboratory assistants and technicians, 2 per cent in electrical and allied trades, 3 per cent in other manufacturing, farming, mining, transport and the like, 8 per cent clerical and office staff, 4 per cent fire brigade, police, sales and service, recreation and sport and the like. We should like to see these figures raised, but when 1 per cent represents 250 people they represent in themselves a sizeable university. The problem is one of the spread of information. A survey in January 1971 showed that only 20 per cent of manual workers had so much as heard of the Open University. We shall hope to remedy this.

One or two other figures may be of interest. Men greatly outnumbered women among the applicants, by nearly 3 to 1: this was a surprise. The oldest student admitted was 78; the largest age-group applying were those from 26 to 34. A survey of students taking preparatory courses, such as NEC/BBC Gateway courses, showed that well over a third of those had finished with formal education by the age of 16 or younger; as many as 52 per cent of the women taking these courses finished their education at 18; among 'housewives' this figure was 64 per cent.

It is pertinent here to draw attention to the question of the possible ad-mission of qualified school-leavers. The battle of the bulge is on us as much as if we were middle-aged sedentary businessmen. We could wish that the Open University had been given three to five years to find its feet. But by that time the eligible entrants for conventional universities will have doubled, and there is no predictable possibility of coping with them in the conventional way. The Open University offers an extraordin-arily inexpensive way of training graduates, astronomically cheaper than other universities. Even with an 80 per cent dropout (which is not likely) the figures would compare favourably – and that without taking into account the fact that Open University students are feeding into the GNP, and are not drawing on local authorities for such substantial sums for board and subsistence. In this way the Open University is an 'obvious' to help. But there are problems. Will a system designed for the unqualified mature student be suited to the qualified 18-year-old? And what is the effect of adding qualified 18-year-olds to a university which requires no qualification? And would it not devalue the Open University if it became a universal sixth choice and last line of defence – for most 18-year-olds will prefer full-time education if they can get it? The university has ex-pressed its willingness to look at the problems.

Basic Principles (II): Openness in Curricula

Secondly, the Open University is open over curricula. The Planning Committee early came to the view that the education offered should be built up from a broad, strongly integrated base; it is some answer to the 'disintegration' which G. B. Jeffery deplored in his Eddington lecture of 1949. Furthermore, they decided that the British system of a course which is largely determined throughout and ends in a once-for-all examination was too inflexible, and the American system of a multiplicity of small courses, each self-contained, rating anything from 1 to 5 credits and adding up to 180 credits in all, was too fragmented. They therefore came to a view which tries to bring together the best in both systems. Students should graduate on 6 credits, or 8 for an honours degree, a credit representing the successful achievement of a course lasting a full year and carrying the academic weight of about half a normal university year's work. The evaluation of a student's work is partly by continuous assessment and partly by an examination at the end of each course; to prevent continuous assessment being continuous examination a student will be assessed only on his half-dozen or so best pieces, and this gives him room to experiment with his approaches. A student may (not necessarily will) be permitted to take two credits in a single year: no more. Students who have already acquired qualifications at a higher level may be exempted from not more than three credits. The degree offered is that of BA; there is good precedent for this at Oxford and Cambridge, and no other nomenclature would suit all possible combinations of subjects. Standards will be validated at all levels by External Examiners.

Two of these credits must be obtained in the foundation courses, so that a student will have taken courses in more than one faculty. We have not solved the problem of Sir Charles Snow's 'Two Cultures': the majority of students have opted for Science and Mathematics or for Social Sciences and Arts. A fifth foundation course, in Technology, will be added in 1972; the sixth faculty, of Education, does not propose to offer a foundation course. These foundation courses are an attempt at an integrated approach to the work of each faculty. Thus the social scientists, entitling their course 'Understanding Society', bring together five different views of man – the economic, sociological, psychological, political and geographic – in asking 'three fundamental questions: why people live in societies; how people live in societies; and what kind of problems they face'. The scientists offer an introduction to science; they aim 'to present and explain some of the concepts and principles of importance in modern science and to show how science, technology and society are interrelated', and 'discuss a selection of topics from the general areas of physics, chemistry, biology and geology' in such a way as to show how these disciplines are related to and depend upon each other, and to show what is common, in method, technique, and philosophy, and what is specific to each'; nothing quite like this integrated approach to science at university level has ever been essayed before, and international scientists in Unesco are particularly excited by it. The mathematics course is a highly original presentation of mathematics which (to risk a prophecy) may well revolutionize the teaching of mathematics; the aim is 'to explain not only what mathematics *does* – the various ways in which mathematics can be of use in other fields – but also what mathematics *is*'. The arts faculty claim four aims in their course on humanities: '(a) to awaken interest in and enthusiasm for the study of man, his history and his cultural achievements; (b) to raise questions about the possible relations between technological development, social organization, religion, thought and the arts; (c) to help students towards intelligent reading and assimilation, the clear expression of critical judgments, and habits of intellectual analysis and synthesis; (d) to guide in basic methods, e.g. the handling of source material, the evaluation of a work of art or literature, clear and logical thinking.'

It is this integrated approach which has proved the most exciting aspect of working on the courses. It is an appalling fact that the majority of academics have had no experience of working with those in other disciplines. It is true that the effects of this are limited by the faculty structure, and there is little interfaculty cross-fertilization as yet, though we are hoping to develop a number of interfaculty courses, such as 'History of Science' or 'Design'. Meantime the arts faculty is proud to have on its books two chemists, who will bear prime responsibility for the history of science course, and who are meantime building the history of science appropriately into the arts courses.

Integration may of course mean many things, and we would not claim to have achieved it in the fullest sense. With a limited staff we have to cut our coats according to our tailors. Our tailors vary from those who try to apply to the study of man and his achievements an extended form of the sort of integration involved in traditional classical studies, where, in reading Plato, say, language, literature, philosophy, history, religion and the arts are inextricably intertwined and only artificially to be separated, or those who, specialists themselves in historical studies, are prepared to take an all-embracing view of history, to those at the other end who believe in the sacrosanctity of their own disciplines but are prepared to share in an interdisciplinary course. Plainly you do not achieve integration by aligning the traditional disciplines in snippets side by side, and sometimes we have been reduced to this – not only in the arts faculty. But sometimes we have achieved more, and we think that we have done it without reducing the rigour of the demands properly made by the individual disciplines.

It may be interesting to catch a glimpse of the arts faculty at work. The original draft syllabus was presented to the course-team for the foundation course, who were at the time all the members of the faculty. It was, very properly, torn to shreds, and out of the new proposals a fresh draft was drawn up. This too suffered a similar *sparagmos*, until gradually out of weeks of patient discussion an agreed syllabus emerged. This was broken into blocks of basically two weeks' work for the student, and each block assigned to a working-group, consisting of the academic primarily responsible, at least one other academic normally from a different discipline interested in this area, an educational technologist, and representatives of the BBC, of whom more in a moment. These decided on the part to be covered by correspondence material, radio and television respectively. Each part of this would go through several drafts under the gently merciless scrutiny of the other members. Often it was tested by prospective students, who were refreshingly candid when they found it dull or difficult. Finally it had to pass the whole course-team, which met weekly for a year and a half. Other faculties have worked in slightly different ways: all have acknowledged their corporate responsibility for the end product.

At the second level, the integrated or interdisciplinary approach will remain. The arts faculty is offering period studies, a total view of the period, its history, thought, literature, art, music, religion, science. The mathematicians propose a course in linear mathematics. Other faculties are offering combinations of half-courses in something which looks more like the traditional disciplines, though those proposed in educational studies are 'Personality, growth and learning', 'School and Society', and 'Environment and learning'. A student will be able to graduate on two foundation courses, followed by two second-level courses in each of his two faculties. If so, he will have had an extraordinarily good general education. But he need not take more than one second-level course and can if he prefers proceed to more advanced specialist studies. These are for the most part barely a gleam in a father's eye; the gleams include Computer Science; Statistics; War and Society; The Novel; Systems Engineering; and many other widely diverse and exciting themes.

Basic Principles III: Openness in Methods of Presentation

Thirdly, the Open University is open as to methods of presentation. This is the most obviously exciting part of the work. The original conception of the University of the Air had to be modified, partly because television is an exceedingly expensive medium, partly because the amount of air time available on either radio or television at hours when full-time workers can listen is strictly limited. One of the important pieces of basic research has been applied to students enrolled for preparatory courses to ascertain the best hours of listening. Of these students 78 per cent had

BBC2 at home, 67 per cent had VHF radio. About 80 per cent were still at home at 08.00, and could have heard or watched a 07.30 transmission; the figure does not reach 80 per cent again till 18.30, and at 17.30 it is only 50 per cent. There were interesting and important statistics about those who missed programmes through unforeseen circumstances. It is interesting to note that, listening habits apart, only half the students reserved a regular time for study; times for study were found by about 40 per cent on weekday evenings, and about 50 per cent at weekends fairly equally divided between morning, afternoon and evening. The Open University is working on the basis of about 10 hours a week from a student in all for a single course.

The overall system is without precise precedent, but the Planning Committee examined such precedents as were available. Probably the closest parallel is at Armidale, New South Wales. There students who are unable to attend the normal university courses are enabled to take degrees through correspondence material and radio teaching. There is an important summer school, and it was largely through the experience at Armidale that this was built into the Open University. At Armidale students are matriculated; on the other hand they are taking courses designed for conventional teaching, and they do not have the use of television. They experience about a $33\frac{1}{3}$ per cent dropout in the first year, and thereafter their results are marginally better than those of students in the conventional situation: the motivation is of course very strong. Other experience was drawn on – the use of broadcasting for pre-university courses in Japan, Munich and Chicago; the engineering courses sponsored by the state broadcasting organization and the Ministry of Education in Poland and supported by Unesco; Radio-Sorbonne; the massive correspondence enterprise of the University of South Africa; the excitingly experimental use of television at Boston; and many others.

The university has initially entered into a contract with the BBC for the provision of radio and television programmes. The Open University is not a BBC university; technically, it employs the BBC to do part of its work; in practice there is, and has been from the first, a genuine partnership. BBC producers are full members of course-teams and working groups, and play a full part in all the discussions which shape the course; they are far more than technical advisers on a single aspect. Each foundation course has, in round figures, one half-hour radio programme and one half-hour television programme each week (they are in fact slightly shorter). In later years the amount will decrease, but it will remain significant; the third level course on 'War and Society' is planning an extensive use of archive film, for example.

The use of the media is very varied. There are four obvious uses. First, to present material which should be seen and heard. Even here we had surprises. Two obvious uses might seem to be for drama and fine art. But drama is expensive, and twenty-five minutes is not a long time, and fine art is limited by lack of colour, fleeting images, and the small screens some students will possess. Secondly, television and to a lesser extent radio are important for their impact on students. Material could be presented in other ways, but – the medium is, in measure, the message. Thirdly, broadcasting can be used to personalize an otherwise impersonal situation. Disembodied teachers take on a voice and presence. Fourthly, the student himself can be made to feel that he is sharing with others in a teaching situation. This has been brilliantly exploited by Professor G. N. A. Vesey, who conducts philosophy seminars in which the viewer can really feel that he is a participating member.

The scientists' main problem has been to ensure that a student without regular access to laboratories has adequate experimental experience. They have done this in a variety of ingenious ways. In the first place observational and to some extent experimental science can be explored in everyday life – the garden, the cooker, the bicycle and motor car are obvious possibilities. Secondly, each student is supplied with a brilliantly designed home experiment kit: I need only mention the low-cost microscope, no bigger than a large matchbox, with a magnification of 200. The equipment is on loan with a deposit. Thirdly the summer school provides an opportunity for intensive laboratory experience. Fourthly, the primary use of television in science is to expose the students to demonstration experiments. The programmes are thus relatively straightforward and seem in prospect wholly adequate to their purpose.

The most obvious quality of the television programmes in mathematics is the use of animated graphics. It is of course arguable that mathematics *pur sang* is conceptual, and to make it visible is to detract from its essential quality. That would be a highly purist argument, and many will take the mathematics courses who will not be as pure as that. Television can further be used to link the abstractions of mathematics with practical problems. In the social sciences one of the major uses of television is to present a student with interview situations. In arts, two of the most exciting television programmes have been on cast-iron, where the use of the medium, obvious enough, is excellently exploited, and on the background to D. H. Lawrence's life at Eastwood. In radio some of the best programmes have been talks diversified by illustrations read by different voices. Another effective use has been dramatization: one of the best programmes here is a philosophical discussion between Descartes and Princess Elizabeth entitled 'The Princess and the Philosopher'.

Television and radio offered an exciting challenge and opportunity, and it will be seen that care was taken to try to use them effectively in their own way, and not to be content simply to transcribe conventional lectures. Less expected has been the equally exciting nature of the correspondence material. This represents teaching material of a basically new kind. It is beautifully printed in an A4 format (leaving plenty of room for a student's own notes) with copious illustration. For each week's work a student receives a booklet of 12,000 words or more: if two or more weeks' work deal with the same topic they may be bound together to form a substantial book. The systematic exposition of mathematics through this medium is really revolutionary: so is the programmed logic which is a part of the arts course. One technique has been devised by the arts faculty, chiefly through Arthur Marwick, the Professor of History, and the educational technologists (whose work is an important feature of the university's system, encouraging staff to spell out the aims and objectives of each unit and each element within it, advising on methods of presentation, and evaluating work through developmental testing). This is to provide students with constant challenges to react to what is presented to them and then to comment (without having seen it) on their reaction. Plainly this can be done in a simple way to test assimilation of factual material: a student can be asked questions and subsequently told answers. The excitement comes when critical judgement is involved. We have found the means of inviting a critical response, and then saying something like: 'There is no absolute right or wrong here. But surely you should have said A, B and C; if you did not, read the basic material again. If you said X or Y I think you have entirely misunderstood the point at issue; again you should go back. For the rest, here is my view. If you differ from it think again about the material to see whether there are points you've missed. If you have points which I've missed, well done.' In this way correspondence material is much more like a seminar or tutorial than a book.

Books are necessary, and publishers have been co-operative in putting out prescribed books at an exceedingly low price. Some of these, mostly in the form of anthologies or readers, have been specially issued for the courses. Early signs suggest that these are already making their impact on individuals and institutions outside the Open University. The Open University is on a scale unprecedented in higher education in Britain, and it has been agreed that courses shall run for four years without fundamental revision, so that substantial sales of prescribed books are virtually guaranteed.

Plainly, what the Open University cannot provide is continuous face-to-face contact between students and teachers; the Open University exists for those who by definition cannot have this and will have nothing except what the Open University can give. The primary aim must be to provide an academic education of the highest possible quality. Equally it is important to make it as personal as possible. This is done in a variety of ways. First there are summer schools, hosted by other universities during the summer months. For the foundation courses these are obligatory unless exemption is explicitly granted (for the bed-ridden or prisoners, for example). They provide a week's intensive university experience in the middle of the course: the university year coincides with the calendar year. Then there is the correspondence-tuition, using part-time tutors to correct written assignments in such a way as to help the student to a better understanding and improved presentation. There are study-centres in the main towns and cities where students can congregate of an evening to listen to the broadcasts and discuss them together, to meet counsellors ('moral tutors') who can give them general guidance as to their work, and occasionally to meet part-time class-tutors within their own academic field. Television, and to a lesser extent radio, offer strong possibilities of making teaching personal. And the arts faculty has gone a long way to personalizing correspondence material by identifying authors, using a conversational tone, and not being afraid to expose disagreement within the course-team and to challenge the student to disagreement. The system can never be fully personal; nor in fact are the conventional universities. But it can be made as personal as possible.

Conclusion

There are many aspects of the Open University I have not here touched on. One important one is the use of a computer for the selection procedure and for the maintenance and analysis of student records. This is a technological university for a technological age. An American visitor said 'We think of you in Britain as living in the nineteenth century; and then we find among you a university of the twenty-first century'. Another is our awareness that the future may well lie not with public broadcasting but with the development of video-tape, and we are keenly watching progress here. Another is the world potential of our products and experience, which has led to the appointment of a Director of Marketing. The potential is enormous, whether for the whole system, whole courses, or elements within the courses of all sorts, shapes and sizes. An early sale was of science kits to the new technological university established at Benin in Nigeria.

Nothing has done more to reconcile the academics in the conventional universities to this experiment than the quality of staff attracted. There were over 1,200 applicants for the first 30 posts. It would be invidious to name individuals, but it is clear that the staff provide a combination of the highest academic attainments with a readiness to experiment with new methods.

In the Eddington lecture already mentioned Professor G. B. Jeffery identified three marks of the true university:

1. It should be a temple of knowledge, one and indivisible, and all who enter it should know to what the temple is dedicated.

2. It should be inspired by a social purpose. It does not exist for the intellectual comfort of its senior members. It exists to serve the wider social community within which it is set, especially in relation to the promotion and sustaining of the intellectual life of that community.

3. It should be a place of education, that is to say, a place in which young people are prepared in body, mind and spirit for service in other spheres of activity, usually outside the university.

Of all the universities of Britain the Open University would seem most plainly to fulfil these ends.

30

Universities and their Range of Concern

Warren B. Martin

On every hand commentators say that the American university cannot have it both ways; it must be this or that, stand here or there, take one path or another. They say: that if the university responds favourably to advocates of affective education, then the quest for certainty must be surrendered; that if the principle of reductionism is adhered to, then seeing the gestalt, acknowledging existential wholeness, developing a tolerance for ambiguity, accepting complexity or even contradiction, become impossible; that if the institution is faithful to its sociopolitical involvements, the concept of the university as a centre of independent thinking goes out the window.

We are also told: that realism and idealism have always been mortal enemies, as have probity and permissiveness; that a community imposes constraints on its members, and that therefore individualism is a threat to collectivity; or, if primary value is placed on the other side, that collectivity is a threat to individualism; that if the university is large enough to carry out its research and service functions, it will be too large to allow for the intimacy and person-centredness of a small college; that the experimental is always a critical conscience to continuity, order, and the pre-eminence of the conventional.

You cannot have it both ways, they say.[1]

The University as Multidimensional

That a university should decide what it is and what it is not is incontrovertible. What is disputable is that it must decide to be a unidimensional institution rather than a multidimensional one, a place characterized by commitment to uniformity rather than by commitment to pluralism. There should be single-purpose institutions, usually colleges, but there is no reason why a university cannot seek to make provision for alternate perspectives and differing programmes. Indeed, as we move into a time when transmission of knowledge need not involve a teacher, when research will be carried out by institutes, when service functions are handled by external agencies, then the only future for the university will be to do what is not being done elsewhere. And this is the job of synthesis: integrating new fields of knowledge with each other, as well as with those that came before; combining the theoretical and the practical, the pure and the applied research; merging and meshing the interests and concerns of societies, cultures, and human nature. Nowhere else is this intellectually stimulating, socially relevant work likely to be done.

The goal has not been achieved. The multiversity is not a model for what is required, nor, we know now, was it even a harbinger of things to come. In the multiversity, the emphasis was on the mind, with depreciation of the emotions; methodological favouritism was rampant; the preference was for theoretical knowledge over the applied, for the autonomous research scholar over the group-oriented teacher. Furthermore, while the diversity of American higher education has been a trumpeted theme, what actually existed was procedural diversity, not substantive; organizational differentiation, not ideational. At the level of assumptions, values, and goals, universities have been monotonously uniform; philosophical, methodological, stylistic conformity has characterized academic life. Theoretically, that which represented 'the other way' might be dealt with, albeit usually with a shrug of the shoulder, but, practically, the university has had a one-dimensional orientation. The action has been one way.[2]

A university facing the future, however, can and must have it both ways. It will employ in the educational processes both the cognitive and affective domains of learning – drawing on rational *and* emotional aspects of human nature; it will show regard for the methodological principle of parsimony, but also acknowledge existential plenty – accepting the challenge of reductionism while asserting the necessity for expansionistic probes that posit abundance; it will mix realism and idealism – handling sociopolitical conditions in the context of aspiration and vision; it will show the necessity for both probity and privilege – the legitimacy of standards as well as occasions for transcending them; it will feature individualism and community – self-authentication, but as a prelude to interpersonal relationships.

The new 'balanced' institution of the future will also be characterized by certain organizational components. It will be large and small – providing, within a setting of complexity and diversity, opportunity for simple yet purposeful 'consent units'. It will occupy space, have a discreet campus, yet also develop external degree programmes – exploding the notion that learning takes place only at specified times in prescribed ways for certain age groups. It will combine the conventional and the experimental – accepting the contemporary condition of uncertainty and confusion, in which most are holding to the old ways while some are seeking after something different – and will make provision for both.

The tendency toward dichotomization of the university's structures and functions is the result, at a time of uncertainty, of extreme reactions by present ideational combatants. Critics of established institutional conditions and educational objectives emphasize the need for radical change, and sometimes have ideas about how to effect it. But their assumption that the institution is incapable of substantive alternation moves them to dramatize deficiencies and call for the discard of existing practices while insisting on a leap of faith toward whatever they propose. Defenders of the *status quo*, meanwhile, are so incensed by futurity that they often scorn reform, calling it faddism, or change for the sake of change, while romanticizing the past or absolutizing the present.

The Synthesis of Diversity

What is needed now is not further polarization, but fresh efforts at creative syntheses. On most issues – the interaction of mind and body in learning, behaviouristic and humanistic methodologies, realism or idealism in educational philosophy, external standards and internal motivation, the authority of the person as compared with that of the crowd, the comparative advantages of largeness and smallness, the setting, timing, and styles best suited for learning, conventional instruction compared to innovative approaches to it – on these and other issues, the fact of the matter is that all sides are 'right'. This is not to say that there is no wrong, but rather to assert that on most problems confounding educators today, rival disputants have essential contributions to make to the resolution of these problems.

To be more specific, it is evident that if the skills needed by minorities – and they are rightly insisting on education for mastery of skills – are to be supplied, or if the machines of the technological society are to be serviced and improved, or if the momentum of scientific advances in many fields is to be sustained, or if communication and interaction between differing cultures are to have the vigour and clarity that make for understanding and mutual appreciation, then the university must posit the authority of the human mind and emphasize respect for the life of reason. To sacrifice reason is to surrender the right to disciplined criticism. To depreciate the mind is to put down mankind, for the mind is one of man's distinguishing characteristics. An irony of the present movement against cognitive rationality is that its best spokesmen are among our most persistent reasoners.

Yet these critics have a point and, by now, have it well documented. The university has contributed to the fragmentation of man by concentrating on his intellect and ignoring or minimizing his emotions. The intuitive, spiritual, affective qualities of man have been allowed to atrophy. Human sensibilities have been dulled and weakened. Whereas historically, institutions of higher learning showed interest in the whole man – body, mind, and spirit – that holistic, inclusive approach was lost as attention focused on a dispassionate, intellectually rigorous, scientific methodology which excluded the scholar's point of view unless it emerged as the consequence of research, and which scorned 'enthusiasm' as a contaminant.

There was need to redress the balance. But the concern for correctives has, in some quarters, been carried too far. Reports circulate that academic departments at some institutions have become sensitivity training centres or centres of anti-reason or of unapologetic irrationality. Going to this extreme is as much a violation of the western tradition – encompassing Greek, Hebraic, and Christian thought – as was university practice in the recent past. Exclusive attention to the emotions cannot meet our needs any better than exclusive attention to reason.

Reconciliation of these two equally valid emphases is possible. To be sure, in certain subject matter areas of the curriculum such as languages and natural science, concentration must remain on linear, sequential, cognitive learning methodologies. But hopefully, attention can also be given to the role of the non-cognitive, acknowledging its effect on topics chosen, inferences drawn, and the uses made of rationally-oriented study.

In other sections of the university's programme, attention may concentrate on the emotions more than on the intellect, or on the way the emotions can lead to employment of the mind rather than, as before, conceiving of the intellect only as a monitor of the emotions. There will continue to be tension between those who would bring the emotions into the service of the intellect and those who want the intellect to serve the emotions, but these perspectives are essentially complementary, indeed essential to each other, if universities facing the future are to serve the whole man in a complex society and make that society humane.

A serious internal threat to the modern university is pressure, usually at the departmental level, toward methodological uniformity. It is not uncommon for a philosophy department to be 'captured' by, say, adherents of analytic philosophy, and with the consequence that a phenomenological existentialist has no chance for appointment there. Such conformity can become absolute, so that if, perchance, a tenured well-established scholar who had been in the analytic ranks were persuaded to join the existentialists, it is likely that despite professed loyalty to the principles of tenure and academic freedom, he would be frozen out of the fellowship and 'forced' to leave that department. It is equally likely that educational psychology departments committed to behaviourism, or Stimulus-Response, associational, and mediation theory, will criticize or even scorn organizationalists or rule-learning theorists. The principal of parsimony must be served.

This is a time, however, when the scientific methodology is being charged with contributing to our most serious social problems, when the academic mentality is judged as small-bore and boring ('more and more about less and less'), carried to levels of everything and nothing. Without surrendering either the methodology or the accomplishments of the modern scientific era in both the natural and behavioural sciences, there does seem to be reason to acknowledge the need for openness toward alternative methodologies. Conditions of our day may not call for starting over, but they certainly indicate the need for opening up, for probing differing approaches to scholarship and social service. Nature does not adhere to the principle of parsimony; nature is more often characterized by abundance, even extravagance, one seed taking root for every ten thousand dropped. Perhaps our need today is to make the university a natural organism featuring methodological options, especially during a period of uncertainty when anxiety about the adequacy of what we have done and the ways we have done it is matched by a new surge of creativity, primarily among the young operating in a context of hope. Let the behaviourists, therefore, work with their detailed analyses while the conceptualists, or those scholars striving for more humanistic research models, move to cluster and integrate, synthesize and apply what has been learned.

The Problem of Standards

The American university has always been a curious mixture of realism and idealism. Faculties became adroit in internal politics as institutional policies were being shaped by external pressures from business, industry, and agriculture; from state, church, and home. Financial considerations have probably decided more faculty debates than have academic goals. On the other hand, universities idealistically have sought institutional independence. From the medieval period when authorities in the University of Paris began playing off church officials against state officials to achieve a rough and tenuous freedom, the goal has been to make the university a centre of independent thinking, in the idealistic belief that only so can the institution best serve society. Idealism also figured in the definition of the university as a repository of culture, transmitter of essential knowledge, centre of criticism and creativity, training ground not only for vocations and professions, but also for the preparation of an intellectual and social elite from which societal leadership could be expected to come. There is less reason to fear the concept of the university as an ivory tower if everybody understands that this institution is no better than its foundations, foundations inevitably set on the rock of social reality.

The trouble with permissiveness is that it requires standards against which the claims of permissiveness can be made, by which the practice of permissiveness may be tested. As is true with so many aspects of modern life, permissiveness stands up only by leaning on that which it is trying to tear down. The university, therefore, cannot survive without standards, without criteria for evaluation, without concepts of probity or rectitude.

Yet to acknowledge this is not to argue for the continued dominance of conventional standards. Research has exposed manifold deficiencies in established criteria of excellence. Most student testing programmes, such as those provided by the Educational Testing Service, have been reliable only in showing whether or not, given the existing norms and practices, the people tested are likely to succeed in college. It is, of course, precisely at this point that challenges are being raised. Other measures of other qualities, aptitudes, and interests have been lacking, are now emerging, and must be employed. While the majority of students respond to conventional standards, a growing minority needs and deserves new indices of accomplishment and recognition of different types of accomplishment. New measures of institutional purpose and vitality are also needed.★

Viewing the problem of standards from another perspective, Kierkegaard and other philosophers, Jung and other psychologists, Kohlberg and other researchers, have all posited a level of human maturity at which the individual, in full awareness of social norms decides to transcend them – in the name of a higher law or an inner motivation. For the life of the university, this means that there should be established procedures for achieving institutional objectives, and that most persons and organizations will adhere to them gladly. But there should also be provision for self-designed objectives, individualized procedures operating in the context of situational ethics. In a university characterized by the concept of pluralism, believing in diversity, seeking a character best designated as future-oriented, there need be no single standard for all groups; rather, a recognition that all groups should determine standards appropriate for their missions. Thus there would be a plenitude of probity, and probity in the context of plenitude.

Individualism and Community

The same synthesizing of alternatives should also characterize the university's approach to the claims of individualism and of community. Martin Buber pointed out that individual freedom and self-authentication are necessary prerequisites to meaningful community. A person must determine who he is in order to know what he has to contribute in the group. But this freedom, said Buber, is a footbridge, not a goal. The tragedy of our time is that we have not passed over into true community. Individualism has become rampant, sliding off into radical subjectivism, making possible only a community of convenience, a place which utilizes

---

★ Educational Testing Service is actively engaged in designing and field testing such instruments. Two recent examples are the Institutional Goals Inventory and the Institutional Functioning Inventory.

services in order to get something done. What is needed is a community of conviction, a place where things get done by people who have come together in order to be something.

A unidimensional university is not the answer. Rather, within the larger community, where the key shared commitments would be to process and pluralism only, there would be vital sub-units, consent groups, communities of conviction. Recent research shows that the federated college plan, the cluster college concept, other mechanisms for decentralizing a monolithic university into smaller, purposeful communities, all provide viable alternatives that show promise for meeting the need.[3]

These same ideas respond to the question of how a university facing the future can be large in total numbers and yet small in operational units. Reformulated programmes and colleges, within which a student would spend perhaps 60 per cent of his time, with the remainder distributed through courses or activities available elsewhere in the university, would make possible the realization of a purposeful community in which every student could become acquainted with both the realities of pluralism and the meaning of diversity. More need not mean worse – it can be made to mean different, and perhaps better.

This organizational configuration also encourages innovative or experimental sub-units within the university at the same time that traditional or conventional programmes are maintained. The extended degree notion is one exciting form of change, as are holistic problem/theme curriculum models, programmatic research by student-faculty teams, learning in various time blocks, and other available options.

I repeat my assertion: on most of the issues confronting a university facing the future there is need for the insights and action programmes that are currently being offered by theoreticians, researchers, and practitioners, who, regrettably, consider each other's views as irreconcilable. There are limits even to pluralism, but for the areas of concern in the preceding paragraphs, contenders have contributions to make. Indeed, only so can there be a future-oriented university, one that has it both ways.

The University of the Pacific

The University of the Pacific, California's first chartered institution of higher education, is an example of a university that has been trying in recent years to have it both ways. And, to date, it is a story of success. Pacific could have been content to be a first-rate liberal arts college. Many faculty, alumni, and at least one prestigious evaluation committee, believed that the best future for this institution would be as the College of the Pacific. But under the leadership of President Robert Burns a different future was envisioned: Pacific would become a full university with a conventional range of professional schools and graduate programmes, and it would become an innovative university, featuring the cluster college concept. If American post-secondary education needed to personalize and vitalize the undergraduate experience, then at Pacific small academic sub-units granted the freedom to be different would help to meet that need. Hence came into being Raymond College (1962), Covell College (1963), and Callison College (1967), each with a distinctive undergraduate curriculum served by separate facilities and faculties. If higher education in America also needed an extension of graduate and professional programmes beyond the baccalaureate degree, then Pacific would address itself to that need. Hence, professional programmes established early in music, education, and engineering, have more recently become full-fledged professional schools. A School of Pharmacy (1955), School of Dentistry (1962), and the School of Law (1966) have been initiated or acquired, and, in addition, the Graduate School offers the Doctor of Philosophy degree in a few fields and the Master of Arts in several others.

One of the corollaries of this extensive programme development has been a geographical expansion of the university. At present, in addition to the main campus at Stockton, major locations include San Francisco and Sacramento.

The core of this educational complex has been and remains the College of the Pacific (COP) – the oldest, largest, most diversified of the university's undergraduate colleges. From 1911 to 1961, the total institution carried the name, College of the Pacific, and few programmes beyond those in the arts and sciences were available. Beginning with the establishment of the cluster colleges (1962), COP (now the central college of arts and sciences within the University of the Pacific) underwent an identity crisis: would COP become a college with its own distinctive characteristics or would it be simply a service unit for the rest of the university's programmes?

One of the most interesting and important developments at this university during the past five years has been the emergence of the College of the Pacific as a separate and distinctive entity.[4] And this has occurred as a direct response to challenges posed by the cluster colleges on the one hand and the professional schools on the other. The attention in the innovative undergraduate sub-units to educational philosophy, curriculum innovation, and a spirit of community compelled faculty and students in COP to clarify their own attitudes and actions. The muscle of the professional schools, especially affecting resource allocations, compelled administrators in COP to give closer attention to their own resources.

Today, momentum that in the 60s seemed to be with the cluster colleges – they were getting national attention, had character, were receiving preferential treatment – has in the early 70s swung over to the College of the Pacific. Encouraged by an academic vice-president, John

Bevan, who sensed the need for fresh endeavour in this component of the university, and guided by a skilful dean, William Binkley, who worked with a student-faculty committee, the College of the Pacific has not reduced its services to other schools and colleges of the university, but has designed and implemented a different curriculum for itself. In consequence, an ethos has emerged, a sense of community, a cogent rationale for the work of the college that has greatly increased the vitality of that institution. At the same time, the cluster colleges have been put on notice that they can no longer claim centre stage.

At the University of the Pacific, the pertubational theory of organizational change and institutional growth has been put to the test, and found to be effective; the university is experiencing growth and improvement through the tension of differences. The most conspicuous change in the College of the Pacific affects the freshman year programme. Freshmen select three pairs of thematically-linked courses from four areas: historical-cultural studies, behavioural and social sciences, natural sciences, and creative-communicative arts. The Introductory Year Programme, Information and Imagination: a Programme of Disciplined Synthesis, may be illustrated as shown in Table 1.

The college has also gone to a 4-1-4 calendar, allowing study during the month of January in one subject-matter area, on campus or off, without the usual classroom restraints.

As the College of the Pacific has now shown the cluster colleges that they have no corner on innovation and that they cannot rival COP in options available to students, so, *vis-à-vis* the professional schools, the college has made it clear that the traditional service functions, while not abandoned, will hereafter exist only where services offered are consistent with COP's resources and do not violate the integrity of that school's character.

There are obvious dangers for all parties in the developments taking place at the University of the Pacific. It has been important for each of the university's components to become strong enough to relate to the others with confidence. But in allowing sufficient autonomy to each unit to establish its own place, there is the peril that the university could become only a collection of disparate segments or separate programmes. At present, there is the question of what this university *qua* university is or should be. Is it simply a holding company for several distinct and competing units, even a conglomerate? Or is the university finding its character in the pluralistic and process orientation which should characterize universities facing the future?

No less difficult to answer is the question of the best governance configuration for a university committed to change. Thus far the University of the Pacific has been able to expand its professional offerings and

TABLE 1

Areas	Creative-Communicative Arts		Natural Sciences		Historical-Cultural Studies		Behavioural Sciences	
Themes	Existentialism	Creativity	Pollution	Technology	Revolution	Alienation	Urbanization	Human Rights
Paired Courses	Philosophy, Literature	Psychology, Art	Biology, Geology	Engineering, Physics	History, Literature	Religion, Political Science	Sociology, Political Science	Psychology, History

establish undergraduate innovations from a conventional hierarchical governance matrix. But as new units press for stability, the old governing plan may prove unable to effect change. Perhaps one challenge, as this university plans for the future, is to think creatively about a more balanced pattern of governance that will be certain to facilitate rather than inhibit the achievement of a future-orientation.

Nevertheless, despite the often provisional, *ad hoc*, short-term nature of planning that has brought this university to its present status, UOP has, better than most American universities, succeeded in creating a setting where it is possible to have it both ways. The cognitive is featured in most programmes, but affective education has found a place. The methodologies of behaviouristic parsimony and existential plenty are both present. Realism and idealism abound, albeit there has been a tendency to give more attention to launching programmes than to their effective implementation; the reach has exceeded the grasp. The faculties have grappled, and continue to struggle, with the issue of the extent to which academic and social standards for students, and professional criteria for faculty, should be uniform across programme, college, and school lines. The cluster colleges have been given 'intervals of innovation' within which to test options, to select from the plenteous variations that may provide new and better standards. Pacific does make provision for individualism and community, for the large diversified programmes and small unified ones, for the conventional and the innovative.

Conclusion

In a day when educators can no longer say, 'This is the way, walk ye in it', the best strategy is to multiply the options, allowing provisions for those who think they have answers as well as for those who have only questions. Above all, the either/or mentality must be transcended. Lawrence Stone has shown that any system of thought that polarizes is dysfunctional because it contradicts the way ideas work to achieve change:

> New ideas permeate old ones, run underground and pop up in unexpected places, mingle surreptitiously, or even coexist side by side without either conflict or conflation. One system of beliefs or values rarely challenges another directly and finally overthrows it in a single cataclysmic struggle. It is more a matter of guerrilla warfare, secret infiltration, and eventual mutual accommodation.[5]

A university facing the future must make provision to have it both ways, so that new syntheses can emerge and radical alternatives can be tested, so that it can be true to its traditions of pluralism and diversity, so that truths will prevail.

REFERENCES

1. For a lucid expression of certain dimensions of this thesis, see Robert Nesbit, 'Great Books and Great Snippets: The Cult of Individuality', *Change*, January–February, 1971, pp. 44–8.
2. See Warren Martin, *Conformity: Standards and Change in Higher Education* (San Francisco: Jossey-Bass, 1969).
3. For research-informed consideration of the cluster college concept, see Jerry Gaff, *The Cluster College*, San Francisco: Jossey-Bass, 1970, and Warren Martin, *Alternative to Irrelevance*, Nashville: Abingdon Press, 1968.
4. For comparative analyses of certain cluster colleges, including Raymond College, with certain more conventional institutions, including the College of the Pacific (comparisons based on data collected five years ago), see Martin, *Conformity*, op. cit., pp. 24–8 and seriatim thereafter.
5. Lawrence Stone, 'The Ninnyversity?' *New York Review*, January 28, 1971, p. 23.

Index

(n indicates footnote reference)